CW00631764

FAO
GUIDELINES

Integrated coastal area management
and
agriculture, forestry and fisheries

FOOD AND AGRICULTURE ORGANIZATION OF THE UNITED NATIONS
Rome, 1998

Editing, design, graphics and desktop publishing:
Publishing Management Group,
FAO Information Division

The designations employed and the presentation of material in this publication do not imply the expression of any opinion whatsoever on the part of the Food and Agriculture Organization of the United Nations concerning the legal status of any country, territory, city or area or of its authorities, or concerning the delimitation of its frontiers or boundaries.

P-00
ISBN 92-5-104132-6

All rights reserved. No part of this publication may be reproduced, stored in a retrieval system, or transmitted in any form or by any means, electronic, mechanical, photocopying or otherwise, without the prior permission of the copyright owner. Applications for such permission, with a statement of the purpose and extent of the reproduction, should be addressed to the Director, Information Division, Food and Agriculture Organization of the United Nations, Viale delle Terme di Caracalla, 00100 Rome, Italy.

© **FAO** **1998**

PREPARATION OF THIS DOCUMENT

The preparation of these guidelines has mobilized the FAO Inter-Departmental Working Group on Integrated Coastal Area Management (IDWG/ICAM), as well as a number of experts drawn from international institutions and universities.

The guidelines have been technically edited by Nadia Scialabba, Secretary of IDWG/ICAM, working in the Environment and Natural Resources Service of the FAO Sustainable Development Department. It is based on drafts prepared by Louise F. Scura, David Insull, Cormac Cullinan and Nadia Scialabba (Part A), Andrew Dorward and Abdelghani Souirji (Part B), Paul Vantomme and Mette Løyche-Wilkie (Part C), Stephen Cunningham and Olivier Thébaud (Part D), and Caroline Blatch and Cormac Cullinan (Part E), whose contributions are very much appreciated. Special thanks also go to Michael Cracknell, Gloria Soave and Anne Aubert.

Scialabba, Nadia (ed.). 1998. *Integrated coastal area management and agriculture, forestry and fisheries. FAO Guidelines.* Environment and Natural Resources Service, FAO, Rome. 256 p.

ABSTRACT

These guidelines address the incorporation of agriculture, forestry and fisheries planning into integrated coastal area management (ICAM). The external or internal environmental effects that each of these sectors generate, as well as the environmental impacts originating outside these sectors and affecting them need to be taken into account in sector plan formulation. These guidelines examine issues specific to the agriculture, forestry and fisheries sectors, and suggest the processes, information requirements, policy directions, planning tools and possible interventions that are necessary for ICAM.

Sustainable development of coastal areas involves enhancing national capacities for integrated coastal resources management. Any coastal development strategy will be influenced by the respective strengths of the bargaining positions of the many parties involved. These guidelines aim at improving the bargaining position of the agriculture, forestry and fisheries sectors, in order to allow them to take a proactive stance, seek to clarify and quantify trans-sectoral impacts and formulate and coordinate appropriate management interventions.

These guidelines advocate coordinated sectoral management according to commonly agreed goals and objectives for coastal area development. Negotiation, conflict resolution, and participatory planning are central elements.

Part A of these guidelines introduces the general concepts involved in ICAM and focuses on major issues common to coastal agriculture, forestry and fisheries. The legal framework and institutional arrangements for ICAM are outlined. Attention is drawn to the need for appropriate institutional coordination, information bases, analytical techniques and processes when dealing with the interaction and conflicts of interest between different sectors and user groups. The iterative process for developing ICAM strategies and plans is emphasized.

Parts B, C and D identify the distinctive characteristics and requirements with respect to ICAM for the agriculture, forestry and fisheries sectors, respectively. The focus is on interactions among the sectors, information requirements, and policy and planning needs for ICAM.

Part E examines conflicting claims over the allocation and use of coastal natural resources that can lead to the degradation of the environment. It proposes alternative mechanisms to facilitate the resolution of conflicts that may arise in the context of ICAM.

Key words: Integrated coastal area management; coastal zone management; coastal agriculture; coastal fisheries; coastal forestry; dispute resolution; conflict management; participatory planning.

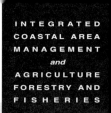

INTEGRATED
COASTAL AREA
MANAGEMENT
and
AGRICULTURE
FORESTRY AND
FISHERIES

Contents

INTEGRATED
COASTAL AREA
MANAGEMENT
and
AGRICULTURE
FORESTRY AND
FISHERIES

Contents

PART **D**

INTEGRATION OF FISHERIES
INTO COASTAL AREA MANAGEMENT

PART **E**

CONFLICT RESOLUTION
IN INTEGRATED COASTAL AREA MANAGEMENT

vi

Note: detailed contents are at the beginning of each of Parts A, B, C, D and E.

INTEGRATED
COASTAL AREA
MANAGEMENT
and
AGRICULTURE
FORESTRY AND
FISHERIES

User's guide

RATIONALE

At present, one-quarter of the world's population of some 5.9 billion live in coastal areas and most of the largest urban concentrations are on the coast. The current coastal urban population of 220 million is projected to almost double in the next 20 to 30 years. Unless appropriate action is taken by governments and users of coastal resources, population pressure and associated levels of economic activity will further increase the already evident overexploitation of coastal resources and environmental degradation of many coastal habitats. In many developing countries, this trend is further exacerbated by widespread extreme poverty and unemployment. Furthermore, conflict often arises from competing and antagonistic uses of resources, or from the displacement of traditional users of coastal resources by new economic activities.

Integrated coastal area management (ICAM) offers a means of balancing the competing demands of different users of the same resources and of managing the resources to optimize the benefits to be derived on a sustainable basis that is consistent with a country's goals.

In many countries, sector-oriented line ministries have the mandate, technical competence and professional experience to conserve, manage and develop coastal resources. Commitment on the part of some ministries is a condition for the successful adoption and application of truly integrated plans for the conservation, management and development of coastal resources. In addition to as the institutional capacities to undertake their tasks, the ministries must also have staff with a sufficiently flexible approach for constructive collaboration across ministries.

These guidelines describe the institutional options, policy processes, planning mechanisms and issues specific to the agriculture, forestry and fisheries sectors, respectively, with regard to ICAM. Since there are many approaches to resolving the often difficult institutional problems that arise when countries seek to adopt ICAM, guidance is proposed, rather than recipes.

Perhaps the most critical lesson to be learned from what is still fairly limited experience in ICAM is the need for adequate human and financial resources to be made available. In most cases, this calls for a reallocation of funds, rather than additional funding. However, line ministries understandably find it difficult to shift priority away from their traditional, sector-based issues to cross-sectoral ones.

Experience also points to a need to distinguish between coastal management *strategy*, which describes the goals and the means of achieving those goals, and *plans*, which express the objectives in terms of details, targets, policy instruments, necessary human and financial resources and time-frames.

The guidelines suggest that the responsibility for the preparation of an ICAM strategy (which provides the basis for sectoral plans) should lie with a lead, coordinating organization or body. The preparation of plans and the implementation of the strategy should be the responsibility of the line ministries. Alternatively, a new organization responsible for the design and implementation of ICAM plans might be established by government. The guidelines also suggest that such plans should not stand alone but should be an integral part of sectoral development, resource management and research activities. Plans should be flexible and adjusted periodically as more information becomes available or new issues are addressed.

INTEGRATED
COASTAL AREA
MANAGEMENT
and
AGRICULTURE
FORESTRY AND
FISHERIES

User's guide

OBJECTIVES AND SCOPE OF THE GUIDELINES

The aim of these guidelines is to enhance the contribution of the agriculture sector to the integrated management of coastal areas. The agriculture sector, as broadly defined, is comprised of the subsectors of agriculture (including crops and livestock), forestry (including timber, non-wood forest products and wildlife) and fisheries (including capture fisheries and aquaculture). The guidelines also provide an introduction to this approach for those who are not familiar with integrated management.

Specifically, the guidelines are intended to help to develop awareness in the agriculture sector line agencies and among resource users of: 1) the external or internal environmental effects that each sector may generate; and 2) the environmental impacts originating outside the sector and felt in one or more of the subsectors. In addition, the guidelines indicate ways for planners and resource users in each of the subsectors to take these impacts into account in plan formulation. Since any ICAM strategy will be influenced by the respective strengths of the bargaining positions of the many parties involved, the guidelines seek to improve the bargaining positions of the agriculture, forestry and fisheries subsectors. Other major interested parties include industry, urban areas and dwellers, the tourist sector, industrial ports, sea transport (including oil transport) and mining.

The guidelines should be useful, even where there are no formal institutional and organizational arrangements for integration and coordination for ICAM. Line agencies can take a proactive stance, and seek to clarify and quantify trans-sectoral impacts, as well as formulating and coordinating appropriate management interventions. This, in turn, will help to develop a constituency for more formal organizational arrangements for ICAM and the adoption of appropriate management strategies.

The goal of the guidelines is, therefore, to assist countries to achieve sustainable development of their coastal resources by contributing to:

- enhancing national institutional capacities for ICAM;
- integrating planning and management of the agriculture, forestry and fisheries subsectors into coastal area management;
- preventing and controlling environmental degradation in coastal areas.

TARGET AUDIENCE

The guidelines are intended particularly for planners in the agriculture, forestry and fisheries subsectors who are concerned with development planning and natural resource management in marine coastal areas or in areas adjoining large inland water bodies. In addition, they are intended for officials in agencies with responsibilities for planning and investment in coastal areas. Finally, they target all those who are concerned with sound environmental conservation and management in coastal areas.

STRUCTURE OF THE TEXT

The ambition of the document is to provide guidance on the processes, tools and possible interventions to be used in the integration of the agriculture sector into coastal area management. Since the audience is so broad, in Part A, the main text is complemented with figures, boxes and tables. These contain either general background information (yellow background) or somewhat more technical details (light-blue background). The four following parts are illustrated mainly with case studies and examples contained in boxes.

INTEGRATED
COASTAL AREA
MANAGEMENT
and
AGRICULTURE
FORESTRY AND
FISHERIES

User's guide

The guidelines are presented in five parts:

Part A focuses on major issues common to the three subsectors, as well as perspectives and approaches to ICAM. It includes a brief discussion of the main techniques and tools used that are common to integrated policy and planning in agriculture, forestry and fisheries. Aspects of the legal framework of ICAM that are equally applicable to all three subsectors are also included.

Parts B, C and D contain technical issues and requirements specific to agriculture, forestry and fisheries, respectively, with regard to their interactions with other (sub)sectors and their incorporation into ICAM.

Part E examines issues and tools for negotiation and conflict resolution relating to the use of natural resources.

The purpose of Part A is to introduce the general concepts involved in ICAM, and to provide an operational context for agricultural, forestry and fisheries planning in coastal areas. Attention is drawn to the need for appropriate information bases, analytical techniques and processes to cope with the interactions and conflicts of interest between different activities, (sub)sectors and interest groups. Some of the analytical techniques and institutional procedures that can be applied in agriculture, forestry and fisheries are broadly similar, and these are described in Part A.

The purpose of Parts B, C and D is to identify the distinctive characteristics and the requirements for planning in the agriculture, forestry and fisheries subsectors within ICAM. However, because the information requirements in each subsector are substantially different, Parts B, C and D also consider particular features of information required for planning within the context of ICAM.

Terms with which some readers may not be familiar are explained in the text and/or in the Glossary. Further reading and bibliographical sources can be found in References. An Index is provided to assist readers to find specific subjects in the text.

THE PLACE OF THE FAO GUIDELINES WITHIN OTHER INITIATIVES

These FAO guidelines support the United Nations Conference on Environment and Development (UNCED) 1992 Earth Summit Agenda 21, Chapter 17, Programme Area A, "Integrated management and sustainable development of coastal and marine areas, including exclusive economic zones". The guidelines are also relevant to other chapters of Agenda 21.[1]

The guidelines are complementary to FAO Fisheries Technical Paper No. 327, *Integrated management of coastal zones* (1992). The intention of the earlier publication was to provide some immediate support to UNCED Agenda 21, Chapter 17, Programme Area A, by identifying government actions that can lead to the effective management of coastal resources across the broad range of uses of coastal areas (from agriculture to water control and supply).

ix

---

[1] These are: Chapter 10, "Integrated approach to the planning and management of land resources"; Chapter 11, "Combating deforestation"; Chapter 12, "Managing fragile ecosystems: combating desertification and drought"; Chapter 13, "Managing fragile ecosystems: sustainable mountain development"; Chapter 14, "Promoting sustainable agriculture and rural development"; and Chapter 18, "Protection of the quality and supply of freshwater resources: application of integrated approaches to the development, management and use of water resources".

INTEGRATED
COASTAL AREA
MANAGEMENT
and
AGRICULTURE
FORESTRY AND
FISHERIES

User's guide

These guidelines examine more closely the issues peculiar to the agriculture sector, and describe the policy directions, planning tools and information requirements for policy formulation that are available to planners in these sectors. As such, they are the first "sectoral guidelines" among a number of guidelines so far prepared for ICAM.

A review of progress achieved in the implementation of the ICAM concept since the Earth Summit indicates that it has become a central organizing concept in a number of international agreements formally lacking a coast emphasis (e.g. the Biological Diversity Convention) and that several international entities have developed ICAM guidelines. Cicin-Sain, Knecht and Fisk (1995) compared the coastal management guidelines developed by five different international entities (i.e. OECD in 1991, the World Coast Conference Report in 1993, the World Bank in 1993, Pernetta and Elder for IUCN in 1993 and UNEP in 1995), based on ten major variables that were considered important in the design and implementation of ICAM (often referred to as integrated coastal management – ICM) programmes. These ten variables were: the scope/purpose (the major aspects covered); principles; definition of the management area; the functions of ICM; the legal basis for ICM; horizontal integration (mechanisms for intersectoral coordination); vertical integration (mechanisms for intergovernmental integration); financial arrangements; prescriptions on the use of science; and capacity building.

Based on their comparisons, the authors developed a "Consensus set of ICM guidelines" (see Table 1). These guidelines reinforce the consensus but recognize that horizontal and vertical integration cannot be successfully achieved without building the capacity of individual sectors to address trans-sectoral impacts. Thus, the guidelines strengthen the constituent components of the mosaic of users in coastal areas and focus on coordinated sectoral management along commonly agreed goals and strategies. Another conviction expressed in these guidelines is the importance of negotiation and conflict resolution in participatory development planning.

A major international workshop on ICM in tropical countries, held in 1996 in Xiamen, China, discussed the lessons learned from successes and failures experienced with ICM efforts. The workshop generated: 1) an overview of the processes of formulating, designing, implementing and extending ICM within the East Asian region as well as to other regions; and 2) a set of good practices in the formulation, design and implementation of ICM initiatives (IWICM, 1996).

Sorensen (1997) critically reviewed the definitions, achievements and lessons of national and international ICM efforts. He reported that, in the past three decades, ICM practice has involved approximately 90 coastal nations which have been engaged in a least 180 programmes, projects or feasibility studies but that relatively little information has been generated on what works, what does not work and why. He stressed the importance of factors such as: formulation of a better consensus on definitions, concepts and achievement measurement; determination of lessons that can be derived from cross-national comparisions and the transferability of these lessons to international, national, and subnational institutions; and development of new and improved information exchange networks.

INTEGRATED
COASTAL AREA
MANAGEMENT
and
AGRICULTURE
FORESTRY AND
FISHERIES

User's guide

TABLE 1

A consensus set of integrated coastal management guidelines

Purpose of ICM	The aim of ICM is to guide coastal area development in an ecologically sustainable fashion.
Principles	ICM is guided by the Rio Principles with special emphasis on the principle of intergenerational equity, the precautionary principle and the polluter pays principle. ICM is holistic and interdisciplinary in nature, especially with regard to science and policy.
Functions	ICM strengthens and harmonizes sectoral management in the coastal zone. It preserves and protects the productivity and biological diversity of coastal ecosystems and maintains amenity values. ICM promotes the rational economic development and sustainable utilization of coastal and ocean resources and facilitates conflict resolution in the coastal zone.
Spatial integration	An ICM programme embraces all of the coastal and upland areas, the uses of which can affect coastal waters and the resources therein, and extends seaward to include that part of the coastal ocean that can affect the land of the coastal zone. The ICM programme may also include the entire ocean area under national jurisdiction (Exclusive Economic Zone), over which national governments have stewardship responsibilities under both the Law of the Sea Convention and UNCED.
Horizontal and vertical integration	Overcoming the sectoral and intergovernmental fragmentation that exists in today's coastal management efforts is a prime goal of ICM. Institutional mechanisms for effective coordination among various sectors active in the coastal zone and between the various levels of government operating in the coastal zone are fundamental to the strengthening and rationalization of the coastal management process. From the variety of available options, the coordination and harmonization mechanism must be tailored to fit the unique aspects of each particular national government setting.
The use of science	Given the complexities and uncertainties that exist in the coastal zone, ICM must be built upon the best science (natural and social) available. Techniques such as risk assessment, economic valuation, vulnerability assessments, resource accounting, benefit-cost analysis and outcome-based monitoring should all be built into the ICM process, as appropriate.

Source: Cicin-Sain, Knecht and Fisk, 1995.

INTEGRATED
COASTAL AREA
MANAGEMENT
and
AGRICULTURE
FORESTRY AND
FISHERIES

PART

A

ISSUES, PERSPECTIVES, POLICY AND PLANNING PROCESSES FOR INTEGRATED COASTAL AREA MANAGEMENT

INTEGRATED
COASTAL AREA
MANAGEMENT
and
AGRICULTURE
FORESTRY AND
FISHERIES

BOXES

FIGURES

TABLES

ISSUES, PERSPECTIVES, POLICY AND PLANNING PROCESSES FOR INTEGRATED COASTAL AREA MANAGEMENT

PART A

INTEGRATED
COASTAL AREA
MANAGEMENT
and
AGRICULTURE
FORESTRY AND
FISHERIES

1. The need for integrated coastal area management

1.1 DEFINING COASTAL AREAS

Coastal areas are commonly defined as the interface or transition areas between land and sea, including large inland lakes. Coastal areas are diverse in function and form, dynamic and do not lend themselves well to definition by strict spatial boundaries. Unlike watersheds, there are no exact natural boundaries that unambiguously delineate coastal areas.

Geologically, continental margins are of two types: active margins where the edge of a continent happens to be at the edge of an oceanic plate (e.g. the west coast of South America); and inactive margins where the transition from continental lithosphere to oceanic lithosphere is within a plate rather than at a plate edge (e.g. the Atlantic). Coastal areas are therefore characterized by the vertical accretion of near-shore land. This depends on several factors: sediment supply from rivers or from the sea; the width of the shelf, or the proximity of a submarine canyon through which currents remove sediments; and the strength of

3

INTEGRATED
COASTAL AREA
MANAGEMENT
and
AGRICULTURE
FORESTRY AND
FISHERIES

PART A

ISSUES, PERSPECTIVES, POLICY AND PLANNING PROCESSES FOR INTEGRATED COASTAL AREA MANAGEMENT

1. The need for integrated coastal area management

longshore currents and incidence of cyclones, both of which transport and redistribute sediments along the coast. Sedimentation is the major geological activity that shapes coasts, but human-induced land subsidence is having an increasing impact on coastal morphology.

Nevertheless, for management purposes, a variety of landwards and seawards boundaries, ranging from fairly narrow and precise ones[1] to much broader and more nebulous ones,[2] have been utilized around the world. Management boundaries are pragmatic, being influenced by the geographic scope of relevant management concerns, including biophysical, economic, social, institutional and organizational aspects. Therefore, the boundaries of a coastal area may change over time for management purposes, as the issues to be faced become more extensive or complex and require more far-ranging solutions.

It has been suggested that a distinction be made between the terms "coastal zone" and "coastal area". The term "coastal zone" would refer to the geographic area defined by the enabling legislation for coastal management, while "coastal area" would be used more broadly to refer to the geographic area along the coast that has not yet been defined as a zone for management purposes. In the United States, earlier attention to management in the coastal zone gave rise to the term "coastal zone management" (CZM). As experience was gained of the multifaceted character of many of the issues and the consequent need to adopt an holistic approach to management, the term was revised to "integrated coastal zone management" (ICZM). This term continues to be used by many authorities, including the World Bank.

The multifaceted approach to the management of coastal resources has become known as integrated coastal management (ICM). Pernetta and Elder (1993) have described it as meaning "the process of combining all aspects of the human, physical and biological aspects of the coastal zone within a single management framework". However, they have preferred the term "holistic coastal management" to emphasize that "careful planning and management of all sectoral activities simultaneously will result in greater overall benefits than pursuing sectoral development plans independently of one another."

In practice, laws concerning coastal management seldom unambiguously or precisely define the coastal zone. Thus, the boundaries of the relevant management area can, and usually do, change over time without regard to the enabling legislation. In addition, few nations have comprehensive coastal zone management policies. As a result, different coastal areas within the same nation can fall under the jurisdiction of different coastal management plans and their boundaries can be variously defined by prevailing management issues in the locality.

In these guidelines, the term "coastal area" is preferred to "coastal zone" to refer to the geographic entity covered by an integrated coastal management plan. Such coastal management takes place at two levels: the national, or subnational, level, where national goals, strategies, institutional arrangements and legislation may be determined and put into place; and the local, or area, level, where area-specific goals, objectives, plans and their implementation are the focus of attention.

The use of integrated coastal area management (ICAM) makes explicit the fact that degradation of coastal resources may result from activities outside the coastal zone, as defined at the beginning of these guidelines. Where issues are deemed to arise in a watershed, ICAM may, subject to the appropriate institutional arrangements, extend outside the coastal area.

1.2 THE ECONOMIC AND ENVIRONMENTAL IMPORTANCE OF COASTAL AREAS

Favourable biophysical and climatic conditions, together with the ease of communication and navigation frequently offered by coastal sites (by sea or up river valleys), have encouraged human settlement in coastal zones since prehistoric times.

---

[1] For instance, in Sri Lanka, the coastal zone is defined as encompassing 1 km seawards of the mean low waterline and 300 m landwards of the mean high waterline, extending to a maximum of 2 km inland in the case of rivers, lagoons or estuaries. Similarly, coastal areas in the Association of Southeast Asian Nations (ASEAN) countries are defined using arbitrary distances, in connection with administrative or political boundaries and physical landmarks or selected environmental units (Scura *et al.*, 1992).

[2] For example, under French law, a coast is loosely defined as a geographic entity that calls for specific zoning and land-use protection and development (Boelaert-Suominen and Culinan, 1993).

PART A

INTEGRATED
COASTAL AREA
MANAGEMENT
and
AGRICULTURE
FORESTRY AND
FISHERIES

ISSUES, PERSPECTIVES, POLICY AND PLANNING PROCESSES FOR INTEGRATED COASTAL AREA MANAGEMENT

1. The need for integrated coastal area management

1.2.1 Economic role

Many of the world's major cities are located in coastal areas, and a large portion of economic activities, with the exception of agriculture, are concentrated in these cities. The coastal zone is an area of convergence of activities in urban centres, such as shipping in major ports, and wastes generated from domestic sources and by major industrial facilities. Thus, traditional resource-based activities, such as coastal fisheries, aquaculture, forestry and agriculture, are found side by side with activities such as industry, shipping and tourism.

The potential for economic opportunities in coastal cities is a strong attractive force, fuelling immigration, often from economically depressed rural areas. As a result, in the future much larger, younger populations can be expected in the coastal areas of developing countries. These future coastal residents will demand employment, housing, energy, food, water and other goods and services, thus presenting a substantial development challenge.

Against this demographic backdrop, coastal areas are extremely important for the social and economic welfare of current and future generations, as coastal resources support key economic and subsistence activities. The economies of most developing countries are currently very dependent on natural resources, for agriculture, fisheries and forestry subsectors,[3] mining, oil and gas extraction, marine tourism and ocean transport. Many of the world's most productive agricultural areas are located in river deltas and coastal plains. In particular, the deltas' food productivity[4] exceeds local consumption needs and eventual delta disturbance can result in national economic shock waves that reach far beyond the delta.

Although, in the future, coastal areas will become more urbanized, and the economies of developing countries will undoubtedly diversify to some extent through industrialization, dependence on coastal resources is likely to remain strong. Industrial development often entails the processing of agricultural, fishery and forestry products, together with oil refining and textile manufacture. These diversified economic activities are often also dependent on coastal resources and, as economic diversification increases and makes the component sectors more interdependent, conflicts over natural resources and the environment will tend to develop.

1.2.2 Environmental role

Coastal areas are also important ecologically, as they provide a number of environmental goods and services. The peculiar characteristic of coastal environments is their dynamic nature which results from the transfer of matter, energy and living organisms between land and sea systems, under the influence of primary driving forces that include short-term weather, long-term climate, secular changes in sea level and tides.

Marine, estuary and coastal wetland areas often benefit from flows of nutrients from the land and also from ocean upwelling which brings nutrient-rich water to the surface. They thus tend to have particularly high biological productivity. Moreover, coastal areas frequently contain critical terrestrial and aquatic habitats, particularly in the tropics. Such habitats together comprise unique coastal ecosystems, support a rich biological diversity and frequently contain a valuable assortment of natural resources. Examples of such habitats are estuarine areas, coral reefs, coastal mangrove forests and other wetlands, tidal flats and seagrass beds, which also provide essential nursery and feeding areas for many coastal and oceanic aquatic species.

It is estimated that 90 percent of the world's fish production is dependent on coastal areas at some time in their life cycle. In addition, these areas support large numbers of migratory and non-migratory waterfowl and shorebirds, and endangered reptiles, such as turtles and alligators. The advantages of maintaining their biological diversity have been formally recognized.[5] Water quality is related in different ways to key coastal

---

[3] The economic and environmental roles of agriculture, forestry and fisheries are briefly described in Section 1.7. More details are in Sections 1 of Parts B, C and D.

[4] For example, in Viet Nam, 50 percent of the national rice production comes from the Mekong delta in the south and 20 percent is produced in the Red River delta near Hanoi.

[5] In, for example, the Convention on Biological Diversity, introduced at the United Nations Conference on Environment and Sustainable Development, Rio de Janeiro, June 1992, which entered into force on 29 December 1993, and the 1995 Jakarta Mandate on Biodiversity.

INTEGRATED
COASTAL AREA
MANAGEMENT
and
AGRICULTURE
FORESTRY AND
FISHERIES

PART A

ISSUES, PERSPECTIVES, POLICY AND PLANNING PROCESSES FOR INTEGRATED COASTAL AREA MANAGEMENT

1. The need for integrated coastal area management

demands; some examples are illustrated in Figure A.1.

Physical features of coastal ecosystems, such as reefs and belts of mangrove, are important for the mitigation of the effects of natural disasters, such as storm-tide surges, shoreline retreat or floods. These features also play an essential role in natural processes, such as land accretion, and help to control coastal erosion and other damage arising from wind and wave action.

Even when coastal areas do not provide unique biological ecosystems, their location at the sea/land interface has recreational and aesthetic values which, in many countries, support valuable tourism activities, as well as providing attractive sites for industrial development and human settlements. The recreational and aesthetic values of coastal areas are increasing in developing countries as coastal tourism develops and domestic demand rises with increasing real incomes. Unique and appealing vistas, sandy and rocky beaches, pristine blue water, wetlands and coastal forest, and the associated wildlife, coral reefs and multiple recreational activities supported by these areas are major attractions of coastal areas.

The mouth of a river heavily polluted by sewers of overcrowded towns and cities, West Africa

1.3 ENVIRONMENTAL THREATS TO COASTAL AREAS

The most common problems of coastal areas, resulting from both natural and anthropogenic stresses, are illustrated in Figure A.2.

The dynamics of alluvial landscapes and natural sedimentation patterns that determine the nutrient and energy flows in coastal areas are increasingly being modified by human activities, in particular those that affect water flows (dams, increased water extraction, deviation of rivers) and erosion, especially that caused by deforestation. This prevents or slows down vertical accretion, thus aggravating salt-water intrusion and impairing drainage conditions in riverine, delta or estuarine areas. It reduces or blocks sediment supply to the coast itself, which may give rise to the retreat of the coastline through wave erosion. Coastal areas are also prone to threats from natural causes such as tidal surges and sea-level rise.

The worst scenario projects a sea-level rise of 95 cm by the year 2100, with large local differences (resulting from tides, wind and atmospheric pressure patterns, changes in ocean circulation, vertical movements of continents, etc.) in the relative sea-level rises. The impacts of sea-level rise are therefore expected to be

Aerial photo of Saint Louis, Senegal

PART A

ISSUES, PERSPECTIVES, POLICY AND PLANNING PROCESSES FOR INTEGRATED COASTAL AREA MANAGEMENT

INTEGRATED
COASTAL AREA
MANAGEMENT
and
AGRICULTURE
FORESTRY AND
FISHERIES

1. The need for integrated coastal area management

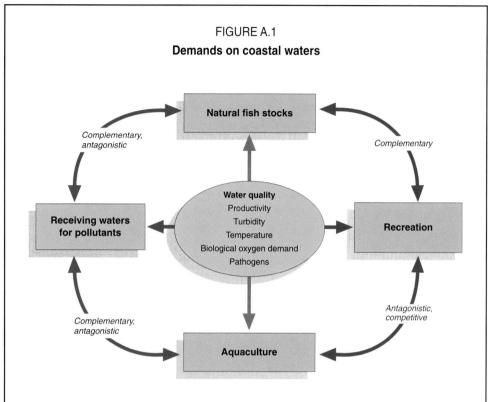

FIGURE A.1

Demands on coastal waters

Note: Among the key water quality parameters are temperature, turbidity, primary productivity, biochemical oxygen demand and concentration of pathogens such as coliform bacteria. The distribution of temperature (along with salinity) provides information on patterns of circulation. In addition, temperature affects the growth rate and distribution of fish populations. The turbidity (like the biochemical oxygen demand) of the water not only determines its recreational value, but is also an indicator of the capacity of water to receive additional nutrients and particulate/dissolved organic wastes. The primary productivity of the water ultimately determines the productivity of commercial stocks of fish, crustacea and molluscs. The concentration of pathogens is, of course, a concern for humans as well as for farmed and natural populations of marine organisms.

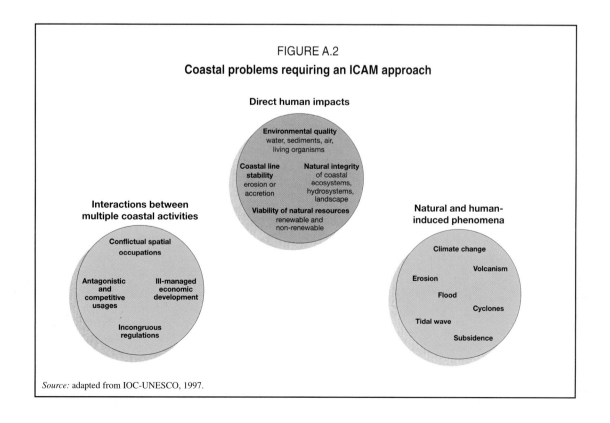

FIGURE A.2

Coastal problems requiring an ICAM approach

Source: adapted from IOC-UNESCO, 1997.

INTEGRATED
COASTAL AREA
MANAGEMENT
and
AGRICULTURE
FORESTRY AND
FISHERIES

PART A

ISSUES, PERSPECTIVES, POLICY AND PLANNING PROCESSES FOR INTEGRATED COASTAL AREA MANAGEMENT

1. The need for integrated coastal area management

more local than global (Warwick *et al.,* 1996). The relative change of sea and land is the main factor. Many cities, for instance, suffer land subsidence as a result of groundwater withdrawal. This may be compounded by sea-level rise, especially since rates of subsidence may exceed the rate of sea-level rise between now and 2100. Under the worst scenario, the majority of the people who would be affected live in China (72 million), Bangladesh (13 million people and loss of 16 percent of national rice production) and Egypt (6 million people and 12 to 15 percent of agricultural land lost) (Nicholls and Leatherman, 1995). Between 0.3 percent (Venezuela) and 100 percent (Kiribati and the Marshall Islands) of the population would be affected (Nicholls, 1993). Even more significant than the direct loss of land caused by the sea rising, are the associated indirect factors, including erosion patterns and damage to coastal infrastructure, salinization of wells, suboptimal functioning of the sewage system of coastal cities (with resulting health impacts), loss of littoral ecosystems and loss of biotic resources. In coastal areas, and particularly deltas, factors such as modified ocean circulation patterns (and their impact on building and erosion of the coast), climate change in the catchment basin and change in coastal climate, not to mention changes in the frequency of extreme events, should be taken into account.

While increased damage to coastal areas will certainly occur, it will be linked more to development (value of assets) than to increased fragility of populations or agriculture. Particularly in small islands, where development leads to a concentration of wealth, there is a risk of high damage being caused by natural disaster events. Where the extremes of one or more variables are involved at the same time, the risks will be very high. Such "time bombs" are to be found in highly vulnerable deltas (which are densely populated and normally feed a large hinterland) that may become very unstable over a short period of time (Gommes *et al.,* 1997).

Wherever rising populations continue to be economically dependent on the primary producing sectors – agriculture, forestry and fisheries – and on other sectors directly dependent on natural resources, such as tourism and mining, the overexploitation of renewable and non-renewable resources, the degradation of ecosystems and the resulting loss of natural resource productivity are of primary concern.

In this context, it is worth noting that marine pollution is derived mainly from land-based sources and the atmosphere (see Figure A.3), with river runoff and land-based discharges directly affecting coastal waters (GESAMP, 1990). More than 90 percent of all chemicals, refuse and other material entering coastal waters remains there in sediments, wetlands, fringing reefs and other coastal ecosystems.

1.4 DEMOGRAPHIC AND OCCUPATIONAL PRESSURES

According to the 1994 distribution of population in relation to the distance from the nearest coastline, 20.6 percent of the world's population lives within 30 km of the coast, and 37 percent within 100 km (Gommes *et al.,* 1997). As a result of migration to coastal areas, and in particular to coastal cities, the coastal population is growing at a faster rate than the world population; within the next 20 to 30 years, the coastal population is projected to almost double.[6] At present, two-thirds of the world's cities with a population of 2.5 million or more are situated near tidal estuaries (IUCN/UNEP/WWF, 1991) and 220 million people live in the, mostly coastal, megacities. These urban developments are taking up fertile agricultural land and leading to pollution of rivers, estuaries and seas by sewage and industrial and agricultural effluents. In turn, this is posing a threat to coastal ecosystems, their biological diversity, environmental regulatory functions and role in generating employment and food.

Poor people often migrate from inland rural areas and settle along the coast in search of better livelihoods because they cannot find employment elsewhere. They are drawn to coastal areas where resources still tend to be "open access", or freely available, and thus offer sources of income of last resort. One means of relieving the pressures on coastal areas is therefore to improve living conditions in more distant rural areas. Investments in natural resource conservation in inland coastal areas, often made up of hilly and fragile land, will have the double advantage of improving conditions for poor farmers and reducing erosion and siltation. The creation

---

[6] The world's 20 largest coastal urban agglomerations (i.e. Tokyo, New York, Mexico City, Sao Paolo, Shanghai, Bombay, Los Angeles, Calcutta, Buenos Aires, Seoul, Osaka, Rio de Janeiro, Jakarta, Metro Manila, Karachi, Lagos, Istanbul, Lima, Bangkok and Dacca) are expected to increase from a total population of 216.9 million in 1990 to 353.5 million in the year 2015. (UN, 1994).

PART A

INTEGRATED
COASTAL AREA
MANAGEMENT
and
AGRICULTURE
FORESTRY AND
FISHERIES

ISSUES, PERSPECTIVES, POLICY AND PLANNING PROCESSES FOR INTEGRATED COASTAL AREA MANAGEMENT

1. The need for integrated coastal area management

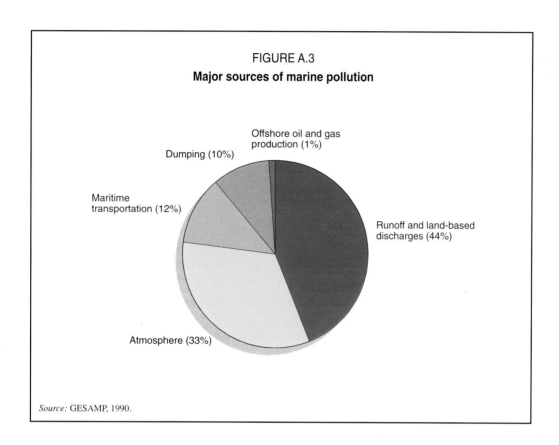

FIGURE A.3
Major sources of marine pollution

Offshore oil and gas production (1%)

Dumping (10%)

Maritime transportation (12%)

Runoff and land-based discharges (44%)

Atmosphere (33%)

Source: GESAMP, 1990.

Mangrove fuelwood
transport fleet, Conakry,
Guinea

Young boy entering mangrove forest to
collect shrimp fry for shrimp farming,
Sunderbans, Bangladesh

INTEGRATED
COASTAL AREA
MANAGEMENT
and
AGRICULTURE
FORESTRY AND
FISHERIES

PART A

ISSUES, PERSPECTIVES, POLICY AND PLANNING PROCESSES FOR INTEGRATED COASTAL AREA MANAGEMENT

1. The need for integrated coastal area management

of non-agricultural employment and the introduction of appropriate management systems will further improve the situation.

The World Resources Institute developed an index of development-related threats to coastal ecosystems, drawing on 1995 digitized map data, and defined coastal zones as including the land area within 60 km of adjacent near-shore waters. The index is based on five globally available georeferenced indicators of potential anthropogenic threats:

- cities with populations of more than 100 000: captures potential threats from coastal development, sewage, and industrial pollution;
- major ports: measures the potential threats from species introductions (through the release of ballast water), the potential for oil spills and industrial pollution;
- population density: measures potential threats from coastal development and pollution;
- road density: an indirect measure of access to coastal resources and coastal development;
- pipeline density: measures the potential threat of oil pollution and of spills of other industrial wastes.

It is important to note that, as the above indicators measure pressure rather than condition, the results do not imply that these areas have actually been degraded. In addition: the impacts of fishing, deforestation and agricultural activity are not covered; human activities beyond 60 km of the coast were not considered; the study did not include the relative sensitivities of different ecosystems to disturbance; data quality was better for some regions than for others; data modelling and mapping added additional uncertainty to the results; and pressures may have been underrepresented where they have a cumulative effect. The current study was also at too coarse a scale to guide national management and planning activities and the intention is to develop a set of more comprehensive, finer-resolution indicators.

Keeping in mind these limitations, Table A.1 shows that 86 percent of Europe's and 69 percent of Asia's coasts are at high or moderate potential risk of degradation.

1.5 SECTORAL INTERDEPENDENCIES IN COASTAL AREAS

The coastal resource system is interdependent and interrelated and has direct and indirect connections with inland resource systems. For instance, production of fish may be dependent on the habitat for juveniles provided by mangrove swamps, and the health of a coral reef may be related to the filtering properties of the mangrove ensuring that only clear water reaches the reef. Conversely, a coral reef may die as a result of being covered with silt from soil erosion, perhaps occurring many miles upstream, caused by inappropriate forestry or agricultural practices. Mangroves, coastal dunes and reefs may protect coastal agriculture from erosion or storm surge, for example.

Ill-managed economic development in coastal areas is likely to create serious problems related to water pollution, degradation of critical habitats, depletion of natural resource stocks and other effects. When this occurs, the much publicized benefits of growth such as increased employment and rising nominal incomes will be undermined by increased costs in the areas of health, productivity and aesthetics.

Economic activities consist in changing resources or inputs into products or services. Thus, all activities directly or indirectly affect and interact with their environment (i.e. ecological, economic and social systems). For example, air and water temperatures determine the types of agriculture, forestry and fisheries that are possible and affect productivity, while market characteristics affect their viability.

Such interactions may be categorized as being synergistic, complementary, competitive or antagonistic (see Box A.1). Integrated coastal area management aims at maximizing synergistic and complementary interactions and minimizing competitive and antagonistic ones.

1.6 CAUSES OF ECOSYSTEM DEGRADATION AND NATURAL RESOURCE LOSS IN COASTAL AREAS

Ecosystem and natural resource damage in coastal areas, and hence reduced environmental goods and services, stem from increasing demands on resources (especially local demand arising from demographic pressure) and unsustainable management practices. The causes of ecosystem or natural resource damage in coastal areas can be analysed according to three interrelated "failures": market failure (of which a related issue is property rights); policy or intervention failure; and information failure (Turner and Jones, 1991).

ISSUES, PERSPECTIVES, POLICY AND PLANNING PROCESSES FOR INTEGRATED COASTAL AREA MANAGEMENT

PART A

INTEGRATED
COASTAL AREA
MANAGEMENT
and
AGRICULTURE
FORESTRY AND
FISHERIES

1. The need for integrated coastal area management

BOX A.1
Basic interactions between economic activities

Two or more activities may be **synergistic** when their interaction results in an increase in economic activity (or well-being) or environmental benefits greater than the sum of their individual results. For example, tree conservation on land cleared for agriculture not only provides wood and non-wood products, stabilizes the soil and generates agricultural products, but also leads to a more rational and complete use of soil fertility and energy, enhances synergetic relations between species, minimizes the risk of pests and diseases and diversifies economic opportunities.

Complementarity between two activities exists when they share the same resource(s) or the same facilities without conflict and when one activity provides inputs to another. For example, there is complementarity when a forest industry supplies timber for boat building or wood for the smoking of fish or when agricultural by-products are used in the feeding of cultured fish.

In contrast, a **competitive** interaction most commonly occurs when two or more activities have a shared requirement for a resource in limited supply, resulting in conflict. A competitive interaction may be

either reciprocal or one-sided. An example of reciprocal competition is when farmers and urban dwellers draw on the same groundwater supply, each suffering from the subsequent shortage of water or its increasing salinity. An example of one-sided interaction is where water is drawn off for irrigation upstream, thus affecting the flow of water downstream with the consequent damage to fishery habitats (e.g. the damage to the spawning habitat of Caspian Sea sturgeon as a result of diversion of water in the Russian Federation and the Islamic Republic of Iran).

An **antagonistic** interaction occurs when the output of one activity degrades resources or modifies the environment in a way that harms another activity. For instance, pollution resulting from urban, industrial or agricultural activity that affects fisheries (killing fish, destroying fish habitats and infecting fish with substances dangerous to human health). Antagonistic interactions, like competitive ones, may be one-sided or reciprocal. A reciprocal antagonistic interaction is when the overexploitation of a renewable resource leads to its depletion beyond an economic harvesting level with the consequent loss of livelihood of the former harvesters.

TABLE A.1
Percent of coastlines under potential threat[a]

Region	Low [b]	Moderate [c]	High [d]
Africa	49	14	38
Asia	31	17	52
North and Central America	71	12	17
South America	50	24	26
Europe	14	16	70
Former USSR	64	24	12
Oceania	56	20	24
World	**49**	**17**	**34**

Notes:
(a) Threat ranking depicts potential risk to coastal ecosystems from development-related activities in 1995.
(b) Low potential threat: coastal areas with a population density of less than 75 people/km^2, a road network density of less than 100 km of road/ km^2 or no pipelines known to be present.
(c) Moderate potential threat: coastal areas with a population density of between 75 and 150 people/km^2, a road network density of between 100 and 150 km of road/ km^2 or a pipeline density of between 0 and 10 km of pipeline/ km^2.
(d) High potential threat: coastal areas falling within a city or major port footprint or having a population density exceeding 150 people/km^2, a road network density exceeding 150 km of road/ km^2 or a pipeline density exceeding 10 km of pipeline/ km^2.

Sources: World Resources Institute, 1996; Bryant *et al.,* 1995; http://www.wri.org/wr-96-97.

INTEGRATED
COASTAL AREA
MANAGEMENT
and
AGRICULTURE
FORESTRY AND
FISHERIES

PART A

ISSUES, PERSPECTIVES, POLICY AND PLANNING PROCESSES FOR INTEGRATED COASTAL AREA MANAGEMENT

1. The need for integrated coastal area management

1.6.1 Market failure and property rights

Market prices frequently fail to reflect the true cost of a good or a service and so send incorrect signals to the marketplace; sometimes, putting a price on a good may be impossible. Such situations represent market failure.

An example of incorrect market signals is the lack of internalizing of the cost of conversion of mangrove forest to agriculture or aquaculture because the costs of the conversion do not internalize externalities. Mangrove may be taken over by landless rural people seeking to make a living. But where users (e.g. companies) pay the owner for the (use of the) land, it has often been seen that in future years productivity will decline, there will be saline intrusion and/or storm damage will occur inland because of the absence of the protection that the mangrove provided. None of these negative factors will be reflected in the purchase price. The cost of destroying the mangrove may well have to be borne, not by whoever destroys it, but by someone else; in this case, market failure is even more pronounced. Widespread destruction of mangroves can lead to siltation of estuaries and ports or eutrophication of coastal waters; such impacts, which originate outside the places they affect and are almost invariably negative, being referred to as negative "externalities".[7]

The term "property right" (see Box A.2) refers to a legally enforceable right that may arise from legislation or unwritten common law or customary law. A distinction should be made between property rights as such and *de facto* situations of access to a resource because it is not owned by anyone (for instance fish or wild animals prior to capture) or because the owner (who may be the state) does not exercise the right to exclude others from access to the resource. The issue of property rights arises most frequently when a good or service cannot be priced.

For any property regime, it is essential that an authority system (e.g. state authority or traditional leaders) can meet the expectations of rights holders. When the authority system breaks down, management of the natural resource fails, and the entire system changes (i.e. common property degenerates into open access). The authority mechanisms and capacity to enforce compliance ensure compliance with, and integrity of, the property regime (Bromley and Cochrane, 1994).

Maribot Beach,
Saint Lucia

Flooded farmland,
Bangladesh

12

---

[7] See Glossary.

PART A

INTEGRATED
COASTAL AREA
MANAGEMENT
and
AGRICULTURE
FORESTRY AND
FISHERIES

ISSUES, PERSPECTIVES, POLICY AND PLANNING PROCESSES FOR INTEGRATED COASTAL AREA MANAGEMENT

1. The need for integrated coastal area management

BOX A.2
Market aspects of property regimes

From an economic perspective it is convenient to distinguish four main types of property regimes affecting natural resources.

State property refers to resources that are managed by the state, either directly or by delegating authority to local bodies. State property may consist of both resources that are owned by the state but that are capable of private ownership, and public resources that cannot be privately owned and that the state must manage in the public interest. The seashore and the territorial waters of most countries fall into the category of public resources and, in some countries, public resources also include freshwater and land. Indeed, it is generally believed that all societies originally treated land in this way. This concept is summed up in the remark of a West African chief that "Land belongs to a vast family of which many are dead, few are living, and countless numbers are still unborn" (cited by Simpson, 1976).

The state determines the rules of access to state property and, generally, a controlling agency ensures such access is respected. The state may lease the natural resource to groups or individuals under specified conditions and for a specified period. For example, grazers may have access to state pastureland, or a mining company have the right to mine minerals on state land. Where a long-term lease is granted, the regime might resemble private property. On the other hand, short-term leases provide no incentives to the concessionaire to practise conservation. Where rules of access are not enforced, because of a lack of personnel and finance, logistical problems or corruption, such resources become (factually though not legally) open access regimes.

Open access regimes refer to situations where no-one controls access to a resource and anyone can exploit it. No-one has rights to the resource but neither does anyone determine or enforce norms for its use. As a result, such resources tend to be used opportunistically and no-one manages them since there is no incentive to use them prudently. Thus, open access tends to entail overexploitation – the benefits of a greater harvest accrue to an individual (or group) while the cost (diminishing stocks) will be shared by all. Open access regimes are often the result of institutional failures that undermine former collective or individual regimes.

Common property refers to situations where a group of co-owners have exclusive rights of access to a resource for specific or general purposes (e.g. to draw water for irrigation or to use land for cultivation or grazing). Such groups are social units that can vary in nature, size and internal structure. The group determines membership which usually implies some common cultural norms. Internal authority systems usually apply sets of rules and codes of conduct. Groups vary widely but are typically "social units with definite membership and boundaries, with certain common interests, with at least some interaction among members, with common cultural norms and often their own endogenous authority systems" (Bromley and Cernea, 1989). Tribal groups, subvillage groups, small pastoral groups and kin systems are examples of common property regimes. The group, having a common interest and rules, generally shares resources fairly and manages them sustainably. In the case of commonly owned land, customary tenure systems usually identify leaders who allocate specific areas of land to individuals or families from the group who, in turn, have specific rights and duties in respect of that land and retain it for as long as it is productively used. However, there is a risk of "free riding", individuals being tempted to overexploit their share of the resource while counting on others to observe the rules. Such defections should be treated with strong punitive action.

Private (alienable) property includes property owned by individuals or legal entities, where owners can exclude others, transfer ownership and manage and invest knowing that good stewardship will bring in long-term benefits. Private owners will usually have an economic incentive to use their property prudently and sustainably. However this is not always the case and the prospect of obtaining high returns in the short term may cause some private owners (particularly absentee owners, who may be investors with high capital mobility) to exploit resources unsustainably. In practice, private owners are often constrained by legal rules that place restrictions on their freedom to exploit their resources (e.g. legislation governing air or water pollution levels from factories).

13

INTEGRATED
COASTAL AREA
MANAGEMENT
and
AGRICULTURE
FORESTRY AND
FISHERIES

PART A

ISSUES, PERSPECTIVES, POLICY AND PLANNING PROCESSES FOR INTEGRATED COASTAL AREA MANAGEMENT

1. The need for integrated coastal area management

Property and use rights are fundamental to the allocation of natural resources, as they determine who has the legal right to control access to the resource. In ICAM, the issue arises when ways of preventing environmental degradation or overexploitation (such as mangrove conversion or overfishing) are being sought. However, the response may vary according to circumstances. For example: the state may choose to enforce an existing ownership right over mangroves to prevent conversion; the distribution of property rights could be changed (e.g. use rights may be granted to a limited group of users, or state-owned resources could be sold); or legislation could be introduced to restrict the rights of private owners where these are causing harm.

One of the areas where open access is most prevalent in coastal zones is in fisheries. Very often, any citizen of the state has, in effect, free access to fisheries. The result in recent years is that most fisheries are fully or overexploited. A newcomer entering such a fishery may have a better vessel and fishing gear than current fishers and may, as a result, be able to fish profitably. The newcomer's increased wealth, however, will be made at the expense of the more poorly equipped fishers.

In recent years, the degradation of open access resources has led to an increased awareness of the value to society of these resources. Much attention is therefore being given to establishing or rebuilding institutions to manage access to threatened resources to help to protect society from negative resource externalities.

The existence of private or common property or exclusive use rights may lead to undesirable environmental and other impacts. For example, the holding of private property rights by entrepreneurs investing in shrimp cultivation in some coastal areas of South and Southeast Asia and of Latin America has, in some cases, resulted in destruction of wetland forests, water pollution and the marginalization and dislocation of resource-poor people. Where population pressure increases, through migration for instance, and pure survival is the issue, it will often be difficult to ensure compliance with various property regimes that endeavour to exclude one group or another.

In a perfect market situation (which only exists in textbooks) resources would be allocated to their correct societal use. In practice, resources usually have multiple uses valued differently by different potential users (forest dwellers need wood for heating and cooking

while environmentalists defend trees *per se*; a logging company may see only the value of the exploitable trees, while local communities are aware of the forest's non-wood resources such as medicinal plants, wildlife and insects, and its role in absorbing CO_2 or producing oxygen). Excluding people from access to essential resources, especially when survival itself depends on that access, has a high social cost and, indeed, eventually becomes impossible.

Owing to the difficulty of accounting for the environmental goods and services of a given resource, especially in the long term, and the social values placed upon them by different user groups, the market will be a poor guide to management decisions. Appropriate management will depend on the circumstances and interactions of social, economic and biophysical institutions.

1.6.2 Policy failure

Policy failure is the single most important cause of natural resource loss and ecosystem degradation. Policy failure is usually driven by the pursuit of short-sighted economic gain and lack of awareness of the long-term implications of non-intervention.

In most cases, policy failure means policies have not responded to actual or threatened degradation in the resource base or ecosystems, or have not taken account of local views. This leads to weakening of the institutions needed to cope with the situation; absence of a legal framework or weak enforcement capabilities for example. Such situations may apply to coastal resources which therefore become open to overexploitation.

Resource loss and ecosystem degradation will only be halted if appropriate policies are adopted and implemented. Growing awareness of the environmental, social and economic consequences of policy failure that are of global concern, such as global warming or loss of biological diversity, is fortunately beginning to put pressures on governments to rectify present polices and create an appropriate policy environment.

More specifically, the following measures should be adopted:

- legislation related to the long-term sustainability of the natural environment;
- decentralized structures established on the basis of effective participation at local level;

PART A

ISSUES, PERSPECTIVES, POLICY AND PLANNING PROCESSES FOR INTEGRATED COASTAL AREA MANAGEMENT

INTEGRATED
COASTAL AREA
MANAGEMENT
and
AGRICULTURE
FORESTRY AND
FISHERIES

1. The need for integrated coastal area management

- incentives for producers;
- provision of support that cannot be covered from local resources.

In the current context of globalization and interdependence, international institutions often impose policy reforms related to market forces, which do not always take account of the needs of nations whose bargaining power is weak. Global environmental concerns and the international exchange of goods and services are, however, governed by conventions and agreements that influence national and local decision-making. While economic efficiency and competitiveness are clearly important, local-level concerns ought to be voiced in the macropolicy arena in order to reflect and respect environmental, cultural and economic diversity.

Sustainability (or unsustainability) can be measured by the sum of the various human, economic and natural resources, where the degree of use, exchange and trade among them will vary according to the values given to each. The interactions between resources, and the degree of substitutability, therefore ultimately depend on the acceptability of trade-offs between resources. In farming systems, trade-offs exist between productivity, stability, resilience and equity. The different properties of a system and their importance to different groups will determine the trade-off patterns. As farm systems evolve in response to their own logic, as well as to changes in society, agricultural innovations may initially be rejected because of socio-cultural constraints to their adoption, but will be adopted rapidly if economic circumstances change (e.g. capital, labour, markets, support services). In other words, the sustainability of a system depends on circumstances, that is, on contingency.

1.6.3 Information failure
Sound policies require sound information. Frequently in developing countries, information is lacking, especially in such areas as renewable resources and, more particularly, on the status of renewable resources (especially fisheries), natural resource dynamics, land-use and tenure patterns, institutional, social and cultural conditions, and levels of investment in coastal areas. Similarly, environmental monitoring, for example of water quality, is often scant.

Perfect information will never be available even in the most advanced countries; for example, it is often extremely difficult to determine if a decline in fish catches in a particular area is caused by the effect of sedimentation of habitat, overfishing, natural factors or all three. However, the more information is available, the better the basis for policy decisions.

Lack of information can be a contributory factor to policy failure. For example, policy-makers may take the view that their country is too poor to afford conservation of renewable resources or ecosystems, and would opt for economic development even if it destroys some of the country's natural capital. The attitude may be different if policy-makers are aware of the full economic value of the resource under threat and take account of the value of all the goods and environmental services it provides.

The routine collection and analysis of information is costly, in both human and financial terms. But, insofar as policy decisions cannot be taken without adequate information, it must be made available. The cost of gathering information can be contained by identifying as precisely as possible the information requirements related to coastal areas that are under threat.

However, lack of adequate information should not be a reason for inaction. Useful action can be taken even where only relatively superficial information is available and there are often good arguments for taking a precautionary approach[8]: "when in doubt, protect". In order to overcome these difficulties gradually, research requirements should be built into the strategy or plan, encompassing information gathering and strengthening staff capacities to analyse and compute various types of information and to analyse interactions.[9]

Policy-makers need tools to assist them in policy-making and planning, especially to gauge whether their actions are likely to result in sustainable development. Some attempts to create indicators of ecological sustainability and quality of life have been made by a number of institutions.[10] Such indicators, however, must be used with caution as situations are always highly complex and the quantification of the environment – and more especially its monetization – is fraught with difficulties.[11]

15

---

[8] See Section 2.2.4 and Box A.5.
[9] See Section 2.3.5.
[10] See Section 2.3.6.
[11] See Box A.24.

INTEGRATED
COASTAL AREA
MANAGEMENT
and
AGRICULTURE
FORESTRY AND
FISHERIES

PART A

ISSUES, PERSPECTIVES, POLICY AND PLANNING PROCESSES FOR INTEGRATED COASTAL AREA MANAGEMENT

1. The need for integrated coastal area management

Once policy-makers, planners and resource users agree on the issues, criteria for thresholds of resource degradation can be established. Factors here will include social and economic considerations, such as the time, expense and level of detail that is being aimed at. In addition, estimates and common sense based on experience, training and intuition will also often provide a satisfactory basis for decisions.

1.7 AGRICULTURE, FORESTRY AND FISHERIES IN COASTAL AREAS

Most developing countries are characterized by a fast-growing population and workforce. The rate of growth of the world's economically active population, between 1990 and 2000, is 1.86 percent per year (ILO, 1998). While nearly half of this workforce is absorbed in the agriculture, forestry and fisheries subsectors, an increasing amount of labour will seek employment in non-farm occupations. Finding productive and remunerative employment for these workers will be one of the main challenges of the twenty-first century.

The development of non-farm jobs in villages and small towns closely linked to agriculture and farm-produce processing is a powerful way of relieving pressure on coastal areas. It is especially efficient as the cost of job creation in rural areas is much less than in urban areas.[12] It has the added advantages of:

- creating or maintaining employment related to the primary sector in coastal areas (through both agriculture and small agro-industry activities);
- stabilizing rural employment and communities;
- contributing to the overall distribution of wealth;
- reducing environmental damage;
- promoting traditional and informal activities;
- promoting links between agriculture and industry;
- reducing the cost of service activities.

However, while non-farm rural job creation will relieve pressures, the population of coastal areas will inevitably continue to increase. Worldwide, the ratio of economically active population in agriculture is declining (52 percent in 1980, 47.5 percent in 1995).

Some of the major similarities and differences of degree of management, type of access and production cycle between the agriculture, forestry and fisheries subsectors are shown in Table A.2. Table A.3 shows economic activities in the agriculture, forestry and fisheries subsectors that have an impact on environmental and social concerns within or outside the subsector in which the activities are taking place. The main consequences of mismanagement in coastal areas in general are felt in health, productivity and aesthetics. Some of these issues are intrasectoral, such as depletive/destructive resource uses. Others are often transsectoral, such as loss of habitat and environmental degradation. Figure A.4 represents the agriculture sectoral/subsectoral location of activities and the degree to which activities and their impacts are taken into account in subsectoral planning and management.

1.7.1 Agriculture

In some coastal areas, and especially in small islands, agricultural production makes an extremely important contribution to the local economy or to national agricultural production. In countries such as Egypt and Bangladesh, the river deltas, with their fertile alluvial soils, play a major role in the agriculture sector.[13]

Whatever the situation, there are a number of reasons for giving agriculture particular attention in integrated coastal resource management planning. Among these are the following:

- agriculture has major positive, but also potentially negative, effects on the coastal environment. Sustainable agricultural policies are therefore needed to minimize the negative impacts of inland agriculture on coastal areas;
- agriculture is usually concerned with the production of food, and thus has strategic and political significance for food and livelihood security. Often, however, in coastal areas, urban growth, the high value of urban goods and services and the political importance of urban centres marginalize coastal agriculture and attract labour away from primary-sector activities. Protecting and maintaining peri-urban agriculture in coastal areas can make a substantial contribution to providing food to cities (particularly large ones) and creating employment;

---

[12] A comparison made by the World Bank between urban and rural projects in Africa, Asia and the Pacific and Latin America found that the average investment cost per job was 17 times higher in urban projects than in rural ones (World Bank 1978).

[13] See Part B, Section 1.

PART A

ISSUES, PERSPECTIVES, POLICY AND PLANNING PROCESSES FOR INTEGRATED COASTAL AREA MANAGEMENT

INTEGRATED
COASTAL AREA
MANAGEMENT
and
AGRICULTURE
FORESTRY AND
FISHERIES

1. The need for integrated coastal area management

TABLE A.2

Differences and similarities between agriculture, forestry and fisheries

	Agriculture		Forestry		Fisheries	
	Settled crop/livestock	Extensive grazing	Planted	Natural	Aquaculture	Capture
Degree of management and labour/capital inputs in production (not harvesting)	Medium to high	Low	Medium to high	Low to high	Medium to low	Low to high
Resource base and access	Land Exclusive	Land Open, common property	Land Exclusive/ open	Land Open, common property	Land/water* Exclusive/ open	Water Open/ common/ exclusive property
Biological stock and access	Crops and livestock Exclusive	Livestock Exclusive	Trees Exclusive/ open	Trees and wildlife Open, common property	Fish Exclusive/ open	Fish Open/common/ exclusive property
Production cycle	< Annual/ biennial	Annual/ biennial/+	> 10 years	> 100 years	< Annual/ biennial	> 10 years

* Aquaculture may rely on wild breeding stock.

Fishers pulling nets, Cape Verde

17

Deforestation through shifting cultivation, Brazil

1. The need for integrated coastal area management

TABLE A.3
Impact of agriculture, forestry and fisheries activities on coastal areas

Area of impact/ subsector	Use or activity	Environmental or social change	Impact of social/ economic concern
Estuary, harbour and inshore water quality impacts			
Agriculture	Diversion of rivers for irrigation	Reduced water flow in rivers, increased estuary salinity, decreased estuary circulation	Decreased fish yields
Agriculture	High use of pesticides	Toxic pollution of estuaries and inshore waters	Decreased fish yields
Agriculture	High use of fertilizers	Increased amount of nutrients entering the water leading to eutrophication of rivers, estuaries and inshore waters	Decreased fish yields
Agriculture	Excessive cropping or grazing on watersheds	Watershed erosion, river turbidity, sedimentation of fish habitat in estuaries and inshore waters, floodplain deposition and beaches covered with sediment	Decreased fish yields, silting of navigation channels, increased flood hazard, and decreased tourism attraction
Groundwater quality/quantity			
Agriculture Coastal aquaculture	Withdrawal of groundwater at a greater rate than natural recharge	Salt-water intrusion of aquifer leading to increased salinity, contamination of groundwater	Reduction in the water available for use, risk to human health
Mangrove and other coastal wetland impacts			
Agriculture Coastal aquaculture	Reclamation of mangrove for rice paddy	Destruction of mangrove, filling and canalization	Reduced fish yields, reduced filtration capability, increased risk of shore erosion, increased risk from flooding, increased risk of storm damage
Forestry	Mangrove harvesting for building materials, fuelwood, woodchips	Harvesting at a level greater than the sustainable yield	Decreased timber yield in successive harvests, decreased fish yields, reduction or loss of rare or endangered species, reduction in non-timber forest products used or traded by forest dwellers
Agriculture	Draining of salt marsh and coastal wetlands (in temperate countries) for grazing and cropping	Lowering of land surface and accelerated rise in sea level	Increased frequency and extent of flooding, increased beach erosion, increased salinity in coastal soils and in upstream "wedges", increased need for "hard" coastal defences
Coral reef and atoll impacts			
Agriculture Forestry	Irresponsible agricultural and/or forestry practices in coastal watersheds	Watershed erosion, turbidity and siltation of coral reefs	Decreased fish yields, decreased tourism and recreational value
Fisheries	Fishing with dynamite, muro-ami fishing	Coral reef destruction	Decreased fish yields, decreased tourism and recreational value
Fisheries	Intensive localized fishing effort	Harvesting targeted species at a level greater than sustainable yield	Decreased yield of associated fish species
Beach, dune and delta impacts			
Agriculture	Grazing of livestock	Destruction or removal of dune stabilizing vegetation	Initiation or increase of dune migration on to agricultural land, urban and infrastructure development
Agriculture	Diversion of rivers for irrigation	Decreased supply of beach material to the shoreline	Initiation or increase of shoreline erosion, decreased productivity
Social impacts			
Aquaculture	Commercial shrimp farm development	Acquisition of land used by peasant farmers/fishers, unfair contract arrangements	Creation of landless people, lack of equity, social conflict
Fisheries	Competition between inshore and offshore fishers for the same stocks	Overfishing	Decreased fish yields, social conflict
Agriculture	High use of pesticides	Toxic pollution of inshore resources	Potential human consumption of toxic fish
	Intensive use of nutrients	Eutrophication	Reduction in recreation and tourist attraction
	Agro-industries	Toxic effluents	Reduction in recreation and tourist attraction

Source: after Sorensen and McCreary, 1990.

PART **A**

ISSUES, PERSPECTIVES, POLICY AND PLANNING PROCESSES FOR INTEGRATED COASTAL AREA MANAGEMENT

INTEGRATED
COASTAL AREA
MANAGEMENT
· *and*
AGRICULTURE
FORESTRY AND
FISHERIES

1. The need for integrated coastal area management

FIGURE A.4

Relationships between the location of activities and their incorporation into subsectoral (agriculture, forestry, fisheries) planning within the agriculture sector

Activities	Within subsector	Ouside subsector, within sector	Outside sector
Within subsector	Usually included in subsectoral planning and management	Seldom included in subsectoral planning and management	Seldom included in subsectoral planning and management
Ouside subsector, within sector	Sometimes included in subsectoral planning and management	Typically ignored in subsectoral planning and management	Typically ignored in subsectoral planning and management
Outside sector	Sometimes included in subsectoral planning and management	Typically ignored in subsectoral planning and management	Ignored as irrelevant

Binder-Eil, Somalia

INTEGRATED
COASTAL AREA
MANAGEMENT
and
AGRICULTURE
FORESTRY AND
FISHERIES

PART A

ISSUES, PERSPECTIVES, POLICY AND PLANNING PROCESSES FOR INTEGRATED COASTAL AREA MANAGEMENT

1. The need for integrated coastal area management

- agriculture may also provide raw materials to industry located in coastal areas and may therefore have considerable economic significance. In particular, fostering the linkage between agriculture and tourism offers opportunities in both sectors for demand and supply of food, beverage and employment.

Planning for coastal agricultural activities must make explicit allowance for the wide range of farmers' interests and activities, including non-farm activities, the limited flexibility that farmers have in production decisions, their high vulnerability to adverse environmental change and the importance of non-commercial considerations in their decision-making. The complexity of these factors makes participation or consultation particularly important in coastal area planning where it impinges on agricultural activities. In particular, planning in coastal areas must account for such special characteristics of agriculture, such as the following:

- it includes a broad range of activities with a variety of types of product (crops and livestock, food and industrial raw materials), enterprises (from smallholdings to large commercial enterprises) and production processes (intensive, extensive);
- it makes a variety of contributions to the local economy, social cohesion and the maintenance of the cultural traditions of a society;
- it is dependent on natural growth processes and, to a greater or lesser extent, on land and its associated natural resources and environment.

Small-scale agriculture in many developing countries deploys strategies that are governed by complex considerations among which economic factors may rank very low. Last but not least, it is essential to take the special requirements of gender fully into account.[14]

1.7.2 Forestry

Coastal forests in developing countries are mainly mangroves, which cover an estimated 15.5 million hectares worldwide. Other coastal forested ecosystems include savannah woodlands, dry forests and rain forests. Commercial production from mangroves is comprised of building materials, such as poles and timber, and numerous non-forest products. Savannah woodlands and dry forests are used primarily for grazing, while rain forests are used for their commercial timber.

The value of mangroves is primarily environmental and social, rather than economic. An important part of the value of mangroves lies in the environmental services provided by their unique habitat which is host to significant biological diversity and provides spawning and nursery grounds for many species of commercially valuable fish. Mangroves also act as a sediment trap, a source of nutrients to inshore waters, and help to protect areas against shoreline erosion and surge-tide damage.[15]

Economic activities associated with forests, even inland, may be critical to the environmental health of the coastal area. In particular, excessive cutting and extraction of timber on steep slopes will result in severe erosion, which is likely to lead to turbidity in rivers carrying away the displaced topsoil, and sedimentation of fish habitats, such as seagrass beds and coral reefs, degrading and ultimately destroying them. In Bacuit Bay, the Philippines, for example, the benefits of logging activities on mountain slopes are outweighed by the loss in tourism and fishing value resulting from the degradation of offshore reefs.

Coastal forests are often perceived as an obstacle to development, rather than a resource to be supported. As absolute priority is often given to the immediate and most pressing economic needs, medium- and long-term gains may be overlooked.

1.7.3 Fisheries

The fisheries sector often accounts for a significant proportion of GDP, up to 5-10 percent in the economies of many developing coastal nations. Revenue earned by some small island developing states from the exploitation and processing of their fisheries resources accounts annually for more than 50 percent of public-sector revenue. The sustainable development of coastal fisheries (which, for example, represent less than 10 percent of total catch in the Pacific but, significantly, 70 percent of local consumption) will determine the ability of many coastal communities to survive. A large proportion of the total fish production of many coastal

20

---

[14] See Part B, Section 2.1.

[15] See also Part C, Section 1.3 and Boxes C.1, C.2 and C.3.

PART A

ISSUES, PERSPECTIVES, POLICY AND PLANNING PROCESSES FOR INTEGRATED COASTAL AREA MANAGEMENT

INTEGRATED
COASTAL AREA
MANAGEMENT
and
AGRICULTURE
FORESTRY AND
FISHERIES

1. The need for integrated coastal area management

countries is usually derived from coastal fisheries.[16] At the local level, the fisheries sector provides a livelihood to the population and also contributes to food security. Annual average per caput consumption of fish is 9 kg in developing countries, 27 kg in developed countries and 50 kg in many small island states (most of the population's animal protein intake). Coastal areas everywhere provide habitat for about 90 percent of marine fish in commercial and subsistence fisheries, at all or some stages in the lives of the fish.

Conventional fisheries management has been concerned only with problems generated within the fisheries sector. Planning in coastal areas has to take account of the specific features of small-scale and artisanal fisheries, including the risk of overexploitation by "last resort" fishers (poor people with no other source of livelihood). Solutions include the creation of jobs in other coastal sectors or support to help fishers to fish further offshore thus relieving pressures on inshore areas. Increasingly, policy reforms aiming at the conservation of coastal resources and habitats take the form of revitalizing traditional fisheries management systems with a view to incorporating them into management planning.[17]

Coastal aquaculture has been growing in a number of industrialized and developing countries, particularly in parts of Southeast and East Asia and parts of Latin America, and there is considerable scope for development and expansion in other regions. However, while coastal aquaculture is gaining economic importance in many countries, it can also have damaging consequences if it is poorly managed.[18] Moreover, it is susceptible to environmental change originating in actions outside the sector. Coastal aquaculture must be environmentally managed and absorbed into the coastal management planning process.[19]

---

[16] There are some exceptions, e.g. Kenya and the United Republic of Tanzania, which derive the greater part of their fish production from Lake Victoria.

[17] For more details see Part D, Section 1.1 and Box D.8.

[18] See also Part D, Section 1.4.

[19] For example, Article 10 of the Code of Conduct for Responsible Fisheries is concerned with the integration of fisheries into coastal management planning.

PART A

ISSUES, PERSPECTIVES, POLICY AND PLANNING PROCESSES FOR INTEGRATED COASTAL AREA MANAGEMENT

INTEGRATED
COASTAL AREA
MANAGEMENT
and
AGRICULTURE
FORESTRY AND
FISHERIES

2. The process of integrated coastal area management

2.1 PURPOSE OF INTEGRATED COASTAL AREA MANAGEMENT

The sustainable development concept commonly strives to maintain or restore a "balance" between the natural and human environments without any agreement on spatial or temporal benchmarks. Besides the fact that it is impossible to freeze the biosphere in its present state for future generations or attempt to restore an equilibrium of the past, changes in world population density and distribution and national or local economies impose a concept of evolution. As a result, the myth of equilibrium is replaced by variability, uncertainty, precaution and irreversibility.

Development involves management in time and space of the interactions between economic and ecological, and social and natural variability, where ecosystems and the lifestyles they support can exist side by side. The purely conservationist approach has given way to a more dynamic, progressive and development-oriented perception, with a view to closer integration between conservation and development. The ecosystem is a

matter of concern to a plurality of actors, and has to support a plurality of resources and uses. The issue is therefore a matter of coordination between these uses and the users (Babin *et al.*, 1997).

Coastal resources management includes a wide array of management practices such as: land-use planning; legal, administrative and institutional execution; demarcation on the ground; inspection and control of adherence to decisions; solution of land tenure issues; settling of water rights; issuing of concessions for plant, animal and mineral extraction (e.g. wood and non-wood products, fishery resources, hunting, peat); and safeguarding of the rights of different interest groups (e.g. traditional and indigenous people, women).

Coastal area management is too complex to be handled by traditional sectoral planning and management. To be effective, planning for integrated coastal area management (ICAM) must be coordinated between sectoral implementing agencies. A balanced management perspective is needed in which intersectoral relationships are fully understood, trade-

23

Meeting of Matale
District Group,
Sri Lanka

INTEGRATED
COASTAL AREA
MANAGEMENT
and
AGRICULTURE
FORESTRY AND
FISHERIES

PART A

ISSUES, PERSPECTIVES, POLICY AND PLANNING PROCESSES FOR INTEGRATED COASTAL AREA MANAGEMENT

2. The process of integrated coastal area management

offs recognized and anticipated, benefits and alternatives critically assessed, appropriate management interventions identified and implemented, and necessary institutional and organizational arrangements worked out. This is the essence of ICAM.

Integrated management refers to management of sectoral components as parts of a functional whole, with resource users, not stocks of natural resources, as the focus of management. This focus highlights the need for the active participation of communities. Relevant line agencies must be involved so as to mitigate cross-sectoral impacts and adjust sectoral development portfolios to make them consistent with integrated coastal management goals.

ICAM programmes should be tailored to fit the institutional and organizational environment of the countries or regions involved, including the legal, political and administrative structure, cultural patterns and social traditions. It can be started as a strategy for an entire country, or can focus initially on special management areas selected on the basis of priority of management issues, their tractability to management interventions and the level of private or government support locally, regionally or nationally.[20]

The management programme can be comprehensive or selective in the issues it includes. There is no single correct way to organize and implement ICAM strategies and plans. Each country will develop its own customized plan, as evidenced by the diversity found in existing programmes worldwide. Nevertheless, there are some basic features that are common among them.

The objectives of ICAM, along the lines endorsed by Heads of State at the Earth Summit are in Box A.3.

2.2 THE LEGAL FRAMEWORK

2.2.1 The role of law in ICAM

The role of law in the successful implementation of ICAM is frequently overlooked or inadequately appreciated. The long-term prospects of an ICAM initiative will be seriously jeopardized if, first, it is not based on a clear understanding of the legal and institutional arrangements governing coastal management and, second, appropriate legal mechanisms are not used to implement it.

Implementing ICAM may involve changing the way

existing institutions operate, creating new institutions, changing the rights of users of coastal resources, and introducing new mechanisms to regulate human activities within, or that may affect, coastal areas. This will almost invariably require repealing or amending existing legislation and frequently enacting entirely new legislation. The transition may also give rise to new conflicts between implementing agencies, between implementing agencies and other stakeholders in the coastal area, and between stakeholders. In addition, legislation can be used to provide tools and mechanisms to enable and facilitate the integrated management of coastal areas and to establish mechanisms for resolving disputes.[21]

2.2.2 Rights to own and use coastal resources

ICAM policy-makers will frequently have to decide whether to change the regime governing property or user rights in order to attain their objectives. They must therefore understand the nature and function of different property regimes, the existing regimes and how governance arrangements function; without this, serious policy errors can be made.[22]

The concept of ownership has been described as a "container" of a number of rights in relation to the property, for example: the right to possess it, to use it, to enjoy its fruits, and to dispose of it (e.g. Simpson, 1976). The owner may transfer particular rights to other parties for a period on agreed terms (rent a tract of land for grazing for three years, for example) but the container of ownership remains with the owner; even if all rights have been transferred for the time being, ultimately they will revert to the owner.

---

[20] See Figure A.5.

[21] See Part E.

[22] For example, Mathiews (1995) argues that the complete collapse of the cod fishery in Newfoundland is at least partially attributable to inappropriate Canadian Federal fisheries policy which was heavily influenced by Hardin's "tragedy of the commons" thesis. Hardin incorrectly equated common ownership with open access to a resource and concluded that, as population grew, overexploitation of the resource was inevitable. As a result Canadian Federal Fisheries authorities were prejudiced against existing common property regimes managed on a local basis by inshore fishing communities and instead introduced a system of federal licensing designed to restrict the number of individuals involved in fishing (rather than, for example, limiting the activities of large offshore trawlers). This policy was spectacularly unsuccessful in preventing the overexploitation of the resource.

PART A

ISSUES, PERSPECTIVES, POLICY AND PLANNING PROCESSES FOR INTEGRATED COASTAL AREA MANAGEMENT

INTEGRATED
COASTAL AREA
MANAGEMENT
and
AGRICULTURE
FORESTRY AND
FISHERIES

2. The process of integrated coastal area management

FIGURE A.5

The different spatial management scales of ICAM

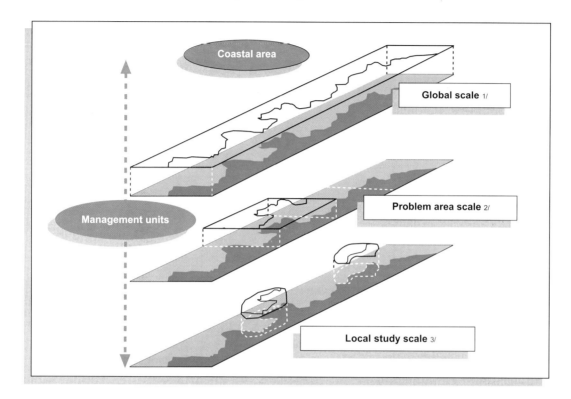

Notes: The boundaries of a managed coastal area may change as different problems are addressed. Influencing factors may be biophysical, economic, social, jurisdictional and/or organizational in character.

[1] National or subnational level scale: could be a bay, entire archipelago or whole coast under national jurisdiction. Ideally, a national policy (goal and strategy) with different routes of implementation, according to intracountry socio-political and biophysical differences.

[2] Problem area scale: defined on the basis of prevailing management issues or administrative level of support.

[3] Local study scale: one or more pilot sites selected for special studies (e.g. specific geographic sites of natural, cultural or economic significance) or for demonstration purposes.

Source: adapted from IOC/ICSU/WMO, 1997.

BOX A.3

UNCED objectives for ICAM

The 1992 United Nations Conference on Environment and Development (UNCED) provided significant support for integrated management of coastal areas. Chapter 17 of Agenda 21, "Protection of oceans, all kinds of seas including enclosed and semi-enclosed seas, coastal areas and the protection, rational use and development of their living resources" outlines a commitment by coastal nations to "integrated management and sustainable development of coastal areas and the marine environment under their national jurisdiction". Paragraph 17.5 of Programme A of Chapter 17 sets out the objectives of integrated coastal area management as being to:

- provide for an integrated policy and decision-making process to promote compatibility and a balance of uses;

- identify existing and projected uses of coastal areas and their interactions;
- concentrate on well-defined issues;
- apply preventive and precautionary approaches in planning and implementation;
- promote the application and development of methods that reflect changes in value resulting from uses of marine and coastal areas, including pollution, marine erosion, loss of resources and habitat destruction;
- provide access, as far as possible, for concerned individuals, groups and organizations to relevant information and opportunities for consultation and participation in planning and decision-making at appropriate levels.

**INTEGRATED
COASTAL AREA
MANAGEMENT
and
AGRICULTURE
FORESTRY AND
FISHERIES**

PART A

ISSUES, PERSPECTIVES, POLICY AND PLANNING PROCESSES FOR INTEGRATED COASTAL AREA MANAGEMENT

2. The process of integrated coastal area management

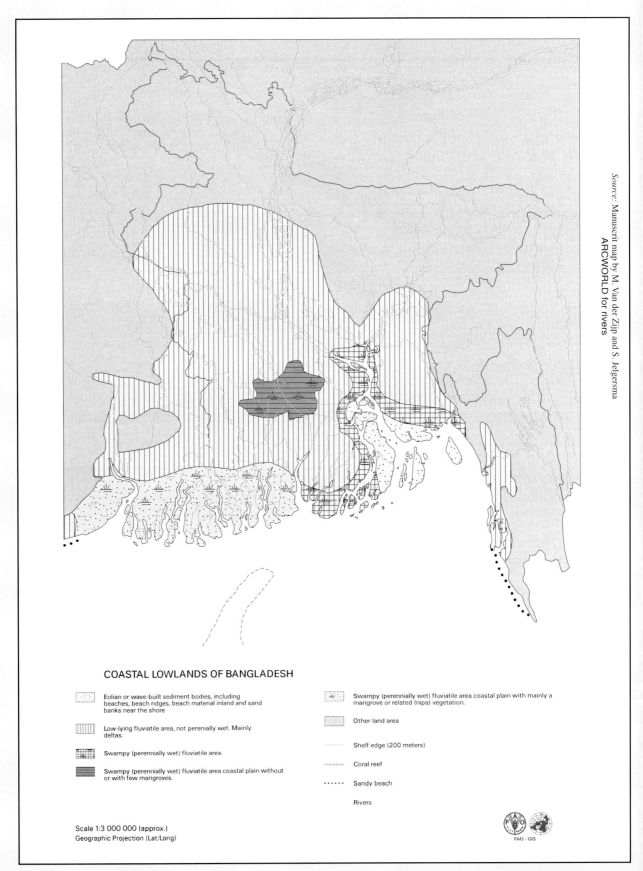

Source: Manuscrit map by M. Van der Zijp and S. Jelgersma
ARCWORLD for rivers

COASTAL LOWLANDS OF BANGLADESH

Eolian or wave-built sediment bodies, including beaches, beach ridges, beach material inland and sand banks near the shore

Low-lying fluviatile area, not perenially wet. Mainly deltas.

Swampy (perennially wet) fluviatile area.

Swampy (perennially wet) fluviatile area coastal plain without or with few mangroves.

Swampy (perennially wet) fluviatile area coastal plain with mainly a mangrove or related (nipa) vegetation.

Other land area

------- Shelf edge (200 meters)

.... Coral reef

• • • • • Sandy beach

Rivers

Scale 1:3 000 000 (approx.)
Geographic Projection (Lat/Long)

FAO - GIS

Map of coastal lowlands of Bangladesh

PART A

ISSUES, PERSPECTIVES, POLICY AND PLANNING PROCESSES FOR INTEGRATED COASTAL AREA MANAGEMENT

INTEGRATED
COASTAL AREA
MANAGEMENT
and
AGRICULTURE
FORESTRY AND
FISHERIES

2. The process of integrated coastal area management

Property rights are created and enforced by society for particular purposes. They define the relationship between a person (an individual or a legal entity such as a company) and a thing (which may be physical or intangible). Legal systems typically distinguish between types of ownership by reference to both the subject (i.e. the owner) and the object of the right. The categories vary between legal systems but many legal systems incorporate distinctions between:

- things that cannot be owned, for example, air or the sea which are common to everyone (*res communes*) and property such as the seashore which is held by the state for the benefit of the public (*res publicae*);
- things that are unowned but can be owned (such as wildlife before capture);
- things in respect of which full ownership rights exist and that may be freely bought and sold (this "alienable property" is often referred to as "private property" but in fact it may be owned by the state as well as by private individuals or corporations).[23]

Discussions of property regimes often focus on the various categories of person who hold the rights; they thus sometimes lose sight of the fact that the characteristics of the property regime are determined both by the category of person holding the right (e.g. the state, a group with common rights, or a private individual or legal entity) and by the nature of the property (thing) in question.

When property rights are discussed from an economic perspective, distinctions are often made between state property, private property, common property and open access regimes.[24] Legal analyses, however, tend to concentrate on distinguishing between different ownership regimes such as public property, common property, unowned resources and alienable property (private property).

However from the perspective of natural resource management, the identity of the legal owner of a resource is not usually the crucial issue. In addition, the categories used in Box A.2 can overlap. For example, from a factual perspective there may be open access to a resource regardless of whether, legally, it is subject to state, common or private ownership. It is therefore important to ensure that the categories used for

analysing property regimes do not obscure the most relevant distinctions from a management perspective.

From an ICAM perspective, rather than classifying property rights in coastal areas on the basis of legal or economic categories, it is usually more useful to identify: a) who has the legal right to manage the resource (which is distinct from, though related to, who the owner is); b) whether or not the use or exploitation of the resource is in fact controlled; c) who the management authority is; and d) on what terms access to the resource is granted.

2.2.3 Evaluating regulatory frameworks for ICAM

An initial assessment of existing regulatory frameworks will usually aim to evaluate the extent to which existing laws, property and use rights and institutional arrangements will promote or hinder the attainment of the objectives of the coastal management programme and identify any required modifications.

Most laws apply primarily to a particular sector or human activity (e.g. fishing) and are administered by the line ministry or government agency responsible for that sector. However, since ICAM is concerned with area management, it will usually be necessary to review a wide range of laws, administrative regulations, institutional practices and customary laws. These would typically include laws that:

- define the rights and duties of owners and users of coastal resources (e.g. the constitution and laws governing land tenure and water use rights);
- govern the management and exploitation of natural resources (e.g. laws regulating land tenure, rural and urban development and planning, land and water use, mining, oil and gas exploitation, industrial development, pollution control, tourism, fishing, forestry and agriculture);
- promote the conservation and protection of the environment, wildlife and biological diversity;
- provide a structure within which human and other resources can be organized and coordinated for the purpose of attaining long-term strategic objectives (e.g. laws relating to national planning and economic development);
- establish mechanisms for averting or resolving disputes concerning the use of coastal resources (e.g. laws or procedures that provide for the use of

27

---

[23] See Part E, Section 2.1.
[24] See Box A.2.

INTEGRATED
COASTAL AREA
MANAGEMENT
and
AGRICULTURE
FORESTRY AND
FISHERIES

PART A

ISSUES, PERSPECTIVES, POLICY AND PLANNING PROCESSES FOR INTEGRATED COASTAL AREA MANAGEMENT

2. The process of integrated coastal area management

techniques such as conciliation, mediation and arbitration.[25]

The obligations, principles, standards and recommendations contained in international agreements and documents provide a useful measure against which to evaluate national legal frameworks for ICAM. In some instances, it will be important for drafters of national laws to take into account the provisions of binding international treaties, such as the United Nations Convention on the Law of the Sea[26] and others.[27] In addition, useful guidance in preparing ICAM policies and legislation can be obtained from the provisions of a variety of non-binding international documents such as the Earth Summit agreements and the Code of Conduct for Responsible Fisheries (which includes Article 10 on "Integration of fisheries into coastal area management") and others.[28]

Some of the specific issues that should be considered in reviewing laws that affect the management of coastal areas are set out in Box A.4.

In developing a framework for ICAM it is important to avoid simply adding further layers of bureaucracy

28

Women training,
Hio, Benin

Fishers planning
coastal microprojects,
Hio, Benin

---

[25] See Part E.

[26] Concluded on 10 December 1982, at Montego Bay, and put into force on 16 November 1994.

[27] There are a number of other international conventions with relevance to coastal areas including: the Convention on Biological Diversity (Rio de Janeiro, 5 June 1992) which came into force on 29 December 1993; the Convention for the Protection of the World Cultural and Natural Heritage (Paris, 16 November 1972) which came into force on 17 December 1975; the Ramsar Convention on Wetlands of International Importance especially as Waterfowl Habitat (Ramsar, 2 February 1971) which came into force on 21 December 1975; and the United Nations Framework Convention on Climate Change (New York, 9 May 1992) which came into force on 24 March 1996. Regional conventions may also be relevant, particularly those concluded under the UNEP Regional Seas Programme which covers 13 regions of which eight currently have binding international framework conventions, nine have action plans, and a number of other action plans, framework conventions and protocols are under negotiation.

[28] Relevant non-binding international instruments include the Rio de Janeiro Declaration on Environment and Development of 16 June 1992; Agenda 21 concluded on 16 June 1992 at Rio de Janeiro (particularly Chapter 8, which deals with the importance of providing an effective legal and regulatory framework, and Chapter 17, which deals with the protection of oceans, seas and coastal areas); the non-legally binding Authoritative Statement of Global Consensus on the Management, Conservation and Sustainable Development of all Types of Forests, concluded on 13 June 1992 at Rio de Janeiro; and the 1995 "Jakarta Mandate" adopted by the second Conference of the Parties to the Convention on Biological Diversity.

PART A

INTEGRATED
COASTAL AREA
MANAGEMENT
and
AGRICULTURE
FORESTRY AND
FISHERIES

ISSUES, PERSPECTIVES, POLICY AND PLANNING PROCESSES FOR INTEGRATED COASTAL AREA MANAGEMENT

2. The process of integrated coastal area management

BOX A.4
**Considerations for integrating
the legal framework**

In assessing the degree of integration of an existing or proposed legal framework for coastal management, it is helpful to consider the following questions:

- Is the scope of the legislation broad enough to encompass: a) the geographical area relevant to the ICAM initiative (geographical jurisdiction); b) the institutions and individuals who have the powers to control coastal resources (jurisdiction over legal persons); and c) the subject matter necessary to achieve ICAM (e.g. environmental quality and protection, economic development and the conservation of marine and terrestrial living resources)?
- Do the substantive laws, rights and duties accord with the overall policy objectives? (For example, a right of unrestricted public access to the coast may conflict with a policy objective to protect fragile coastal ecosystems.)
- Do procedural law provisions and administrative procedures ensure that all relevant information will be taken into account and that holistic (as opposed to sectoral) criteria will be used in planning and decision-making?
- Are there procedural mechanisms for ensuring the consistency of the legal rules and criteria applied by different institutions and at different levels in the governmental or administrative hierarchy?

Landing site development committee meeting, after having obtained legal right to protect the site from encroachment of real estate development, Conakry, Guinea

29

Fishers' group leaders and fisheries officers setting priorities, Kamsar, Guinea

INTEGRATED
COASTAL AREA
MANAGEMENT
and
AGRICULTURE
FORESTRY AND
FISHERIES

PART A

ISSUES, PERSPECTIVES, POLICY AND PLANNING PROCESSES FOR INTEGRATED COASTAL AREA MANAGEMENT

2. The process of integrated coastal area management

and legal complexity. The principle of integration should also be applied to the legal and institutional framework, reducing overlaps and producing a more streamlined and effective governance structure. This means that the proposed legal framework itself should be comprehensive, holistic in approach and internally consistent.

The impact of laws on society is largely determined by the way those laws are implemented and enforced. In order to gain a proper understanding of how a regulatory system actually functions, it is essential to analyse the institutional framework in conjunction with the relevant laws.[29]

2.2.4 Legal principles to support ICAM

While it is inappropriate to transplant a law from one legal system to another – particularly where the social context and legal traditions are very different – principles used in one system can often be usefully adapted and applied in other legal systems. A number of principles – most of which are derived from international environmental law – that either have been, or could be, incorporated into national laws in order to promote ICAM are outlined in Box A.5. The focus is on those principles that are likely to provide practical guidance to the drafters of national legislation rather than on attempting to discuss all relevant principles.[30]

2.2.5 Legal mechanisms used to achieve ICAM objectives

A great variety of legal instruments have been used to promote ICAM objectives. However, identifying appropriate, practical legal mechanisms to give effect to the concepts and principles such as sustainable development that underlie ICAM remains one of the major challenges facing legislative drafters. This section discusses some legal mechanisms that may be useful.[31]

Mangrove regrowth after introduction of improved livestock waste management measures. Cumulative effects of waste effluents had destroyed the mangrove facing the Strait of Malaya, Malaysia.

Unchecked flash floods carrying away precious topsoil, Tunisia

---

[29] The institutional framework for ICAM is discussed in Section 2.3.

[30] For other examples and for a fuller discussion of this issue see Boelaert-Suominen and Cullinan, 1994.

[31] Ibid .

INTEGRATED
COASTAL AREA
MANAGEMENT
and
AGRICULTURE
FORESTRY AND
FISHERIES

PART A

ISSUES, PERSPECTIVES, POLICY AND PLANNING PROCESSES FOR INTEGRATED COASTAL AREA MANAGEMENT

2. The process of integrated coastal area management

BOX A.5
Legal principles to support ICAM

The precautionary principle. The essence of this principle is that, in situations where there is reason to believe that something is causing serious or potentially irreparable environmental harm, preventive action should be taken immediately, even in the absence of conclusive scientific evidence. Principle 15 of the Rio Declaration calls upon states to apply the precautionary approach stating that: "Where there are threats of serious or irreversible damage, lack of full scientific certainty shall not be used as a reason for postponing cost-effective measures to prevent environmental degradation." As Boelaert-Suominen and Cullinan (1994) point out, "the precautionary principle is particularly appropriate in the context of ICAM because of the vulnerability of many coastal resources (and hence the likelihood of irreparable harm occurring swiftly) and because scientific knowledge about the complex web of interconnected biological processes found in coastal systems is far from complete." One of the ways in which this principle can be applied in national law is to require developers to bear the onus of satisfying the authorities that a proposed development will not cause significant harm to the environment. This would mean that in situations where the environmental impact of a project is uncertain, it would not be authorized. The current position in many countries is that consent must be given unless the authorities have evidence that harm will result.

The principle of preventive action. This principle requires action to be taken to avert known or quantifiable harm. Preventive measures are usually justifiable on the basis that it is cheaper, safer and more desirable to prevent environmental harm occurring than to rectify it later (if, indeed, this is possible). The application of this principle can be seen in legal requirements for environmental impact assessments, development permits and consents.

The polluter pays principle. This principle is concerned with ensuring that the social costs of environmental degradation are borne by those responsible for the environmental degradation rather than by society at large. There is no universally accepted formulation of this principle and the extent to which it is applied varies significantly. In most instances the application of the principle is limited, for example by stating that polluters are only responsible for the costs necessary to reduce pollution to within prescribed limits.[32] In the coastal context, the principle should result in improved allocation of scarce resources by imposing on the user the full cost of any use of a resource (including the cost of any incidental damage to the environment).

Responsibility not to cause transboundary environmental damage. Water is not only the most important component of coastal ecosystems, it is also often shared by more than one country. Thus, the management of aquatic resources, such as fish stocks, and the

control of marine pollution frequently have transboundary implications. Probably the most fundamental obligation of states that share a natural environmental resource is, as far as possible, to avoid creating adverse environmental effects beyond their own borders, or at least to reduce such effects to a minimum.[33]

Rational and equitable use of natural resources. Many international legal texts incorporate the principle that the use and management of natural resources generally, or of particular resources such as fisheries, should be "rational". One way to apply this principle in the context of ICAM is to fix priorities among coastal-dependent activities when granting development rights. Giving weight to activities that, by their very nature, are dependent on their situation close to the sea is a first step in the process of allocating coastal resources rationally.[34] Where a resource is shared by more than one country (typically an international watercourse or fishery) international law also emphasizes that the community of interests of co-users of the resource gives rise to an obligation to negotiate in good faith to bring about an equitable allocation of the resource. Such principles of international law may be usefully incorporated into national law, and can serve as a useful general guide for decision-makers in such situations.[35]

Public involvement. There has been a worldwide trend to provide increased public access to environmental information and to require consultation with interested or affected members of the public when preparing new policies or authorizing developments that may affect the natural environment. The case for public involvement in coastal management is even stronger than in other areas because the public is usually a significant user of coastal areas and in some countries may even be considered to be the owner of areas such as the shoreline.[36]

---

[32] The European Community formulation states that: "natural or legal persons governed by public or private law who are responsible for pollution must pay the costs of such measures as are necessary to eliminate pollution or to reduce it so as to comply with the standards or equivalent measures laid down by the public authorities." Council Recommendation 75/436/EURATOM, ECSC, EEC of 3 March 1975, Annex, para. 2; OJ L 169, 29.6.1987, p. 1.

[33] See the "Draft Principles of Conduct in the Field of the Environment for the Guidance of States in the Conservation and Harmonious Utilisation of Natural Resources Shared by Two or More States", UNEP/IG. 12/2 and UNEP/GC. 6/17, approved by the General Council Decision of 19 May 1978 and by UN General Assembly Resolution 34/186 of 18 December 1979.

[34] The principle is expressed in United States Congressional Declaration of Coastal Zone policy and is also found in the legislation of several other countries. For example, the 1988 Spanish Shores Act provides that within 100 m landwards from the landwards limit of the seashore "Generally, only works, installations and activities which by their very nature may not be located elsewhere or which provide services necessary or convenient for the use of the coastal public property will be permitted".

[35] For example, the Coastal Zone Management Act in the United States provides incentives for states to implement management policies to bring about "wise use of the land and water resources of the coastal zone" (section 303 (2)) and to ensure that management programmes contain mechanisms "assuring that local land-use and water use regulations within the coastal zone do not unreasonably restrict or exclude land uses and water uses of regional benefit" (section 306 (d) 12).

[36] The importance of public consultation is emphasized by paragraph 17.6 of Agenda 21 which provides that local and national mechanisms established to ensure integrated management and sustainable development of coastal and marine areas and their resources "should include consultation, as appropriate, with the academic and private sectors, non-governmental organizations, local communities, resource user groups, and indigenous people".

INTEGRATED
COASTAL AREA
MANAGEMENT
and
AGRICULTURE
FORESTRY AND
FISHERIES

PART A

ISSUES, PERSPECTIVES, POLICY AND PLANNING PROCESSES FOR INTEGRATED COASTAL AREA MANAGEMENT

2. The process of integrated coastal area management

Guiding the exercise of administrative discretion.
Legislation dealing with natural resource management will often mandate a line ministry or executive agency to prepare management or development plans and establish procedures for granting authorizations. Usually the executive agency or official responsible will have wide discretion as to how these duties are performed. However, in some instances it may be helpful to stipulate various general principles that the executive agency or official must take into consideration. This technique has the advantage of requiring important but legally imprecise principles to be formally considered.[37] The disadvantage is that the enforcement of such provisions may be difficult, particularly where non-governmental organizations and members of the public do not have legal standing to challenge the validity of plans and administrative decisions in court.

Changing rights to own and use coastal resources.
Property rights are a fundamental component of any system for allocating or managing natural resources.[38] If it is clear that the existing property regime in the coastal area will obstruct or prevent the attainment of the desired objectives, it may be desirable to redistribute the relevant rights (where possible). This may give rise to an obligation to pay compensation. Adjusting property regimes can be politically sensitive and legally complex. Therefore, before undertaking any radical restructuring, it is important to ascertain whether or not problems such as environmental degradation are in fact a consequence of an inappropriate property regime or are attributable to other factors, such as poor management.

In many cases it is the management regime rather than the ownership regime that is critical.[39] For example, asserting state control over coastal resources may appear to be an obvious way of implementing ICAM. In theory, if much of the coastal area is public land, access to beaches and other coastal resources will be assured and

the integrity of the coast maintained.[40] However, if the public has a legal right to use the area in the absence of careful state management, intensive public use can result in environmental degradation. Furthermore, most analysts agree that the tendency during the 1970s and 1980s to shift control over local natural resources from local user groups to central government has generally not resulted in effective natural resource management (Bromley and Cernea, 1989).

Existing property regimes may have been superimposed on traditional customary law rights which, until recently, were often simply ignored. In recent years there has been increasing recognition of at least some of the traditional legal rights asserted by indigenous people over natural resources and of the fact that the principles that they embody are often useful in promoting sustainable management and equitable allocation.

The distribution or redistribution of rights to own and use coastal resources can have a significant impact on coastal management. Some of the legal mechanisms used in this regard include:

- reasserting public ownership and control over coastal areas or initiating expropriation or acquisition programmes to bring important areas under public ownership or control;
- recognizing customary or indigenous rights over resources and devolving certain powers to manage those resources to traditional authorities or local organizations representing users;
- imposing restrictions on private ownership rights, for example, by providing for public servitudes or easements over private land to facilitate access to the seashore and requiring landowners to obtain official authorization for undertaking certain activities, particularly where these are likely to have a significant impact on the coastal landscape and environment.

---

[37] For example, many of the principles in international environmental law texts such as the principle of intergenerational equity (Rio Declaration, Principle 3) and the principle of the interdependence of environment and development (Rio Declaration, Principle 4).

[38] See Section 2.2.2.

[39] Ibid.

---

[40] The term "public land" is used here as a generic term to refer to various legal concepts of collective public land tenure that exist in different legal systems, such as *res communis, domaine publique,* crown lands and public trust lands. In recent years various initiatives to protect coastlines have led to ancient principles of public ownership being reasserted in a number of jurisdictions including Costa Rica, Spain, France and its overseas dominions (Guyana, Guadeloupe and Martinique in the Caribbean and Réunion in the Indian Ocean), and Sri Lanka.

ISSUES, PERSPECTIVES, POLICY AND PLANNING PROCESSES FOR INTEGRATED COASTAL AREA MANAGEMENT

PART A

INTEGRATED
COASTAL AREA
MANAGEMENT
and
AGRICULTURE
FORESTRY AND
FISHERIES

2. The process of integrated coastal area management

Establishing protected areas. One of the most common legal mechanisms used in coastal area management is the formal designation of an area of particular ecological importance as a protected area in which special conservation and management measures will be applied. The protected area may be designated for a particular purpose (e.g. preservation as a wilderness area), but protected areas that permit multiple uses, subject to controls, are becoming more common. It is always preferable to consult current (traditional) users of the area regarding the establishment of protected areas and to associate them with the management of such areas.[41] Excluding them can lead to hardship for them and/or violent reactions. This is an extremely useful mechanism particularly when it is used proactively to conserve important resources before they become degraded. However, legal difficulties are sometimes encountered in establishing protected areas that cover areas of both land and sea, and in managing and controlling activities outside the protected area that have an impact on the area itself.

Zoning and coastal setback lines. Most land-use planning systems rely on designating areas (zones) in which only certain specified activities or land uses (e.g. agriculture) will be permitted. This is a proactive mechanism (as opposed to project-specific environmental impact assessments (see Box A.6) which are reactive in nature) and can be useful in coastal management if plans are regularly updated and development restrictions enforced. A particular type of zoning commonly used in coastal management involves prohibiting or restricting certain activities or uses of coastal resources (e.g. erecting buildings) within a defined strip of land between the shoreline and a "setback line". This mechanism can be used for a variety of purposes including conserving natural habitats, guaranteeing public access to the shore and promoting tourism. It tends to be favoured by legislators because it is relatively straightforward to enforce, is popular with

---

[41] Many wildlife or biological reserves bring few or no benefits to the inhabitants and, in addition, can create severe social stress (loss of traditional livelihoods). Contrary to common perceptions, local inhabitants often contribute strongly to conservation and, when this fails, it is frequently not owing to irresponsible conduct on the part of such populations.

BOX A.6
Environmental impact assessment (EIA) and cumulative environmental impact assessment (CEIA)

An increasing number of countries have introduced legislation requiring an **EIA** to be conducted before certain developments will be authorized. Requiring EIAs is particularly useful in the context of ICAM because this mechanism is inherently cross-sectoral in philosophy, preventive in nature and specifically concerned with evaluating the linkages between human activity and the environment. However, this technique has its limitations. EIAs are primarily designed to make relevant information available to a decision-maker; merely requiring the submission of an EIA report does not in itself provide any legal control over environmentally harmful activities. It is therefore essential that the decision-maker has the power to refuse to grant development consent, or to impose enforceable conditions when granting the consent on the basis of the information in the EIA report, and that these powers are exercised when appropriate. Compliance with conditions imposed in the administrative consent must also be monitored and enforced. Furthermore, in coastal areas the cumulative impact of many different activities, some occurring in distant catchment areas, is frequently far more significant than the effects of local developments. As a result, cumulative environmental impact assessments, strategic EIAs of regional and local development plans and policies and appropriate zoning of development areas may be more effective than project-specific EIAs. Finally, competence in undertaking EIA, or in evaluating EIA reports, is not always available locally.

CEIA may be applied in coastal areas that suffer from the cumulative impact of numerous actions. The justification of CEIA is that, even where there is an effective EIA, the EIA frequently does not protect ecosystems against incremental degradation effects, partly because the actions may be too small to justify an individual EIA and partly because of a commonly occurring willingness to accept a little degradation. The purpose of CEIA is threefold: to give individuals advance notice of how adverse cumulative impacts will be considered; to allow regulators to decide whether an incremental change is acceptable; and to increase the capability of regulators to control or influence small-scale activities and projects that would not be considered under the conventional EIA procedure. Cumulative effects on the agricultural sector will increase as the scale of development increases. Hence, planners in agriculture, forestry and fisheries have a particular interest in cumulative effects and, therefore, in CEIA. This is because the effects often extend for long distances downstream, beyond the obvious direct impacts of a project, and also because multiple small-scale actions may have even greater adverse effects on natural systems than a few large-scale projects will have. The problems with CEIA are that there is not yet a generally accepted comprehensive methodology and, often, reference to cumulative effects in environmental management laws is absent. In addition, there is frequently a reluctance on the part of resource managers to consider cumulative effects which, in turn, may be the result of a range of factors such as the perceived need to give greater priority to other issues, the absence of the necessary mandate, or a lack of data.

INTEGRATED
COASTAL AREA
MANAGEMENT
and
AGRICULTURE
FORESTRY AND
FISHERIES

PART A

ISSUES, PERSPECTIVES, POLICY AND PLANNING PROCESSES FOR INTEGRATED COASTAL AREA MANAGEMENT

2. The process of integrated coastal area management

people inland and is often an extension of existing legal principles related to public access to the coast.

Key issues to consider in evaluating the legal framework for ICAM are summarized in Box A.7.

2.3 THE INSTITUTIONAL FRAMEWORK

During the policy process for ICAM, goals and objectives are determined and the means to achieve them are formulated in strategies and plans. The process will vary considerably from one country to another, depending upon the size of the country, the issues to be considered, the institutional framework, cultural background and many other considerations. In general, however, the setting of area goals and the strategy to achieve them is undertaken by a coordinating agency in conjunction with the concerned line ministries, other government agencies and representatives of other stakeholders. The plans through which the strategy is implemented are formulated by the responsible executing agencies, usually the line ministries and subnational and local governments, often in conjunction with non-governmental organizations. Consultation with local people is highly desirable but rarely undertaken. The line ministries, therefore, are critical to the process, both through their contribution to the formulation of the goals and strategy and to its implementation.

Experience shows that when ICAM plans are prepared as stand-alone plans – distinct from national or subnational development plans and from sectoral development and renewable resource management plans – it is difficult to find the human and financial resources to implement them. In contrast, when ICAM is an integral part of sectoral development and renewable resource management plans, this problem may often be less pronounced.

2.3.1 Definition of the boundaries of ICAM

In adopting the principle of ICAM, governments have to decide whether to apply ICAM at the area, subnational or national level. Coastal countries, especially small island countries, will need to adopt a national ICAM policy, and some may opt also to have a national ICAM plan. Many other countries will have specific ICAM plans only for certain threatened parts of the coast.

However, the absence of an ICAM plan does not

Fishers ply their trade, Mekong River, Laos

Farmer standing next to a gully that has eaten away part of her property, Lesotho

ISSUES, PERSPECTIVES, POLICY AND PLANNING PROCESSES FOR INTEGRATED COASTAL AREA MANAGEMENT

PART A

INTEGRATED
COASTAL AREA
MANAGEMENT
and
AGRICULTURE
FORESTRY AND
FISHERIES

2. The process of integrated coastal area management

BOX A.7
Issues in evaluating legal frameworks for ICAM

The following list of questions is intended to give an indication of some of the issues that are useful to consider in evaluating regulatory frameworks for ICAM. It is not an exhaustive checklist.

The planning process
- Is there a body that has a legal mandate to prepare development or management plans for the coastal area – even if these are not specifically conceived for ICAM purposes?
- Does the planning body have adequate powers to prepare the plans?
- Are the coastal area and scope of the plans defined?
- Is there a legally prescribed process that must be followed to prepare, approve, review and amend the management plans and does it provide for effective public participation?
- What is the legal status of the plans and policies? For example, is the plan binding on other agencies or does it merely provide guidance for decision-makers?
- Does the planning process take into consideration regional and international commitments?
- Are there mechanisms for encouraging and enforcing compliance with the plans?

Existing rights and obligations
- Are the rights of existing owners and users of the coastal areas – including the rights of groups who have traditionally used coastal resources – clearly defined and legally enforceable?
- Is the existing distribution of public and private rights to own and use coastal land and resources conducive to protecting environmental quality and long-term sustainable development, including ensuring equitable access and use by the current generation and intergenerational equity?
- How will implementation of the plan be affected by existing rights?

- How will implementation of the plan affect existing rights?
- How can existing customary law rights be incorporated into, or recognized by, the new regime?
- Are further limitations on the existing rights of private owners necessary, and justifiable, in order to attain ICAM policy goals, and will it be necessary and possible to pay compensation for affecting these rights?

Implementation
- Are there clearly identified bodies mandated to implement the plans and do they have the necessary legal powers to do so?
- Are there processes for consultation and coordination between relevant agencies and for resolving interagency conflicts?
- Does the legal system as a whole provide suitable legal mechanisms to implement the plan?
- Do other laws conflict with or hinder the attainment of ICAM objectives? For example, inadequate controls on deforestation or harmful agricultural practices in the catchment area may result in increased sedimentation in rivers with negative consequences for coastal areas.
- Are there adequate mechanisms to encourage and enforce compliance? For example do the relevant authorities have the necessary powers and capacity, including powers of enforcement in exclusive economic zones in accordance with international law, are the sanctions sufficient to deter illegal or undesirable activities and, where appropriate, are there incentives for self-regulation by local stakeholders?
- Is the legislation that is proposed to facilitate ICAM consistent with the legal system as a whole, consistent with international commitments, clear, equitable and enforceable, bearing in mind financial, institutional and other constraints?

Polluted waters in Java
Harbour, Indonesia

2. The process of integrated coastal area management

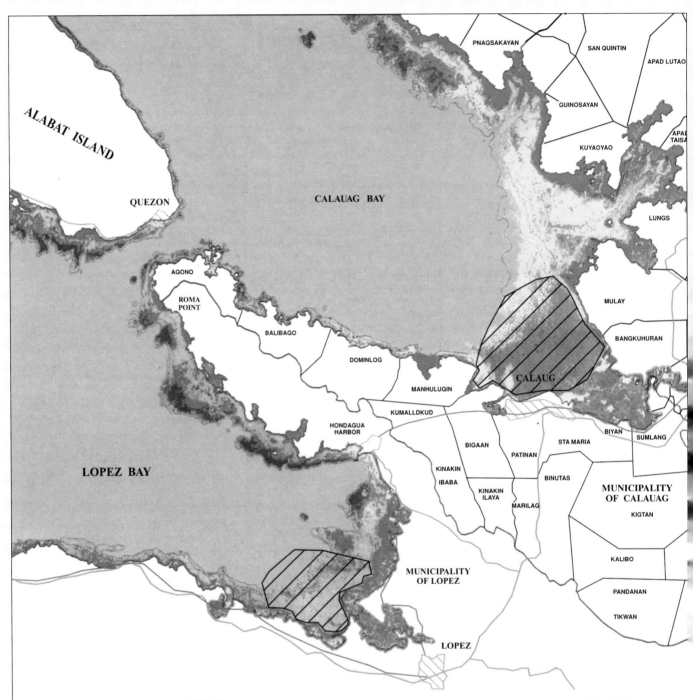

In the tidal area, the colour orange represents degraded areas, mainly mangroves, which should be rehabilitated. The yellow represents dry bare lands, mostly idle aquaculture ponds which require ground survey. In shallow water, the mapping of areas covered by coral (violet tones) and seagrass (green tones) is very useful for assessing fish habitat and monitoring destruction of coral.

Scale 1:50 000

Satellite data for coastal map for planners
Calauag and Lopez Bays, the Philippines

PART A

ISSUES, PERSPECTIVES, POLICY AND PLANNING PROCESSES FOR INTEGRATED COASTAL AREA MANAGEMENT

INTEGRATED
COASTAL AREA
MANAGEMENT
and
AGRICULTURE
FORESTRY AND
FISHERIES

2. The process of integrated coastal area management

necessarily imply that coastal resources are not managed; sectoral plans, plans for environmental management or local community management may fulfil coastal management requirements successfully.

In most coastal states, there are differences in climatic, biophysical, economic, social, political, institutional and cultural variety among different parts of the coast. Therefore, different resource allocation decisions and, perhaps, different routes to implementing them will be required. Moreover, with the exception of small island states, the complexity of national coastal areas makes it impractical to manage at the national level.

In most countries, therefore (other than for small states), coastal management is usually undertaken at the area level.[42] For the purpose of management, the boundaries of a managed coastal area may change as different problems are addressed. There is much to be said therefore, for area boundaries being determined pragmatically and flexibly. The factors influencing a boundary may be biophysical, economic, social, jurisdictional and/or organizational in character.

Experience of successful integrated coastal management points to the need to ensure that the area under management encompasses the source of the environmental changes that have an adverse effect in the coastal area.[43] Some areas defined for integrated coastal management may be relatively small. Others may be larger than some countries.[44] Although ICAM is usually area-based, it is desirable to have a national ICAM outline plan to ensure a proper legal framework, integration with national development planning, and funding. Funding for ICAM can come largely from

adjustments to existing sectoral budgets and investment plans.

It is as well to limit initial attempts at ICAM to small selected pilot sites, which provide an opportunity to explore the broader institutional requirements and demonstrations prior to the expansion of ICAM to larger and more complex sites.

Under an area-based approach, progress in implementation will vary considerably within a country and the final results will differ from place to place. Areas where there is most experience of ICAM will be a number of stages ahead of others where it has been applied at a later date. The severity of issues to be faced and the performance of institutions in applying ICAM will also vary greatly. The main concern is that they all share the same national goals and strategy.[45]

2.3.2 Types of governance and institutional arrangements

Few countries actually start with comprehensive, enabling legislation for coastal area management on a nationwide basis, perhaps because legislation often significantly lags behind problems. Many countries take a more expedient, piecemeal approach in which existing laws and policies are amended or coordinated by means of interagency guidelines, or new, complementary laws are enacted.[46]

Few countries have the capacity to deal with nationwide management of coastal areas initially, and programmes need to be adapted to local situations. If organized correctly, pilot site plans can be used as a testing ground for domestic capabilities in technical, institutional and organizational approaches for managing coastal areas.

Effective management intervention is dependent on the existence of appropriate institutions and organizations. A major question is the adequacy of existing arrangements for management planning and implementation. Where these arrangements are found inadequate or constraining, changes can be gradually introduced. For practical purposes, management activities will initially have to be adapted to existing institutions and organizations, and adjustments phased over the longer term.

37

---

[42] There are exceptions. For example, Sri Lanka has developed a Coastal Zone Management Plan (CZMP) for the country which covers archaeological, historic, cultural, scenic and recreational resources. The plan places most emphasis on the control of erosion, coral and sand mining and reef protection. However, in a second generation management plan, coastal resources management is being devolved to district and local level and special area management plans are being developed and implemented for specific geographic sites of natural or economic significance.

[43] For example, the Chesapeake Bay Program in the United States embraces, not only the large area of the bay itself, but also the watershed, which comprises some 166 000 km². However, the causes of air pollution which are having an adverse effect on fish habitat in the bay originate even further inland and are being addressed.

[44] For example, the Australian Great Barrier Reef, which is managed as an entity, extends for approximately 2 200 km and covers an area of 348 700 km².

---

[45] See Figure A.5.

[46] See Section 2.2 for the legal framework

INTEGRATED
COASTAL AREA
MANAGEMENT
and
AGRICULTURE
FORESTRY AND
FISHERIES

PART A

ISSUES, PERSPECTIVES, POLICY AND PLANNING PROCESSES FOR INTEGRATED COASTAL AREA MANAGEMENT

2. The process of integrated coastal area management

There is an enormous range of possible institutional arrangements for ICAM. Broadly, the following distinctions can be made:

- *Multisectoral integration.* This involves the translation of common goals into independent sectoral planning by coordinating the various agencies responsible for coastal management on the basis of a common policy and bringing together various concerned government agencies and other stakeholders to work towards common goals by following mutually agreed strategies.
- *Systematic integration.* Here, an entirely new, integrated institutional structure is created by placing management and development and policy initiatives in a single institution. This requires cooperative goal definition, planning and action.

Coordination tends to be preferred since line ministries are typically highly protective of their core responsibilities, as these relate directly to their power base and funding. The establishment of an organization with broad administrative responsibilities overlapping the traditional jurisdictions of line ministries – as would be the case where management, policy and development functions are integrated within a single institution – is often likely to meet with resistance rather than cooperation. Integration and coordination should be thought of as separate but mutually supporting.

Integration is an important mechanism in coastal area planning and implementation. Three distinct types of integration are important for ICAM: systems integration, functional integration and policy integration:

- *Systems integration* relates to the need to ensure that all relevant interactions and issues, regardless of their origins, are considered.
- *Functional integration* focuses on ensuring that management interventions are consistent with coastal area management goals and objectives.
- *Policy integration* concerns the need to incorporate management policies, strategies and plans with development policies, strategies and plans.

Coordination is an important mechanism in coastal area planning. It brings together disparate resource users, community groups, non-governmental organizations, research institutions and government agencies at various levels, including central, regional and local. The objectives of coordination are to:

- promote and strengthen multi-agency and multisectoral cooperation and communication;
- provide a forum for negotiation and conflict resolution;
- reduce rivalry by minimizing overlaps and gaps in responsibilities.

Coordination on several levels – vertical, horizontal and temporal – is needed as illustrated in Figure A.6:

- *Vertical coordination* refers to cooperation among various hierarchical levels of government: central, regional and local.
- *Horizontal coordination* focuses on gaining cooperation within a specific level of hierarchy, such as at the local level among local government, sectors and various stakeholders.
- *Temporal coordination* refers to achieving optimal phasing of management actions.

It is important that planning for ICAM be incorporated into national economic and sector development plans to ensure appropriate institutional and budgetary support, and to ensure that ICAM goals are compatible with the national and sectoral development and management plans. The hierarchical relationship between national, sectoral and integrated coastal area planning is illustrated in Figure A.7.

2.3.3 Prerequisites for ICAM

Whatever the exact nature of the process, the success of ICAM will revolve around an effective coordinating mechanism[47] and a number of prerequisites.

Establishment of a twin-track process. Regardless of who initiates the ICAM process, the decision to proceed should be taken by a senior government authority to mark the political will to pursue it. Overall goals determined at government level must then be refined at area level into goals and objectives specific to coastal dwellers' needs. Experience at the area level will highlight the need for action (e.g. legislation) in support of integrated coastal management. Lessons learned in the implementation of policies at the area level will feed into the evaluation and adjustment of national goals and strategies. In other words, the top-down and bottom-up processes mutually influence and feed into each other.

---

[47] See Section 2.3.4.

PART A

INTEGRATED
COASTAL AREA
MANAGEMENT
and
AGRICULTURE
FORESTRY AND
FISHERIES

ISSUES, PERSPECTIVES, POLICY AND PLANNING PROCESSES FOR INTEGRATED COASTAL AREA MANAGEMENT

2. The process of integrated coastal area management

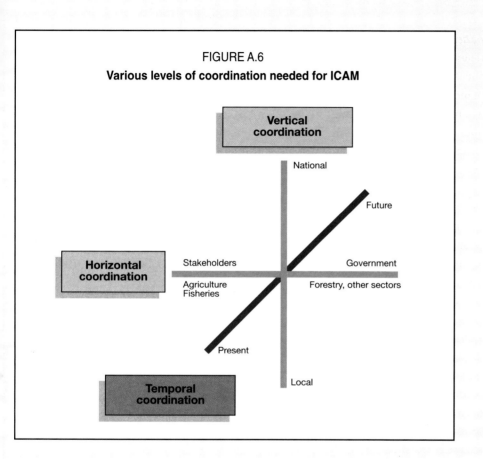

FIGURE A.6

Various levels of coordination needed for ICAM

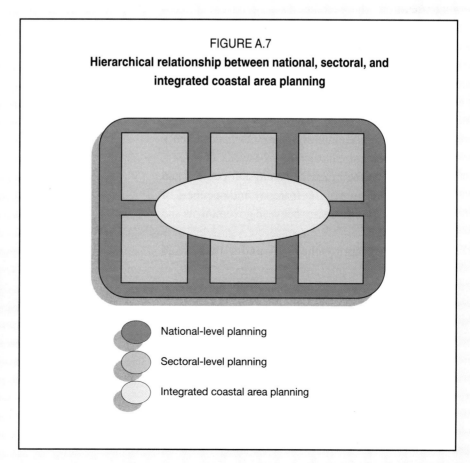

FIGURE A.7

Hierarchical relationship between national, sectoral, and
integrated coastal area planning

INTEGRATED
COASTAL AREA
MANAGEMENT
and
AGRICULTURE
FORESTRY AND
FISHERIES

PART A

ISSUES, PERSPECTIVES, POLICY AND PLANNING PROCESSES FOR INTEGRATED COASTAL AREA MANAGEMENT

2. The process of integrated coastal area management

Establishing an iterative policy process. The policy process involves continuous learning. Among the factors are: experience in the application of various policy instruments; new information provided by environmental monitoring and research; developments in economic and social activities; and revised objectives, according to emerging new factors. Given the long-term nature of much of the research, it is recommended to make provision for research in the strategy and plan; the results will be used in subsequent periodic reviews of plans. As confidence in the ICAM process widens, planners may address more complex issues calling for more research and more learning.

Public involvement. ICAM brings together a variety of social actors, ranging from resource users and communities to legal, recognized or customary institutions, from various hierarchical levels. Figure A.8 illustrates the major groups of social actors at play. It is possible to identify various levels or types of public involvement:

- information sharing in the form of dissemination to groups affected or interested in a decision;
- consultation, where feedback is sought from affected groups and interested parties prior to the making of decisions;
- participation by multiple stakeholders in the decision-making process itself.

The latter varies from shared decision-making (consensus building), to collaborative decision-making (co-partnership), and empowerment (self-management). Public involvement can therefore be weak or strong, depending upon the broader institutional context and the nature and degree of transparency and openness of the communication processes between governments and citizens.[48]

Participatory approaches fall under two broad categories:

- traditional efforts based on ancient rituals and culture/traditions of people. These efforts are long-lasting structured around human development in harmony with nature and the cosmic world and meet requirements through existing endogenous funding channels;

40

Crowded fishing
port, Morocco

Processing of dried fish for
export, Guinea

---

[48] See Table A.4.

PART A

ISSUES, PERSPECTIVES, POLICY AND PLANNING PROCESSES FOR INTEGRATED COASTAL AREA MANAGEMENT

INTEGRATED
COASTAL AREA
MANAGEMENT
and
AGRICULTURE
FORESTRY AND
FISHERIES

2. The process of integrated coastal area management

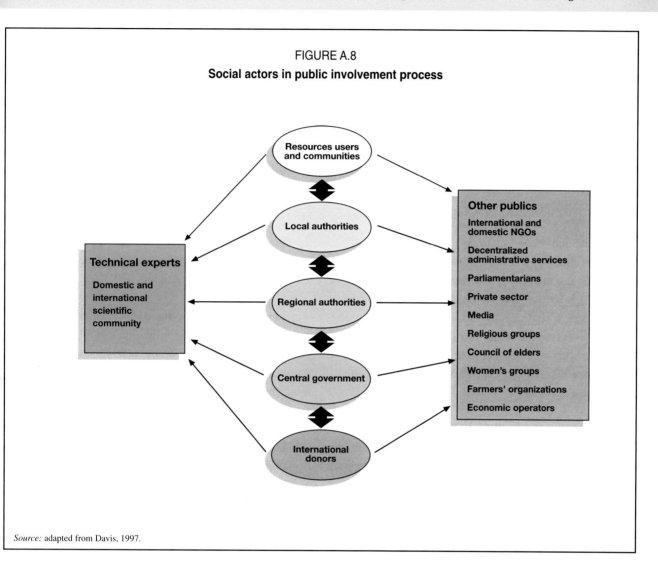

FIGURE A.8

Social actors in public involvement process

Source: adapted from Davis, 1997.

TABLE A.4

A typology of participation

Types of participation	Characteristics of each type
Manipulative participation	Participation is simply a pretence.
Passive participation	People participate by being told what has been decided or has already happened. The information that is shared belongs only to external professionals.
Participation by consultation	People participate by being consulted or by answering questions. The process does not concede any share in decision-making, and professionals are under no obligation to take people's views into consideration.
Participation for material incentives	People participate in return for food, cash or other material incentives. Local people have no stake in prolonging technologies or practices when the incentives end.
Functional participation	Participation is seen by external agencies as a means to achieve project goals, especially at reduced costs. People may participate by forming groups to meet predetermined objectives related to the project.
Interactive participation	People participate in joint analysis, development of action plans and formation or strengthening of local groups or institutions. Learning methodologies are used to seek multiple perspectives, and groups determine how available resources are used.
Self-mobilization	People participate by taking initiatives independently of external institutions to change systems. They develop contacts with external institutions for the resources and technical advice they need, but retain control over how resources are used.

Source: Pretty *et al.,* 1995.

INTEGRATED
COASTAL AREA
MANAGEMENT
and
AGRICULTURE
FORESTRY AND
FISHERIES

PART A

ISSUES, PERSPECTIVES, POLICY AND PLANNING PROCESSES FOR INTEGRATED COASTAL AREA MANAGEMENT

2. The process of integrated coastal area management

• facilitated efforts helped in various ways by development agents. These efforts are either coopted (by incentives, policy instruments or demanding free labour in return for development aid) or coerced participation. They are usually successful on a short-time basis but not sustainable in the long term, both in terms of participation of people and future efforts/commitments.

One of the key elements for successful projects (which fall under the second category) is working towards a higher (cosmic) human dimension, where project activities are integrated into the culture of people (for example, by converting, where appropriate, the various operational activities into rituals as a duty to the king and/or a service to the god). The participatory process can develop an innovative mix of traditional and "imported" expertise, according to each specific context (Sharma, 1997).

2.3.4 Institutional coordination for ICAM

Criteria for the selection of the coordinating institution. Experience in ICAM suggests that line ministries with sectoral responsibilities change or adjust very slowly within the framework of an ICAM initiative. Furthermore, formal institutional coordination works well only within relatively narrow limits, especially until experience and confidence in the process are acquired by the line ministries. In these circumstances, the selection of the most appropriate institution is a critical part of the process as a whole. Among the criteria that should be considered in this selection are the following (after Dick Osborne and Associates, 1993):

• compatibility of the institution's mandate with its proposed functions as the coordinating agency;
• capacity to lever funding for ICAM from concerned ministries or a combination of national sources and donor funding;
• institutional experience in multisectoral planning or, preferably, integrated planning;
• long life expectancy and ability to survive changes in government;
• strong constituency base and ability to perform well in negotiations with line ministries in the ICAM process;
• a strong institutional capacity for ICAM driven by the culture, morale and technical competence within

the organization, rather than dependence on a few committed individuals;
• a holistic approach to policy issues;
• adaptability to new procedures and policy instruments;
• willingness to involve local communities.

Few coordinating institutions will comply with all these criteria. There are perhaps as many ways for countries to select a coordinating institution as there are countries undertaking ICAM through a coordinated approach. Different examples of countries' approaches are illustrated in Boxes A.8 and A.9.

Requirements for effective coordination. There are many prerequisites for coordination to work effectively. Dick Osborne and Associates (1993) have listed the more important as being:

• adoption of a holistic approach;
• agreement on goals at central, area and sector levels;
• agreement on respective roles, jurisdictional boundaries, provision of resources and responsibilities at different levels of governance;
• provision for effective negotiation (bargaining) between different levels of governance, between these and the line ministries, between ministries, and between government and civil society groups that use and manage coastal resources.

The establishment of effective channels of communication and coordination between line ministries and other stakeholders will, for example, allow for the following:

• information sharing and transfer;
• joint education and training, when appropriate;
• joint assessment and acceptance of costs and benefits of environmental changes and proposed policy interventions, when appropriate;[49]
• learning from policy experience;

---

[49] This may be of critical importance. It provides for ministries to undertake jointly the valuation of natural resources and cost-benefit analysis of options for their conservation, management and development potentials and to adopt a system of arbitration relating to their use when agreement cannot be reached between the agencies concerned.

PART A

ISSUES, PERSPECTIVES, POLICY AND PLANNING PROCESSES FOR INTEGRATED COASTAL AREA MANAGEMENT

INTEGRATED
COASTAL AREA
MANAGEMENT
and
AGRICULTURE
FORESTRY AND
FISHERIES

2. The process of integrated coastal area management

BOX A.8

Selection of the coordinating agency for ICAM in Kenya

Kenya selected its coordinating agency in three stages. Originally, the Kenya Marine Fisheries Research Institute (KMFRI) was selected as the lead institution on the basis of its knowledge of many coastal biophysical interactions and its experience of coastal fisheries, as well as its long-standing relationships with two of the international agencies involved, UNEP and FAO. However, its narrow mandate hampered progress and early in the project the lead institution function was transferred to the Coast Development Authority (CDA).

CDA was established just two years prior to the inception of the project to plan and coordinate development projects in the Coast province and the exclusive economic zone. However, while the CDA's mandate (related to land use and management of water and other marine resources) was broad, relevant and endowed

with regulatory powers, it had a number of shortcomings. CDA lacked experience in working with other agencies, had relatively weak institutional capacity, lacked expertise in any relevant area and did not have a policy on ICAM.

CDA maintained a good working relationship with KMFRI and both developed good working relationships with other agencies with a strong interest in the sound management of the area. These included the Kenya Wildlife Service, the Fisheries Department, the Public Health Department and the municipality of Mombasa, within which the area falls. These agencies, together with stakeholders, have formed an informal coastal resources management committee. The combined experience and institutional capacity of these agencies amounts to a considerable force for sound coastal management.

BOX A.9

Selection of the coordinating agency for ICAM
in the Philippines

The Lingayen Gulf was the site in the Philippines for the Coastal Resources Management Project jointly sponsored by the Association of Southeast Asian Nations (ASEAN) and the United States. In 1986, four institutions were identified to implement the Philippines' component of the project. While each had considerable technical competence, none had experience in formulating a coastal management plan and, in 1990, the National Economic Development Plan (NEDA) was designated as the lead agency.

This project ended in 1992 with the main output in the Philippines being the Lingayen Gulf Coastal Management Plan. Implementation, however, did not begin until 1994 with the issue of an executive order creating the Lingayen Gulf Coastal Area Management Commission.

The membership of the Commission is representative of the principal central and local government interests in the area. It is

composed of the Secretaries of the Departments of Environment and Natural Resources (DENR) (chairman), Agriculture (vice chairman), Interior and Local Government, Trade, Industry and Tourism, and National Defence, the Director-General of the National Economic Development Authority, the governors of the two provinces concerned and the mayors of the concerned local governments. DENR provides the technical secretariat of the Commission, headed by an executive director.

The Commission serves as an advisory body to the President and its responsibilities include the preparation of ten- and twenty-year Integrated Master Plans for the Gulf.

The Commission also has some executive powers, including the institutionalization of an integrated environmental permit and licensing system and an incentive system based on the "polluter pays" principle.

INTEGRATED
COASTAL AREA
MANAGEMENT
and
AGRICULTURE
FORESTRY AND
FISHERIES

PART A

ISSUES, PERSPECTIVES, POLICY AND PLANNING PROCESSES FOR INTEGRATED COASTAL AREA MANAGEMENT

2. The process of integrated coastal area management

Mulberry fields with fish ponds in
the Pearl River Delta are artificial
ecological systems in the Chinese
tradition, China

Pens for rearing fish,
Thailand

- joint project and policy monitoring and evaluation;
- participation by all stakeholders;
- balance between top-down and bottom-up processes.

Role of line ministries in ICAM. Staff in line ministries are conventionally sectorally oriented. For ICAM, however, they should understand the need for a holistic approach and be professionally equipped to discuss and negotiate with officials in other agencies. In order to achieve this, training courses should be designed for staff on the need for ICAM and the role of their line ministry in ICAM as a whole and in specific ICAM plans.

Ministries will naturally wish to protect and promote the interests of their respective sectors. They have the incentive and are in a good position to observe the impacts in their sector that are generated internally or arise from activities in other sectors.[50]

The aims of line ministries should be to:

- minimize the generation of negative externalities originating within their sector and having harmful environmental or social effects in other sectors;
- identify and assess, with the available information, current and potential environmental impacts on their sector that may be generated by economic activities in other sectors;
- create public and government awareness regarding these impacts with a view to their minimization;
- coordinate within their own ministry and with other relevant line ministries at central, regional and local levels;
- through a thorough analysis of censuses and surveys and, if necessary, the carrying out of additional specific surveys, make available quantitative and qualitative assessments of the labour force and total population concerned;

---

[50] Some caution has to be exercised at this point. These guidelines suggest that resource users and ministry officials within a sector are often in the best position to record changes that are taking place and to suggest where these changes may originate. However, they are not always in the best position to monitor environmental changes scientifically (it may, for example, be beyond the financial resources of a fisheries ministry to monitor water quality) and it may not always be possible, even with long-term monitoring, to identify with certainty the causes of changes in renewable resource stocks or of ecosystems.

PART A

INTEGRATED
COASTAL AREA
MANAGEMENT
and
AGRICULTURE
FORESTRY AND
FISHERIES

ISSUES, PERSPECTIVES, POLICY AND PLANNING PROCESSES FOR INTEGRATED COASTAL AREA MANAGEMENT

2. The process of integrated coastal area management

- assess the population-supporting capacity of the sector, and its prospects, in the light of population projections and assumptions regarding productivity;
- review the performance and constraints of the respective subsectors in the light of biophysical and economic conditions.

As well as seeking to remove or mitigate the generation of environmental changes that have harmful effects in other sectors, line ministry managers should seek to remove externalities that are internalized within the sector in which they occur.

Several potential weaknesses in institutional arrangements for ICAM will have to be overcome by the coordinating mechanism. Line ministries will not always have the necessary expertise and resources available and they will naturally tend, in the beginning, to give priority to purely sectoral considerations.[51] Appropriate priorities will become clearer once the objectives and policies of the integrated coastal area strategy have been incorporated into the objectives and policies of each sectoral plan.

Role of resource users and non-governmental organizations (NGOs). There are several prerequisites for the successful involvement of resource users:
- an institutional framework in which property rights are allocated to a group of users who, in turn, have an obligation to manage them sustainably;
- an institution, of which resource users are part, that is able to command their support and loyalty and to exercise management authority over them;
- where necessary, training, scientific and technical advice provided by the relevant line ministry to the users, as well as support for the enforcement of management decisions;
- development of appropriate skills and disciplines by the management institution and adoption, with the support of the relevant line ministry, of sound management principles, rules and regulations;
- a clear definition of the area to be managed, and the involvement of all resource users in the management group.

Local NGOs can be valuable partners by:
- providing useful lines of transmission from the local community to the authorities and vice versa;
- helping to keep management focused on local issues;
- contributing to the formulation and implementation of strategies and plans.

Local management will have all the more chance of success when the area devolved or under co-management is relatively small and clearly defined, with a relatively small number of resource users and where rights of ownership or use are exclusive. Commonly managed fisheries of lagoons or areas of reef, for example, frequently work well when the appropriate institutions are in place (Willmann and Insull, 1993).

In many countries, line ministries with responsibility for the management of renewable resources are entering increasingly into a range of cooperative partnerships with resource users for the management of resources. Such partnerships must be based on clear responsibilities and accountabilities on the part of all those involved. In these cases, line ministries will already be working with the resource users. Wide-ranging and true participation (rather than consultation in a predetermined context) with resource users, and a demonstrable willingness of planners to take account of resource users' attitudes and preferences by involving the users in the management process, will usually give good results.

While devolved management is frequently the most effective approach to management, the burden on government continues to be high. Local managers require a constant flow of information on which they can base their management decisions and, frequently, they require support in the form of enforcement by government, especially to stop encroachment by "outsiders". In most situations, the institutions responsible for implementation of management require considerable training and technical support. For these reasons, the recognition of the role of line ministries by resource users is important, especially as certain vital functions can be fulfilled only by the public sector. The involvement of resource users in coastal management is relatively more effective where the state is ready to grant exclusive ownership or user rights to a group of

45

---

[51] Figure A.4 illustrates this tendency.

INTEGRATED
COASTAL AREA
MANAGEMENT
and
AGRICULTURE
FORESTRY AND
FISHERIES

PART A

ISSUES, PERSPECTIVES, POLICY AND PLANNING PROCESSES FOR INTEGRATED COASTAL AREA MANAGEMENT

2. The process of integrated coastal area management

resource users and where the conditions outlined above can be met.[52]

Creating a constituency for ICAM. ICAM often calls for detailed knowledge of conditions in the area, perhaps extending back over many years. This information will rarely be available in quantitative form, gathered over many years. Local knowledge is an invaluable complementary source of information, and institutional mechanisms for ensuring that the knowledge of resource users is properly taken into account should be a concern of line ministries.

The resolution of resource-use issues almost invariably results in losers as well as winners. When resource users are required to reduce or halt activities that they may have been undertaking for generations, it is essential that they fully understand the reasons. This understanding can only come about if they are fully involved in all the processes. Line ministries should ensure that resource users are represented in the planning committees that are established to support the planning process in ICAM.[53]

When resource users are required to surrender resource use, appropriate compensation[54] should be provided. Line ministries should include adequate provisions in their budgets, along with the necessary legal and institutional adjustments. It is never easy to achieve fairness and equity in such situations.

Successful management of natural resources requires a conviction on the part of those affected by management change that they can influence the process and that the proposed management measures are equitable and fair. Without this perception of legitimacy, or constituency building (Olsen, 1993), there is a strong likelihood that proposed management measures will fail. Indeed, those affected may even sabotage the measures.

Creating a constituency for ICAM is one of the chief aspects of the policy process. Support from the private sector, including individual stakeholders, and from communities and special interest groups is essential. Accordingly, community leaders, members of the community and trade organizations should be targeted.

The full participation of resource users will often

Women at work in a field
in the Tirana plain,
Albania

---

[52] See Box A.10.
[53] See Sections 1.6.1 and 2.3.3 and Table A.4.
[54] See Section 2.2.5 and Box A.4.

PART **A**

ISSUES, PERSPECTIVES, POLICY AND PLANNING PROCESSES FOR INTEGRATED COASTAL AREA MANAGEMENT

**INTEGRATED
COASTAL AREA
MANAGEMENT**
and
**AGRICULTURE
FORESTRY AND
FISHERIES**

2. The process of integrated coastal area management

BOX A.10
Community-based resource management and co-management

In the past, resources were always community-managed. It is therefore not surprising that community-based resource management still tends to succeed today, when properly set up.

When devolving management responsibility on local communities, it is always advisable to draw on indigenous knowledge and resource management practices. In some cases, it may be necessary to adopt enabling legislation. Similarly, assistance may be needed for communities to develop managerial and organizational skills adapted to current conditions.

Usually, when direct government intervention in resource management is deemed necessary, government staff's attitudes and approach will need to be seriously revised. Local management will not work if civil servants maintain a superior approach and consider local people as beholden to them.

In South Asia, fisheries communities have undergone significant socio-economic and cultural change as a result of their incorporation into larger national and international processes that have altered community relationships in coastal villages. Support for overcoming these dislocations was provided through measures including aquarian reform and community development aimed at building new relationships. Aquarian reform consisted of granting stewardship to workers and owner-workers so that the coastal waters would regain their status as community property.

Community development involved better organization of fish marketing in order to increase incomes, better credit arrangements, access to improved education and health facilities, and skills training for the young and for women.

Source: extracted from Pomeroy, 1994.

**Rural radio extension,
Madagascar**

47

INTEGRATED
COASTAL AREA
MANAGEMENT
and
AGRICULTURE
FORESTRY AND
FISHERIES

PART A

ISSUES, PERSPECTIVES, POLICY AND PLANNING PROCESSES FOR INTEGRATED COASTAL AREA MANAGEMENT

2. The process of integrated coastal area management

BOX A.11

The steps of the patrimonial approach

Inception (requires a mediator to stimulate dialogue and negotiation):
- identification of stakeholders, including interested but absent third parties;
- debate on present trends;
- debate on the ecological, economic, and social (non-)acceptability of present trends.

Definition of goals and objectives (requires mediation):
- discussion of very long-term (patrimonial) objectives (25 to 30 years);
- legitimization process where stakeholders appropriate the product of their negotiations and establish a "social contract";
- ritualization (a ceremonial proper to the local culture).

Strategy formulation (requires mediation and expert advice, namely for scientific evaluation of scenarios and appraisal of economic feasibility):
- stakeholders elaborate medium-term management scenarios towards the very long-term objective (including uses, access, control, transferability, distribution rules and sanctions);
- selection of management tools;
- legitimization of the result through public restitution of terms of agreement to a recognized authority.

Plan formulation
Executive details to implement decisions taken on agreed scenarios, including establishing a negotiated management structure. For example, tasks incumbent on the structure are to implement decisions taken regarding matters such as control over access and to exclude outsiders, notifying the applicable sanctions to the authority responsible for enforcement.

Source: adapted from Weber, 1996.

---

highlight conflicting interests affecting coastal resources that are difficult to reconcile. Through mediated dialogue, perceptions could be confronted and negotiated among stakeholders to define long-term patrimonial objectives in coastal areas.

Patrimonial mediation[55] seeks to inverse the process of negotiation by obtaining the common agreement of a group on the long-term future they desire. The quest for agreement about the long-term, as an attempt to put short- and medium-term undertakings into perspective, endows a community heritage dimension where actions can be organized to shape the future along common objectives. The aim is to enable the actors to compare and discuss their perceptions (which are equally legitimate and equally subjective) and the commonly held disagreement on the prolongation of present trends. Once the goal is agreed upon by a group, and thus legitimized, short-term scenarios of use, access and control of resources can be established, including comparative viability and costs. Agreed scenarios thus transform the desired patrimonial objective into possible "constitutional" choices. Ultimately, a management structure is established to implement decisions taken on agreed scenarios. This approach, which requires much patience and skill, ensures interaction and self-mobilization and is based on an endogenous social contract where actors conform to the product of negotiation.[56]

2.3.5 Building capacities for ICAM
Institutional capacity to manage the ICAM process.[57]
The institutions contributing to ICAM should have the collective capacity to allocate resources according to the goals and strategic approach adopted. The engine to drive the process includes well-trained and experienced staff. The capacity to manage the process can be developed as part of the strategy. Not all individual participating organizations will – or should be able to – satisfy this requirement, but it is important that the system as a whole is able to deliver the following services (Olsen, 1993; Dick Osborne and Associates, 1993):

---

[55] More information on mediation characteristics and processes can be found in Part E, Section 4.1.4.
[56] See Box A.11 and Box A.12.
[57] See Section 2.3.4.

PART A

ISSUES, PERSPECTIVES, POLICY AND PLANNING PROCESSES FOR INTEGRATED COASTAL AREA MANAGEMENT

INTEGRATED
COASTAL AREA
MANAGEMENT
and
AGRICULTURE
FORESTRY AND
FISHERIES

2. The process of integrated coastal area management

BOX A.12
Patrimonial mediation in Madagascar

In Madagascar, the policy of transferring the management of renewable natural resources, under contract, to rural communities has, since October 1996, been governed by Law 96-025 providing for local management of renewable resources. The management of forests, wild fauna and flora (both aquatic and terrestrial), water and rangeland coming within the state domain or territorial communities can thus be handed over to local entities.

The Law creates a regulatory framework for the so-called GELOSE (*gestion locale securisée* – security in local resource management) contracts. Such contracts are entered into by the state along with the commune or the base rural community. A contract provides for:

- the transfer, under contract, of the management of a renewable natural resource within a demarcated community area to a given rural community;
- the rendering of relatively secure land tenure (by public record), where all parties will have been able to make an input, regarding individual or community land occupancy throughout the territory concerned.

The objective is to put an end to uncontrolled access by making rural communities responsible for the resources in their area. A contract can only be stipulated at the free request of the community concerned. The contract must promote the use of the resource and the enhancement of its value for the benefit of such communities or communes. A contract implies that negotiation has taken place between the government, the community occupying the territory

(commune) and the local community – on the basis of patrimonial mediation. The community or commune is assisted in the process by a qualified environment mediator of its choice. The mediator is chosen by the rural community on the basis of personal qualities, and has no power over the parties beyond the confidence generated in others by an ability to listen and mediate. There is no *a priori* preclusion of any actor in the social or economic life of the locality. The process inevitably requires consideration on the part of the community as to the long-term use of the different areas making up the territory it occupies. The relevant contracts are made for a trial period of three years and are renewable. Administrative monitoring is provided for ten years.

The commune awarded the contract ensures that obligations are complied with. It is also required to secure exclusive access for members of the community undertaking the management. The GELOSE contract ratifies the use and management rights of the rural community as holders of the usufruct.

The formula endows the legitimate with the force of law; it allows communities to become prime beneficiaries and dynamic elements in local development. It also seeks to release local initiative and restore assurance and responsibility to local actors.

GELOSE is a constituent – horizontal – element in the Environment Plan of Madagascar and is associated with the support for regionalized management and land area approach that is required to facilitate regionally negotiated planning of development activities.

Source: Babin *et al.,* 1997.

49

Shrimp fishing boats ready for the next catch after some weeks of closed season in order to protect the fry, Hell-Ville harbour, Madagascar.

INTEGRATED
COASTAL AREA
MANAGEMENT
and
AGRICULTURE
FORESTRY AND
FISHERIES

PART A

ISSUES, PERSPECTIVES, POLICY AND PLANNING PROCESSES FOR INTEGRATED COASTAL AREA MANAGEMENT

2. The process of integrated coastal area management

BOX A.13

Key GESAMP[58] findings on the role of natural and social sciences in ICAM

Among the findings, the most salient points are as follows:

- competent management of a complex ecosystem interrelating with significant human activities will have more chances of success where the scientific basis for processes is known;
- science can support ICAM by taking an issue-driven approach in which scientists seek to provide managers with information useful for solving relevant problems;
- close and continuing working relationships between managers and scientists are essential in determining the required information that can be provided by natural or social scientists;
- there are limits to the ability of science to provide the information required by managers for setting objectives and targets and taking actions in situations of uncertainty; recognizing this and establishing appropriate mechanisms would avoid tensions between managers and scientists;
- managers and scientists should work together to achieve community support and the participation of resource users in the design and conduct of research related to management decisions that will affect them;
- research related to management problems should ensure that the objectives are realistic, taking account of available resources and the explicitly stated time-frame;
- science funded by ICAM programmes should be subject to peer review;
- relevant scientific knowledge that is available elsewhere should be documented before new research is initiated;
- simple and inexpensive technology can often effectively meet the needs of scientists and managers;
- the presentation and application of science must be sensitive to the local culture;
- developing countries should develop a national cadre of natural and social scientists to ensure that the available science can be applied, whether or not foreign scientists are involved.

[58] The Joint Group of Experts on the Scientific Aspects of Marine Environmental Protection (GESAMP) is an advisory body of experts nominated by the following sponsoring agencies and programmes in the United Nations System: the International Maritime Organization (IMO), Food and Agriculture Organization of the United Nations (FAO), the United Nations Educational, Scientific and Cultural Organization, Intergovernmental Oceanographic Commission (UNESCO-IOC), the World Metereological Organization (WMO), the World Health Organization (WHO), the International Atomic Energy Commission (IAEA), the United Nations (UN) and the United Nations Environment Programme (UNEP).

Source: extracted from GESAMP, 1996a.

- an equitable and efficient decision-making process;
- use of the best available knowledge about how the relevant ecosystems function;
- participation of resource users, and all those affected by management decisions, in the decision-making process;
- capacity to resolve differences of interest;
- ability to employ economic policy instruments strategically;
- integrated, simple and effective regulatory instruments;
- public investment for the protection of coastal ecosystems and management of renewable resources.

Government line agencies rarely have expertise in participatory methods and integrated natural resource management. Thus, forming a team that is proficient in strategy and methods requires in-service training. During implementation, local staff should be exposed to a variety of learning experiences, including brief courses, internal workshops and seminars, experience-exchange events and study tours. It is important that training of local staff be included in the terms of reference of consultants (national or international). In addition, the participatory monitoring and evaluation process should have a continuing educational and formative orientation by identifying lessons learned and further learning needs. A mix of hiring *ad hoc* project staff and mobilizing professionals from relevant line agencies and institutions would allow higher efficiency and wider dissemination of the approach among local institutions.

Because coastal problems involve a range of actors and a multiplicity of complex interrelated issues, an institutional capacity to resolve conflicts and institutional supervision will be required to manage the participation and relationships of interested parties and the different interests represented, as well as to identify suitable options and agree on objectives and means to attain them. Depending on local circumstances (traditional practices and principles) consideration should also be given to establishing funding mechanisms for conflict resolution (in order to cover the costs of appointing mediators or experts, or simply of running negotiations) and providing training and education for third parties to mediate, facilitate or arbitrate in disputes. Administrative procedures and

INTEGRATED
COASTAL AREA
MANAGEMENT
and
AGRICULTURE
FORESTRY AND
FISHERIES

PART A

ISSUES, PERSPECTIVES, POLICY AND PLANNING PROCESSES FOR INTEGRATED COASTAL AREA MANAGEMENT

2. The process of integrated coastal area management

dispute resolution offices or commissions might also be established to anticipate and resolve conflicts arising within and between institutions.[59]

The role of research and environmental information. Identifying critical issues in ICAM requires information.[60] Taking decisions on the most appropriate use of resources usually requires additional information. The contributions of science and, in particular, research, have been specifically addressed by the Joint Group of Experts on the Scientific Aspects of Marine Environmental Protection (GESAMP).[61]

In most countries, there is scope for developing ICAM strategies without high additional expenditures on data collection and research for information. In the early years of ICAM in many countries, it is better to focus on issues that are resolvable in the short to medium term and do not depend on long research programmes for a solution. Depending on local conditions, a phased approach to ICAM can be adopted, with increasing levels of integration and complexity.

In many countries, ICAM data collection and research can usually be implemented by existing research institutions. Often, however, a redirection of research is necessary and this may present difficult choices. In many of these situations, it is very useful to consult users of research in conjunction with scientists about the process by which research plans are drawn up and on the setting of information and research needs. This should not be done by researchers alone. A consultative process can result in additional research capacity becoming available within existing budgets while, in cases where research is handicapped by lack of laboratory equipment or a travel budget, finding additional funds for ICAM information collection and research may require a shift in budgetary allocations to research.

Equally difficult problems may arise in many countries over institutional responsibilities and capacities, both of which may be linked to the issues of financial resources. With regard to the former, the

---

BOX A.14
The Great Barrier Reef Marine Park Authority Programme, Australia

The leading goal of the Great Barrier Reef Marine Park Authority Programme is the conservation of Australia's Great Barrier Reef. The major issue is the runoff from farmland of nutrient- and sediment-enriched water.

High levels of cooperation have been achieved between the Authority, farmers' organizations and state government agencies responsible for primary industry. Experience has shown that if cooperation is achieved in carrying out research into a problem, it is likely to extend into defining and applying ways of resolving the problem.

The Authority has established a reefwide monitoring programme and a multi-institutional, interdisciplinary research programme which aims to develop a complete understanding of the origins of these nutrients and sediments so that corrective action can be taken if necessary. The objective in relation to land-based sources of pollution has been to limit them to levels that do not cause significant changes in the reef ecosystem using as a baseline information collected in 1929-1931.

The most important element in the strategy has been the involvement of farmers' organizations in cooperative research projects with the Authority and other organizations. Research has shown greatly increased nutrient levels since 1932, the sources of these nutrients and their effect on corals. The research also showed that levels of erosion and nutrient loss from sugar cropping can be (greatly) reduced by changes in farming practice – changes that have been voluntarily adopted by most sugar farmers on irrigated land on the coast of Queensland.

Source: extracted from Kelleher, 1996.

---

[59] See Part E, Sections 5 and 6.
[60] See Section 1.6.3.
[61] See Box A.13. The contribution of research to addressing coastal problems is illustrated in Box A.14.

INTEGRATED
COASTAL AREA
MANAGEMENT
and
AGRICULTURE
FORESTRY AND
FISHERIES

PART A

ISSUES, PERSPECTIVES, POLICY AND PLANNING PROCESSES FOR INTEGRATED COASTAL AREA MANAGEMENT

2. The process of integrated coastal area management

monitoring of water quality, for example, may be primarily in the immediate interest of the fisheries or the tourism sector and in the longer-term interest of society as a whole. It would be unreasonable, however, and probably beyond the financial resources of the sector institutions concerned, for the fisheries or the tourism line ministries to bear full financial responsibility for water quality monitoring. As mentioned in earlier sections, a part of the coordination process is to reach agreement on respective roles, jurisdictional boundaries, provision of resources and responsibilities.

In many countries, the immediate constraint on ICAM is the prevalence of weak institutional capacities. Shortages of skills and experience are often less severe in subject areas related to sectoral disciplines than cross-sectoral ones (e.g. environmental and social sciences) and therefore it will be difficult to apply holistic and participatory approaches. These comparative strengths and weaknesses reflect earlier perceived needs in line ministries and research institutions when the need for economists trained in, for example, the valuation of natural resources, was not apparent. Staff weaknesses can be solved by retraining of selected staff, either in-country or outside the country and/or recruitment of suitably trained new staff.

2.3.6. Sustainability indicators

Indicators are increasingly used to provide a convenient description of the current state or condition of a resource, as well as to gauge performance and predict responses. They need to be developed according to their perceived applications and this requires reliable statistics and raw data.[62] Indicators are used to monitor and evaluate what is changing, the processes by which change is occurring and the sustainability of beneficial changes. Different types of indicators exist, depending on the scale (global, national, local) and the level of aggregation.

Indicators of ecological sustainability (e.g. land suitability, pollution impacts) can be combined with economic data to construct scenarios based on available information. By including in the cost of production the cost of the deterioration in the natural resource base, policy choices can be made aimed at mitigating the negative impacts on natural resources and this will help to allocate resources more efficiently. Placing a reasonable value on the costs and benefits of preserving natural resources is essential in order to make a workable estimate of externalities or indirect costs.

Human development indicators. Indices to measure human development and the quality of human life are proposed by the United Nations Development Programme (UNDP) Human Development Index. The index combines factors such as longevity (associated with health and nutrition) and educational attainment with income, to generate a weighted index of "essential" living standards. Factors of quality of life cover basic human biophysical needs such as food, clothing and shelter, and satisfaction of basic socio-economic needs, such as access to essential goods and services (health, education) and equity in employment, income and wealth distribution. But quality of life also includes activities that have an impact on the environment or on other factors, and that are perceived as benefits (e.g. recreation opportunities, biological diversity or aesthetics), costs or risks (e.g. exposure to, and magnitude of, environmental contamination or hazards).

Environmental indicators. The International Union for the Conservation of Nature and Natural Resources (IUCN) has developed indicators for conserving life-support systems and biological diversity, ensuring the sustainable use of renewable resources, minimizing the depletion of non-renewable resources and keeping within the carrying capacity of supporting ecosystems.[63]

Performance indicators. There is a growing understanding that sustainability depends on the emphasis placed by development programmes on enhancing the capacity of groups, organizations or societies to understand and solve the problems they face. The indicators needed to measure changes in the capacity or the performance of groups, organizations or societies are not well established but efforts are beginning (e.g. the Organisation for Economic Co-operation and Development – OECD) to develop

---

[62] See Figure A.9.

[63] Refer to IUCN/UNEP/WWF, 1991.

PART A

ISSUES, PERSPECTIVES, POLICY AND PLANNING PROCESSES FOR INTEGRATED COASTAL AREA MANAGEMENT

INTEGRATED
COASTAL AREA
MANAGEMENT
and
AGRICULTURE
FORESTRY AND
FISHERIES

2. The process of integrated coastal area management

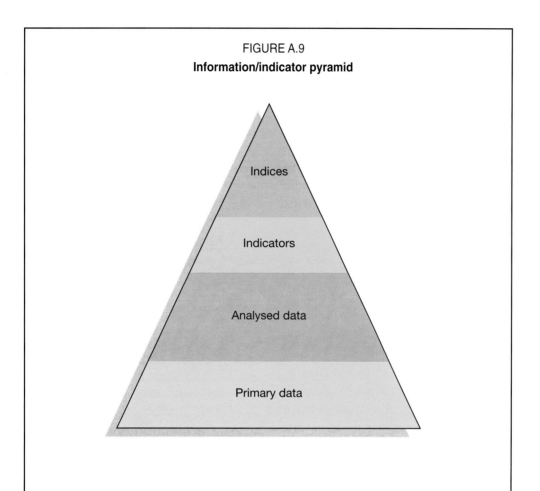

FIGURE A.9

Information/indicator pyramid

Note: Measurements of events or phenomena produce raw data. After analyses, primary data produces statistics. Statistics become indicators when they are tied to a specific problem or application. If indicators are aggregated according to a formula, they become indices (e.g. Human Development Index, Air Pollution Index, UV Radiation Hazard Index, Water Quality Index).

Source: WRI, 1996.

A rainbow over the hills of the Blue Mountains, looking north from Keith Hill, Jamaica

INTEGRATED
COASTAL AREA
MANAGEMENT
and
AGRICULTURE
FORESTRY AND
FISHERIES

PART A

ISSUES, PERSPECTIVES, POLICY AND PLANNING PROCESSES FOR INTEGRATED COASTAL AREA MANAGEMENT

2. The process of integrated coastal area management

process-oriented indicators as well as effective systems and tools for performance reviews. In the case of monitoring, the question is whether only the "what" should be monitored (i.e. outputs and results) or also the "how" (the process as such – systemic, participatory, consensual – including the role and responsibilities of all the parties involved). Hence, performance indicators might include information on coordination mechanisms, performance incentives and standards, available financial resources, control over allocation, skills, information exchange mechanisms, etc.

Interdependence indicators. Efforts are also under way to develop indicators of dynamic relationships, where the most important indicator is the degree of interdependence between human beings and the natural environment. This approach is based on the recognition of the fact that individuals' "dependence" on local resources is related to the degree of capital mobility. For example, the flexibility entrepreneurs have within the globalized economy to move investments rapidly from one country to another. When capital is not mobile, tenants would tend to preserve the value of an environmental asset in time, and derive the exclusive benefits of their work and investments. When capital is mobile, and social constraints are lacking, the investor has little interest in preserving the ecosystem and the owner would tend, consciously, to continue an unsustainable practice (i.e. maximizing short-term yields) and then move on to another area to exploit (Weber, 1996).

Pressure-state-response indicators. The most widely used framework for sustainability indicators at present is the pressure/state/response (PSR) indicator[64] which addresses the chain of events that lead to environmental impacts:
- *pressure* refers to driving forces that create environmental impacts (e.g. a given agro-industrial process is decreasing water quality);
- *state* refers to the condition(s) that prevail(s) when a pressure exists (e.g. the result of decreased water quality is that fish die);
- *response* refers to the mitigation action(s) and levers that could be applied to reducing or eliminating the

Cow grazing near swamp at
Tangalla, Sri Lanka

Sea-salt extraction,
Thailand

54

---

[64] See Figure A.10.

PART A

ISSUES, PERSPECTIVES, POLICY AND PLANNING PROCESSES FOR INTEGRATED COASTAL AREA MANAGEMENT

INTEGRATED
COASTAL AREA
MANAGEMENT
and
AGRICULTURE
FORESTRY AND
FISHERIES

2. The process of integrated coastal area management

FIGURE A.10
The pressure-state-response (PSR) framework

The PSR framework provides a convenient representation of the linkages between the pressures exerted on natural resources by human activities (pressure box), the changes in quality of the resource (state box) and the responses of these changes as society attempts to release the pressure or to rehabilitate resources that have been degraded (response box). The interchanges among these form a continuous feedback mechanism that can be monitored and used for assessment of natural resource quality.

- *Pressure indicators* can be developed by using statistical (census) databases, often available nationally.
- *State indicators* can be developed from usually dispersed individual, specialized data banks (e.g. digitized soil maps),

supplemented with data from other sources such as estimates obtained from physical process models (e.g. the Erosion Productivity Impact Calculator of the United States Department of Agriculture), remote sensing and related techniques (e.g. aerial photographs, field identification of indicator plants).

- *Response indicators* can be developed by evaluating activities undertaken in response to the problem identified. Information on these initiatives is available from government departments, the records of NGOs, companies, etc. and also from PRA inquiries.

Because of local requirements and priorities, indicators should be location-specific and geo-referenced at appropriate scales using geographic information system (GIS) techniques.

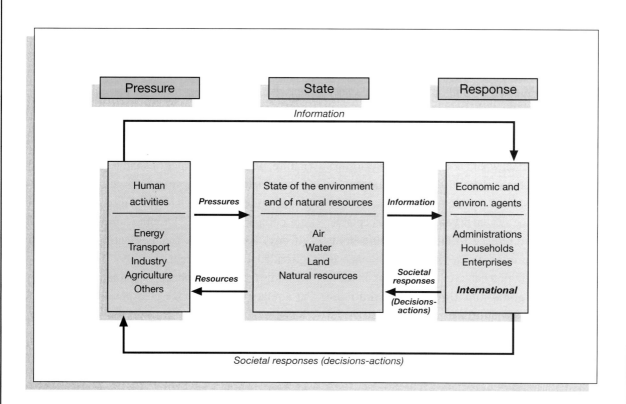

Source: extracted from FAO, 1997b

INTEGRATED
COASTAL AREA
MANAGEMENT
and
AGRICULTURE
FORESTRY AND
FISHERIES

PART A

ISSUES, PERSPECTIVES, POLICY AND PLANNING PROCESSES FOR INTEGRATED COASTAL AREA MANAGEMENT

2. The process of integrated coastal area management

impacts (e.g. water treatment and technology adjustment would enhance water quality).

In response to the call made in Agenda 21 of the Earth Summit to develop and use indicators of sustainable development, the Commission on Sustainable Development has produced a set of methodology sheets for indicators, following the PSR framework. Those developed or in progress for coastal areas include three driving force-type indicators – population growth in coastal areas, discharges of oil into coastal waters and releases of nitrogen and phosphorus into coastal waters – and two state-type indicators – maximum sustainable yields for fisheries and algae index (UN, 1996). No response-type indicators are proposed but ICAM effectiveness in improving coastal ecosystems and livelihoods could be a useful consideration.

Pressure and response indicators are generally considered at sectoral (or subsectoral) level and therefore relate directly to the policy arena. State indicators relate to changes in the condition and quality of natural resources. The application of the PSR approach to ICAM entails identifying key coastal issues for each cluster of indicators, in particular for the policy-related questions that must be answered. After identifying the shortlist of strategic indicators associated with key issues (which would normally reflect priorities as perceived from the various stakeholders), targets for each indicator should be developed, as well as thresholds where the system may become unacceptable. Monitoring with reference to targets and thresholds makes it possible to assess sectoral performance in relation to coastal maintenance or degradation. In cases where reliable goals and thresholds cannot be developed, trends in performance still provide useful information.

The major shortcoming of the PSR framework is that it does not capture the interactions and trade-offs between the economic and environmental dimensions of the development equation. State indicators fail to capture processes, trends and performance. PSR relates better to the long term (e.g. when addressing long-standing issues, where pressures have been exerted for a long time, leading to a chronic "state of nature" that reflects a degree of dynamic equilibrium between pressure, response and state). The PSR concept does not capture the direction of the trend in the pressure and state, the rate of change of the pressure or state or

the time lag between the moment the pressure is applied (or changed), and the moment at which the effect is fully reflected in the state. Garcia (1996) proposes to describe the situation of an exploitable system in terms of pressure, state and response, by indicators of level, change and structure.[65]

Selection of indicators. Not everything that happens can or should be monitored. Data collection and monitoring should be pragmatic and based on selection criteria such as timeliness, relevance and cost-effectiveness (See Box A.16). In addition to agreement on selection criteria, consensus is required on the data and derivation methodology to be used in establishing indicators, including a delimitation of the allowable fluctuation of the indicator. Indicators could be directly representative, indicative of, or a proxy for, the factor considered important. Complex changes may be highlighted by choosing a limited number of suitable indicators that are regularly monitored and compared with previous readings back to the baseline for each one. It is therefore essential for baseline conditions to be established at the very outset for people's attitudes (both users' groups and advisory staff) and socio-economic and biophysical conditions. To determine the nature, direction and rates of change, assessments need to be done on a recurring basis and compared with baseline data. After each round of monitoring, the results are compared with the baseline condition, differences (if any) are analysed, trends identified and feedback provided to management.

While the development of sustainability indicators is at a relatively early stage, it is possible to design and implement systems that provide decision-makers with the information necessary for resource management and for anticipating, and acting upon, change. "Menus" of potential indicators have been developed for specific sectors (health, agriculture, environment). However, there is a tendency to put aside those checklists of potential indicators and rely instead on the clear identification of specific problems to be solved in each specific case. The clear and precise identification of criteria used to describe a specific problem should lead to the identification of the specific indicators of change. (Le Blanc, 1997).

---

[65] See Box A.15.

PART A

ISSUES, PERSPECTIVES, POLICY AND PLANNING PROCESSES FOR INTEGRATED COASTAL AREA MANAGEMENT

INTEGRATED
COASTAL AREA
MANAGEMENT
and
AGRICULTURE
FORESTRY AND
FISHERIES

2. The process of integrated coastal area management

BOX A.15
Indicators of level, change and structure

Indicators of level reflect the spatial and temporal evolution of key system variables expressed as absolute values (e.g. fishing capacities, revenues, employment, number and importance of conflicts) or in the form of ratios (e.g. between virgin and present biomass, or between fishery and agricultural revenues). They measure the final response of the system or of one of its components. They integrate a large number of interactions and reflect directly the performance of the system, if used in conjunction with peer-established sustainability criteria. However, indicators of level (e.g. stock abundance) in isolation may not provide information on whether the system is stable, improving or worsening, nor on the action eventually required.

Indicators of change indicate the direction and rate of change of key indicators. Combined with indicators of level, they give a dynamic perspective to otherwise static indicators and would be particularly useful for early warning systems.

Indicators of structure refer to the functional elements of a system. When referring to institutions, they are called institutional indicators. The sustainable nature of an exploitation system, management set-up or development strategy can be assessed against a checklist of desirable and undesirable system properties relating to:

- objectives retained for management or development (e.g. sectoral production targets, requirements for environmental conservation);
- the management planning process with its institutions and mechanisms (e.g. availability of data, establishment of mechanisms for effective people's participation, existence of dispute resolution mechanisms);
- the management approach and measures (e.g., access regulations, economic incentives/disincentives);
- management implementation (e.g. built-in process of periodic evaluation, surveillance system).

Source: extracted from Garcia, 1996.

BOX A.16
Selection of sustainability indicators

Among the criteria guiding the selection of sustainability indicators for ICAM are the following:

- **Policy relevance**: ensure the indicators address environmental changes of primary concern in the country or area where they are being applied.
- **Predictability:** provide information that anticipates environmental change and thus allows decisions to be taken before change becomes irreversible.
- **Interdependency:** provide information that clearly links cause and effect and reflects the dynamism between the ecological, social and economic environments in order to allow a better understanding of how they affect each other and the driving forces that need to be measured.
- **Measurability**: provide information expressed in quantitative or qualitative terms so it can be either convertible to a monetary value (and therefore related to national accounts) or used for informed decision-making.
- **Performance:** ensure human and institutional capacity are able to manage the policy and planning process effectively through participatory and transparent approaches.

INTEGRATED
COASTAL AREA
MANAGEMENT
and
AGRICULTURE
FORESTRY AND
FISHERIES

PART A

ISSUES, PERSPECTIVES, POLICY AND PLANNING PROCESSES FOR INTEGRATED COASTAL AREA MANAGEMENT

2. The process of integrated coastal area management

One difficulty in selecting (and aggregating) indicators is related to value judgement. Scientific evidence and a precautionary approach, as well as considerations of local cultural preferences, should play a central role in the process of achieving agreement on indicators.

2.4 THE POLICY AND PLANNING PROCESS IN ICAM

The ICAM process evolves through successive completion of cycles. Each cycle addresses management issues, formulates and implements strategies and plans, and monitors and evaluates performance.

The first cycle usually begins with the most urgent issues and has a limited geographical and institutional coverage. Through successive cycles, the scope and scale of the strategy and plan are increased to incorporate new and more complex problems and stakeholders. Performance review (including monitoring and evaluation) is an integral element throughout the process. Performance review not only suggests regular revisions and adjustments during the implementation phase, but represents the motor that moves ICAM plans into successive cycles. Thus, as achievements are consolidated and confidence is gained, there will be an evolution from a small ICAM (demonstration) project to an expanded application leading to a fully fledged, effective, national coastal programme.[66]

The end products of the ICAM policy and planning process are the formulation and implementation of a strategy. As stressed earlier in this document[67] there is no single way to organize ICAM strategies and plans. Whether a given country chooses to start with a local demonstration project, coordinate "expanded" sectoral plans (that contain an ICAM part), or create an entirely new integrated plan, it is important that the process leading to the formulation of the coastal strategy involves all stakeholders so that any implementation route follows agreed goals and objectives.

These guidelines focus on the issues and requirements that lead to plan formulation. The assumption is that an appropriate strategic basis and plan(s) will lead to sound implementation.

The ICAM process should be viewed as long-term, continuous and iterative, as shown in Figure A.11. The

Villagers help to pull a fishing net, which has been set in a semi-circle, from open boats in the Arabian Sea about 500 m off the beach, India

Mapping and analysis of remote sensing data, India

---

[66] See Figure A.5.
[67] In Sections 2.3.1 and 2.3.2.

PART A

ISSUES, PERSPECTIVES, POLICY AND PLANNING PROCESSES FOR INTEGRATED COASTAL AREA MANAGEMENT

INTEGRATED
COASTAL AREA
MANAGEMENT
and
AGRICULTURE
FORESTRY AND
FISHERIES

2. The process of integrated coastal area management

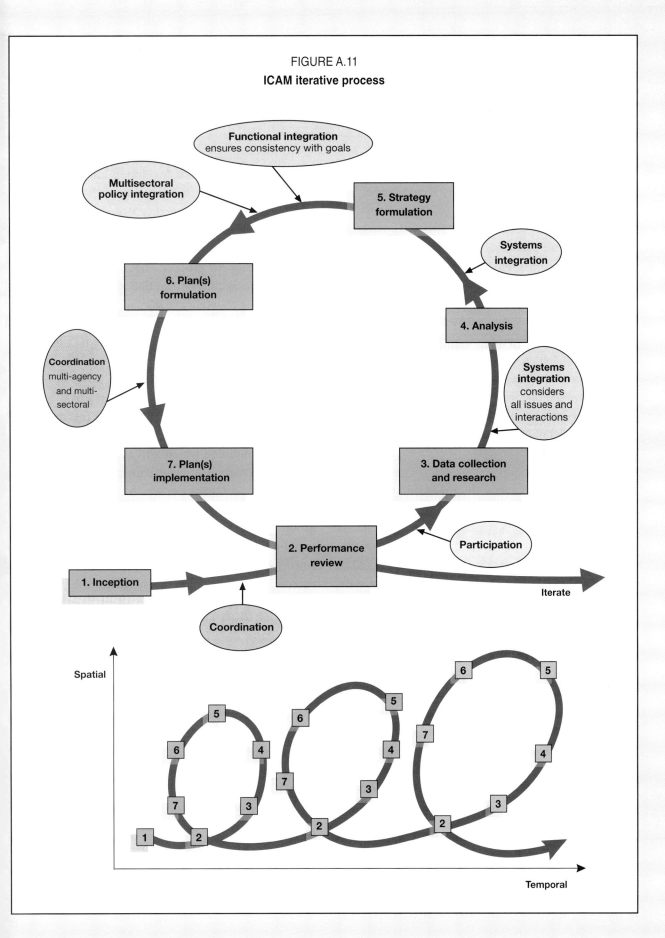

FIGURE A.11
ICAM iterative process

INTEGRATED
COASTAL AREA
MANAGEMENT
and
AGRICULTURE
FORESTRY AND
FISHERIES

PART A

ISSUES, PERSPECTIVES, POLICY AND PLANNING PROCESSES FOR INTEGRATED COASTAL AREA MANAGEMENT

2. The process of integrated coastal area management

process is divided into steps, for which individual definition varies slightly between authorities but that, in principle, are as follows:

- inception;
- performance review;
- data collection and research;
- analysis;
- strategy formulation;
- plan formulation/absorption into sectoral plans;
- plan implementation.

Throughout the process, negotiation will constitute a base for sound participatory decision-making, and conflict resolution should be based on the dominant cultural values. Negotiation, at different levels and involving a variety of actors, will be necessary between: the different views represented by sectoral planners; the different interest groups present in coastal communities; different population groups, with various expectations for solutions, who face a range of different institutional, operational and financial constraints; the needs felt by local actors and the normative needs as identified by the technical staff of collaborating institutions.[68]

2.4.1 Inception

Concept paper. In general, ICAM is initiated with a concept paper. In most instances, the originating agency will have an appropriate mandate, for example, for regional planning or, perhaps, for the environment. One of the reasons for this is that such an agency would be likely to have a cross-sectoral mandate to institute the iterative process involving all the stakeholders likely to be involved. However, an inception paper may be produced by, for example, a sectoral agency or a group of individuals outside the public sector with a strong interest in the conservation and management of the coastal area; their aim would be to persuade other government agencies that integrated management is required.[69] The agency that initiates the ICAM process will not necessarily be the one that will subsequently lead it.

The inception paper should identify the reasons for adopting an ICAM approach, describe in broad terms

what it is intended to achieve, identify the main actors (line ministries, local municipalities, resource users, NGOs, etc.), indicate how the proposal will be developed, identify a possible coordinating mechanism, and estimate the cost and time required to develop an ICAM strategy.

The preparation of this paper should be an iterative process in which it is developed and refined by government agencies in cooperation with all other key interested parties. It is important that all of the affected groups be identified early and invited into the process from the very beginning.

The decision to proceed should be taken by the government, including the line ministries with an interest in the planning and management of the coastal area(s) concerned. At this point, regional efforts or international assistance can play a catalytic role (Post and Lundin, 1996).

Committees. After approval has been given by the government, the line ministries involved, together with representatives of other stakeholders, might form a steering committee which will fulfil a guiding and facilitating function throughout the process. In addition to the steering committee, which will include senior officials representing their ministries and civil society group leaders, a management committee might be established, comprised of representatives of those with an active concern in the planning process, which will coordinate work on a day-to-day basis.

2.4.2 Performance review

The pitfalls of the main evaluation methods currently in use (*ex post* economic analysis, subjective scoring methods, impact evaluation and multicriteria analysis) are that they are usually carried out when programmes/ projects have been completed and that they are weak in the evaluation of externalities and the effects on those who bear them, therefore they do not detect the longer-term impact of an initiative. While evaluation is based on results at, or soon after, project completion, externalities often become evident only after several years. Consequently, evaluation does not enable feedback during the implementation stage.

In the case of a long-term programme such as ICAM, it may be appropriate to carry out periodic monitoring and evaluation to provide information for the remaining

---

[68] See Part E.
[69] For subsectoral justifications and interactions, see Sections 1 and 2, respectively, in Parts B, C and D.

PART A

ISSUES, PERSPECTIVES, POLICY AND PLANNING PROCESSES FOR INTEGRATED COASTAL AREA MANAGEMENT

INTEGRATED
COASTAL AREA
MANAGEMENT
and
AGRICULTURE
FORESTRY AND
FISHERIES

2. The process of integrated coastal area management

period of implementation, as well as an input into the next generation of policy measures. To attain the highest level of participation and commitment, stakeholders could gradually become their own monitors and evaluators, after appropriate training. The context will determine the timing and smooth integration into the process evolution, the choice of methods and the contracting of the proper resources.

Performance review comprises participatory monitoring and evaluation[70]. Performance review has two focuses: the assessment of the implementation process, with special concern for participants' and/or sectors' collaborative relationships; and the evaluation of preliminary results, including the technical quality of the work, the cost/benefit balance and the initial outcome of joint efforts to improve natural resource management.

Participatory monitoring is the systematic recording and periodic analysis of information that has been chosen by stakeholders. Its main purpose is to provide information during the life of the project, so that adjustments and/or modifications can be made if necessary. It is important that monitoring starts at the early stage of articulation and implementation. It will assist, initially, in refining the intended achievements expressed in the concept paper and, later in the process, in: redefining goals and objectives; developing monitoring questions; determining direct and/or indirect indicators that will answer the monitoring questions; deciding which information gathering tools are needed; who will do the monitoring and when periodic analysis will take place; modifying organizational arrangements; and reassigning resources. Downstream, it will assist in evaluating the progress of the process itself.

Participatory evaluation is an opportunity for stakeholders to stop and reflect on the past in order to make decisions about the future. It allows stakeholders to plan what is to be evaluated, decide how evaluation will be done, carry out the evaluation, analyse the information and present the evaluation results. Evaluation must involve all those associated in the project and their collective counsel should be elicited regarding the way in which the project can be improved in the next phase. Participatory evaluation takes into

---

BOX A.17
Participatory assessment, monitoring and evaluation

Participatory assessment, monitoring and evaluation (PAME)[74] is an adaptive and dynamic approach that encourages, supports and strengthens communities' existing abilities to identify their own needs and objectives and then monitor and evaluate to adjust these within a project time frame. PAME is a combination of three interlinked components: a concept, backed up by participatory methods and participatory tools for information gathering.

Four methods are used in the PAME approach:
- assessment: community site selection, community problem analysis, participatory baselines;
- monitoring: participatory monitoring and on-going evaluation;
- evaluation: participatory evaluation events (i.e. stop and reflect on what has happened in the past in order to make decisions about the future);
- feedback: analysis of information and communication of results.

These are valuable means for:
- providing feedback on the joint decision-making process with the indigenous point of view;
- documenting local actors' perception of the work performed;
- changing attitudes;
- developing a broader grassroots capacity-building strategy – reviewing joint efforts in a controlled setting can provide local actors with several opportunities (for discovering their own potential and limitations);
- discussing the nature and origin of internal and external conflicts;
- strengthening capacity for negotiation within and outside the community.

---

[74] For further reading, see Davis-Case, 1989.

---
[70] See Box A.17.

INTEGRATED
COASTAL AREA
MANAGEMENT
and
AGRICULTURE
FORESTRY AND
FISHERIES

PART A

ISSUES, PERSPECTIVES, POLICY AND PLANNING PROCESSES FOR INTEGRATED COASTAL AREA MANAGEMENT

2. The process of integrated coastal area management

account overall and immediate objectives, their continued relevance and the effectiveness of the activities. Stakeholders are also required to review their own performance. As such, evaluation becomes part of the strategy as an immediate mid-course correction. Action is therefore inherent to the process and the evaluator is a process facilitator. In this way, there is an orientation towards the future and towards planning (and the investment of time and effort in change) and evaluation parallel planning.

The whole planning process needs to take account of issues such as: economic valuation of environmental costs and benefits; risk and uncertainty; anticipation of events that might seriously affect performance (including policy changes and other exogenous factors); and identification of the performance indicators to be monitored. Features vital to achieving sustainability include the generation of information during implementation, and building a consensus (or coalition) for change among the stakeholders, as well as creating problem-solving and institutional capacities. Participatory monitoring and evaluation can strongly contribute to achieving these.

2.4.3 Data collection and research

Coastal profile. The product of the data collection and research stage is termed the coastal profile by some authorities and is referred to below by this term. The purpose of this stage is to collect the baseline information and seek to facilitate an understanding of the relationships between key factors in order to identify and prioritize management issues properly (Scura *et al.*, 1992). A typical coastal profile includes information highlighting the problems and causes for concern in the coastal area, related to the social, biophysical, institutional and organizational characteristics of the area. This information is used in the subsequent stage (Analysis).[71]

The preparation of a coastal profile is analogous to the sector review, or stocktaking stage, in conventional sector studies. As in sector studies, it is important to focus on essential information.

Based on the criteria set during the initial performance review for information collection and indicator selection,[72] the information required may be categorized as being concerned with:

- biophysical characteristics of the area;
- social issues and related economic linkages, including level of investment in coastal areas;
- the governance framework, embracing laws and institutional characteristics.

Biophysical characteristics. The purpose of this part of the profile is to establish the environmental health of the area and its impact upon the coastal communities specifically and upon society at large.

Biological information will include: biological resources (e.g. biomass, primary and secondary productivity, diversity, distribution and abundance of living resources, indicator species); major habitats and ecosystems (including ecological relationships that determine productivity); reproduction sites (e.g. nurseries, exchange zones); and the presence of special species and areas (e.g. rare, threatened, endangered).

Physical information will include: geomorphology (coastal type and nature); coastal oceanography (tides, sedimentary dynamic); coastal climatology (winds, rainfall); hydrography (watersheds, sediment inputs); surface hydrology (hydric balance, soil occupation); topology hydrogeology (flux); and geochemistry (mineral elements).

While much of the above information will be provided by the economic sectors using coastal resources (e.g. agriculture will have readily available information on soil, topography, water supply, land use, climate; forestry will have information on the status of coastal forest resources and the carrying capacity for wildlife; fisheries will have information on patterns and trends in the magnitude and distribution of fish populations, water quality, changes in critical habitats, etc.), a particular effort should be made to provide information on patterns of natural resource use in space and time, flows, variability, resilience, interactions and impacts.[73]

Social and economic issues. In this part of the profile the aim is to evaluate the impact of human activities on coastal ecosystems and the demand put on coastal

---

[71] See Section 2.4.4.

[72] See Sustainability indicators in Section 2.3.6.
[73] Sections 3 of Parts B, C and D provide detailed suggestions on information available within sub-sectors.

PART A

ISSUES, PERSPECTIVES, POLICY AND PLANNING PROCESSES FOR INTEGRATED COASTAL AREA MANAGEMENT

INTEGRATED
COASTAL AREA
MANAGEMENT
and
AGRICULTURE
FORESTRY AND
FISHERIES

2. The process of integrated coastal area management

resources. Human activities in terms of population (demographic occupation, employment), infrastructures, economic and qualitative values of resource use patterns (e.g. urbanization, industrialization, tourism, mining, fisheries, agriculture), land and sea tenure, existing types of management, and historic and current use patterns, will be assessed.

Social problems and their causes will be identified. In particular, attention should be focused on problems that arise from actual or potential competition for resources (or conflict over space), resource dependency, the incidence of externalities, and relevant economic linkages. Different user types and priority needs, potential benefits, constraints, the number of people deriving livelihoods from coastal resources and alternatives should also be considered.

Measurement of the contribution of coastal activities to household income could be made by establishing baseline data on: return on capital; return on labour; return on land; gross returns; cash expenditure; labour demand through the year; and assessment of economic viability and risks. These will be used to monitor change through periodic reviews.

The assessment of factors that affect decisions on the use of coastal resources includes: market distortions and the effects of policies (e.g. prices, government intervention, subsidies, trade barriers and exchange rates); income distribution; land and other assets; and political accounting.

Governance characteristics. The purpose of this part of the profile is to identify the legal[75] and institutional mechanisms that form the governance framework in order to identify constraints and opportunities for ICAM. A tabulation by the Untied States Environment Protection Agency of institutional information that might be sought includes the following:

- components of the institutional structure (e.g. line ministries, other relevant official bodies such as provincial and local administrations and statutory bodies, community organizations, NGOs), including their institutional mandates, financial and human resources applied to the ICAM area and links with other bodies;

- the administrative and decision-making processes, including legislation and regulations, and the level of enforcement;
- public health and water quality standards and regulations;
- management policies for renewable resources (agriculture, forestry, fisheries, habitat protection, water, etc.);
- management policies for non-renewable resource (coastline management, minerals and oil extraction, etc.);
- urban, industrial, transport and infrastructure development policies;
- finance mechanisms relevant to the ICAM area (sources of revenue and revenue management);
- public investment related to ICAM;
- land-use planning.

Specific role of sectoral agencies. The roles of the line ministries in this stage are to ensure that available information is fed into the process and sectoral issues and that concerns are adequately taken into account. Resource planners and managers from relevant line ministries or agencies are valuable sources of information. Sector studies prepared by line ministries are often available and typically contain the most detailed and accurate information available at the time of their preparation.

Subsector-related (agriculture, forestry and fisheries) information to be included in a coastal profile may include:

- socio-economic features characterizing resource-dependent activities (e.g. resource users, relevant linkages between resource users and others, quantitative and qualitative assessment of the labour force and total population concerned, conditions of entry into and exit from employment in the subsector, population-supporting capacity of the subsector in the light of population projections and productivity assumptions);
- the biophysical aspects of the area (e.g. state of the resources, levels of exploitation and intra- and intersectoral impacts);
- the existing organizational and institutional (including legal) provisions for management (e.g. descriptions of the conditions of resource access), and performance and constraints of subsectors in the light of biophysical and economic conditions.

63

---

[75] For evaluation of the regulatory framework, see Section 2.2.3 and Boxes A.4 and A.7.

INTEGRATED
COASTAL AREA
MANAGEMENT
and
AGRICULTURE
FORESTRY AND
FISHERIES

PART A

ISSUES, PERSPECTIVES, POLICY AND PLANNING PROCESSES FOR INTEGRATED COASTAL AREA MANAGEMENT

2. The process of integrated coastal area management

Specific subsectoral information requirements are found in Parts B, C and D.

Information requirements. In information collection, there is a need for a balance between subjective sources of information (perceptions of stakeholders) and objective ones (mainly quantitative primary data and secondary data). The latter consists of secondary data (obtained from existing sources) and primary information (obtained in the course of the preparation of the coastal profile).

Very often, there will be gaps in the information for the coastal profile that cannot be filled in the short term. Where research is required to fill gaps, it should be treated as it would be in a sectoral planning process, i.e. it should be included in the plan.

Coordination between the different agencies involved in ICAM will allow the location of information sources. Where information is not readily available, concerted action will allow data generation needs in respective work plans and budgets to be taken into account or the use of information from other sectors participating in ICAM, thus avoiding the costly duplication of efforts.

The monitoring of data clearly imposes a burden on states, particularly poorer countries, even when it involves information that might be expected to be collected in the normal course of coastal management. While the biophysical data generally fall within the experience of scientists and officials in the relevant government agencies, the collection of socio-economic information, through surveys, rapid appraisal and sources of quantitative information, is often outside their experience. The responsible line ministries should link with other organizations that could provide such information or acquire the capacity to undertake this kind of work.

Tools used in information collection include: published and unpublished reports of line ministries (referred to above), other secondary sources of information, public inquiries, participatory and rapid appraisal of coastal areas, biophysical tools, measuring and monitoring tools, and GIS.[77] The tools and techniques used for public involvement are described briefly in Box A.20. A methodological framework for organizing and analysing information for ICAM has been developed by IOC and is shown in Figure A.13.

64

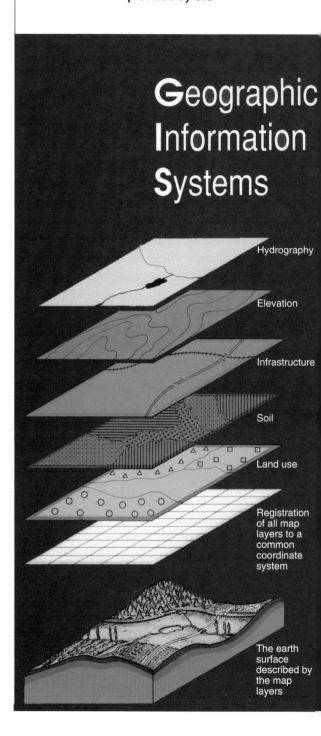

FIGURE A.12

Overlay of different maps of the same location provided by GIS

Geographic
Information
Systems

Hydrography

Elevation

Infrastructure

Soil

Land use

Registration of all map layers to a common coordinate system

The earth surface described by the map layers

---

[77] See Figure A.12 and Boxes A.18 and A.19.

PART A

INTEGRATED
COASTAL AREA
MANAGEMENT
and
AGRICULTURE
FORESTRY AND
FISHERIES

ISSUES, PERSPECTIVES, POLICY AND PLANNING PROCESSES FOR INTEGRATED COASTAL AREA MANAGEMENT

2. The process of integrated coastal area management

BOX A.18

Remote sensing and geographic information systems (GIS)

Remote sensing covers all techniques related to the analysis and use of data from satellites (such as Meteosat, NOAA-AVHRR, Landsat, MOS-1, SPOT, ERS-1 and Soyouz) and of aerial photographs. Remote sensing can be extremely useful for assessing and monitoring the condition of coastal areas, particularly in archipelagos where conventional survey techniques are usually difficult and expensive. Remote sensing can also provide information on such topics as water quality in bays and estuaries, providing a better understanding of the ecology and biology in such areas. The traditional collection of biophysical parameters in coastal areas (especially by ground- or sea-based systems) is expensive and time-consuming and the information available to key users is often incomplete and inadequate. Furthermore, the information available at present is not adequate to permit a well-defined, geographic approach to managing the coastal environment or to distinguish between the impact of increased human activity and other impacts such as climate change. Analysis of remote sensing data can provide an important input to GIS.

Satellite earth observation data. These data integrate surface and earth observation measurements and data over time and can play a major role in providing information on quality parameters, covering particularly: the coastline (the single interpretation of the imagery could lead to an excellent and geometrically correct baseline map of the coast); the intertidal area (mapping principal vegetation categories such as grasslands and healthy and degraded mangroves); and the shallow-waters area, including bottom types (sparse and dense grass, as well as live and damaged coral, could be distinguished to a depth of 10 m) and bathymetry (up to 40 m depth). The derived information (including also primary productivity, chlorophyll concentration, temperature and turbidity) allows such practical applications as: updating nautical charts; localizing near-shore sea resources (e.g. shells, seaweeds); selecting potential sites for sea farming; assessing and monitoring the environment (particularly degraded resources); and assessing existing aquaculture activities (e.g. water-filled and idle ponds).

Compared with information acquired by traditional methods (e.g. aerial photographs) these data offer several advantages: they provide synoptic coverage of vast extents of coastline (from 3 600 to 34 000 km^2 in one high-resolution satellite image, depending on the type of satellite); data can be acquired for the same area at a high rate of repetition (twice or three times a month) thus permitting monitoring; various wavelengths imagery, visible and non-visible, provide accurate information on vegetation conditions, even on shallow water features; data can be obtained in any part of the world without encountering administrative restrictions; and, from the economic point of view, satellite-derived information has been found to be two-thirds the cost of panchromatic aerial photographs but the execution times for mapping are the same (one year) for both techniques. Satellite data techniques stress the importance of using digital data and of having excellent ground support for calibration with accurately positioned sample points visited on the sea, near-shore and land. This approach enables a data source,

currently limited to research laboratories and programmes, to be converted into valuable information for use in coastal decision-support systems. Such an approach has, therefore, both commercial and environmental benefits.[76]

Geographic information systems. GIS are computer-assisted systems that can input, retrieve, analyse and display geographically referenced information useful for decision-making. They have been widely used for different types of natural renewable resources and protected area conservation and planning. In general, the main benefits include (Kam, *et al.*, 1992):

- the ability to integrate data of various types (graphic, textual, digital analogue) from a variety of sources, (e.g. overlays of social information on maps showing levels of resource depletion);
- a greatly enhanced capacity for data exchange between different disciplines and sectors, compared with more established procedures;
- a greatly enhanced capacity for data analysis compared to manual methods;
- the ability to test and compare different scenarios in the computer;
- the ability to update large amounts of data, including graphic information, quickly;
- the ability to handle and store large volumes of data.

In its application to coastal planning, GIS can portray boundaries and deal with enormous differences in scale, especially when working with one map.

GIS software has developed rapidly in the last few years with object tool kits that enable domain-specific applications with GIS functionality to be developed quickly and efficiently. In addition, improvements in the capabilities of hardware and commercial off-the-shelf software have increased the potential access to such systems and reduced the time and cost of developing them. By taking advantage of these technological changes, it is now possible to obtain sophisticated graphical visualization of data and produce high-quality maps of environmental conditions.

The choice of a particular GIS for ICAM is dependent on the type of mapping that is required and the functions of the respective systems that are regarded as most appropriate to the particular application. In many situations, however, limitations on the use of GIS are not imposed by the functions of the relative systems but by the availability of appropriate data and the level of skill in using a system. When GIS is used in ICAM, the coordinating agency must have the capacity to:

- introduce a system, if one is not already in place;
- train managers in its use;
- maintain and update it;
- familiarize line ministries in the coastal area with the type of information required and the forms in which it should be made available.

For line ministries, the imperatives are to:

- understand the assistance that GIS can provide to them in their management and conservation roles;
- provide the information required by GIS in the forms in which it is most useful.

65

---

[76] For more detailed information see Lantieri, 1998; and Populus and Lantieri, 1991. Examples of coastal maps derived from satellite data are on pages 26 and 36.

INTEGRATED
COASTAL AREA
MANAGEMENT
and
AGRICULTURE
FORESTRY AND
FISHERIES

PART A

ISSUES, PERSPECTIVES, POLICY AND PLANNING PROCESSES FOR INTEGRATED COASTAL AREA MANAGEMENT

2. The process of integrated coastal area management

BOX A.19

Integrated coastal analysis and monitoring system (ICAMS)

The ICAMS project is supported by the European Commission and consortium partners (i.e. United Kingdom, Irish, Greek and international organizations such as FAO). The project stems from work carried out, both individually and collaboratively, by consortium members over many years. ICAMS is driven by the needs of end-users and integrates existing capabilities into its applications, including the use, as far as possible, of existing technologies. An evaluation of the entire programme will be made in the context of its relevance to European policies and international scientific programmes, and its potential for technology transfer to developing countries. To demonstrate that ICAMS is applicable to a range of coastal issues, the application aspect of the pilot project is divided into three separate, but related investigations, at different sites in Europe and with different environmental concerns, including coastal pollution, eutrophication and fisheries management.

Although there is general consensus that information derived from satellite ocean colour data could dramatically improve the information available on some biophysical parameters, there are barriers to its effective use that could threaten to confine the data to the research laboratory rather than allowing it to play an important role in the operational management of coastal areas. These barriers include poor access to data, limited frequency of measurement, absence of local calibration/validation, insufficient integration with other data sources and inadequate analysis and dissemination approaches. In particular, there is a wide gap between the potential user community for information on water quality and the means for delivering that information.

ICAMS proposes to bridge this gap by developing, testing and evaluating a system that will transform time series of oceanographic satellite imagery into water quality and resource maps of the coastal area. These environmental and resource maps will be used in comparison with maps and data of the human exploitation of similar coastal waters. Such detailed spatial and temporal data will provide a decision aid for end-users who manage the often conflicting demands of human exploitation that affect coastal water quality. They will also help to decide whether changes in water quality have been caused by weather conditions or by natural or human-related pollution sources.

More specifically, ICAMS will support: intelligent selection and ingestion of ocean colour and temperature data from several satellite sources; conversion into water quality information relevant to the needs of the pilot project end-users; integration and assimilation with a variety of other data from satellites, surface measurements and end-user archives in order to produce water quality maps; and end-user access to a comprehensive analysis package to visualize and manipulate the four-dimensional nature of the information. The data quality will be enhanced further by calibration through comparison with measurements from ships and buoys. Transmission of this information in nearly real time through a satellite data messaging system will also allow local interpolation of the results deriving from the available ocean colour coverage. The full potential of satellite imagery as a tool to monitor and analyse the coastal environment cannot be realized without the integrated, multivariate processing that characterizes ICAMS.

Source: www.eos.co.uk/ICAMS.

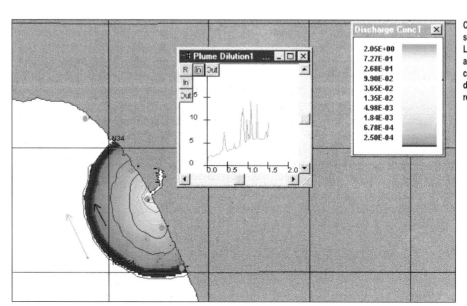

Coastal runoff plume simulation of the city of Los Angeles, USA. Sewers are the major source of coastal pollution. The red dots along the coast represent beaches.

INTEGRATED
COASTAL AREA
MANAGEMENT
and
AGRICULTURE
FORESTRY AND
FISHERIES

PART A

ISSUES, PERSPECTIVES, POLICY AND PLANNING PROCESSES FOR INTEGRATED COASTAL AREA MANAGEMENT

2. The process of integrated coastal area management

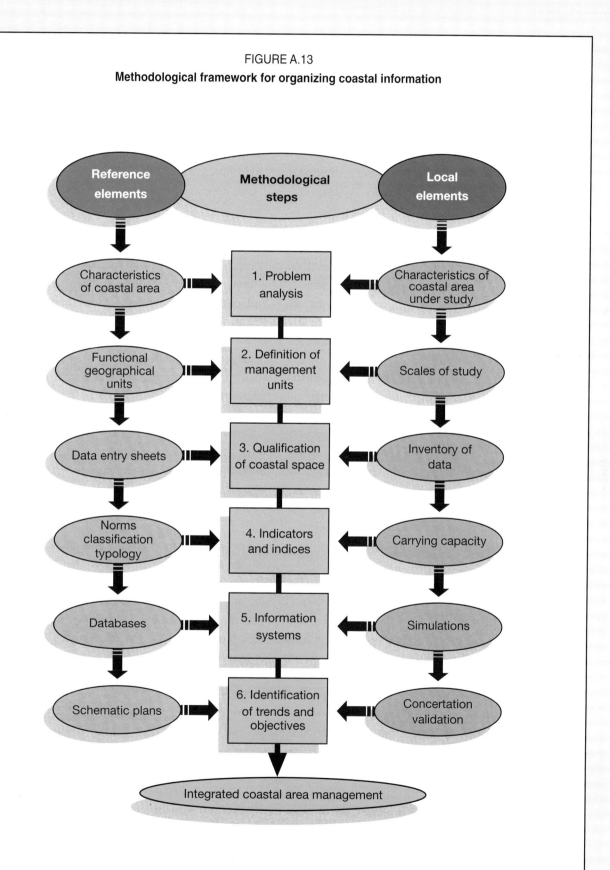

FIGURE A.13

Methodological framework for organizing coastal information

Source: IOC/ICSU/WMO, 1997.

INTEGRATED
COASTAL AREA
MANAGEMENT
and
AGRICULTURE
FORESTRY AND
FISHERIES

PART A

ISSUES, PERSPECTIVES, POLICY AND PLANNING PROCESSES FOR INTEGRATED COASTAL AREA MANAGEMENT

2. The process of integrated coastal area management

2.4.4 Analysis

An analysis for ICAM extends cross-sectorally to focus on the following:

- descriptions of problems or causes for concern, with particular emphasis on interactions across sectors, including estimates of their respective costs as incurred by society (societal costs);
- the extent to which current policies and institutional structures (strengths, weaknesses, synergism, conflicts and gaps) adequately address problems or causes for concern;
- a statement of possible actions that determines how these problems and causes for concern can be resolved or their effects mitigated to improve the situation.

Having regard to the fact that this stage is issue-driven, GESAMP has summarized the tasks to be addressed by an ICAM team, which should include the concerned line ministries, as follows:

- estimating the relative influences of human-incurred and natural factors in causing particular changes to coastal systems and resources;
- characterizing the likely short- and long-term consequences for society of existing trends in the condition and use of the coastal environment;
- assessing the social and economic costs and benefits that stem from various options for the use and exploitation of coastal resources and amenities;
- formulating approaches to mitigate or reverse environmental degradation.

Evaluation of problems. The first of these functions is related to the allocation of coastal resources. For example, if a lumber company is allowed to fell trees in the watershed and this will result in soil erosion which, in turn, may destroy a coral reef, in a sense the coral reef is being allocated to the lumber company.

In practice, most resource-allocation decisions are made on socio-political grounds, but the valuation of natural resources and social and economic analysis can be an important input into this process. Valuation and analysis can be used to identify who will benefit and who will lose and to show the costs and benefits of the proposed options and the alternatives. Analysis can also establish a common framework within which economic, social, cultural, political and ecological information can be evaluated on a common basis and management issues can be prioritized. In other words, valuation and analysis

provide information to decision-makers to assist them in evaluating the trade-offs between development options that have environmental and social effects within or outside the sectors in which they arise.

Evaluation of institutional responses. The second of these functions is to determine what can be done about environmental problems and causes for concern.

One approach to this is to identify each problem or cause for concern with the appropriate parts of the institutional infrastructure. For example, the problem of agricultural runoff may be relevant to only three of the elements in the institutional infrastructure: relevant laws and regulations, the agriculture extension service, and public investment in environmental awareness programmes. In contrast, most elements in the institutional infrastructure, including for example, management of natural resources, land-use planning and financing mechanisms, may have to be called upon to address problems such as overexploitation of renewable natural resources.

Cross-referencing of problems and causes for concern with the relevant elements in the institutional infrastructure provides the basis for an analysis of the effectiveness of the response of institutions. As noted by the United States Environmental Protection Agency, the purpose of such an institutional analysis is not the overall effectiveness of the institutions being considered but the identification of their strengths and weaknesses in relation to the problems and causes for concern and the quality of their responses to a specific problem.

Evaluating coastal activities requires assessment of their positive and negative effects (socio-economic and environmental) in the context of the prevailing goals for sustainable development, national development and sectoral objectives. Tools used in this process include institutional capacity analysis system (Box A.21), cost-benefit analysis (Box A.22), multicriteria analysis (Box A.23), economic valuation of natural resources (Box A.24), environmental impact assessment and cumulative environmental impact assessment (Box A.6).

Establishment of a learning process. In order to improve understanding of the biophysical and socio-economic impacts of policies and to monitor change, reliable records should be kept of data and analysis.

PART A

ISSUES, PERSPECTIVES, POLICY AND PLANNING PROCESSES FOR INTEGRATED COASTAL AREA MANAGEMENT

INTEGRATED
COASTAL AREA
MANAGEMENT
and
AGRICULTURE
FORESTRY AND
FISHERIES

2. The process of integrated coastal area management

BOX A.20
Tools and techniques for public involvement

Participatory techniques create conditions for the exchange of knowledge, facilitate visualization of overall interactions and improve interdisciplinary teamwork. All techniques depend for their success on the ability of the facilitator to elicit group participation. The choice of particular methods and tools will depend on the tasks to be handled and the levels of society targeted and is therefore highly contextual.

Social communication and information dissemination. This includes the use of printed materials (brochures, newsletters, displays), the media (radio, television, newspapers), public information sessions and public information centres (open houses, site visits). The aim is to keep the public informed about what is being planned, and explain those plans.

Rapid appraisal. Rapid rural appraisal (RRA) and participatory rapid appraisal (PRA) approaches can gather local knowledge, assess attitudes and preferences, identify problems and brainstorm potential solutions. Some of the techniques and tools include:[78]
- preference ranking and scoring (e.g. matrix ranking, rating, sorting);
- diagrams and graphics (e.g. Venn diagrams, flow charts, decision trees, pie charts);
- mapping (e.g. thematic, resource or historical maps);
- understanding process and change (e.g. time lines, seasonal calendars, process diagrams);
- structured observation (e.g. transect walks);
- checklists or semi-structured interviews targeting key informants or selected groups;

- strengths, weaknesses, opportunities and threats (SWOT) analyses;
- meetings and workshops are of key importance to discussion, analysis of findings and restitution of results to the community;
- rapid appraisal of coastal environments (RACE) modifies RRA techniques and allied modes of research to: hasten the analysis of management problems and issues during inception, verify the output of formal research during analysis and formulation, and assist formal monitoring and evaluation procedures.[79]

Interactive analysis and planning. Social assessment (SA) is an iterative process that begins with stakeholders' analysis and involvement in the collection and analysis of information, the selection of priorities, design of plans, adjustment of early ideas and application of these plans. Objectives-oriented programme planning (ZOPP) involves a multidisciplinary team approach that studies multisectoral problems, discusses social groups and institutions' interests, forecasts anticipated impacts and risks and specifies the inputs and costs of the contributions required by each party. The jointly designed ZOPP is an aid for dialogue between partners concerning the aim and objective of their cooperation, and is the basis for a learning process that develops from analysing joint experiences. The process is supported by external moderators and incorporates the main interest groups and decision-makers.

Conflict resolution and management techniques. Facilitation, conciliation, negotiation, mediation and arbitration (described in Part E).

---

[78] Related selected references: Davis-Case, 1989, Townsley, 1993; Pretty, 1997; GTZ, 1988.

[79] For further reading, see Scura *et al.*, 1992.

69

Government agencies
and fishers' associations
setting up a coordination
body for coastal
activities, Gambia

INTEGRATED
COASTAL AREA
MANAGEMENT
and
AGRICULTURE
FORESTRY AND
FISHERIES

PART A

ISSUES, PERSPECTIVES, POLICY AND PLANNING PROCESSES FOR INTEGRATED COASTAL AREA MANAGEMENT

2. The process of integrated coastal area management

Crops in the Peruvian coastal flatlands that have been
ruined by flooding, the eroded and deforested
mountain sides having been unable to hold the rush of
waters.

Rebuilding traditional terraces as part of soil
conservation programme, Peru.

BOX A.21
Institutional capacity analysis system (ICAS)

The nature, strengths and weaknesses of organizations, as well
the context in which organizations function, need to be understo
before interventions are planned and executed. The institution
capacity analysis system (ICAS) is a tool that helps to investiga
specified capacities of organizations from the point of view of t
particular functions the organization(s) will have to perform.

Essentially ICAS goes through three phases:

1. Determining the specific tasks to be carried out that derive direc
from the stated objectives.

2. Assessing the institutional capacity gaps in the five most cruc
dimensions of the institutions to be involved, which are:
- the national (or other applicable) policy environment, laws a
  regulations;
- inter-institutional relationships;
- the "internal organization" (distribution of functions, interr
  organization and management, physical and financial capacit
- the appropriateness of personnel policies and rewa
  arrangements;
- skills, expertise, information (in relation to the tasks to
  performed).

Thus, the analysis moves from the general context, via an analys
of the organization, to the specific skills and incentives require
Each dimension is scored on a five-point scale, indicating t
severity of the "institutional capacity gap".

3. Determining whether, taking account of the noted capacity gap
the envisaged activities can take place. If so, deciding whi
particular gaps need to be addressed in order to achieve t
objectives. This can result in an institutional development strate
that focuses on highly specific interventions aimed at overcomi
any deficiencies.

ICAS centrally involves the staff of the concerned organizations.
fact, the preference is to train and work through them. The meth
makes use of standardized formats and semi-structured interviev

Source: de Graaf, 1997.

ISSUES, PERSPECTIVES, POLICY AND PLANNING PROCESSES FOR INTEGRATED COASTAL AREA MANAGEMENT

PART A

INTEGRATED
COASTAL AREA
MANAGEMENT
and
AGRICULTURE
FORESTRY AND
FISHERIES

2. The process of integrated coastal area management

BOX A.22
Cost-benefit analysis (CBA)

CBA is a basic classical tool in project appraisal and will be familiar to many readers. In area planning, CBA has a role in providing an input into the decision-making process in relation to relatively large changes which are under consideration, such as the drainage of coastal wetlands and conversion of agricultural land for urban development. CBA involves an appraisal of costs and benefits; if benefits exceed costs, the project is, in principle, acceptable. Otherwise it is not (Pearce *et al.*, 1989).

There are potential problems in applying CBA to environmental issues, in particular as regards the discount principle underlying CBA.[80] Among the means of dealing with some limitations inherent to CBA are:

the use of improved valuation techniques;[81]

incorporating environmental considerations into the planning process. For instance, the management of renewable resources should be required to be sustainable, and the rents from the use of non-renewable resources should be reinvested in resources that will compensate for the exhaustible resource;

incorporating a sustainability constraint such as requiring that the overall effect of a programme should have as small an adverse environmental impact as possible.

The basic formula used in CBA involves a value for the environmental consequences of a project (negative or positive). A prime requirement, therefore, is the integration of environmental values into CBA. This is especially important in ICAM, where the environment is a critical factor.

Useful reading on CBA includes Sugden and Williams, 1978; and Sassone and Schaffer, 1978.
See Box A.24.

Fisheries development unit
reviewing progress of coastal
microprojects, Benin

BOX A.23
Multicriteria analysis (MCA)

MCA begins with the specification of options to be examined and the criteria that are deemed to be of importance in their evaluation. The advantages and disadvantages of each option are compared through an assessment of their effects. Each effect is measured in a common unit across all options using either quantitative or qualitative criteria. Weightings for each criterion may be introduced, indicating the relative importance of each criterion in the analysis.

An advantage of MCA over CBA, is that it can take into account broader considerations such as the distribution of associated costs and benefits among different groups within society. Furthermore, unlike CBA, it does not require a monetarization of effects, nor does it focus exclusively on the measurement of efficiency. These advantages apply particularly to countries where the database is weak, economic activities are directly dependent on natural resources and distribution concerns are strong. MCA may be argued to perform better than CBA in accounting satisfactorily for sustainability objectives.

Methodologically, however, MCA suffers from its dependence on the specification of appropriate criteria and the specification of weights. However, these weaknesses can be overcome to some extent by undertaking sensitivity analysis in which preferred options can be tested and information provided on factors that have a critical effect on the ranking of options.

Source: Resources Assessment Commission, 1992.

INTEGRATED
COASTAL AREA
MANAGEMENT
and
AGRICULTURE
FORESTRY AND
FISHERIES

PART A

ISSUES, PERSPECTIVES, POLICY AND PLANNING PROCESSES FOR INTEGRATED COASTAL AREA MANAGEMENT

2. The process of integrated coastal area management

BOX A.24
Economic valuation of natural resources

Unfortunately, the techniques and methods for evaluating natural systems have shortcomings: they require much time since they rely on the collection of extensive ecological, sociological and economic data; many countries simply do not have the human and financial resources needed for such an exercise, or the time to undertake it, given the speed with which problems accumulate; and environmental goods cannot be costed in monetary terms. In the final analysis, society must make value judgements and set them aside from economic calculations. More specifically, such methodologies are derived from the neo-classical economics framework and are subject to the criticism levelled at this framework when applied to the environment: the underlying values such as the pursuit of individual self-interest and profit maximization are not compatible with sustainable development; and risk, uncertainty and distributional issues within and between generations are inadequately dealt with. In addition, each individual technique has its own methodological and data problems.[82]

However, as many decisions affecting the environment are taken on the basis of cost-benefit analysis, environmental valuation techniques have proved to be valuable tools for incorporating environmental impacts into traditional analysis and thereby improving the decision-making process at project, sectoral and national levels.

Ecosystems are valued according to different types of values: direct use values are derived from the direct use of a system's goods and services (e.g. timber) ; indirect use values comprise all the ecological functions within a system (e.g. coastal wetlands as a means of flood control); option values are seen as extra insurance against the risk of losing goods and services (e.g. for providing future genes for plant breeding); existence values are placed on the intrinsic value of a system (e.g. a rare habitat); and bequest values upon the desire to preserve the inherent characteristics of a system for future generations for non-use purposes. Option, existence and bequest values are particularly difficult to convert into monetary terms and have to be described qualitatively.

Keeping in mind that common sense remains the best guide for evaluating natural resources, there are a variety of methodologies for assigning a monetary value to environmental goods and services (and thus to the economic costs and benefits of environmental impacts of certain actions and activities). These methodologies can be roughly divided into direct and indirect valuation techniques. The following is a brief description of their usefulness and limitations with reference to ICAM .

Direct valuation techniques. Such techniques attempt to estimate the monetary value of environmental benefits or losses directly from the preferences of the individuals involved. Direct techniques do not necessarily require a prior assessment of the (actual or potential) physical environmental change as they are based on people's perception of risk or change as revealed by their market behaviour or in their response to surveys. Direct valuation techniques comprise: contingent valuation; hedonic pricing approach; and travel cost method.

Contingent valuation. This approach seeks to elicit information on environmental preferences, directly from individuals, using surveys, questionnaires or experimental techniques, which collect information either on the "willingness to pay" (WTP) for an increase in the provision or quality of an environmental good or service, or the minimum "willingness-to-accept" (WTA) compensation to forego such beneficial change. The approach is based on hypothetical behaviour, rather than observed behaviour and thus depends on the respondents having a good understanding of why environmental preferences are solicited and interpreting the contingent valuation method question and scenario in the same way as the writer of the question. The strengths of this technique are that it can be applied in most contexts; it is frequently the only technique possible; and it is the only technique that can measure existence values (as such values are unrelated to any form of use, they cannot be captured by actual or surrogate market behaviour). An underlying weakness is that it does not use observation of actual market behaviour and does not test consumers' effective demand by requiring them to back up their opinions with cash. The values elicited depend on whether the changes are presented as gains or losses. Several types of survey format exist, each subject to varying degrees of bias, and there are some difficulties in determining the appropriate total population concerned. In practice, this technique has been found to be most useful for evaluating changes in amenity, air and water quality, wildlife and biological diversity among a well-informed and concerned population, and it thus has several applications within ICAM.[83]

Hedonic pricing approach. This approach seeks to elicit individuals' preferences directly, but from market information rather than from surveys. It is thus based on actual rather than hypothetical behaviour. As many environmental goods and services do not have their own markets, surrogate markets are used. Two methods are commonly used: the property value approach, which is based on the assumption that differences in environmental quality will be reflected in housing prices; and the wage differential approach, where the labour market is used to reflect the value of different characteristics associated with working conditions and occupations. Both methods require an extensive amount of data and the ability to manipulate it, and the assumptions regarding perfect markets and fixed supply do not hold in many cases. Neither method captures the existence and option values. The wage differential approach can, in principle, be used to value human life in the context of risk of death from pollution but, in practice, the method has several methodological problems. Within ICAM, the property value approach might provide useful data on the benefits of local environmental changes in air and water quality or noise pollution.

Travel cost method. The travel cost method also seeks to elicit information on the demand for an environmental resource directly, using a combination of surveys and surrogate markets. More specifically, the travel cost method infers consumers' willingness to pay for environmental goods and services from the time and expense involved in travelling to them. Data requirements may be large and the technique does not capture the option price with certainty, neither does it capture the existence value, indirect benefits enjoyed by people who never

---

[82] As is in the case with many economic issues, there is no general agreement on the economic valuation of natural resources. For theoretical or empirical discussions of economic valuation, see Schaffer, 1978; Mitchell and Carson, 1989; and United States Department of Commerce, 1993.

[83] For further reading, refer to Winpenny, 1991.

PART A

ISSUES, PERSPECTIVES, POLICY AND PLANNING PROCESSES FOR INTEGRATED COASTAL AREA MANAGEMENT

INTEGRATED
COASTAL AREA
MANAGEMENT
and
AGRICULTURE
FORESTRY AND
FISHERIES

2. The process of integrated coastal area management

actually visit the site or the commercial use value (beach vendors for instance) of recreational sites. The travel cost method is commonly applied to parks, forests, beaches, wetlands and coral reefs, but has also been used to evaluate the demand for unpriced goods, such as fuelwood or clean water in developing countries, based on the time spent in their collection.[84]

Indirect valuation techniques. These techniques rely on a prior assessment of the physical environmental changes, followed by an estimation of the monetary value of such changes. Where the changes are adverse, these techniques thus seek to establish a physical relationship between the environmental damage (response) and some cause of the damage, e.g. pollution (dose), followed by a monetary valuation based either on information obtained from actual or surrogate markets or on a determination of the individuals' WTP, to avoid the damage, or WTA compensation, to suffer the damage.[85] Indirect valuation techniques comprise: changes in production; foregone earnings; opportunity costs; preventive expenditures; replacement costs; and shadow projects.

Changes in production. This technique uses actual market prices to evaluate an environmental effect or disturbance. Environmental quality is viewed as a factor of production. Changes in environmental quality lead to changes in productivity and production costs, which in turn lead to changes in prices and levels of output, which can be observed and measured using actual market prices (or the prices of close substitutes where no market exists). Two steps are involved: estimation of physical effects (through laboratory or field research, controlled experiments or statistical regression analysis); and an estimation of the monetary values of physical impacts. The method is relatively easy to carry out and forms the basis for the majority of appraisals of conservation measures. However, in some cases, the physical relationship between activities affecting the environment and output, costs or damage is not well established, and it is often difficult to disentangle the effect of one cause from that of others and to distinguish between the effects of human-incurred and natural degradation. Within ICAM, the technique is useful in many situations of environmental degradation where there are actual effects on agricultural, forestry or fishery outputs. These include soil erosion, deforestation, loss of wetlands and other natural ecosystems, and the production effects of air and water pollution. This technique can also be used to determine the value of improved farming techniques.

Foregone earnings. Also termed the human capital approach, this technique attempts to calculate the health costs of air pollution and other adverse environmental conditions. Such costs comprise foregone earnings through premature death, sickness or absenteeism, increased medical expenses, and psychic costs. For this technique to be valid, important conditions must hold: the direct cause and effect relationship must be established; the illness is of limited duration, does not threaten life and has no serious long-term effects; and the economic value of the lost productive time is calculable and the cost of health care known. The technique is relatively easy to apply and is the most common technique for evaluating the economic costs of illness.[86] Within ICAM the technique is useful for the evaluation of air and water pollution and of the health effects of new reservoirs, irrigation systems, etc.

Opportunity costs. A popular and widely applicable technique which measures the foregone benefits of selecting one option rather than another, it is particularly useful in cases where it is difficult to estimate the monetary value of the loss of a natural ecosystem. Instead of such a value, the opportunity costs of preserving the area concerned are measured in terms of the development benefits foregone. Rather than completing a cost-benefit analysis, the decision-maker is then asked to make the subjective decision: are the foregone developing benefits likely to exceed the preservation benefits? Within ICAM, this technique is particularly useful where proposed developments threaten pristine environments such as wetlands, natural forests and coral reefs.

Preventive expenditures. Rather than attempting to put a monetary value on environmental benefits themselves (through WTP/WTA estimates), the preventive expenditure technique is based on actual expenditure incurred to prevent, eradicate or reduce adverse environmental effects. This technique is based on the assumption that the victim of environmental damage will be prepared to incur preventive or mitigative expenditure until the costs of doing so are at least as great as the perceived benefits obtained (equal to the environmental damage costs). Information on preventive expenditure can be derived from: direct observations of actual spending; collection of information on WTP to guard against an impending environmental threat; or by obtaining professional estimates on a process that has physical effects that are well perceived and for which there is the possibility of prevention. The disadvantages are that actual expenditures are constrained by the ability to pay and the assumption that the actual expenditure equals the environmental damage costs may not hold. Existence and option values are not captured. Within ICAM, it can be used to evaluate the costs of air, water and noise pollution and soil erosion on residential areas, agricultural, forestry and fishery production.

Replacement costs. The is an *ex post* valuation approach that estimates the replacement or restoration costs once environmental damage has taken place. Such costs can then be taken as a minimum estimate of the presumed benefits of programmes for protecting or improving the environment. The boundary between this approach and the preventive expenditure approach is not always easy to uphold and the limitations above apply also to this technique. In some instances, it will be useful to make separate estimates of preventive expenditure and replacement costs and the effects of no action (using the effects on production technique) and to compare them in order to decide whether it is more sensible to try to prevent degradation, to risk that it happens and try to restore the damage, or to do nothing at all. This method is commonly used to justify the costs of soil conservation measures.

Shadow projects. This technique can be viewed as a special type of the replacement cost technique. It involves the identification and costing of a supplementary or "shadow" project designed to offset the environmental damage. This technique is more reliable than WTP estimates for environmental services, which people find hard to value, such as carbon sequestration by forests which offsets the greenhouse effects of carbon emissions.

73

[84] See Mitchell and Carson, 1989.
[85] See Shogren *et al.*, 1994.
[86] See Freeman, 1979; Tietenberg, 1994; and Pearce and Turner, 1990.

Sources: extracted from Hufschmidt *et al.*, 1983; Winpenny, 1991; and Richardson and Nurick, 1994.

INTEGRATED
COASTAL AREA
MANAGEMENT
and
AGRICULTURE
FORESTRY AND
FISHERIES

PART A

ISSUES, PERSPECTIVES, POLICY AND PLANNING PROCESSES FOR INTEGRATED COASTAL AREA MANAGEMENT

2. The process of integrated coastal area management

Agencies involved in ICAM should therefore establish baseline studies with which future assessments are to be compared.

2.4.5 Strategy formulation

In most cases of ICAM, strategy formulation will be undertaken by the coordinating institution, working through the steering and management committees.

At this stage of the process, the overall goals stated in the inception paper, and the issues and options identified during the performance review and data collection and analysis phases, are translated into specific objectives[87] and a strategy for coastal management, including tools and instruments required to reach the policy objectives. The strategy will demonstrate the linkages between objectives and research and monitoring requirements and should be consistent with identified needs and constraints for development, and with sectoral and overall development goals.

During the strategy formulation phase, details on implementation procedures, schedules and cost sharing are negotiated and finalized with each concerned interest group. The strategy should represent a synthesis of information collected with all the available means and activities agreed upon between local communities and other partners (local authorities, line agencies, NGOs, etc.). Since the strategy should become an integral part of the follow-up by line agencies, it must be as clear and readily applicable as possible. GIS seems to be a particularly useful tool in this respect, offering a unique opportunity for easily retrieving and processing spatial data and information for planning and extension purposes.

In many cases a strategy for a coastal area must emphasize secondary economic development, such as surrendering natural resources to tourism or to urban or industrial development. Where this is so, such choices will be made only after an exhaustive analysis of the trade-offs, including the costs and benefits of adopting the selected strategy. Where possible, in the context of sustainable development, planners will endeavour to avoid loss or degradation of natural resources when pursuing economic development. In order to reach agreement on trade-offs, negotiations with stakeholders can take place within the coordinating committee where arbitration will facilitate acceptance of the inevitable choices. In any case, ICAM requires that the potential benefits and risks associated with various management options be made explicit to the actors involved.

When the long-term objectives have been defined, the following considerations should govern the setting of short-term objectives:

- only attainable objectives should be set, relating to relatively few major issues;
- other, less tractable issues may be addressed at a later stage by fixing and attaining modest objectives, confidence should be established in ICAM before larger, more politically sensitive issues are tackled;
- when programmes of research and training are required, they should comprise part of the strategy, have well-focused objectives and be refined and incorporated into relevant research and training plans;
- agreements reached on monitoring and evaluation procedures should be incorporated in a performance plan.

In describing the means by which the goals and objectives will be met, the ICAM strategy should identify the instruments to be used. In particular, the strategy stage is the point at which to consider the rationale for the selection of instruments that will implement policies. Those instruments are: direct government investment; institutional and organizational arrangements; command and control instruments; economic or market-based instruments; and societal instruments.[88]

Policy instruments may work either directly or indirectly. Table A.5 shows some examples. The indirect approach seeks to influence resource users' actions. Barbier (1992) has concluded that with economic instruments the uncertainty usually concerns the reduction in environmental damage, whereas with regulatory controls the uncertainty is over the costs of reduction.

The ICAM strategy will usually be approved by all the ministries concerned, together with the agreement

---

[87] Examples of stated objectives are in Box A.25.

[88] See Box A.26.

PART A

ISSUES, PERSPECTIVES, POLICY AND PLANNING PROCESSES FOR INTEGRATED COASTAL AREA MANAGEMENT

INTEGRATED
COASTAL AREA
MANAGEMENT
and
AGRICULTURE
FORESTRY AND
FISHERIES

2. The process of integrated coastal area management

BOX A.25
Examples of stated objectives in ICAM

In the Bolinau Community-Based Coastal Resources Management Project (which is site-specific) in the Philippines, the stated objectives are:

- empowerment of local communities, through community organization, environmental education and institutionalization, in order that they function effectively as stewards of their coastal resources;
- food production and income generation aimed at improving livelihoods;
- establishment of linkages with similarly motivated groups with a view to setting goals for changes in policies and laws and lobbying for their adoption.

Source: Gomez and McManus, 1996.

In the Ecuador Coastal Resources Management Programme (which was countrywide), the stated objectives were to:

- create and mobilize constituencies for improved coastal mana-gement both at the community level and within central government;
- improve management through governance structures and processes at the community level and within the central government;
- build indigenous capacity;
- experiment with resource management techniques at a pilot scale in five special area management zones to discover and demonstrate promising approaches to priority coastal manage-ment problems.

Source: Olsen, 1996.

BOX A.26
Instruments for policy implementation

Policy instruments vary from minimum flexibility, control-oriented, maximum government involvement (e.g. regulations, sanctions, charges, taxes and fees) to maximum flexibility, litigation-oriented and increased private initiative (e.g. final demand intervention, such as performance rating, strict liability legislation). In between these two extremes lie moderately flexible market-oriented instruments (e.g. tradable permits). For ICAM, the following categories could be considered.

Direct government investment. This takes two forms: "hard" investment in physical infrastructure, such as water treatment plants; and "soft" investment, such as in research and information, training, resource management and public education.

Institutional and organizational arrangements. These include appropriate legislation relating to the responsibilities and powers of the various institutions involved and provision of the governance arrangements. Care has to be taken that any proposals for changes to legislation and regulations are consistent with existing legislation.

Command and control instruments. These are regulatory instruments relying largely on legal enforcement to obtain satisfactory results. The advantages of command and control instruments include a general preference for them over economic instruments by resource users and by governments. There are a number of reasons for this preference, among which are their familiarity, clarity and perceived certainty, and the perceived absence of undesirable effects on inflation, income distribution and international competitiveness. However, they suffer from often being relatively costly to implement and economically inefficient, substituting decisions on resource use by the government for decisions by resource users.

Economic or market-based instruments. These also rely on regulation but differ from command and control instruments in that they work with the market, that is, the tendency of resource users to respond to financial incentives or disincentives. Economic instruments are usually more efficient than command and control instruments. However, considerable care must be taken in their design, and considerable research is required, for instance to determine the efficiency of transferable quotas or tradable pollution permits. The revenue aspects of taxes and fees for less wealthy governments should not be underestimated.

Societal instruments. The main features of societal instruments are the promotion of civil society organizations, the creation of new channels for public involvement and citizen activism (including greater citizen access to courts for civil suits, for example related to the protection of environmental goods against economic options). In many developing countries, the conditions for such involvement are still far from being fulfilled.

INTEGRATED
COASTAL AREA
MANAGEMENT
and
AGRICULTURE
FORESTRY AND
FISHERIES

PART A

ISSUES, PERSPECTIVES, POLICY AND PLANNING PROCESSES FOR INTEGRATED COASTAL AREA MANAGEMENT

2. The process of integrated coastal area management

TABLE A.5
Examples of policy instruments used in response to some common issues in ICAM

Issue	Category	Direct	Indirect
Pollution	EPI	Effluent charges; tradable permits deposit/refund systems.	Removal of subsidies encouraging resource consumption; taxes on inputs or outputs; subsidies on the use of substitutes and abatement inputs; performance bonds; tradable effluent quotas.
	CAC	Prohibitions on improper waste and effluent disposal; emission limits; environmental quality standards (e.g. for water and air); licensing systems; integrated pollution control systems.	Regulation of equipment, processes, inputs and outputs; imposition of technical standards; efficiency standards for inputs or processes; bans or fixed quotas on inputs or outputs; reporting requirements; environmental impact assessment requirements; land-use zoning.
	DGI	Waste collection, treatment and disposal.	Research and development; technical assistance; education.
	IOA	Creation and extension of institutional jurisdiction and responsibilities; increasing institutional capacity; monitoring; enforcement.	Creating civil liability for pollution damage and for clean-up costs; creating rights for the public to gain access to information and to institute legal actions.
Non-optimal resource exploitation	EPI	Tradable fishing quotas; stumpage fees (royalties); water use charges.	Removal of subsidies encouraging resource consumption; introduction of subsidies to encourage reduced consumption, reuse and recycling; taxes on resource utilization; marketing board margins; licence fees; concession fees.
	CAC	Non-tradable fishing quotas; logging quotas or bans; obligations to rehabilitate or reforest sites.	Regulation of fishing vessels, fishing gear, fishing area, fishing season; regulation of logging area; reporting obligations.
	DGI	Fisheries enhancement.	Research and development; technical assistance; education.
	IOA	Establishment and clarification of legal responsibilities and duties of institutions; increasing institutional capacity; monitoring; enforcement.	Preparation and implementation of integrated coastal management plans and policies; clarification of legal rights to own, use and manage resources; involvement of resource users in decision-making and planning; devolving management authority to local level; establishment of conflict resolution mechanisms.
Habitat degradation	EPI	Taxes on exports of coral; subsidies on use of fuels as alternatives to wood and charcoal.	
	CAC	Restrictions on habitat conversion (e.g. mangrove); prohibitions on harmful activities (e.g. blast fishing, muro-ami, coral harvesting) and restrictions on potentially harmful activities (e.g. inshore trawling, scuba diving); creating legal obligations to rehabilitate and restore degraded areas.	Restrictions on rights of private landowners; establishment of protected areas; system of consents for developments in coastal areas; zoning of coastal areas; coastal set-back lines; environmental impact assessment requirements; regulation of sale and export of products from protected natural resources (e.g. coral).
	DGI	Infrastructure and management of parks and protected areas; reef seeding; mangrove rehabilitation.	Research, technical assistance, education.
	IOA	Establishment and clarification of institutional jurisdictional responsibilities; increasing institutional capacity; monitoring; enforcement.	Preparation and implementation of integrated coastal management plans and policies; clarification of legal rights to own, use and manage resources; creating rights for the public to gain access to information and to institute legal actions; involvement of resource users in decision-making and planning; devolving management authority to local level; establishment of conflict resolution mechanisms.

EPI: economic policy (or market-based) instruments.
CAC: command and control instruments.
DGI: direct government involvement (or investment).
IOA: institutional and organizational arrangements (including societal instruments).

Source: adapted from Grigalunas and Congar, 1991; and Scura *et al.*, 1992.

PART A

ISSUES, PERSPECTIVES, POLICY AND PLANNING PROCESSES FOR INTEGRATED COASTAL AREA MANAGEMENT

INTEGRATED
COASTAL AREA
MANAGEMENT
and
AGRICULTURE
FORESTRY AND
FISHERIES

2. The process of integrated coastal area management

BOX A.27
Guidelines for coastal development
affecting ecosystems

- Designate critical habitats and species for special protection or status.
- Locate development that is not coastal-dependent away from important coastal ecosystems areas.
- In addition to avoiding unnecessary negative impacts on coastal ecosystems, establish shoreline setbacks or buffer zones aimed at avoiding damage to development from coastal and riverine natural hazards.
- If the coastal area must be developed, locate and design sites to avoid vulnerable coastal ecosystems and habitats.

- Incorporate buffer zones whenever development close to vulnerable ecosystems cannot be avoided.
- Avoid breeding and nesting seasons when undertaking construction work.
- Design infrastructures so as to avoid blocking water circulation.
- Dispose of effluents, runoff and discharges in a manner that avoids pollution of ecosystems.
- Require compensation for ecological losses caused by development; where possible, provide for replacement of lost habitat.

**Flamingoes on the
Salamanca Island
game reserve,
Columbia**

INTEGRATED
COASTAL AREA
MANAGEMENT
and
AGRICULTURE
FORESTRY AND
FISHERIES

PART A

ISSUES, PERSPECTIVES, POLICY AND PLANNING PROCESSES FOR INTEGRATED COASTAL AREA MANAGEMENT

2. The process of integrated coastal area management

of the other stakeholders, such as communities, industry organizations and municipalities. Useful approaches for strategy formulation are the patrimonial approach and other public involvement methods.[89]

2.4.6 Plan formulation/absorption into sectoral plans

When it is working well, the ICAM planning process is a dynamic one. New information and new analysis is likely to result periodically in the need either to modify existing objectives or to develop new ones; the process is essentially one of continuous learning.

ICAM plans should evolve from ICAM strategies just as sector plans evolve from sector strategies. The plan outlines the sequence within a time-frame of necessary management actions, financial and workforce requirements to implement the actions, and the mechanisms for monitoring and evaluation. Success will depend heavily on the provisions made for ensuring compliance with plan provisions; the chances of voluntary compliance will depend on the level of public involvement in the planning process.

Where ICAM is institutionally integrated, the integrated body will have funds to implement the strategy by developing an ICAM plan.

Where ICAM is coordinated[90] (the most likely option), the strategy is the basis for line ministries to build plans for the implementation of those parts of the strategy for which they are responsible. The translation of the strategy into sector-based plans will depend critically on those ministries, their competence, their mandates and their control over funds for conservation, management and development.

Sector plans should include:

- short- and medium-term objectives in support of the strategy's goals and objectives to address areas where sectoral resource management might be improved and cross-sectoral impacts mitigated;
- a description of the policy instruments in terms of how they will be applied, the cost of introducing them and the expected benefits, and an identification of the human and financial resources required;
- a statement of the time-frame for the ICAM part of the sector plan.

Details of subsectoral policy instruments are found in Section 3 of Part B and Sections 4 of Parts C and D.

Plans for ICAM that are part of sector plans will be consistent with:

- the relevant research strategies and plans;
- local, regional and national development plans;
- the national environmental policy or national environmental action plan, where such a policy or plan exist.

However, ICAM plans will gradually influence national environmental plans.[91]

In some countries, difficulties may arise in reconciling the dynamism in the ICAM planning process, represented by the flow of information resulting in revision of objectives, with the conventional sectoral planning process in which sector plans, linked to national plans, are normally for a fixed four- or five-year planning term. In this situation, care should be taken to ensure that there is sufficient flexibility in the sectoral planning process to accommodate likely changes in the plan. Ideally, ICAM planning can be best accommodated in sectoral planning where the sector plan is rolled forward from one year to the next.

Coordination of sectoral plans will take place within the coordinating institution where representatives of line ministries and other organizations are involved in implementing the plan. This will ensure that, together, the implementing agencies encompass all aspects of the strategy and avoid overlapping or contradictory actions.

The plan for the coastal area, or the sectoral plans, should indicate the time-frame and resources needed for each activity. When new institutions, or significant modifications to existing institutions, are proposed, a smooth transition from the current situation to the new one must be provided for.

In the integration of ICAM strategy into sector plans, suitable sustainability and performance indicators should be provided.[92]

2.4.7 Plan implementation

This important stage in the process is often the most neglected. Implementation often presents difficulties resulting from the higher priorities perceived by line

---

[89] See Boxes A.11 and A.20, respectively.
[90] See Section 2.3.2.

[91] See Section 2.3.3.
[92] See Sections 2.3.6. and 2.4.2.

PART A

ISSUES, PERSPECTIVES, POLICY AND PLANNING PROCESSES FOR INTEGRATED COASTAL AREA MANAGEMENT

INTEGRATED
COASTAL AREA
MANAGEMENT
and
AGRICULTURE
FORESTRY AND
FISHERIES

2. The process of integrated coastal area management

FIGURE A.14

ICAM management stages

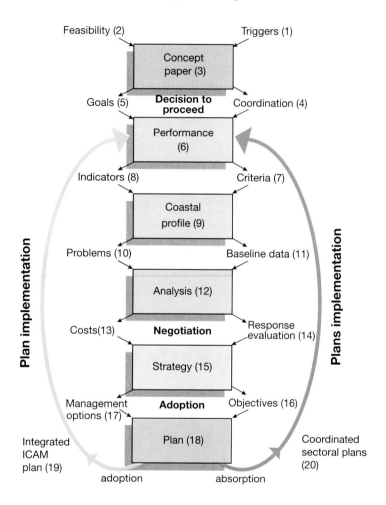

(1) Triggers of the ICAM process include: an environmental incident, decline in productivity, a planning opportunity, a sustainability concern, etc.

(2) Feasibility: assesses coastal issues and management needs and appraises economic feasibility.

(3) Concept paper: the product of the inception phase that identifies the main actors and coordination mechanism: (4) broadly defines the intended achievements; and (5) proposes time horizon and costs.

(6) Performance review: defines who, how and when data will be collected: establishes (7) evaluation criteria; identifies data to be collected; and monitors (8) indicators . As information is generated and stakeholders' capacity is strengthened, the performance review assess the ICAM process and evaluates results.

(9) Coastal profile: the product of the data collection and research phase where: (10) problems, causes of concern and management issues are defined; and (11) baseline data are established.

(12) Analysis: evaluates problems and (13) societal costs; (14) evaluates institutional responses to spot management gaps and needs; and produces a statement of possible actions.

(15) Strategy: translates goals into (16) specific agreed objectives; and defines (17) management options that include negotiated management procedures, rationale for selecting policy instruments, as well as performance research and training plans.

(18) Plan: formulation of (19) a new integrated ICAM plan; or (20) absorption into sectoral plans that contain a statement for the time-frame and budgetary commitment allocated to their ICAM part.

ministries consistent with their conventional, sector-oriented roles. Such difficulties should be anticipated and overcome before the implementation stage is reached. The plan can only be effectively applied when sanctioned at the highest level.

The main steps in the implementation phase include decision-making relative to adopting the plan, budgetary commitment, and monitoring and supervision.[93]

Integration and coordination mechanisms are essential throughout these phases.

For monitoring to be efficiently carried out, policy measures should be formulated with appropriate indicators. Periodic monitoring also provides much of the information required for the evaluation of ICAM plan performance. Performance review evolves management towards more refined ICAM cycles.

---

[93] See Section 2.4.2.

3. Summary guidelines

3.1 PREMISE

Coastal areas are diverse in function and form, dynamic and important both economically and ecologically.

Minimizing the societal costs associated with the growth of coastal areas requires a more integrative approach than that at present adopted in most countries. The term "sustainable development" has provided a socially desirable goal, but it has not given guidance for a course of action to attain that goal. One thing is certain: sustainable agricultural development is not simply the combination of sustainable agriculture, sustainable fisheries and sustainable forestry since, individually, these subsectors do not take into account trans-sectoral issues that affect them and are affected by them.

Critical evaluation of trade-offs between subsectors (and non-agricultural sectors) and among development alternatives is essential to guide public policies in this regard. Standard, sector-based development planning does not allow for adequate identification and evaluation of such trade-offs. In contrast, integrated coastal management planning, because of its more comprehensive nature, provides the opportunity for inclusion of the broader impacts, and the evaluation of their benefits and costs.

Integration of the agriculture sector into coastal area management therefore involves going beyond traditional subsectoral management – and even beyond the broader mandates of sustainable sectoral management – in which agriculture, fisheries and forestry are managed as separate entities. Integrated management is broader in its intrasectoral focus and also includes relevant extrasectoral issues.

Although conventional sectoral planning often results

INTEGRATED
COASTAL AREA
MANAGEMENT
and
AGRICULTURE
FORESTRY AND
FISHERIES

PART A

ISSUES, PERSPECTIVES, POLICY AND PLANNING PROCESSES FOR INTEGRATED COASTAL AREA MANAGEMENT

3. Summary guidelines

in unsustainable development, the information generated by sectoral agencies for their own planning purposes can be an extremely useful input to planning of a more integrative nature. Furthermore, even if planning is integrated, implementation is often still within the mandate of the various sectoral agencies. Therefore, active involvement of these agencies in the integrated planning process and coordination of the implementation of these and their other activities are essential.

3.2 GENERAL ICAM PRINCIPLES

There are inseparable links between development and environment that have the potential to be at once complementary or conflicting. Natural resource and environmental problems are often as much consequences of inappropriate development as they are by-products of unmanaged growth. In sustainable development, long-term developmental and environmental goals are complementary.

Incentives originating in market prices or policies can provide valuable guidance for activities in coastal areas. However, such incentives may have unintended side-effects or promote activities that may be inappropriate from a societal perspective. These problems are referred to as market or policy failures.

Conventional sectoral planning does not take adequate account of the externalities generated by the sector or by those that affect it but originate in other sectors. An integrative approach to development planning in coastal areas involves correcting for market and policy failures and reducing the magnitude of, and the costs associated with, these transectoral impacts.

With ICAM, component sectors are managed as part of a functional whole, the primary focus being based on resource users rather than resource stocks.

The objectives of integrated management are to ensure that multisectoral development has the fewest possible negative impacts and the least possible long-term societal costs.

Some trade-offs among competing coastal activities are inevitable and should be anticipated. The societal costs associated with these trade-offs can be handled through well-balanced management which assesses the relative costs of the trade-offs, arrives at a consensus among stakeholders on appropriate management actions, and implements these actions to minimize the trade-offs.

Sectoral line agencies play an important role in both ICAM planning and implementation. Line agencies are key players in: identifying transectoral impacts; negotiating with other line agencies, community groups and resource users; agreeing on trade-offs among alternative development proposals; and assessing the feasibility and efficacy of alternative management interventions.

3.3 ICAM CHARACTERISTICS

The management of coastal areas is a long-term, dynamic and iterative process. Plans (including their spatial and temporal scope) require periodic revision in the light of new information and changing circumstances. Everybody involved in the planning process should recognize that it is a learning process in which flexible attitudes are essential. The continuous nature of the planning process should, therefore, be explicitly incorporated in funding and organizational arrangements.

The planning process should be multisectoral and integrate all issues relevant to the current stage of development of the area, with a particular focus on cross-sectoral issues.

The types of management issues that predominate are a function of the mix of the development activities in an area and are, therefore, closely correlated with economic development. A management plan should be proactive, not merely reactive, anticipating and including management issues that are likely to arise in future, having regard to the resources in the area and the development direction being pursued.

An important part of the coastal management process is made up of actions at the local level. All stakeholders must be able to participate in the planning process to ensure that: 1) it is as equitable as possible and takes their concerns into account (given the need for compromise and trade-offs); and 2) they understand the connections between the different elements of both the process and the plan and understand how their actions can contribute to the achievement of the common good, or detract from it.

ISSUES, PERSPECTIVES, POLICY AND PLANNING PROCESSES FOR INTEGRATED COASTAL AREA MANAGEMENT

PART A

INTEGRATED
COASTAL AREA
MANAGEMENT
and
AGRICULTURE
FORESTRY AND
FISHERIES

3. Summary guidelines

3.4 POLICY AND PLANNING PREREQUISITES FOR ICAM

Coastal areas should be defined pragmatically for management purposes. Definitions should encompass all the relevant management issues to be addressed, including the biophysical, economic, social, institutional and organizational aspects.

Responsibility for the management of coastal areas is usually shared between a number of different ministries, some with sectoral responsibilities and others with jurisdictional ones. Although integrated coastal management will probably initially focus on a few major management issues, it should aim at policy integration during the policy-making phases.

Coordination of management actions undertaken by various agencies and stakeholders is critical to overall plan integrity and effectiveness. An appropriate body will be given overall responsibility for coordination.

Management plans should originate from within the management area, subject to the overarching goals of the government for coastal management and to budgetary limitations.

Coastal area management strategies and plans should be integrated with sectoral, local, regional and national development plans, sectoral resource management plans and national environmental plans.

Management actions should take account of local needs and constraints and should strive to establish a balance between conservation and development.

An integrated management plan must be tailored as far as possible to fit into existing institutional and organizational arrangements. These include political and administrative structures, legal frameworks, cultural attitudes and social traditions. Existing institutions and organizations, government and non-governmental, involved in the management of coastal resources or having jurisdiction over coastal resources, should be fully considered. If they are found to be inadequate to meet the needs of integrated management, action should be taken to establish a legal and administrative environment (including clarification of roles and provision of funding and training) conducive to effective cooperation between individuals, communities, government organizations and NGOs.

In integrated coastal management, the responsibilities of the coordinating organization and of the cooperating organizations should be clearly defined and overlaps and conflicts in organizational jurisdictions should be minimized. Appropriate authority and budgets should be allocated to these organizations.

In many instances, different interests in a coastal area may have similar objectives but will award them differing levels of priority. The planning process has to include mechanisms aimed at reconciling these differing priorities.

The allocation of resources is essentially a political process, based on the interests of different groups, as expressed through the consultative process. Economic valuation of resources and ecosystems can provide a rational basis for allocation and facilitate the political process. Values that cannot be quantified can be expressed qualitatively.

Property rights governing coastal resources should be clearly and unambiguously defined.

Information collection should be restricted to that directly needed for planning purposes.

Research and environmental monitoring should be directed towards the provision of improved information for improved plan formulation and implementation. Support for research, especially where funding is limited, should be restricted to research that contributes to essential information requirements and policy needs.

In addressing management issues, management should use a cost-effective combination of societal instruments, command-and-control measures, economic policy instruments and direct public-sector investment and provide the appropriate institutional and organizational framework.

3.5 MAIN STEPS IN DEVELOPING ICAM PLANS

Inception. A concept paper will initially be prepared by a government institution or other authoritative interest group, identifying actors from both government and non-governmental institutions involved in natural resource use. The concept paper should respond to a defined need and purpose. A steering and a management committee are then established, with representatives from all concerned parties, to guide and coordinate the process. The committees should be based where they can have the greatest influence on the national development system (e.g. ministry of planning). The need for an ICAM strategy, as the best response to well-identified problems, must be evident.

83

INTEGRATED
COASTAL AREA
MANAGEMENT
and
AGRICULTURE
FORESTRY AND
FISHERIES

PART A
ISSUES, PERSPECTIVES, POLICY AND PLANNING PROCESSES FOR INTEGRATED COASTAL AREA MANAGEMENT

3. Summary guidelines

Performance review. Monitoring, at the early stage of articulation and implementation, is the most important management tool, satisfying the iterative nature of the process. Periodic evaluation focuses on the effectiveness in the operating mode, with particular attention to the proper evaluation of environmental externalities. Performance indicators ought to be identified early in the process.

Data collection and research. Each subsector represented in the committees prepares baseline information on the resources, the environmental impacts and the institutional structures proper to coastal resource management which would then be used to form a coastal profile.

Analysis. The biophysical and socio-economic environments, interactions within the coastal ecosystem and various economic sectors, and constraints, opportunities and possible alternatives for sustainable development are identified and attempts made to analyse and understand them.

Strategy formulation. The ICAM strategy to be adopted is developed by the steering and management committees on the basis of the broad goals identified in the inception paper and on information collected. The strategy defines long-term objectives and identifies policy instruments to reach the agreed objectives. It is paramount for the objectives to be those of the people implementing the strategy, and so they are set following broad-ranging consultations and debates. Objectives can be refined as the strategy progresses. There must be high-level political support for the strategy.

The process itself, and its costs and likely benefits, must be fully understood. The commitment of key participants is essential and, if some cannot be induced to participate, a more limited strategy can be considered with a view to bringing others on board as the strategy gains in momentum and support.

Plan formulation. The ICAM strategy, once agreed, is translated into plans at the sectoral level; this involves conventional sectoral planning being upgraded to address cross-sectoral concerns and prevent adverse environmental impacts. Policy measures will have been taken, during the formulation stage, to anticipate difficulties and provide for changes in circumstances not foreseen by the plan.

Plan implementation: During implementation, new information and periodic monitoring and evaluation will lead to revisions of objectives and management interventions, as provided for during plan formulation.

INTEGRATED
COASTAL AREA
MANAGEMENT
and
AGRICULTURE
FORESTRY AND
FISHERIES

PART

B

INTEGRATION OF AGRICULTURE INTO COASTAL AREA MANAGEMENT

INTEGRATED
COASTAL AREA
MANAGEMENT
and
AGRICULTURE
FORESTRY AND
FISHERIES

PART B

INTEGRATION OF AGRICULTURE INTO COASTAL AREA MANAGEMENT

INTEGRATED
COASTAL AREA
MANAGEMENT
and
AGRICULTURE
FORESTRY AND
FISHERIES

Executive summary

Agriculture in coastal areas often plays an important role and, as elsewhere, it occupies the major share of available land. Coastal areas often provide excellent soil and climatic conditions for agriculture. Apart from its evident function in providing food to coastal populations, agriculture also often provides raw materials to industry, which may be established in the area to make the most of port facilities. Agricultural products may find markets in the tourism sector, although this is not always as strong a link as is sometimes assumed. Agriculture also provides livelihoods for coastal populations, including those of coastal cities.

Coastal agriculture often benefits from favourable environmental conditions, from generally good land and sea communications, and from the development of industry and tourism in coastal areas. However, it also faces constraints related to the proximity to the sea, including: the risk of saline air and water; poor water quality and insecure supplies caused by upstream activities; and severe competition for available coastal land.

The agriculture sector influences, and is influenced by, other sectors. These interactions may be positive, but are often negative, and revolve around competition for land, water, capital and labour. The negative influences of agriculture on other sectors include pollution of fisheries by agrochemicals and silting of coral reefs and ports resulting from land erosion. In turn,

agriculture itself may by negatively influenced by pollution originating from outside the coastal area, or it may induce its own negative impacts, for instance by inappropriate irrigation practices which can lead to the intrusion of salt water from the sea.

In order to integrate agricultural planning into overall coastal planning, the first stage is to gather relevant and useful information. This should cover the biophysical and socio-economic environments, interactions with other sectors, governance, and the constraints, opportunities and possible alternatives for the sector.

The next stage is planning, taking account of the special characteristics of coastal agriculture while ensuring that the plan conforms to overall national objectives for agriculture. During this phase, means to reduce or avoid the negative impacts of agriculture on other sectors should be introduced; these may entail revising subsidies, taxation and regulations, while introducing specific support services and reviewing the institutional set-up. The outcome might be changes in cropping patterns and cultivation methods.

Throughout the process, all interested parties and stakeholders should be consulted and involved and close liaison should be maintained with relevant ministries and services dealing with the other sectors.

Coastal area agricultural development plans will address the specific characteristics of agriculture in the area, interactions with other sectors and the importance of sustainable practices.

87

INTEGRATED
COASTAL AREA
MANAGEMENT
and
AGRICULTURE
FORESTRY AND
FISHERIES

1. The role of agriculture in coastal areas

There are many situations in which coastal agricultural production makes an important contribution to the local economy or to national agricultural production. This is the case in many small islands and in many countries where agriculture may be concentrated on the coastal plains or in fertile river deltas, as in Bangladesh and Egypt.

Even where agriculture in a coastal area may not appear to be particularly significant in terms of its contribution to the local economy or to national agricultural production, there are a number of reasons for giving it specific attention when making integrated coastal area plans:

- agriculture is the main user of land and, as a result, agricultural activities can have a significant impact on natural resources in a coastal area, with particularly important effects on the quality and flows of water and on natural habitats;
- where tourism or other capital-intensive activities are developed in coastal areas, land tenure may become fragile for smallholders with limited capacity to defend their interests, or they may be highly tempted to sell productive agricultural land for non-agricultural purposes;
- agriculture may play a key role in the local economy, either through the production of food or by providing raw materials to industry, and thus has strategic and political significance;
- in many developing countries a large percentage of the population is dependent on agriculture for their livelihoods, although this tends to be less significant with regard to coastal populations.

89

PART B
INTEGRATION OF AGRICULTURE INTO COASTAL AREA MANAGEMENT

INTEGRATED
COASTAL AREA
MANAGEMENT
and
AGRICULTURE
FORESTRY AND
FISHERIES

2. The interactions of agriculture with other coastal economic activities and ecosystems

Some particular opportunities and constraints apply to agriculture in coastal areas and these can also have an impact on other coastal economic activities and ecosystems.

2.1 OPPORTUNITIES AND CONSTRAINTS FOR AGRICULTURE IN COASTAL AREAS

2.1.1 Opportunities

The following three particular types of opportunity are identified in Part A of these guidelines as being potentially important in the development of agriculture in a coastal area:

- those arising from the dependence on natural resources resulting from the special characteristics of the coastal environment;
- those arising from the location of the coastal area that makes it a link between land and sea; those derived or secondary opportunities that develop with and from the other two.

Opportunities dependent on natural resources. In many cases, coastal areas offer very favourable environmental conditions for agriculture. This is especially so where coastal areas consist of alluvial accumulation plains. Such areas generally have deep, relatively flat, fertile soils and benefit from a substantial supply of water, from surface and/or subsurface sources. The Batinah and Salalah coastal plains in Oman are a good example; they produce most of the agricultural output of that arid country.

Most coastal areas also have a milder and more humid climate than the interior as a result of the moderating influence of the sea, especially where favourable sea currents occur (e.g. the Gulf Stream along the western coasts of Europe). Such conditions may favour the growth of a particular crop or crops not grown elsewhere in the country.

In marked contrast to capture fisheries and natural forestry activities, coastal agriculture does not normally involve harvesting of coastal resources;[1] its relationship with coastal ecosystems is usually more competitive (for instance, the expansion of agriculture into mangrove forests) and antagonistic (the modification of coastal ecosystems) than exploitative.[2]

Thanks to the diversity of coastal environments, which include both terrestrial and marine ecosystems, coastal populations often draw their livelihoods from a combination of agriculture and fishing, and sometimes also from seasonal work in the tourism sector (which can lead to agricultural labour shortages). Box B.1 describes two Vietnamese systems where agriculture, forestry and, in one case, fisheries are closely integrated.

Opportunities arising from location. Land and sea communications can also have implications for coastal agriculture.

When it is located near the coast, agriculture benefits from reduced transport costs for its produce compared to inland agriculture, whether export or domestic markets are targeted.

Coastal roads may give access to markets for agricultural products, and also facilitate input supplies. Improved roads may allow new areas of land to be brought into cultivation, and new water sources may also become accessible. However, roads in relatively isolated coastal areas are often poor, denying farmers market access or leading to produce reaching consumers in poor condition.

Even in the absence of good roads, produce can be shipped to markets by river as far as the coast and by boat along the coast. This may be the most significant locational advantage of coastal areas.

91

---

[1] Cutting fodder from mangrove forests for livestock and the use of dried fish or seaweed as fertilizers are some exceptions.

[2] For explanations of various relationships, see Part A, Section 1.5 and Box A.1

INTEGRATED
COASTAL AREA
MANAGEMENT
and
AGRICULTURE
FORESTRY AND
FISHERIES

PART B

INTEGRATION OF AGRICULTURE INTO COASTAL AREA MANAGEMENT

2. The interactions of agriculture with other coastal economic activities and ecosystems

BOX B.1

Integration of coastal agriculture, fisheries and forestry in Viet Nam

Two examples of farming systems in Viet Nam illustrate how farmers may develop local integrated systems involving crops, livestock, forestry and fisheries to use available resources effectively, gain advantage of complementary interactions and overcome the constraints faced by each subsector operating on its own.

- On sulphate soils in the south of Viet Nam, *Melaleuca leucandendron*, a tree species tolerant of toxic salts in acid sulphate soils, is planted in rice paddies along with rice. Rice is cultivated for two years under the growing trees, which are thinned at three, five and seven years (for fuelwood and poles) before the main felling at 20 years. *Melaleuca* can tolerate a pH as low as 2.3 in the dry season, and six months of flooding up to 1 m deep during the wet season, when shrimps, fish, eels, snakes, etc. are caught in the plantations. Farmers also keep bees which feed on the white flowers of *Melaleuca*. Twenty percent of a typical *Melaleuca* holding is planted to rice, 10 percent is used for canals, gardens and housing and the remainder is under *Melaleuca* plantation.

- In the coastal areas of the central region of Viet Nam the acid sandy soils are poor in nutrients and humus. During the wet season, heavy rains and typhoons cause flooding, but soils dry out rapidly in the long dry season and become susceptible to wind erosion, leading to sand dune formation and inshore drift affecting agricultural land, roads and villages. In one district, an agroforestry system has been developed for these conditions. Bands of *Casuarina* 80 to 100 m wide are planted next to the seashore, with a 2- to 3-m wide shallow trench separating them from food crops (beans, groundnuts, mulberry). Inland from this are bamboo, rattan and coconut around the villages, with rice and sweet potato fields beyond. The system provides protection from storm damage, wind erosion and drift. It also provides fuelwood as well as improved food production, water supplies, cattle fodder and employment opportunities.

Source: Hoang Hoe, 1991.

Derived or secondary opportunities. Coastal industries and development arising from special ecosystems and/or locational opportunities, may lead to population growth, thus providing derived opportunities for some types of agriculture, with increasing demand for food. When parts of the population are becoming more wealthy, there may also be increasing demand for higher-quality foodstuffs, such as fruit, vegetables, meat and dairy products. Industrial growth may also lead to increased demand for agricultural raw materials.

Tourism may also encourage demand for higher-value, perishable agricultural products, although this demand may not affect domestic markets as much as might be expected. In some small island countries, for example, large hotels are reported to import a high proportion of their food, whereas smaller hotels purchase most from local markets (FAO, 1992).

The impact of both types of increased demand on smallholder agriculture may be small and, as already mentioned, rising land values caused by the development of non-agricultural uses may result in insecurity for smallholders and tenants.

2.1.2 Constraints

Constraints specifically affecting agriculture and agricultural development in coastal areas, arise principally from:
- the direct effects of the proximity of the sea;
- the location of coastal agriculture at the downstream end of river flows;
- the limited space for expansion or relocation and the limited resources in many coastal areas, together with the need to limit the potentially harmful impacts of agriculture on sensitive and important coastal ecosystems.

Proximity of the sea. Many coastal agricultural areas are flat, although others (for example volcanic islands and the Pacific coast of Latin America) may have steep coastlines. Low-lying agricultural land is frequently subject to severe drainage and soil salinity problems caused by high, more or less saline, water-tables, stagnation of rain and runoff water and flooding from rivers or periodic storm surges. There may also be physical damage from wind storms or tidal waves, and sensitivity to airborne salt deposition. Low-lying agricultural lands may also be susceptible to shoreline retreat and flooding as a result of coastal erosion, subsidence or a rise in sea levels which could result from global climatic change. Higher air humidity in coastal areas is favourable to the occurrence and propagation of certain plant diseases and pests that constrain crop growth. Even if the agricultural area is not directly affected, it may be taken over to replace land lost by other sectors.

Another important consequence of the proximity of the sea is the occurrence of tides that induce the

PART B

INTEGRATION OF AGRICULTURE INTO COASTAL AREA MANAGEMENT

INTEGRATED
COASTAL AREA
MANAGEMENT
and
AGRICULTURE
FORESTRY AND
FISHERIES

2. The interactions of agriculture with other coastal economic activities and ecosystems

penetration of sea water far inland in the lower reaches of most coastal water courses during high tides. This causes periodic increases in river water salinity that may preclude or complicate its safe use for irrigation. A good illustration of this is the coastal plain of the Limpopo river, near the city of Xai-Xai, in Gaza province, Mozambique.

In some special circumstances, the coastal climate may be very unfavourable to agriculture. A sizeable part of the coastal areas of Chile and Peru are deserts as a result of the negative influence of the Humbolt cold sea current.

Upstream effects. Supplies of surface water become available to coastal agricultural activities after they have already been used for upstream activities that influence the timing, quantity and quality of river flows. Upstream dams and irrigation schemes can deprive coastal areas of water for irrigation and, by removing silt and regulating floods, may affect the fertility of coastal alluvial agricultural land. Conversely, inland encroachment of agriculture on to forested land, slash and burn practices, overgrazing and inappropriate cultivation methods may increase runoff and erosion in catchment areas, with coastal land affected by increased sediment in rivers, lower dry season river flows and increased flooding. Thus, Bangladesh is highly affected by deforestation in the Himalayas several hundred kilometres to the north. The quality of surface water available to coastal agriculture may also be affected by upstream discharges of industrial and urban effluents and by drainage of chemicals and salts from agricultural land into rivers.

Water availability, use and upstream effects are a critical issue for agriculture (see Box B.2).

BOX B.2
Water: a critical issue in coastal areas

Water is a resource used for a variety of activities which provides: a medium for movement (not only of boats and logs but also of organisms, chemicals and particles); a habitat for aquatic life forms; and a potential source of harnessed power (hydroelectric dams). It can, however, also be a physically destructive force (tidal waves). Inland surface waters reach the sea via the coast where they accumulate in subsurface aquifers which are in dynamic equilibrium with adjacent sea/lake water. Inland and coastal agricultural activities may have a strong impact on water flows and quality, placing high demands on water and affecting catchment areas as the following illustrations demonstrate.

Countries in **the Near East**, with growing populations, standards of living and industrial and agricultural activities, face increasing competition for limited water supplies. Surface water supplies are often limited by low rainfall, and coastal aquifers are a major water source. Groundwater extraction today tends to exceed the natural recharge rate, causing saltwater intrusion into the freshwater stocks. In Qatar, for example, the sea water interface is estimated to be advancing inland as fast as 1 000 m per year. The quantity and quality of water recharge to coastal aquifers may also be affected by the drainage of irrigation water and by the construction of coastal roads and their drainage systems. Saltwater intrusion into coastal aquifers has long-term impacts not only for the sustainability of coastal agriculture, but also for the availability of water to meet growing non-agricultural demand. Measures that may be taken to address these problems include: bans on drilling new wells and on increased extraction rates; improved efficiency in water use in irrigation; the cultivation of crops and cropping patterns with lower water demands; surface water management for improved groundwater recharge; the construction of physical barriers to saltwater intrusion; and the development of alternative freshwater sources (for example, imports or desalinization). There are various technical, financial, political and institutional difficulties associated with each of these measures. Saltwater intrusion is difficult to halt, and even more difficult to reverse.

Belize, in contrast, has ample supplies of high-quality water in rivers draining forested mountains. There are, however, signs of degradation and potential conflict over water. Specific issues concerning agriculture involve growing demands for irrigation water for rice and sugar cane, discharge of organic waste from citrus processing plants, and increasing flooding and sedimentation in rivers (arising from the encroachment of agriculture into the upper forested watershed). This situation causes particular concern about potential adverse effects on the economic and environmental status of the coastal area, which supports an important fishing industry and a developing tourist trade. The killing of fish and damage to coral reefs have already been observed as a result of sedimentation and organic pollution of rivers. Measures proposed to address these problems include the establishment of a legal and institutional framework for water management and environmental protection, adoption of more efficient irrigation methods, development of drainage and water treatment facilities, and monitoring of water quality to control, prevent and remedy water pollution from agro-industrial effluent, agricultural chemicals and municipal waste.

Source: Al Rifai, 1993; Belize, 1992.

93

INTEGRATED
COASTAL AREA
MANAGEMENT
and
AGRICULTURE
FORESTRY AND
FISHERIES

PART B

INTEGRATION OF AGRICULTURE INTO COASTAL AREA MANAGEMENT

2. The interactions of agriculture with other coastal economic activities and ecosystems

Space and resource constraints. Coastal areas are, almost by definition, of limited extension. The special opportunities they may present for agriculture (in deltas or estuaries, or processing and port facilities, for example) decline as activities are based further from the shore, the estuary or the port. Opportunities for expansion or relocation of such agricultural activities are therefore limited, especially when the coast is bounded by mountains. Agricultural development and population growth can only lead to physical concentration and pressures on resources such as water and land.

Space constraints and competition for land and water become more intense with urbanization. Many forms of agriculture require extensive amounts of land to produce relatively low-value outputs. As competition for land intensifies, agricultural activities such as grain crops and livestock grazing tend to be marginalized and replaced, either by non- agricultural activities or by agricultural activities with higher-value outputs, which require higher capital inputs and less land (for example intensive livestock raising or horticulture). Smallholders, unable to invest and intensify, thus tend to lose their land and migrate to the coastal towns.

Similar considerations affect irrigated agriculture where there is growing competition for water; irrigation uses high volumes of water, often inefficiently, to produce relatively low-value outputs. Increasing water scarcity may divert water away from agriculture to residential and industrial uses, and to other types of agriculture. Institutional arrangements for water fees, allocation and distribution ought to be introduced to encourage more efficient irrigation on higher unit-value crops.

Where the marginalization of low-value agricultural production is affecting peasant agriculture, this will lead to increasing pressure on a declining share of land unless non-agricultural employment opportunities are growing fast enough to absorb the labour displaced from agriculture. In any case, increasing pressure on land may lead to overexploitation, with inappropriate land use through the extension of agricultural activities into areas that may not be suitable for agriculture. This problem is not confined to coastal areas, but it may have particularly severe consequences if it affects coastal ecosystems (see Section 2.2.1).

Conversely, rapid development in other sectors may lead to competition for labour, although this is not a problem in many developing countries. If other sectors are perceived as more attractive, capital available for investment in agriculture may become scarce. There may also be competition for produce markets; good communications in coastal areas may facilitate imports of low-cost, high-quality agricultural produce with the consequent loss of outlets for local producers.

2.2 THE IMPACT OF AGRICULTURE ON THE COASTAL ENVIRONMENT

A number of general points can be made about the external effects of coastal agricultural activities on coastal ecosystems and other sectors:

- agricultural activities normally involve competition for, and degradation of, land and/or water;
- many such effects are harmful in that they involve change from conditions to which ecosystems have adapted in each locality;
- damage to coastal ecosystems has wide-ranging implications for the forestry, capture fisheries, aquaculture and tourism sectors which may directly rely on them for natural resources, and for all coastal activities that gain physical protection from them;
- the impact of changes in coastal agriculture is complex, involving the direct and indirect effects of physical, biological, social and economic processes on coastal ecosystems and other sectors;
- many of the external effects of coastal agriculture on coastal ecosystems and other sectors are associated with the intensification, expansion or marginalization of agricultural activities. These are normal (if sometimes undesirable) processes of agricultural and general economic development in coastal areas.

2.2.1 Potential harmful effects of agriculture on the coastal environment

The constraints already discussed occur largely as a result of agricultural activities suffering from one-sided or reciprocal competitive and antagonistic interactions. Under integrated coastal area management (ICAM) agricultural activities are also increasingly constrained by the need for control of their competitive and antagonistic effects on other activities and on special coastal ecological systems. These new constraints are common and must be a major consideration in the planning of agricultural development in coastal areas.

PART B

INTEGRATION OF AGRICULTURE INTO COASTAL AREA MANAGEMENT

INTEGRATED
COASTAL AREA
MANAGEMENT
and
AGRICULTURE
FORESTRY AND
FISHERIES

2. The interactions of agriculture with other coastal economic activities and ecosystems

TABLE B.1

Potential harmful effects of agricultural activities on coastal ecosystems

Activity	Environmental change	Impact of social concern
Estuary flood control, impoundment or diversion of coastal rivers	Increased estuarine salinity, reduced circulation, sediment trapping, decreased supply of beach material to shoreline, shoreline erosion	Reduced crop yields, reduced fish yields, increased water-borne diseases
Agricultural pesticides	Toxic pollution of estuaries and inshore waters	Killing of fish, reduced fish yields, potential human consumption of toxic fish, coral pollution and loss
Fertilizer use	Increased amount of nutrients, eutrophication and pollution of estuaries	Killing of fish, reduced fish yield, coral pollution and loss
Overcropping or grazing in coastal watershed	Watershed erosion, estuary sedimentation and increased turbidity, increased deposition in flood plains	Corals and beaches covered with sediment, coral death, decline in fish yields, decreased recreation and tourism attraction, obstruction of navigation channels with sediments
Irrigation from coastal aquifers	Depletion of coastal aquifers	Saltwater intrusion, contamination of groundwater
Coastal wetlands reclamation	Draining or dyking, physical destruction of habitat, toxic (acid) drainage, change in sedimentation patterns, change in water circulation/drainage, loss of coastal protection (mangroves), increased water-borne diseases	Loss of wetland and forest/wildlife production, loss of biodiversitybiological diversity, loss or rarefaction of endangered species, killing of fish, reduced fish yields, increased storm damage and coastal erosion
Intensive livestock activities	Organic effluent, eutrophication and pollution	Killing of fish, reduced fish yields, coral pollution and loss, reduction in recreation and tourism attraction
Agro-industries	Organic and toxic effluents, eutrophication and pollution	Killing of fish, reduced fish yields, coral pollution and loss, reduction in recreation and tourism attraction
Over-Overgrazing on coastal dunes	Destabilization of dunes	Initiation or increased dune migration on to agricultural or urban areas and on infrastructure

Source: Extracted and modified from Sorensen and McCreary, 1990; and Barg, 1992.
Note: This table is only an indicative list of sketchily described impact chains and is not intended to explain, or list exhaustively, cause-and-effect relationships.

The discussion that follows concentrates on the effects of coastal agricultural activities. However, both inland and coastal activities may have a major impact on coastal ecosystems as a result of upstream processes. The profound influences of inland agriculture on the coast must therefore be recognized and addressed in coastal area management. The proximity of coastal ecosystems and coastal agriculture, however, leads to additional and stronger local interactions. These, as well as the more general upstream effects of both coastal and inland agriculture, are considered in this section.

Table B.1 shows the main ways in which coastal agriculture can adversely affect coastal ecosystems and the natural resource-dependent activities related to them. In particular, the table shows that agricultural activities can have serious and damaging impacts on coastal ecosystems and on human populations. These impacts

may result from resource depletion (such as loss of natural breeding areas or groundwater), from loss of habitat (with associated effects on biological diversity and on the productivity of natural resource-dependent activities), from hazards to human health (associated with contamination of water by chemicals or disease), or from loss of protection against coastal erosion or sand dune migration.

These issues are not unique to coastal agriculture, but are part of the more general problems of development in coastal areas, discussed in Part A of these guidelines.[3]

Dealing with such difficulties in a sustainable way is a major objective of ICAM. Minimizing the negative impact of agriculture must therefore be a particular

[3] See in particular Part A, Section 1 and Table A.3.

INTEGRATED
COASTAL AREA
MANAGEMENT
and
AGRICULTURE
FORESTRY AND
FISHERIES

PART B

INTEGRATION OF AGRICULTURE INTO COASTAL AREA MANAGEMENT

2. The interactions of agriculture with other coastal economic activities and ecosystems

concern to all involved with ICAM and with agricultural planning and management in coastal areas.

In keeping with the discussion in Part A of these guidelines,[4] it is helpful here to distinguish four major processes through which agriculture may have a negative impact on other economic activities and coastal ecosystems:

- competition for land;
- competition for water;
- antagonistic effects;
- secondary socio-economic effects.

Competition for land. Agriculture is the major occupier of land for cultivation and grazing. Associated settlement, buildings, roads and irrigation and drainage works take up still more land. In many coastal areas, significant clearing and drainage of coastal wetlands (swamps and mangrove forests) is taking place for cultivation. This may be the result of large-scale projects or continual encroachment by small-scale farmers. Such action results in habitat loss and loss of biological diversity, with wide-ranging effects on fisheries and, in the case of mangrove swamps, on forestry and wildlife. Since, in many cases, the soils of these wetlands are very difficult to manage, yields often decline dramatically after a few years and the land then has to be abandoned, creating pressure for further clearance, drainage and destruction of coastal wetlands.

Coastal wetlands and dunes may also be used for grazing. This may not necessarily result in direct destruction, but it may do if steady degradation continues over several years. Box B.3 describes the effects of grazing and movement of livestock on coastal dunes in Somalia.

Agriculture also suffers from direct competition for land for urban and other uses as mentioned above.[5]

Competition for water. The effects of agriculture on competition for water are discussed in Section 2.1.2, but the use of water for agricultural activities affects other sectors too. Dams and irrigation schemes, inland or near the coast, may reduce surface flows, with effects on the timing as well as the overall volume of river flows. Irrigation and cropping activities in coastal areas

> **BOX B.3**
> **Overgrazing and deforestation: coastal dunes in Somalia**
>
> The Brava and Shamballot areas in Somalia suffer from destabilization of the Old Red Sand Ridge and the formation of shifting coastal sand dunes which are moving inland and encroaching on important irrigated cropland. The immediate causes of dune formation are wind and water erosion of denuded land. Denudation itself, however, is triggered by overgrazing, tree cutting for poles and fuelwood, and movement of livestock from coastal settlements across the ridge to inland grazing areas and back, as well as for nomadic pastoralists' herds, from inland grazing areas across the ridge to coastal water sources.
>
> Dune fixation is extremely expensive. More fundamental measures are needed to address this problem, with an integrated, proactive approach to prevent dune destabilization. Such measures include the establishment of protected stock movement routes, the protection of scrubland from grazing and tree felling, the provision of access to alternative sources of water inland, and promotion of agroforestry systems providing fodder, fuelwood and poles.

may lower the water-table. Where irrigation systems extract groundwater from coastal aquifers these may become exhausted or, more commonly, become increasingly saline as salt water intrudes into them. Reduced or erratic surface and groundwater supplies in coastal areas can pose serious problems to coastal ecosystems, to aquaculture and to industrial and domestic water supply systems (see Boxes B.2 and B.4). Overexploitation of groundwater can also lead to subsidence and greater susceptibility to flooding.

Antagonistic effects. The most pervasive antagonistic effects[6] of agricultural activities tend to be related to water flows. Coastal ecosystems are highly dependent on water, are often sensitive to changes in water quality or quantity, and are located downstream of inland and coastal activities using and discharging fresh water. Moreover, water supplies for residential and industrial users in coastal areas are also often limited.

Intensive agricultural activities – usually related to export-oriented rather than subsistence crops – may result in water pollution through runoff of agricultural

---

[4] See Part A, Section 1.5.
[5] See "constraints" in Section 2.1.2.

---

[6] See Table B.1.

2. The interactions of agriculture with other coastal economic activities and ecosystems

---

> **BOX B.4**
> **Local effects of irrigation on fin-fish and shrimp farms in Indonesia**
>
> Cultivation of fin-fish and shrimps in brackish water ponds is an important earner of foreign currency in Indonesia as well as an important strategy for improving farmers' living conditions in lowland reclamation resettlement areas. The ponds are located along the coastline and supplied with fresh water from the irrigation system. However, water is supplied irregularly, according to overall availability, crop water requirements and irrigation system shutdowns for maintenance. Irregular water supplies constrain production in the ponds and hatcheries and, in addition, water supplies are frequently polluted by the return irrigation flows. Quality and quantity of production, as well as export acceptability, are adversely affected by these problems. It is estimated that, with improved freshwater supplies, a 15 to 25 percent increase in production from existing ponds could be achieved, corresponding to about 50 000 tonnes of exportable shrimps and the creation of 150 000 to 200 000 additional jobs. Without proper water management there is the risk of groundwater contamination and degradation of adjacent land from brackish water infiltration from the ponds.

chemicals. The closer the use of agrochemicals to the coastal area, the higher the risk of it having a negative impact on coastal ecosystems and the more difficult the protection of the area. Similar risks are associated with intensive livestock enterprises and agro-industry.

Soil erosion, which has many causes, increases sediment in watercourses which can silt up ports and cover coral reefs. Conversely, dams trap sediments needed to fertilize coastal areas such as swamps. Dykes and polders trap fresh water required in coastal wetlands. Poorly managed irrigation can lead to saline runoff, or the release of toxic substances that find their way to the coast.

Changes in water quality may have far-reaching effects. Increased sediments in water, for example, are damaging to coral reefs which require clear and clean water (see Boxes B.2 and B.5), but reductions in sediments are damaging to coastal wetlands dependent upon periodic recharge with imported nutrients and organic material. Toxic chemicals and organic wastes in surface water damage, and may destroy, sensitive coastal ecosystems. Downstream aquacultural enterprises may also be damaged, with fish death,

reduced productivity or contamination of produce (see Box B.4). Surface or groundwater supplies for domestic uses may also be contaminated. There may be wider health implications too; in some parts of West Africa falling salinity of previously tidal swamps has resulted in the spread of insect- and water-borne diseases.

Physical disturbance of coastal ecosystems may have other antagonistic effects that do not involve water flows. Many animal species require different habitats at different stages of their life cycle, and need to migrate between them. Disturbance or development in relatively small coastal areas may interrupt migration routes or specific breeding or nursery areas.

Secondary (socio-economic) effects. Table B.1 specifically excludes the secondary effects of agricultural development. These include increased settlement and population growth which in turn can affect the local environment. They may also threaten coastal livelihoods, increasing poverty and forcing people to overexploit the remaining resources available to them (e.g. by draining wetlands, destroying forests, overfishing).

With increasing political and economic interest in environmental protection there is growing pressure to assist farmers in avoiding the negative external effects of agricultural activities. Clearly this requires full information about these effects and, in the light of this information, appropriate planning mechanisms and interventions.

2.2.2 Potential benefits of agricultural development for the coastal environment[7]

There are a number of ways in which appropriate agricultural development can have positive impacts on coastal ecosystems. An appreciable contribution will stem merely from reversing or reducing the competitive and antagonistic effects of existing agricultural activities, for instance by the adoption of irrigation systems or crops that use less water, or crop protection methods that do not rely on persistent biocides. Higher and more sustainable productivity on existing agricultural land may reduce pressures to bring new land under cultivation.

Appropriate agricultural development can also have

97

---

[7] See Table B.2.

INTEGRATED
COASTAL AREA
MANAGEMENT
and
AGRICULTURE
FORESTRY AND
FISHERIES

PART B

INTEGRATION OF AGRICULTURE INTO COASTAL AREA MANAGEMENT

2. The interactions of agriculture with other coastal economic activities and ecosystems

---

BOX B.5
Local effects of agricultural degradation on coastal fisheries in the Philippines

The Central Visayas region in the Philippines provides a dramatic illustration of both direct antagonistic effects and secondary socio-economic effects linking agricultural intensification to coastal ecosystems and the livelihoods of rural coastal people.

"Over 300 years of Spanish settlement and rapid population growth following World War II resulted in near total deforestation of the Central Visayas and extensive corn farming on very steep slopes. The resulting erosion has stripped the slopes of their precious topsoil. Harvests and farm incomes have been steadily declining. Rapid rainfall runoff from bare slopes has increased the frequency and intensity of floods and deposited vast quantities of silt on the once productive coral reefs. Declining farm incomes have encouraged more people to turn to fishing to support their growing families. As a result, the vast coastal fishery resource once thought to be inexhaustible has come under steadily increasing pressure." (Alix, 1989). After detailing further damage to mangrove forests (as a result of overexploitation and conversion to fish ponds), corals (as a result of coral harvesting and fishing techniques that damage corals) and fish stocks (as a result of overfishing and inappropriate fisheries development programmes), Alix comments "many shallow water fishing areas have been abandoned as no longer productive.... As a result, many Philippine fishermen have joined the poorest of the poor".

positive secondary effects, for instance, providing improved livelihoods for rural people can reduce pressure on coastal fisheries and wetlands. Agricultural development may increase the general level of economic activity in a coastal area. Increased demand for agricultural inputs and services and consumption goods and services, and increased supply of food, export crops or industrial raw materials will all contribute to the local economy and stimulate growth and employment in other sectors, with positive secondary effects.

Unfortunately, while higher levels of economic activity in a coastal area can lead to improved livelihoods and reduced pressure on coastal fisheries and wetlands, and can generate wealth for investment in the protection of coastal ecosystems, all too often increasing levels of economic activity in rural coastal areas lead to increasing pollution problems without any easing of the pressure on coastal fisheries and wetlands. Similarly, higher sustainable crop yields can reduce the demand for new cultivated land, but they can also make crop production more attractive and increase the demand for agricultural land. The effects of agricultural development are thus very sensitive to the nature of development and to economic, social and political structures and circumstances. This point will be treated in more detail later in Section 3.2.2 when discussing strategies and interventions that may be used to promote appropriate agricultural development.

TABLE B.2
Potential benefits of agricultural development for coastal ecosystems

Action	Benefit
	Reduced competitive and antagonistic effects
More efficient irrigation systems	Increased water availability for other sectors
Cropping varieties and practices giving higher and/or sustainable yields on suitable land	Increased land availability for other sectors: less cultivation of steep erodable slopes and less clearing and drainage of wetlands
Less cultivation on steep slopes, controlled grazing, conservation practices, appropriate manuring methods, integrated pest management methods	Improved water quality: reduced erosion and nutrient leaching, reduced organic and chemical pollution
	Positive secondary effects
New enterprises or higher productivity leading to improved livelihoods from agriculture	Reduced exploitation and more sustainable use of fisheries and wetlands
	Increased general economic activity
Increased food supplies, demand for agricultural inputs and services, supplies of raw materials for processing, export	Increased incomes, nutrition, employment and wealth in other sectors reducing pressure on fisheries and wetlands

Note: Potential beneficial impacts are shown, but actual impacts will depend upon the nature of changes and on political, economic and social structures.

INTEGRATED
COASTAL AREA
MANAGEMENT
and
AGRICULTURE
FORESTRY AND
FISHERIES

PART B

INTEGRATION OF AGRICULTURE INTO COASTAL AREA MANAGEMENT

3. Agricultural planning in integrated coastal area management

Planning for ICAM must endeavour to cover all relevant sectors as fully as possible. However, coastal ecosystems and economic sectors are complex and often regulated by a range of separate institutions, with different expertise. This complexity makes it impractical for a single institution to carry out detailed planning for ICAM as a single exercise. Once the ICAM strategy and policy options are agreed upon, it is therefore preferable for each subsector to develop its own sectoral plan in conformity with general guidelines.[8] The ICAM parts of the various sectoral plans are then negotiated and harmonized through the coordinating institution.[9] The purpose of this section is to discuss the specific aspects of the agricultural component of ICAM planning, with particular emphasis on information gathering and analysis.

3.1 INFORMATION GATHERING AND ANALYSIS
The information gathering and analysis process should lead to the identification and understanding of:
- the biophysical environment;
- the socio-economic environment;
- governance characteristics;
- sector activities, interactions between agriculture and coastal ecosystems and other sectors;
- constraints, opportunities and possible alternatives.

Table B.3 gives an indicative list of themes to be addressed in the information collection and analysis process. Although almost all the main topic headings listed should be addressed in any agricultural plan, the level of detail required within each heading will depend upon the planning objectives and scope, and upon the features of the particular area being studied. Clearly, if the planning scope were limited to concern with livestock development, for example, the type and amount of information required on cropping activities would not be the same as for a plan focusing on food

crop development. Some information would still be required on cropping activities, however, because of the interactions with livestock production.

3.1.1 The biophysical environment
Soils and water are the chief resources for the majority of agricultural activities, and they are often in short supply in coastal areas. It is therefore essential for planners to obtain adequate information on them. Information on the physical and chemical characteristics of soils, in particular fertility and salinity levels, drainage properties and susceptibility to erosion must be available in the form of narrative reports and maps showing geographic distribution of various types of soil. A detailed topographic map is essential to identify drainage problem areas in coastal lowlands. Information on surface and groundwater resources must make it possible to establish a water balance and identify trends in the quality and quantity of water available to agriculture. Special attention must be paid to salinity levels and to the evolution of the interface between aquifers and sea water.

Apart from basic climatic information, such as precipitation, temperature, relative air humidity, wind speed and solar radiation, it is also important to collect data on storm incidence frequency and magnitude. This information is useful to estimate the feasibility of various agricultural activities and to identify alternative land uses.

Land cover and land-use information facilitates understanding, identification and quantification of the prevailing cropping patterns. However, in many coastal areas, the dominant farm size is small (1 to 3 ha) and many crops are grown in an intricate manner, thus complicating the land cover/use mapping.

Since coastal areas are often narrow strips not exceeding a width of a few kilometres, and are often very heterogeneous, the map scale (for soils, topography, and land cover/use) must be relatively large and should usually vary between 1:5 000 and 1:50 000 according to the desired level of planning detail. Smaller

99

---

[8] See Part A, Section 2.
[9] See Part A, Sections 2.3.4. and 2.4.6 and Figure A.6.

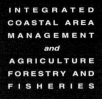

INTEGRATED
COASTAL AREA
MANAGEMENT
and
AGRICULTURE
FORESTRY AND
FISHERIES

3. Agricultural planning in integrated coastal area management

TABLE B.3

Indicative list of relevant information themes to be addressed in agricultural planning for ICAM

Main topics	Themes
Biophysical environment	Soils, topography, drainage, surface and subsurface water supplies, climate, vegetation and land use
Socio-economic environment	
Population	Population size, age and gender distribution, location, growth, migration, literacy, education, health, economic activities, income
Agricultural activities	Kinds, location, employment, natural resource use, kind and value of outputs, production methods and management practices, marketing and processing, seasonal influences, role in household, farming and wider systems
Non-agricultural activities	Range of non-agricultural economic activities, location, employment, natural resource use, output value
Infrastructure	Communications, services, markets
Governance characteristics	
Institutional and legal aspects	Local, regional and national governmental and non-governmental institutions and customary leadership structures, their goals, responsibilities, activities, membership, authority and capacity; access and rights to land and water; environmental legislation and customary laws, their observance and enforcement; labour regulations
Major stakeholders	Principal social and economic actors and representative groups, their goals and strategies
Interactions	
Impact of agriculture on other sectors	Current and anticipated negative and positive effects of agriculture on other sectors
Impact of other sectors on agriculture	Current and anticipated negative and positive effects of other sectors on agriculture
Constraints, opportunities and possible alternatives	Identification of major constraints and opportunities, identification of conflicts of interest at all levels; identification of possible courses of action and outcomes, analysis of costs and benefits to different stakeholders

scales (e.g. 1:250 000) are in most cases inadequate, even for regional coastal planning, as they do not provide enough detail on dramatic coastal features such as tidal flats, dune cordons and smaller wetlands.

It must be understood that, if adequate information on soils, water resources, land use and topography is not readily available, it may take several years and considerable amounts of money to generate. These issues should be taken into account in the work plan and the budget. Other sectors participating in ICAM may have such information, pointing to the need for harmonization in order to avoid costly duplication.

3.1.2 The socio-economic environment

The basic socio-economic information consists of detailed data on population. Current agricultural and related non-agricultural land uses, including resource use and direct and indirect outputs, must be well documented. This must also cover agricultural production and management practices and their seasonal changes. There is often considerable diversity in agriculture within an area, in terms of types and size of production unit (some may be large commercial enterprises while others may be small peasant farms), products, production methods and markets. There may be agricultural activities even in the heart of urban areas and they can also constitute an important secondary source of income and food for the urban population (see Box B.6).

3.1.3 Governance characteristics

The emphasis on wider environmental issues in agricultural development under ICAM requires particular attention to be given to the institutional and legal aspects of land and water management. This is

PART B

INTEGRATION OF AGRICULTURE INTO COASTAL AREA MANAGEMENT

INTEGRATED
COASTAL AREA
MANAGEMENT
and
AGRICULTURE
FORESTRY AND
FISHERIES

3. Agricultural planning in integrated coastal area management

why it is important to gather information on legislation, customary laws and administrative programmes relating to the environment and resource management.[10]

The extent of conflict between laws and programmes, their integration and overlap, and their effectiveness in dealing with environmental issues must be examined in the context of public attitudes towards them. It is paramount to identify the major stakeholders in agriculture and their goals and strategies in order for the planning team to involve them in plan development.[11] Stakeholders' goals and strategy will probably vary considerably according to their socio-economic category. For example, subsistence farmers, the largest agricultural group in many developing countries, have very different goals and strategies from commercial ones. Box B.7 provides an example of subsistence farmers' strategy for minimizing risk. If farmers' goals and strategies are not properly understood, planning proposals may be irrelevant or may even disrupt the fragile natural resource management systems from which farmers derive their livelihoods.

3.1.4 Interactions of agriculture with coastal ecosystems and other economic sectors

Gathering information on agricultural interactions with other sectors and the environment is a very important element in agricultural planning for ICAM. As discussed in Section 2, the positive and negative effects of agriculture and other sectors on each other involve complementary, competitive, antagonistic and secondary[12] elements that may be reciprocal or one-sided. Box B.8 gives an example of competitive interaction for land. Two major tasks are important in gathering information on interactions: identifying interactions that are significant (actually or potentially) between agricultural and other activities; and obtaining information about these interactions and the activities, institutions and people concerned.

Until appropriate ICAM structures and planning mechanisms have been set up, agricultural planners must try to identify significant interactions between agriculture and other sectors. The rural poor, particularly

---

BOX B.6
Urban agriculture and cross-sectoral linkages

Urban agriculture (e.g. garden plots, animal raising in courtyards and in the street) can be an important source of income and food for urban dwellers in sub-Saharan African cities, yet it has been largely overlooked in agricultural development activities until relatively recently (Scott, 1993). Coastal planners should avoid this error.

The neglect of urban agriculture in planning illustrates how significant issues can be ignored if they do not fit into conventional sectoral categories; planners must be imaginative and unconventional in their data gathering and in their investigation of cross-sectoral activities and interactions. In coastal areas a similar situation may arise where many households practise part-time farming, gaining a large part of their income from non-agricultural activities such as fishing. The agricultural activities of such households are easily overlooked – not only may they be classified as fishing households, for example, but it may be very difficult to determine the income gained from agriculture and the resources invested in it.

---

women, often obtain their livelihood from a variety of activities in more than one sector. They may have specific insights and be a valuable source of information on multisectoral interactions. Other potential informants on such interactions include planners, administrators, technicians, business people (in both the formal and informal sectors) and workers.

Adequate attention must also be given to institutional interactions, as there are likely to be institutions in different sectors with conflicting interests, rights and responsibilities. These may involve conflicts at local, regional, national and even international levels.

All information must be available to all stakeholders and, if necessary, help must be provided to the people affected, in order that they understand it and its implications for them.

Agricultural planners must carry out environmental impact assessments, with special emphasis on the effects of irrigation and drainage projects and of pollution induced by agricultural activities.

Box B.9 provides a checklist of issues to be addressed when investigating current and potential agricultural pollution sources that may affect coastal ecosystems, natural resources and other sectors depending on them.

101

---

[10] See Part A, Sections 1.6, 2.2.3 and 2.2.5.
[11] See Part A, Sections 2.2.2 and 2.3.4, Figure A.8 and Box A.11.
[12] See Tables B.1 and B.2 and also Part A, Section 1.5.

INTEGRATED
COASTAL AREA
MANAGEMENT
and
AGRICULTURE
FORESTRY AND
FISHERIES

3. Agricultural planning in integrated coastal area management

---

BOX B.7

Subsistence farmers' strategy to overcome soil and climate limitations in Mozambique

In the coastal district of Xai-Xai, Mozambique, subsistence farmers aim to ensure that food is available at all times. Since their storage capacity is very low, both physically (small capacity and destruction of stored produce by pests and diseases) and financially (they sell little and do not store excess production in the form of money), excess production of good years cannot be used substantially to compensate for the deficit during bad years. Farmers' main strategy to achieve food security is therefore to minimize production risks. This strategy is based on the following:

- **Genetic diversity**. Farmers grow a variety of herbaceous and tree crops. If one crop fails under given environmental circumstances, another will succeed.
- **Land-use diversity**. Farmers diversify their activities and may practise simultaneously crop production, animal husbandry, fishing, production of fermented drinks, collection of reeds in the swamps (to serve in construction), charcoal production ,etc.; if one activity fails others may compensate.
- **Environmental diversity**. Whenever possible, farmers cultivate fields that have complementary edaphic characteristics. They cultivate uplands and lowlands; if the weather is too wet, the uplands will produce and vice versa in case of drought. The Xin'tlavane, which is a narrow strip of land forming the transition between the sandy uplands (Sierra) and the wetlands, is particularly popular among farmers because it is too high to be flooded but low enough to benefit from moisture provided by the relatively shallow water-table.
- **Temporal diversity**. Farmers prefer to grow two crops – one during the cold and one during the hot season – rather than a single crop extending across both seasons, hence if weather

conditions are not favourable during one season, they may be better during the next and the chances of getting a harvest are thus increased.

- **High mobility**. Farmers shift their cropping activities from the uplands to the lowlands according to the prevailing weather (see above). This mobility is made possible by crops such as sweet potato from which the leaves can be harvested as early as two to three weeks after planting the cuttings. These leaves play a key role in food security as they allow farmers to survive until another crop can be harvested.
- **Adaptation to the environment**. Drought-resistant crops, such as pigeon pea, groundnut and cowpea, are replanted in sandy uplands. Crops resistant to waterlogging, such as rice and yams, are planted in the wetlands.
- **Adapted management.** Farmers cultivate on raised beds in the wetlands, intercrop, etc.
- **Adapted nutritional habits**. The importance of leaves in the diet is an important food security measure. Indeed, in case of drought, crops such as cowpea, sweet potato or pumpkin give little fruit/tuber, but their leaves are eaten.
- **Mutual assistance**. Farmers have various mutual assistance practices, such as *kufunana*, by which a group of farmers assist members of the community to carry out their cropping activities, against reciprocity, meals and drinks. This is a very important element in the risk-minimizing strategy because often only limited time is available to complete land preparation and sowing. For example, the heavy clay soils of the alluvial coastal plain can be ploughed (by hand tools or oxen) during a limited time period, because they change quickly from too wet and sticky to too dry and compact.

Source: adapted from Sourji *et al.*, 1995.

3.1.5 Constraints, opportunities and possible alternatives

Planners must be alert to new agricultural opportunities and constraints arising from new settlement, transport, industrial or tourist developments (Table B.4). Agricultural planners in coastal areas should try to obtain information about developments planned in other sectors and should consult them about agricultural plans. A preliminary analysis of the socio-economic and environmental context and stakeholders should allow planners to identify and select a number of potential agricultural land uses that may merge with other sectors' plans.

Thereafter, a land evaluation exercise is usually carried out to determine whether the proposed land uses are suitable in the biophysical and socio-economic context. The final outcome of the land evaluation exercise is a zoning of the coastal area into homogeneous subareas with similar opportunities and constraints for agriculture and other land uses. This information will allow the stakeholders to select the best land-use options (through negotiation and arbitration) and to resolve disagreements and conflicts of interest before the plan proposals are adopted and implemented.

It is very important to identify categories of actors (individuals, institutions, villages, enterprises) with similar interests, activities and problems. Such groups may be classified on the basis of some combination of

PART B

INTEGRATED
COASTAL AREA
MANAGEMENT
and
AGRICULTURE
FORESTRY AND
FISHERIES

INTEGRATION OF AGRICULTURE INTO COASTAL AREA MANAGEMENT

3. Agricultural planning in integrated coastal area management

> **BOX B.8**
>
> **Competition for land between agriculture and coastal wetlands**
>
> A major issue in some developing countries is the political and economic pressure to expand agricultural production and cropland areas to provide food for rapidly growing populations. The coastal wetlands in some countries (such as Indonesia) constitute a major land resource with potential for agricultural production. Drainage and reclamation of this land would be very expensive, financially. But more especially, the destruction of coastal ecosystems would affect natural habitats, biological diversity and activities dependent on these ecosystems. Experience in developing such areas for food production has often not been successful, with acid sulphate soils proving difficult to reclaim and manage productively, and particular social difficulties arising from resettlement programmes.
>
> Conflicts of this nature must be resolved at a national level, with national policies (on food and agriculture, environment, water and resettlement, for example) guiding the extent, nature and location of agricultural development in affected coastal areas. If it is decided that coastal wetlands should be drained and developed for agricultural production, reclamation works, agricultural activities and associated infrastructural and residential developments must be conducted in a way that minimizes the area reclaimed, and protects neighbouring wetlands not designated for development.

agro-ecological zoning (location with respect to the coast or a river, climate, soils, type of produce such as grain crops, sugar, dairy cows, or type of secondary activity, fishing for example) and socio-economic features (scale of activities, family farm or private company, household size, male or female household head for example). Once such a classification has been established, it should be used as a basis for further information gathering and analysis, as well as for defining the groups to participate in the planning process.

3.2 POLICY ISSUES IN COASTAL AGRICULTURAL PLANNING

3.2.1 Aims and objectives

The starting point for any planning must be an understanding and definition of the planning process and objectives. In agricultural planning in coastal areas, broader objectives should be defined with reference to national policies on economic, regional and agricultural

development. These policies should be consistent with one another, and they are likely to be pursued through national, regional and sectoral programmes. In addition, coastal agricultural plans should be consistent with these programmes. Difficulties arise when the different programmes are not consistent. Inconsistencies may not be initially apparent, and reassessment of planning objectives may be needed when the planning process is quite advanced. Planning objectives will also be determined by the political, institutional and administrative support for the planning exercise.

Coastal ecosystems are often fragile and can be irreversibly damaged. In application of the precautionary principle,[13] measures to avoid possible detrimental effects of agricultural development on coastal ecosystems should feature strongly in coastal area agricultural development plans. Agricultural plans must include objectives on the efficient use of land and water, the appropriation of new land for agriculture, and the maintenance (or restoration) of the water flows and stocks and water quality necessary to support coastal ecosystems, as well as on the use of agrochemicals and many other factors.

These objectives must be reflected throughout the plan in: the description of the situation and agricultural problems and opportunities; the choice of ICAM strategy in the specification of development targets, government interventions and resource requirements; and cost-benefit analysis. It is equally important that these objectives be maintained and made operational throughout plan monitoring and implementation; many of the damaging effects of development activities can be reduced if all activities are carried out in a way that is sensitive to coastal ecosystems.

Plans being formulated in the context of ICAM will often contain some elements that may not be found in more conventional agricultural development plans. Table B.5 summarizes the elements that are necessary to ensure that the plans take a broader account of agriculture's position within, and contribution to, the wider coastal economy and environment. Box B.10 suggests means of designing and implementing improvements in agricultural development activities affecting coastal ecosystems.

103

[13] See Part A, Section 1.6.3 and Box A.5.

INTEGRATED
COASTAL AREA
MANAGEMENT
and
AGRICULTURE
FORESTRY AND
FISHERIES

3. Agricultural planning in integrated coastal area management

---

BOX B.9

Information required on agricultural nutrients and pollutants entering river, groundwater and marine systems

Nutrient and pollutant losses from diffuse sources (e.g. cultivated plots):

- appropriate fertilizer (especially nitrogen and phosphorus), solid/liquid manure and biocide types and application rates, for crops and pastures in relation to soil type and/or other environmental characteristics;
- historical data on actual fertilizer, manure and biocide application methods, calendars and quantities from farmers, extension services and suppliers (sales figures and their trends);
- soil fixation levels (including heavy metals), export mechanisms (e.g. surface wash by runoff and/or irrigation water, water percolation, topsoil erosion) and quantification of nutrient and pollutant fluxes from diffuse sources.

Nutrient and pollutant losses from point sources (e.g. dairies, feedlots, processing plants):

- location, type and number of animals raised, waste treatment,

transport and disposal, places and methods of all intensive animal production units;

- location, type and quantity of agricultural produce processed, waste treatment, places and methods of transport and disposal of all agro-industrial processing plants;
- export mechanisms and quantification of nutrient and pollutant fluxes from point sources;
- appropriate waste treatment and disposal methods.

Agricultural sources of sediment load in surface water systems:

- prevailing erosion types and mechanisms in relation to seasonal weather and vegetation cover conditions;
- location and extent of agricultural lands that are affected by each type of erosion process;
- quantification of sediment removal from agricultural lands;
- current and most appropriate soil conservation methods.

TABLE B.4

Potential opportunities and constraints to coastal agriculture

	Opportunities	Constraints
Settlement	Increased labour supply and demand for agricultural produce	Competition for land and water; disturbance of adjacent activities
Road, port and airport construction	Access to new land and produce markets; increased demand for agricultural produce; access to input and labour markets	Loss of land; disruption of surface and subsurface water flows; competition for land, water, labour and other resources as other activities move into the area; easier encroachment on fragile forest and coastal ecosystems; increased competition from imported produce
Rural electrification	Employment; local processing; local service industries; expanded range of technological options; area more attractive to skilled staff	Development of non-agricultural enterprises competing for resources
Industrial development	Employment; infrastructural development; increased demand for food and agricultural raw materials	Competition for land, labour, water and capital; air and water pollution
Rising sea levels		Increased flooding bringing physical damage and soil erosion; permanent loss of land to coastal defences, shoreline retreat and relocation of other activities; salt water intrusion into aquifers
Fisheries development	Employment; improved protein supplies	Competition for land, labour and capital; competition with meat products
Aquaculture	Employment; improved protein supplies	Competition for land, labour and capital; seepage of saline water; water pollution
Tourism development	Employment; markets for agricultural produce; infrastructural development	Competition for labour, land water and capital; increased imports of foods and beverages
Forestry development	Employment; improved supply of fuelwood and building materials; reduced erosion and runoff	Competition for labour, land and capital; restricted grazing

PART B

INTEGRATION OF AGRICULTURE INTO COASTAL AREA MANAGEMENT

INTEGRATED
COASTAL AREA
MANAGEMENT
and
AGRICULTURE
FORESTRY AND
FISHERIES

3. Agricultural planning in integrated coastal area management

3.2.2 Interventions and strategic issues

Changes in the external effects of agriculture can be achieved by a change in agricultural activities or by a change in practices (or technology) for existing activities. Which of these is more appropriate will depend upon local circumstances: the availability of alternative and more desirable activities and technologies; the short- and long-term inputs and outputs associated with them; and the way they fit into local production, economic and cultural systems. For example, where slash and burn methods are being used to produce food crops on marginal land, it is unlikely that alternative crops would be accepted by farmers, but less damaging methods of land clearance, cultivation and regeneration in the production of the existing crops might well be. On the other hand, protection of coastal wetlands from encroachment by agricultural cropping activities, will probably best be achieved by placing limits on these activities.

Voluntary, regulatory and incentive approaches may be used to encourage desired changes in activities or practices.[14] These approaches may involve subsidies, the provision of services, taxation, regulation and institutional development.

Subsidies. Governments have commonly used subsidies to promote particular development strategies. They have commonly been applied to reduce the cost of farm inputs, to raise farm produce prices or to encourage domestic or export demand. Chemical inputs and machinery, for example, have often been subsidized in order to increase production, and withdrawal of a subsidy can be positive, resulting in a fall in use and abuse of harmful agrochemicals. Subsidies may also be applied through the provision of services (see below). Exchange rate controls can act as a subsidy when they distort the prices of imports and exports: an overvalued domestic currency has the effect of "taxing" exports and "subsidizing" imports. Many subsidies in the agriculture sector are decided at the national policy level and they may not be appropriate in coastal area agricultural development plans. Zone-specific subsidies,

105

TABLE B.5

Some elements required in agricultural development plans in the context of ICAM

Plan sections	Elements considered in ICAM plans
Objectives	Sustainable agricultural development Sustainable development of other sectors Protection of coastal resources Social equity
Current situation	Agricultural activities, resources, opportunities and constraint Interactions and trade-offs with other sectors
Development strategies and interventions	Increased agricultural productivity through improved resource use and management Encouragement of efficient and sustainable resource use through the provision of advisory services and appropriate regulation of resource usage within the agriculture sector and between sectors Limitation of negative externalities and promotion of synergistic effects
Development targets	Increased agricultural output while reducing input and resource use Respect for environmental standards, including water flows and quality Maintenance of coastal ecosystems
Government activities	Actions in the agriculture sector Actions in other sectors
Resource requirements	Finance, land, labour force and materials from individuals and private and government organizations in the agriculture and other sectors
Analysis of costs and benefits[15]	Financial and environmental cost-benefit analysis in the agriculture sector Valuation of natural resource stocks and usage Valuation of externalities affecting other sectors
Monitoring and evaluation procedures	Standards and agencies of the agriculture and other sectors

---

[14] See Part A, Box A.26 and Table A.5.

[15] See Part A, Boxes A.22, A.23 and A.24.

INTEGRATED
COASTAL AREA
MANAGEMENT
and
AGRICULTURE
FORESTRY AND
FISHERIES

3. Agricultural planning in integrated coastal area management

---

BOX B.10
Actions to improve agricultural development affecting coastal ecosystems

Agriculture:
- plan upland farm layouts to respect natural drainage patterns;
- encourage sustainable intensification of agriculture on suitable land to reduce pressures on unsuitable dry lands and coastal wetlands;
- in important coastal wetland habitats, only promote crops that are compatible with wetlands, such as taro or rice;
- whenever possible, avoid reclamation of important coastal habitat areas for agricultural development;
- implement soil and water conservation practices to control cropland erosion and surface water runoff;
- utilize fertilizers and pesticides in a manner that will minimize their loss and transport towards coastal areas;
- whenever feasible, promote organic fertilizers, biological pest control and non-persistent biocides.

Feedlots, ranching and range management:
- control livestock population levels on rangelands to avoid denuding the land, soil erosion and sedimentation;
- require replanting and other erosion control measures on rangeland/ranchlands;
- impose stringent pollution control practices and standards on feedlots and other concentrated livestock operations;
- encourage integrated livestock, mixed farming and tree crop systems.

Water development and control:
- regulate groundwater withdrawal to prevent saltwater intrusion, land subsidence and de-watering of bodies of surface water;
- utilize non-structural solutions for flood damage control (flood-proofing, raising structures, setback from flooding zone) to the maximum extent possible;
- design all diversions, dams and impoundment to preserve the existing water quality volume and rate of flow for marshes, estuaries, deltas, etc.;
- design water diversions to accommodate the seasonal migrations of aquatic fauna up- and downstream;
- ensure adequate treatment and disposal of wastes.

Source: modified from Moragos *et al.,* 1983.

106

on the other hand, may be useful. To take one example, irrigation equipment that allows more efficient use of water and less disruption to water flows in a coastal area might be promoted through subsidizing the development, manufacture or import of the equipment, its purchase or installation price, or credit for its purchase and installation. Many subsidy systems can

work against sustainable integrated agricultural development; subsidies that encourage inappropriate land clearance, chemical inputs and drainage and irrigation systems, for example, are common. Subsidy programmes that have such effects should be reviewed.

Provision of services. Agricultural development plans may provide for research, extension, credit, marketing and adequate infrastructure to develop and promote particular activities and technologies. In coastal areas such services may be used to encourage farmers to adopt better soil conservation practices or to use energy sources that do not deplete natural forests. Infrastructure such as roads or irrigation systems may be developed and managed in ways that are intended to minimize damage to soils and water courses. Agro-industrial research may look for ways of reducing effluents from processing plants. Services that are provided to encourage changes in activities and practices in the agriculture (or any other) sector will usually be effective only if users of the services perceive the changes to be in their interests. Recommended practices resulting from research and extension activities must be relevant to farmers' objectives, farming systems and the broader economic and social environment. This in turn calls for the involvement of farmers[16] in setting research objectives and in the design, conduct and evaluation of research activities.

Taxation. Taxes are not commonly prescribed by agricultural development plans; as are subsidies, taxes are more commonly applied at national and regional levels. Their introduction can have far-reaching implications on an economy, and there may be practical, legal and institutional difficulties associated with tax collection.

Regulation. Another approach to limiting the negative external effects of agricultural activities is to control and discourage less desirable activities and practices, through regulation of resource use, activities, practices and products. Regulations may be introduced in a number of ways. Fundamental issues concern what

---

[16] See Part A, Section 2.3.5.

3. Agricultural planning in integrated coastal area management

should be regulated, what form regulations should take, and who should be responsible for their design and enforcement. These issues are closely related and must be considered together.

What should be regulated? Regulations may address use of resources for undesirable activities and practices, the outputs from such activities or their negative effects. Controls may also be imposed directly on activities and practices. If agricultural activities are upsetting water flows to coastal ecosystems, for example, controls on water use or on particularly wasteful irrigation practices or equipment might be appropriate. Blanket controls on irrigation, however, might prevent the introduction of more efficient irrigation systems.

What form of regulations should be introduced? Land-use planning and zoning[17] is a fundamental type of regulation. It may be applied to agricultural activities with or without wider land-use plans for a coastal area as a whole. As applied to agricultural activities, land-use plans may, for example, regulate or prohibit cultivation on steep slopes, near water courses or in coastal wetlands and mangrove swamps. They may require or prohibit irrigation or certain cultivation methods or rotations on different soil types or locations, or set limits on the location of intensive livestock units and agro-industry.

Who should be responsible for regulation? Self-regulation through existing user/producer groups and traditional mechanisms and institutions for managing common property resources is the most effective means of applying regulations, provided that the farmers agree with the objectives.

Institutional development. Taking a definition of institutions as "sets of relationships and rules regarding people's rights and responsibilities", institutional development will often be needed for the effective implementation of subsidies, services, taxation and regulation.[18] Particular attention will need to be paid to water rights and to organizational development and coordination.

Water rights. In view of the importance of competition for water in coastal areas, the establishment of appropriate water rights is often of critical importance to agricultural development in coastal areas. Ideally, water rights should be transferable, enforceable, secure and priced to reflect the full social costs of water use (including all economic and environmental costs to society over time). This normally requires that the state owns all water supplies and then grants rights of use to individuals and organizations. Rights may be granted on the basis of previous use or by permits; they may be transferable; and they may be restricted in terms of type of water use permitted, volume allowed or volume to be left in the water supply system. The time period for which rights are held may also vary. Rights may be granted to individual users through water user groups.

Charges for water may be used to encourage more efficient use. Pricing systems may use a flat rate charge or base the charge on some estimate of water use, such as irrigated crop area. Pricing systems that offer users incentives to practise water conservation are not easy to devise.

Organizational development. Integration and coordination of organizations between different sectors is particularly important with regard to water use and land-use planning. Attention has to be given to coordination between organizations working in the agriculture sector, and to the development of local organizations such as farmers' organizations, cooperatives, water user groups or catchment planning groups. Difficulties in coordinating the activities of different government agricultural departments and agencies (research, extension and veterinary services, for example) are well known in integrated agricultural and rural development projects. Effective coordination is particularly important in coastal agricultural development, and structures and mechanisms must be established to encourage it. This may require the pooling of some resources, the division of some responsibilities between organizations and, where no one organization has particular responsibility for a specific issue, the assignment of new responsibilities. Changing responsibilities may require extensive negotiation between organizations and training and reorientation of some staff.

107

---

[17] See Part A, Section 2.2.5.
[18] See Part A, Section 2.3.5 and Box A.21.

INTEGRATED
COASTAL AREA
MANAGEMENT
and
AGRICULTURE
FORESTRY AND
FISHERIES

3. Agricultural planning in integrated coastal area management

Interventions such as those described above will be effective only if the people involved have the means and the will to make the required changes. Where peasant agriculture is being marginalized and the population dependent on agriculture is increasing, farmers often have no choice but to use whatever resources are available (land, fisheries or wetlands) in whatever way they can to obtain a livelihood. It is then difficult, politically and practically, to enforce regulations, collect taxes or even provide subsidies and services. The only way to reduce the negative impact of agricultural activities is to develop alternative and better livelihoods, either outside agriculture or within the agriculture sector, but with practices that are more productive and less damaging.

Improving the productivity of agricultural activities in favourable areas and developing alternative areas that are suitable for agricultural production are therefore potential strategies to reduce or limit crop production activities that are harmful to coastal areas. In the case of rice production, theoretically the production of upland rice through slash and burn cultivation may be limited if rice yields are increased in irrigated areas, with increased market supplies and lower rice prices. Similarly, the development of inland valley cultivation of rice may provide marginalized farmers with better rice growing opportunities and reduce the need for them to open new land with slash and burn techniques. However, these approaches require marketing and institutional systems that link increases in rice production to lower prices and allow marginalized farmers access to productive land. To be successful, such strategies may require reform of rural policies and institutions (as discussed earlier), including changes in land tenure systems, to give individual farmers and communities more incentives and capacities to invest in sustainable agricultural practices and enterprises. In practice, effective agrarian reform benefiting the poor is very much the exception.

Two fundamental considerations must be addressed in choosing strategies for ICAM in agricultural development planning:

- all interventions must be supported by appropriate institutional and legal frameworks governing the allocation and use of land and water. Lack of security of land tenure profoundly affects farmers' willingness to invest in land improvements, soil conservation and perennial crops, and open access to grazing and forest land encourages overexploitation and degradation;[19]

- the internal factors that cause negative external effects from agriculture must be addressed; for example, problems of poverty or lack of access to resources. A danger with this approach is that the external linkages may then be forgotten.

108

---

[19] See Part A, Box A.2.

PART B

INTEGRATION OF AGRICULTURE INTO COASTAL AREA MANAGEMENT

INTEGRATED
COASTAL AREA
MANAGEMENT
and
AGRICULTURE
FORESTRY AND
FISHERIES

4. Conclusions

Irrespective of the adoption of direct or indirect strategies to address the negative external effects of agricultural activities, all coastal area agricultural development plans should include standards and criteria related to the effects of agricultural activities on soil and water, for example, and should contain targets for reducing negative externalities. These standards and targets have to be backed up by monitoring, reporting and evaluation systems and by staff training to ensure that the control of negative externalities is given due emphasis throughout the planning, implementation and review process. Conversely, in the context of ICAM, agriculture is entitled to reciprocal protection against the negative impact on it of the activities of other sectors.

ICAM requires the coordinated allocation of resources to different activities to maximize their contribution to sustainable development. Decisions about individual activities must take account of both their direct costs and benefits and their effects on other activities.

Planning for the integrated management of a particular coastal area therefore requires:

- systematic examination and understanding of the existing and potential interactions that affect different activities and resources in the area, and analysis of how these interactions are likely to develop over time;
- analysis of the effects of interactions on different activities and on the coastal area as a whole;
- identification of ways of encouraging benefits from complementary interactions and ways of limiting the harmful effects of competitive and antagonistic interactions;
- identification of the costs and benefits of activities that take into account their beneficial and harmful effects on other activities;
- negotiation, arbitration and legislation to encourage a mix of activities that will promote sustainable development in the coastal area as a whole.

This integration must be additional to, and coordinated with, existing sectoral and subsectoral planning.

109

INTEGRATED
COASTAL AREA
MANAGEMENT
and
AGRICULTURE
FORESTRY AND
FISHERIES

PART

C

INTEGRATION OF FORESTRY INTO COASTAL AREA MANAGEMENT

INTEGRATED
COASTAL AREA
MANAGEMENT
and
AGRICULTURE
FORESTRY AND
FISHERIES

PART C

INTEGRATION OF FORESTRY INTO COASTAL AREA MANAGEMENT

INTEGRATED
COASTAL AREA
MANAGEMENT
and
AGRICULTURE
FORESTRY AND
FISHERIES

Executive summary

Forest resources (including wildlife) are substantially different from agricultural or fishery resources, and information, policy and management requirements concerning them are therefore also different from those described in Part B (agriculture) and Part D (fisheries) of these guidelines. Furthermore, forest resources in coastal areas are frequently so different from their inland counterparts as to require different and special approaches to management and conservation. Mangroves and tidal forests for example have no parallels in terrestrial uplands.

Special features of the coastal forestry sector include the following:

- coastal forests comprise a large number of diverse natural and human-created ecosystems;
- there are important links between coastal forests and other terrestrial and marine coastal ecosystems;
- coastal forest ecosystems provide a large number of unpriced services;
- the value of untraded forest products, social use values and indirect use values (environmental services) often far exceeds the value of traded forest products; consequently, option and existence values of coastal forests are likely to be high, although these values are often neglected in land-use and forest management decisions;
- a lack of awareness of the total benefits provided by coastal forests and policy and management decisions are dominated by their direct economic value alone;
- large natural and human-incurred factors threaten the existence of many remaining natural coastal forests and, coupled with a pervading uncertainty, make the management of these forests a complex task;
- a long time-frame is needed in forest planning and management;
- certain forest-related actions are irreversible;
- nost coastal forests are owned by the state, but there is often de facto open access;
- a large number of institutions have jurisdiction over parts of the coastal forest resources;

These issues have important implications for land-use planning and for the management of coastal forests. Recommended actions include:

- sound and clear criteria, based on environmental suitability and on socio-cultural and economic valuation of direct and indirect benefits provided by different uses, must be employed in land-use classification and allocation;
- an integrated, area-based approach must be taken to the planning and management of coastal forest ecosystems, and coordinated between agencies;
- multipurpose management must be introduced for individual forests;
- a precautionary approach to coastal forest management must be employed and strategies and plans must be flexible and must build on local knowledge and expertise;
- responsibility for forest management must be devolved upon local institutions and the capability of these to manage forests for multiple purposes must be strengthened; where traditional forest management systems exist, they should be reinforced;
- public participation should be encouraged in all aspects of coastal forest management planning and implementation;
- research is needed on the interdependence of coastal forests and other coastal ecosystems and on the quantification and mitigation of negative impacts between sectors;
- inappropriate subsidies and other policies adversely affecting the coastal forestry sector should be removed;
- legislation on conservation and development of natural resources in coastal areas should be framed, revised or amended in line with agreed integrated management policies;

The information requirements for policy and planning purposes are outlined and policy instruments that can be used to implement the forestry component of the agreed ICAM strategy are described.

113

PART C

INTEGRATION OF FORESTRY INTO COASTAL AREA MANAGEMENT

INTEGRATED
COASTAL AREA
MANAGEMENT
and
AGRICULTURE
FORESTRY AND
FISHERIES

1. Forests and forestry activities in coastal areas

Forests are defined by the FAO Forestry Department as "all vegetation formations with a minimum of 10 percent crown cover of trees and/or bamboo with a minimum height of 5 m and generally associated with wild flora, fauna and natural soil conditions". In many countries, coastal areas such as beaches, dunes, swamps and wildlands – even when they are not covered with trees – are officially designated as "forested" lands and thus fall under the management responsibility of the Forestry Department or similar agency.

Forest resources (including wildlife) of coastal areas are frequently so different from their inland counterparts as to require different and special forms of management and conservation approaches. Mangroves and tidal forests for example have no parallels in terrestrial uplands. As a result, the information, policy and management requirements concerning integrated coastal area management (ICAM) for forestry are also different.

1.1 COASTAL FOREST ECOSYSTEMS

In each of the climatic regions of the world, inland forests and woodlands may extend to the sea and thus form part of the coastal area. In addition to such formations, controlled by climatic factors, special forest communities, primarily controlled by edaphic factors and an extreme water regime, are found in coastal areas and along inland rivers. Such forest communities include: mangroves, beach forests, peat swamps, periodic swamps (tidal and flood plain forests), permanent freshwater swamps and riparian forests. Of these, the first three types are confined to the coastal area, whereas the remaining types can also be found further inland.

1.1.1 Mangroves

Mangroves are the most typical forest formations of sheltered coastlines in the tropics and subtropics. They consist of trees and bushes growing below the high water level of spring tides. Their root systems are regularly inundated with saline water, although it may be diluted by freshwater surface runoff. The term "mangrove" is applied to both the ecosystem as such and to individual trees and shrubs.

Precise data on global mangrove resources are scarce. Estimates are that there are some 16 million ha of mangrove forests worldwide (FAO, 1994a). The general distribution of mangroves corresponds to that of tropical forests, but extends further north and south of the equator, sometimes beyond the tropics, although in a reduced form, for instance in warm temperate climates in South Africa and New Zealand to the south and in Japan to the north.

Mangrove forests are characterized by a very low floristic diversity compared with most inland forests in the tropics. This is because few plants can tolerate and flourish in saline mud and withstand frequent inundation by sea water.

There are two distinct biogeographic zones of mangroves in the world: those of West Africa, the Caribbean and America; and those on the east coast of Africa, Madagascar and the Indo-Pacific region. While the first contain only ten tree species, mangroves of the Indo-Pacific are richer, containing some 40 tree species (excluding palms).

Most of the animal species found in mangroves also occur in other environments, such as beaches, rivers, freshwater swamps or in other forest formations near water. On the whole, animal species strictly confined to mangroves are very few (crabs have a maximum number of species in mangroves). In many countries however, the mangroves represent the last refuge for a number of rare and endangered animals such as the proboscis monkey (*Nasalis larvatus*) in Borneo, the royal Bengal tiger (*Panthera tigris*) and the spotted deer (*Axix axis*) in the Sundarbans mangroves in the Bay of Bengal, manatees (*Trichechus* spp.) and dugongs (*Dugong dugon*). Mangroves are also an ideal sanctuary for birds, some of which are migratory. According to Saenger *et al.* (1983), the total list of mangrove bird species in each of the main biogeographical regions include from 150 to 250 species. Worldwide, 65 of these

115

INTEGRATED
COASTAL AREA
MANAGEMENT
and
AGRICULTURE
FORESTRY AND
FISHERIES

PART C

INTEGRATION OF FORESTRY INTO COASTAL AREA MANAGEMENT

1. Forests and forestry activities in coastal areas

are listed as endangered or vulnerable, including for instance the milky stork (*Mycteria cinerea*), which lives in the rivers of mangroves.

1.1.2 Beach forests

This type of forest is in general found above the high-tide mark on sandy soil and may merge into agricultural land or upland forest.

Sand dune and beach vegetations are mostly scrub-like with a high presence of stunted tree growths. These coastal forest ecosystems are adapted to growing conditions that are often difficult as a result of edaphic[1] or climatic extremes (strong winds, salinity, lack or excess of humidity). They are very sensitive to modifications of the ecosystem. A slight change in the groundwater level for example might eliminate the existing scrub vegetation. Sand dune and beach vegetations have an important role in land stabilization and thus prevent the silting up of coastal lagoons and rivers, as well as protecting human settlements further inland from moving sand dunes.

The dominant animal species on the adjacent beaches are crabs and molluscs. The beaches are also very important as breeding sites for sea turtles and, therefore, attract predators of turtles' eggs, such as monitor lizards (*Varanus* sp.).

1.1.3 Peat swamp forests

This is a forest formation defined more on its special habitat than on structure and physiognomy. Peat swamp forests are particularly extensive in parts of Sumatra, Malaysia, Borneo and New Guinea, where they were formed as the sea level rose at the end of the last glacial period about 18 000 years ago. Domed peat swamps can be up to 20 km long and the peat may reach 13 m in thickness in the most developed domes. Animals found in peat swamps include leaf-eating monkeys such as the proboscis monkey and the langurs found in Borneo.

1.1.4 Periodic swamps

As with peat swamp forests, these are defined mainly by habitat and contain a diverse assemblage of forest

types periodically flooded by river water (daily, monthly or seasonally). Periodic swamps can be further subdivided into tidal and flood plain forests.

Tidal forests are found on somewhat higher elevations than mangroves (although the term is sometimes used to describe mangroves as well). Such forests are influenced by the tidal movements and may be flooded by fresh or slightly brackish water twice a day. Tidal amplitude varies from place to place. Where the amplitude is high, the area subject to periodic tidal flushing is large and usually gives rise to a wide range of ecological sites. The natural vegetation in tidal forests is more diverse than that of mangroves, although still not as diverse as that of dense inland forests.

Flood plains are areas seasonally flooded by fresh water, as a result of rainwater rather than tidal movements. Forests are the natural vegetation cover of riverine flood plains, except where a permanent high water-table prevents tree growth.

The Amazon, which has annual floods but which is also influenced by tides to some 600 km inland, has very extensive permanent and periodic swamp forests. The alluvial plains of Asia once carried extensive periodic swamp forests, but few now remain as these have mostly been cleared for wetland rice cultivation. The Zaire basin is about one-third occupied by periodic swamp forests, many disturbed by human interventions, and little-studied (Whitmore, 1990).

Throughout the world, flood plains are recognized as being among the most productive ecosystems with abundant and species-rich wildlife.

1.1.5 Freshwater swamp forests

The term is here used for permanent freshwater swamp forests. As opposed to periodic swamps, the forest floor of these is constantly wet and, in contrast to peat swamps, this forest type is characterized by its eutrophic (organomineral) richer plant species and fairly high pH (6.0 or more) (Whitmore, 1990).

1.1.6 Riparian forests

Also called riverine or gallery forests. These are found adjacent to or near rivers. In the tropics, riparian forests are characterized as being extremely dense and productive, and have large numbers of climbing plants.

[1] See Glossary.

INTEGRATED
COASTAL AREA
MANAGEMENT
and
AGRICULTURE
FORESTRY AND
FISHERIES

PART C

INTEGRATION OF FORESTRY INTO COASTAL AREA MANAGEMENT

1. Forests and forestry activities in coastal areas

TABLE C.1
Values related to coastal forests

Use values	Use values	Use values	Non-use values
Direct uses	**Indirect uses**	**Option values**	**Existence and bequest values**
Timber	Nutrient cycling (including detritus for aquatic food web)	Premium to preserve future direct and indirect uses (e.g. future drugs, genes for plant breeding, new technology complement)	Forests as objects of intrinsic value, or as a responsibility (stewardship)
Non-timber forest products (including fish and shellfish)	Watershed protection		Endangered species
Recreation	Coastal protection		Charismatic species
Nature tourism	Air and water pollution reduction		Threatened or rare habitats/ ecosystems
Genetic resources	Microclimate function		Cherished landscapes
Education and research	Carbon store		Cultural heritage
Human habitat	Wildlife habitat (including birds and aquatic species)		

Source: adapted from Pearce, 1991.

In addition to their aesthetic and recreational values, riparian forests are important in preserving water quality and controlling erosion and as wildlife refuges especially for amphibians and reptiles, beavers, otters and hippopotamus. Monkeys and other tree-dwelling mammals and birds are often abundant in riparian forests.

1.1.7 Other coastal forest ecosystems

Other coastal forest ecosystems include: savannah woodlands, dry forests, lowland rain forests, temperate and boreal forests and forest plantations. Many of the natural coastal forests are under severe threat. Most of the lowland rain forests have vanished as a result of the ease with which commercial trees, standing on slopes facing the sea or other accessible coastal waters, could be harvested merely by cutting them down and letting them fall into the nearby water. As a consequence, most coastal dry forests and savannah woodlands have been seriously degraded by overexploitation for fuelwood and construction poles, and conversion to agriculture or to grazing lands through the practice of repeated burning.

Coastal plantations have often been established for both production and protection purposes. As an example of the latter, coastal plantations were established in Denmark as far back as the 1830s to stabilize sand dunes

which were moving inland and which had already covered several villages.

1.2 THE SOCIO-ECONOMIC IMPORTANCE OF COASTAL FORESTS

The total economic value of coastal forests stems from use values (direct uses, indirect uses and option values) and non-use values (existence and bequest values).[2] Table C.1 gives examples of the different values as related to coastal forests. Table C.4 gives examples of valuation approaches applicable to the various types of forest products or services.

Direct use values, in particular the commercial value of timber and other forest products, often dominate land-use decisions. The wider social and environmental values are often neglected, partly as a result of the difficulty in obtaining an objective estimate of these, even though in many cases these values exceed the value of traded and untraded forest products.

Indirect use values correspond to "ecological functions" and are at times referred to as environmental services. Some of these occur off-site, i.e. they are economic externalities and are therefore likely to be ignored when forest management decisions are made.

_____
[2] For a description of these concepts, see Part A, Box A.24.

INTEGRATED
COASTAL AREA
MANAGEMENT
and
AGRICULTURE
FORESTRY AND
FISHERIES

PART C

INTEGRATION OF FORESTRY INTO COASTAL AREA MANAGEMENT

1. Forests and forestry activities in coastal areas

The option existence and bequest values are typically high for coastal forests – especially for tropical rain forests or forests containing endangered or charismatic animal species.

1.2.1 Direct use values of coastal forests

In addition to the activities carried out within the coastal forests (see below), small- and large-scale forest industries are also often found in coastal areas, taking advantage of the supply of raw materials and the ease of transport by waterways and roads, the existence of ports for export, etc. In addition to sawmills and pulp and paper mills, these forest industries may include veneer and particle board factories, charcoal kilns (particularly near mangrove areas), furniture makers and commercial handicraft producers.

There is little information available on the value of marketed goods from coastal forests. In general, their contribution to national gross domestic product (GDP) is small and this fact may lead to their being neglected. Commercial wood production from coastal forests ranges from timber, poles and posts to fuelwood, charcoal and tannin. Non-wood products include thatch, fruits, nuts, honey, wildlife, fish, fodder and medicinal plants. A list of forest-based products obtainable from mangroves is shown in Box C.1.

Accounts of government forest revenues are often a poor indication of the value of the forest products. As an example, in 1982/83, in the Sundarbans mangroves of Bangladesh, some of the royalties collected by the forestry department were exceedingly low: for sundri (*Heritiera fomes*) fuelwood for instance, the market rate was nearly 40 times the royalty rate; and for shrimps the minimum market rate to royalty rate ratio at the time was 136:1 (FAO, 1994a).

Frequently, the value of untraded production (e.g. traditional fishing, hunting and gathering) in mangrove forest areas is substantial, the value often exceeding that from cultivated crops and from formal-sector wage income (Ruitenbeek, 1992).

Other direct use values of the coastal forests include their social functions. Coastal forests provide habitat, subsistence and livelihood, to forest dwellers, thereby supplying the means to hold these communities together, as well as opportunities for education, scientific research, recreation and tourism. Worldwide, the lives of millions of people are closely tied to productive flood

118

BOX C.1
Products obtainable from mangroves

A. Mangrove forest products

Fuel

Fuelwood
Charcoal

Construction

Timber, scaffolds
Heavy construction
Railway sleepers
Mining props
Boat building
Dock pilings
Beams and poles
Flooring, panelling
Thatch or matting
Fence posts, chipboards

Fishing

Fishing stakes
Fishing boats
Wood for smoking fish
Tannin for net/lines
Fish attraction devices

Textile, leather

Synthetic fibres (rayon)
Dye for cloth

Agriculture

Fodder

Paper products

Paper - various

Food, drugs and beverages

Sugar
Alcohol
Cooking oil
Vinegar
Tea substitute
Fermented drinks
Dessert topping
Condiments (barks)
Sweetmeats (propagules)
Vegetables (fruit/leaves)

Household items

Glue
Hairdressing oil
Tool handles
Rice mortar
Toys
Match sticks
Incense

Other products

Tannin to preserve leather and tobacco
Medicines
Packing boxes
Wood for smoking sheet rubber
Fuelwood for salt making, brick making and bakeries

B. Other natural products

Fish/Crustaceans
Honey
Wax
Birds
Mammals
Reptiles
Other fauna

Source: adapted from FAO, 1984a.

PART C

INTEGRATION OF FORESTRY INTO COASTAL AREA MANAGEMENT

INTEGRATED
COASTAL AREA
MANAGEMENT
and
AGRICULTURE
FORESTRY AND
FISHERIES

1. Forests and forestry activities in coastal areas

plains, the associated periodic river floods and subsequent recessions. The socio-economic importance of these areas is especially evident in the more arid regions of the developing world. The seasonal ebb and flood of river waters determines the lifestyles and agricultural practices of the rural communities depending on these ecosystems.

Examples of the educational value of coastal forests are found in peninsular Malaysia, where more than 7 000 schoolchildren annually visit the Kuala Selangor Nature Park, a mangrove area with boardwalk, education centre, etc. (MNS, 1991). In nearby Kuantan, along the Selangor river, a main tourist attraction are evening cruises on the river to watch the display of fireflies and, along the Kinabatangan river in Sabah, cruises are undertaken to watch the proboscis monkeys as they settle in for the night in the riparian forest.

In terms of employment opportunities in coastal forests, ESCAP (1987) estimated the probable direct employment offered by the Sundarbans mangrove forest in Bangladesh to be in the range of 500 000 to 600 000 people for at least half of the year, added to which the direct industrial employment generated through the exploitation of the forest resources alone equalled around 10 000 jobs.

1.2.2 Indirect use values of coastal forests

A prominent environmental role of mangroves, tidal, flood plain and riparian forests is the production of leaf litter and detrital matter which is exported to lagoons and the near-shore coastal environment, where it enters the marine food web. Mangroves and flood plains in particular are highly productive ecosystems and the importance of mangrove areas as feeding, breeding and nursery grounds for numerous commercial fish and shellfish (including most commercial tropical shrimps) is well established (Heald and Odum, 1970; MacNae, 1974; Martosubroto and Naamin, 1977). Since many of these fish and shellfish are caught offshore, the value is not normally attributed to mangroves. However, over 30 percent of the fisheries of peninsular Malaysia (about 200 000 tonnes) are reported to have some association with the mangrove ecosystem. Coastal forests also provide a valuable physical habitat for a variety of wildlife species, many of them endangered.[3]

---

[3] See Section 1.1.

Shoreline forests are recognized as a buffer against the actions of wind, waves and water currents. In Viet Nam, mangroves are planted in front of dykes situated along rivers, estuaries and lagoons under tidal influence, as a protection measure (Løyche, 1991). Where mangroves have been removed, expensive coastal defences may be needed to protect the agricultural resource base. In arid zones, sand dune fixation is an important function of coastal forests, benefiting agricultural and residential hinterland.

In addition, mangrove forests act as a sediment trap for upland runoff sediments, thus protecting sea grass beds, near-shore reefs and shipping lanes from siltation, and reducing water turbidity. They also function as nutrient sinks and filter some types of pollutants.

1.2.3 Option value of coastal forests

The option value of coastal forests – the premium people would be prepared to pay to preserve an area for future use by themselves and/or by others, including future generations – may be expected to be positive in the case of most forests and other natural ecosystems where the future demand is certain and the supply, in many cases, is not.

An example of how mangrove values are estimated is given in Box C.2.

1.3 SPECIAL CHARACTERISTICS OF FORESTS AND FORESTRY ACTIVITIES IN COASTAL AREAS

1.3.1 Diverse natural and human-incurred ecosystems

The term coastal forests covers a wide range of different ecosystems many of which can still be classified as natural ecosystems, although – particularly in the temperate region – they may have been modified through human interventions over the years. However, they still generally contain a greater biological diversity (at genetic, species and/or ecosystem levels) than most agricultural land.

1.3.2 Links with other terrestrial and marine ecosystems

The most important characteristics of coastal forests are probably their very strong links and interdependence with other terrestrial and marine ecosystems.

Mangroves exemplify such links, existing at the interface of sea and land, and relying, as do tidal and flood plain forests, on fresh water and nutrients supplied

119

INTEGRATED
COASTAL AREA
MANAGEMENT
and
AGRICULTURE
FORESTRY AND
FISHERIES

PART C

INTEGRATION OF FORESTRY INTO COASTAL AREA MANAGEMENT

1. Forests and forestry activities in coastal areas

BOX C.2
Net present value of mangrove forestry
and fisheries in Fiji

Using data on the amounts of wood and fish actually obtained from mangrove areas and their market value and harvesting costs, the net present value (NPV) of forestry and fisheries were estimated for three mangrove areas in Fiji, using the incomes or productivity approach with a 5 percent social discount rate and a 50-year planning horizon.

Forestry net benefits

Commercial net benefits were calculated as wood harvested multiplied by market value, minus harvesting costs.

Subsistence net benefits were calculated using the actual amount of wood harvested multiplied by the shadow value in the form of the price for inland or mangrove fuelwood sold by licensed wood concessionaires.

Taking the species composition of the mangrove area into account, the weighted average NPV was estimated for each of the three main mangrove areas yielding the following:
NPV: US$164 to $217 per hectare.

Fisheries net benefits

In only one of the three areas was the fisheries potential judged to be fully utilized and the data are based on this area.

Annual catch (commercial and subsistence): 3 026 tonnes. Area of mangroves: 9 136 ha, thus averaging 331 kg per hectare, equalling $864 per hectare in market value annually.

By taking harvesting costs into account, the following result was obtained:

NPV: $5 468 per hectare, or approx. $300 per hectare per year. This is assuming a proportionate decline in the fisheries. With only

a 50 percent decline (as some of the fish are not entirely dependent on the mangroves) the figure for the NPV is $2 734 per hectare.

Other services

The value of mangroves for nutrient filtering has been estimated, using the alternative cost or shadow project method, by Green (1983), who compared the costs of a conventional waste water treatment plant with the use of oxidation ponds covering 32 ha of mangroves. An average annual benefit of $5 820 per hectare was obtained. This figure is, however, only valid for small areas of mangroves and, as it represents the average, not the marginal value, it should be treated with caution.

The option value and the existence value of mangroves are not captured using the above incomes approach and an attempt to include these values was made by using the compensation approach, as the loss of fishing rights in Fiji caused by the reclamation of mangroves has been compensated by the developers. The recompense sum is determined by an independent arbitrator within a non-market institution. Large variations in recompense sums were however recorded ($49 to $4 458 per hectare) according to the end use and the bargaining power of the owner of the fishing rights. Using 1986 prices the following results were obtained:

Average: $30 per hectare for non-industrial use and $60 per hectare for industrial use.

Maximum: $3 211 per hectare.

By adding the benefits foregone in forestry and fisheries, it can be concluded that the minimum NPV of the mangroves of Fiji is $3 000 per hectare under present supply and demand and existing market and institutional organizations.

Source: Lal, 1990.

---

by upland rivers to a much larger extent than more commonly found inland forest types. Figure C.1 illustrates the mangrove-marine food web.

In the arid tropics, there may be no permanent flow of fresh water to the sea, and the leaf litter and detritus brought to the marine ecosystem by tidal flushing of coastal mangrove areas, where these exist, is the only source of nutrients from the terrestrial zone during the dry season. This further magnifies the role of mangroves in the marine food web. In the Sudan, for example, such a role is considered to be a crucial function of the narrow

mangrove fringe found along parts of the Red Sea coast (Løyche-Wilkie, 1995).

As for the wildlife species found in coastal forests, most are dependent on other ecosystems as well. Mammals may move between different ecosystems on a daily or seasonal basis, water birds are often migratory, and many commercial shrimps and fish use the mangroves as spawning ground and nursery sites but move offshore in later stages of their life cycle. Anadromous species, such as salmon, spawn in freshwater rivers, but spend most of their life cycle in

PART C
INTEGRATION OF FORESTRY INTO COASTAL AREA MANAGEMENT

INTEGRATED
COASTAL AREA
MANAGEMENT
and
AGRICULTURE
FORESTRY AND
FISHERIES

1. Forests and forestry activities in coastal areas

marine waters; catadromous species on the other hand, spawn at sea, but spend most of their life in freshwater rivers. These species probably thus pass through coastal forests at some point in their life.

1.3.3 Large risks and pervading uncertainty

A variety of natural or human-incurred risks and uncertainties affect the sustainable management of coastal forest resources. Some natural risks may be exacerbated by human activities. Uncertainty arises from: the natural variability inherent in coastal forest ecosystems; the incomplete knowledge of the functioning of complex natural ecosystems; the long time-frame needed in forest management; and the

inability to predict accurately the future demands for goods and services provided by natural and cultivated forests.

Natural risks. These include strong winds, hurricanes and typhoons, floods (including tidal waves) and droughts, which can all cause considerable damage to coastal forests.

Global climate change caused by human actions may, through a rise in temperatures, result in "natural" risks such as a rise in sea level, changes in ocean currents, river runoff and sediment loads, and increases in the frequency and severity of floods, drought, storms and hurricanes/typhoons.

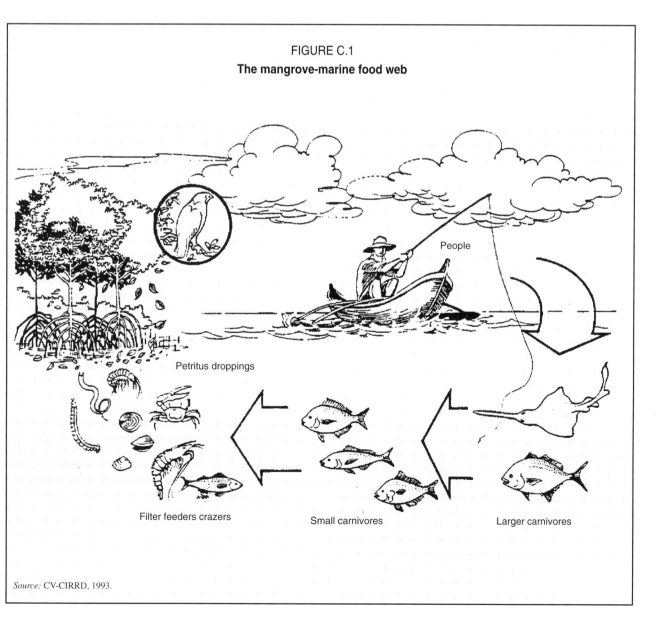

FIGURE C.1
The mangrove-marine food web

People

Petritus droppings

Filter feeders crazers

Small carnivores

Larger carnivores

Source: CV-CIRRD, 1993.

121

INTEGRATED
COASTAL AREA
MANAGEMENT
and
AGRICULTURE
FORESTRY AND
FISHERIES

PART C

INTEGRATION OF FORESTRY INTO COASTAL AREA MANAGEMENT

1. Forests and forestry activities in coastal areas

Human-incurred threats. Human-incurred threats to coastal forests stem mainly from the competition for land, water and forest resources. These include conversion of coastal forest to other uses, building of dams and flood control measures, unsustainable use of forest resources both within the coastal area and further upland, and pollution of air and water.

In many developing countries, deforestation continues to be significant; the annual loss of natural forests resulting from human pressures amounted to an estimated 13.7 million ha in the 1990 to 1995 period (FAO, 1997d). Human-incurred threats to forests are often more pronounced in coastal areas as a result of the relatively high population density of such areas caused by the availability of fertile soils, fishery resources and convenient trade links with other domestic and foreign markets.

Natural variability. One particular uncertainty faced by forest managers relates to the natural variability exhibited by the coastal forest and wildlife resources. Such natural variability can be found at two levels:

- *Between ecosystems*. A number of different forest types are found within the coastal area (see Section 1.1). Each of these has specific management requirements.
- *Within ecosystems*. Although most natural coastal forests are relatively less heterogeneous than the natural inland forest ecosystems, there is still a considerable variation within the individual ecosystems. Natural ecosystems are dynamic and changes in forest structure and species composition occur even without human intervention. In addition, and in contrast to most inland forests, spatial and temporal instability is a main feature of terrestrial-aquatic ecotones.

1.3.4 The long time-frame needed in forest planning and management

The above risks and uncertainty caused by incomplete knowledge are compounded by the long time-frame needed in forest and wildlife management. Trees, and some animals, need a long time to mature: 30 years for mangrove forests used for poles and charcoal; and 150 years for oak (*Quercus*) grown for timber in temperate forests. This long period between regeneration and harvesting makes the selection of management objectives more difficult because of further uncertainty regarding future market preferences for specific forest and wildlife products or services, future market prices, labour costs, etc.

1.3.5 Irreversibility of certain actions

An important characteristic of natural ecosystems (including natural coastal forests) is that once a natural ecosystem has been significantly altered, through unsustainable levels or inappropriate methods of use, it may be impossible to restore it to its original state. Conversion of natural coastal forests to other uses is an extreme example.

It may be possible to replant mangrove trees in degraded areas or in abandoned shrimp ponds, but the resulting plantation will have far fewer plant and animal species than the original natural mangrove ecosystem.

Acid sulphate soils. A particular cause of concern with regard to irreversibility is the high pyrite (FeS_2) content in many mangrove and tidal forest soils, which renders them particularly susceptible to soil acidification when subject to oxidation. This is probably the most acute problem faced by farmers and aquaculture pond operators when converting such forests and other wetlands to rice cultivation or aquaculture ponds, and it makes restoration of degraded areas almost impossible.

Reclamation of acid sulphate soils requires special procedures such as saltwater leaching alternating with drying out, or the establishment and maintenance of a perennially high, virtually constant groundwater-table, through a shallow, intensive drainage system. These may be technically difficult or economically unfeasible.

1.3.6 Issues related to tenure and usufruct

Coastal forests tend to be owned by the state. The inability of many state agencies in the tropics to enforce property rights, however, often means that a de facto open access regime exists, which frequently results in overexploitation of forest resources.[4] This problem is

---

[4] See Part A, Section 1.6.1 and Box A.2. Also Part E, Box E.7.

PART C

INTEGRATION OF FORESTRY INTO COASTAL AREA MANAGEMENT

INTEGRATED
COASTAL AREA
MANAGEMENT
and
AGRICULTURE
FORESTRY AND
FISHERIES

1. Forests and forestry activities in coastal areas

BOX C.3
Mangrove stewardship agreement in the Philippines

One example of successful multipurpose management of a state-owned coastal forest using a participatory approach and aiming to restore the more traditional communal ownership of forests, is the issuing of "Mangrove Stewardship Agreements" in the Philippines. Local communities (or private individuals) obtain a 25-year usufruct lease over a given mangrove area with the right to cut trees selectively, establish new mangrove plantations and collect the fish and shellfish of the area based on a mutually agreed mangrove forest management plan. The Department of Environment and Natural Resources (DENR), which implements this scheme, will assist the local communities and individuals in preparing this management plan if needed. Local NGOs are also contracted by DENR to assist in the initial "Community Organizing" activities, which include an awareness campaign of the benefits obtainable from mangrove areas and an explanation of the steps involved in obtaining a Stewardship Agreement.

only partly overcome by awarding concessions and usufructuary rights as these are often short-term in nature and not transferable and, therefore, fail to provide incentives for investments and prudent use of the resources.

Where the state agency has the ability to enforce laws and regulations and the government has a policy of promoting multipurpose management of state-owned forests, sustainable forest management can be achieved (Box C.3).

1.3.7 Institutional issues

As a result of the variety of goods and services provided by coastal forests and their links with other ecosystems, a large number of institutions often have an interest in, and sometimes jurisdiction over parts of, the coastal forest ecosystems. This raises the risk of conflict between institutions, even within a single ministry.

The forestry department or its equivalent generally has jurisdiction over the coastal forest resources. However, the parks and wildlife department, where it exists, may have jurisdiction over the forest wildlife, and the fisheries department almost certainly has jurisdiction over the fisheries resources found in the rivers within coastal forests, and may regulate the use of mangrove areas for cage and pond culture. Other

institutions with an interest in coastal forests include those related to tourism, land-use planning, mining, housing, ports and other infrastructure.

1.3.8 Lack of awareness of benefits and their economic value

In many countries, there is often little public awareness of the variety of benefits provided by coastal forests, and campaigns should be conducted to overcome this. Mangroves and other swamp forests in particular have often been regarded as wastelands with little use except for conversion purposes. As a result of the low commercial value of wood products compared with the potential value of agriculture or shrimp production, conversion has often been justified, in the past, on the basis of a financial analysis of only the direct costs and benefits. Such analyses, however, do not take into account the value of the large number of unpriced environmental and social services provided by coastal forests, which in many cases far outweigh the value of any conversion scheme.[5]

1.3.9 Implications for the management of coastal forests

The ecological links between coastal forests and other terrestrial and marine ecosystems and the institutional links between the forestry sector and other sectors, must be addressed through an area-based strategy that takes a holistic approach to sustainable development. An ICAM strategy provides the appropriate framework for such an approach.

The nature of coastal forests as described above calls for a precautionary approach[6] to the management of their resources and the adoption of flexible strategies and management plans drawing on the knowledge of the local communities.

The precautionary principle can be incorporated into coastal forest management by imposing sustainability constraints on the utilization of coastal forest ecosystems. Other measures include environmental impact assessments, risk assessments, pilot projects and

123

---

[5] See Part A, Section 1.6.1 and Boxes A.22 and A.24.
[6] See Part A, Section 1.6.3 and Boxes A.3 and A.5.

INTEGRATED
COASTAL AREA
MANAGEMENT
and
AGRICULTURE
FORESTRY AND
FISHERIES

PART C

INTEGRATION OF FORESTRY INTO COASTAL AREA MANAGEMENT

1. Forests and forestry activities in coastal areas

regular monitoring and evaluation of the effects of management. Research, in particular on the interdependence of coastal forests and other ecosystems and on the quantification and mitigation of negative impacts between sectors, is also needed.

Environmental impact assessments[7] should be undertaken prior to conversions or other activities that may have a significant negative impact on coastal forest ecosystems. Such activities may arise within the forest (e.g. major tourism development) or in other sectors outside the forest (e.g. flood control measures). Where there is insufficient information on the impact of proposed management actions, applied research and/or pilot projects should be initiated.

Public participation in the management of coastal forest resources will increase the likelihood of success of any management plan and should be accompanied by long-term and secure tenure/usufruct.

[7] See Part A, Box A.6.

INTEGRATED
COASTAL AREA
MANAGEMENT
and
AGRICULTURE
FORESTRY AND
FISHERIES

PART C
INTEGRATION OF FORESTRY INTO COASTAL AREA MANAGEMENT

2. Interactions

One of the prerequisites of ICAM is the proper identification of the interactions between the coastal forestry sector and other sectors and ways and means to enhance/reduce them. It should, however, be emphasized that the knowledge of such interactions remains incomplete. Ecological research continues to yield new information on interactions between animals and plants within the forest ecosystem, while the impacts of current and future innovations in technology and the resulting changes in use patterns are inherently unpredictable. These impacts may not manifest themselves for many years – especially in the forestry sector with its very long life or production cycle – and the effects, when manifest, may be difficult to attribute to a single cause. Some of the known interactions involving the coastal forestry sector are described below.

2.1 POSITIVE INTERACTIONS BETWEEN THE COASTAL FORESTRY SECTOR AND OTHER SECTORS

2.1.1 Overall economic development

Depending on its relative importance, the coastal forestry sector may provide a stimulus for overall economic development of the coastal area, and could even have an impact upon the economic development of the whole country. Among the potential benefits of sound management of coastal forests is the provision of employment and additional income opportunities for rural people. Coastal forests can also generate foreign exchange through the export of wood and non-wood forest products. Overall economic development may in turn increase the demand for forest products and thereby benefit the forestry sector (or conversely lead to overexploitation).

2.1.2 Fisheries sector

Coastal forests (see Section 1.1) provide leaf litter and detritus for the aquatic food web, in addition to spawning grounds and shelter for various fish and shellfish. The mangrove oyster (*Crassostrea tulipa*) for instance grows on the stilt roots of the *Rhizophora* species. In many developing countries, fishing communities rely on wood from coastal forests for cooking, smoking fish, building materials, boat-building and fishing stakes (see Figure C.2).

Moreover, the mangrove waterways provide an ideal location for small- to medium-scale cage, raft and bottom culture for fish, crabs, lobsters, cockles and oysters. Capture fisheries is also often undertaken on a subsistence basis in the creeks and rivers of coastal forests and in flood plains. The fisheries and forestry sectors may also share the transport infrastructure of the coastal area.

2.1.3 Agriculture and food security

A combination of forestry and agriculture on the same land can be undertaken, and provides mutual benefits. Several different types of agroforestry systems exist.[8] An illustration of the beneficial roles single trees and patches of forests have in maintaining or improving the agricultural carrying capacity of flood plains is given in Box C.4.

In addition, coastal forests protect agricultural land from the actions of winds and waves. In Guyana for example, 90 percent of the population live in a narrow coastal area and the agricultural production from this area accounts for 70 percent of the country's GDP. Mangroves used to protect large parts of this low-lying coastal area, but the mangrove belt has deteriorated, as a result of overexploitation and clogging up of the mangrove pneumatophores with silt originating from the Amazon, necessitating the establishment of expensive sea wall defences (FAO, 1990).

In many coastal areas without natural forest cover, narrow strips of forest are established to protect agricultural land and crops from winds loaded with salt and sand particles; large plantation programmes are often undertaken in areas prone to the encroachment of moving sand dunes. Forests also provide fodder for livestock as well as building and fencing materials.

Animals living in forests contribute to the pollination of crops. For example, several types of pollinating bees and wasps build their nests in the coastal forests and

_125_

---

[8] Several examples of these are provided in Part B, Box B.1.

INTEGRATED
COASTAL AREA
MANAGEMENT
and
AGRICULTURE
FORESTRY AND
FISHERIES

PART C

INTEGRATION OF FORESTRY INTO COASTAL AREA MANAGEMENT

2. Interactions

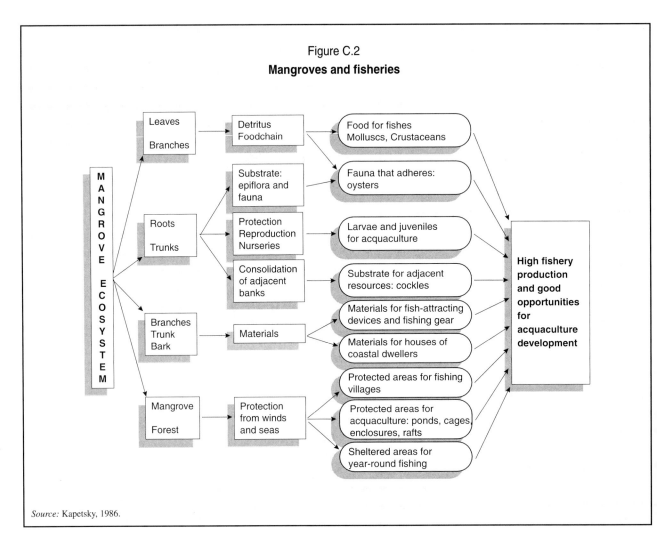

Figure C.2
Mangroves and fisheries

Source: Kapetsky, 1986.

another well-known example is that of the Malaysian cave fruit bat (*Eonycteris spelea*), the only known pollinator of the commercially important durian (*Durio zibethinus*).

Coastal forests also contribute directly to food security by providing game and many other edible forest products such as fruits, nuts and fish. In many countries in arid regions, mangrove forests represent the last remaining wood resource in the coastal area.

2.1.4 Tourism and recreation
When well tended, coastal forests provide additional attractions and recreational facilities that can increase the tourism potential of the coastal area. Lowland rain forests harbour a great number of plant and animal species which may attract tourists, a beach forest may provide welcome shade, and the unique features of the

mangroves or other swamp forests may attract both local and foreign nature tourists.[9]

Activities that are compatible with coastal forest and wildlife management and that may be promoted in coastal forested areas are nature trails, bird watching, botanical studies, nature photography, fishing and river rafting/canoeing/kayaking.

2.1.5 Human settlements
Protection against storms and coastal erosion and the provision of recreational facilities, employment, building materials and fuelwood are some of the positive interactions between human settlements and coastal forests.

---

[9] See also Section 1.3.

PART C

INTEGRATION OF FORESTRY INTO COASTAL AREA MANAGEMENT

INTEGRATED
COASTAL AREA
MANAGEMENT
and
AGRICULTURE
FORESTRY AND
FISHERIES

2. Interactions

BOX C.4
Benefits of single trees or patches of trees for agriculture

An illustration of the beneficial role single trees and patches of forests have in maintaining or improving the agricultural carrying capacity of flood plains is given by the following example of the restoration of seriously degraded flood lands in the Mekong delta in Viet Nam.

Melaleuca leucadendron, a tree 10 to 20 m tall, once covered an area of 250 000 ha in low-lying, seasonally inundated areas in the Mekong delta in Viet Nam. Years of unmanaged harvesting for fuelwood and the clearing of land for other uses gradually reduced and degraded the *Melaleuca* forests. During the war in the 1960s and 1970s, a large portion of the Mekong delta was drained and burned. Once the soil dried out, sulphur rose to the surface, reducing the soil pH to 3.9 or lower. Crops, including rice, could not be grown and local people were forced to leave. After the hostilities, local people made tremendous efforts to restore agriculture on the plain. In so doing, they came to realize that the pH of the soil had to be increased. This could only be achieved through watering the soil with fresh water and planting trees. Fresh water was brought on to the plain by new canals, and millions of *Melaleuca* trees were planted on the most acid soils, since it was the only species that would grow in these conditions. This massive tree planting activity has made the area prosper again also as farmland. In addition, native plant and animal species are gradually returning to the plain. Not only freshwater fish, but also turtles and especially water birds have returned in surprising numbers, thus once again providing a source of food and additional income to local people.

2.1.6 Infrastructure

Forest-based operations can lead to road building and the development of other essential infrastructure works such as ports. Many of the present harbours along a sea shore or river bank originated as timber loading points. In the tropics, mangroves trap sediments and thereby reduce the risk of siltation of shipping lanes and harbours caused by upland deforestation. The coastal forestry sector in turn benefits from access to low-cost marine and inland river transportation systems and from other infrastructure developed to serve the agriculture or fisheries sector. Of course, opening up areas for forestry can also have unwelcome negative effects.

2.1.7 Environment

The wise management of coastal forests will contribute to an improved environmental situation in the region. This is especially valid in erosion-sensitive and mountainous coastal regions. Forest and wildlife management may also contribute to the conservation of the diversity of existing and potential genetic resources. Restoration of degraded areas through tree planting can also contribute to an improved environment.

2.2 NEGATIVE INTERACTIONS BETWEEN THE COASTAL FORESTRY SECTOR AND OTHER SECTORS

As population densities increase, natural resources in coastal areas are subject to high demand and are also facing a larger number of different kinds of user activities. These uses are often incompatible, may result in a wide array of problems and conflicts for coastal resource users and pose difficult choices to decision-makers.

2.2.1 Competitive interactions

The main conflicts stem from competition for land, water, forest products and services for human settlement, agriculture, fishing, forestry, industry, trade, infrastructure works, tourism and amenities between private industries and local people and even between government agencies themselves. The situation is aggravated by the absence of proper coastal land-use planning.

As explained in Part A,[10] negative interactions can be competitive or antagonistic. Examples of competitive interactions between the coastal forestry sector and other sectors are given below.

Fisheries. The conversion of mangrove areas for aquaculture ponds on a large scale in many tropical countries, in particular in Asia but also in Latin America, is a prime example of the competition for land between the forestry and the fisheries sectors.

Agriculture. Many swamp forests and some mangroves have been cleared for cultivation of rice and other agricultural crops because of competition for land. Use

127

---

[10] More specifically in Section 1.5 and Box A.1.

2. Interactions

BOX C.5
Sustained yield forest management

The Matang Mangrove Forest Reserve in Malaysia has been under intensive management since the beginning of the century. The forest is regulated in the appropriate even-aged classes and harvested stands are immediately replanted or, to a limited extent, regenerated naturally; forestation of marginal areas incorporated into the reserve is undertaken exclusively by means of plantation.

Monitoring of the permanent sample plots installed in the reserve has not shown any decline in yields over three rotations (Haron 1981). The incorporation of marginal areas by canalization and plantation has increased the size of the management area over the years. It must therefore be concluded that sustained yield forest management is feasible for at least three rotation periods of 30 years.

With complete crown cover and immediate regeneration of harvested areas, the production of litter fall from the managed forest has been found to be superior to that of natural untouched stands (Ong *et al.,* 1982). Litter fall is an important source of energy in the food web that affects fisheries and other living mangrove-dependent organisms. No significant decline of commercial catches of fish, molluscs and shellfish in the coastal waters adjacent to the Matang Reserve has been reported during the management period.

It would seem most likely that the biological diversity of the original mangrove has been affected in the regulated parts of Matang since only a few preferred species have been used to regenerate harvested areas. Consequently, with this type of management, areas should be set aside in the initial planning stage as reserves

Source: FAO, 1994a.

---

of river water for irrigation purposes may severely limit the amount of fresh water reaching the coastal area and this may adversely affect the viability of mangroves and temporary swamps. Browsing camels, goats and other livestock may damage trees and other forest resources. The establishment of plantations of rubber, oil-palm or fast-growing timber species may in turn decrease the amount of land available for agricultural purposes.

Mining. Peat, sand and other minerals may be established on forested land and destroy the forest or deny access to users.

Tourism and recreation. Intensive, single-species forestry does not provide the type of forest sought for tourism and recreation; not only are such forests not diverse in tree species but wildlife also becomes scarce. Conversely, intensive levels of use of coastal forests for nature tourism and recreation may cause wildlife disturbance, soil compaction or erosion and trampling of rare plant communities.

Other sectors. As a result of the strategic location of coastal areas, pressures on land for human settlements, ports and other infrastructure, industrial and tourism development can become far greater than it is further

inland, placing increased pressure on the remaining natural ecosystems.

Unfortunately, the low value placed on many of the coastal forests (measured only in terms of the value of wood production) means that they are at a disadvantage when decisions on land-use allocation are made. The largest threat currently facing the existing mangroves in the state of Johore in southern peninsular Malaysia for instance, stems from plans to build a second port, a second link to Singapore, an industrial estate and several marinas and residential estates, all requiring the release of land at present classified as mangrove forest reserve; these plans have already been approved or are likely to be in the near future.

2.2.2 Antagonistic interactions

Antagonistic interactions between the coastal forestry sector and other sectors include direct and indirect effects on the forestry sector and adverse effects caused by the sector.

Damage caused by conversion to other land uses. Where conversion of coastal forests takes place, even though individual areas converted to other uses may be small and the effects thus deemed insignificant, the cumulative effects of a fragmentation of the coastal forests on forest resources and biological diversity may

PART C

INTEGRATION OF FORESTRY INTO COASTAL AREA MANAGEMENT

INTEGRATED
COASTAL AREA
MANAGEMENT
and
AGRICULTURE
FORESTRY AND
FISHERIES

2. Interactions

BOX C.6
**Positive environmental effects of sound
forest management**

In the Sundarbans mangroves in Bangladesh, where around 400 000 ha is managed, many species are utilized (sawnwood is a major product) and natural regeneration is promoted.

The regeneration system should maintain biological diversity, but the inherent complexity of the system also makes it difficult to assess if this has in fact happened, although it is assumed that it has. The chief advantage of the forest management of these mangroves is that they have been retained at all. As elsewhere in the tropics, there has been pressure to convert the Sundarbans mangroves to food production, i.e. fish ponds, shrimp farming and agriculture, and to human settlement. The fact that such an extensive area of mangroves is still in existence today, in a country with one of the highest population pressures in the world, is largely the result of the fact that a significant part of the mangroves were reserved at an early stage for forest management.

Nowhere in the world are mangroves more important for the protection of human lives and activities than in the Bay of Bengal, which is periodically affected by typhoons. Consequently, it can be claimed that the management of these mangroves has had a positive impact on the environment.

Natural water-borne feed is also still available for fish and shrimp farmers in the Sundarbans, unlike in some other parts of the world (e.g. Ecuador), where heavy deforestation of mangroves, which are not subject to management, has made it necessary for shrimp farmers to resort to artificial feed in recent years.

Source: FAO, 1994a.

in fact be severe. As a result of strong links with other ecosystems and the many products and services that can be obtained from coastal forests, adverse effects of such conversions extend to other sectors as well.

Damage caused by pollution of water and air. Port and other infrastructure development, industrial and household waste disposal, oil exploitation, mining, dredging and filling may severely disturb, or even destroy, coastal or riverine forested ecosystems as a result of the release of chemical and physical pollutants, including agricultural chemicals, organic waste and untreated aquaculture pond water or acid drainage water, into the air, or into rivers and coastal waters. Chemical pollutants may kill the plants and animals directly or through accumulation in the food chain.

Damage caused by changes in water flow. Such damage may be caused by structures erected to protect the coastal area against erosion from the sea or to control the flooding caused by upland rivers. Changes in water currents may also be caused by dredging and filling. Many wetland and mangrove areas have been destroyed as a result of the construction of coastal protection structures. Such structures can result in large areas of productive wetland and tidal flats being sealed off from marine influences or can deprive the seaward areas of the estuary or lagoon of fresh water. Thus, not only are these protection efforts not always successful, but they also destroy highly productive natural ecosystems. The Farakka dam in India for instance, is blamed for changes in the forest structure in the western part of the Bangladesh Sundarbans mangroves, because of a decrease in the amount of fresh water reaching the forest in the dry season.

Adverse effects of inappropriate coastal forest and forest industry management. Some of the most noticeable and severe effects occur as a result of the clearing of forests. Where this occurs inland along rivers, it often results in increased flood hazards affecting both human settlements and agricultural land. In also usually leads to an increase in the sediment load of rivers and coastal waters through soil erosion and this may adversely affect riverine and coastal fisheries, sea grass beds and coral reefs and may cause siltation of harbours and shipping lanes. Forest clearance along the coast deprives it of protective cover against storms and tidal floods and can open the way to erosion of coastal land by wind and water, intrusion of salt water and/or the destabilization of sand dunes. Valuable spawning and feeding grounds for aquatic species may also be lost when mangroves or riparian forests are cleared. The local population will be affected by a shortage of forest products.

2.3 INTERACTIONS WITHIN THE COASTAL FORESTRY SECTOR

There are also interactions within the coastal forest sector. Natural forests and plantations may improve the microclimate for other plants and provide habitats for many plant and animal species. Animal species may contribute to pollination and seed dispersal, helping to maintain forest biological diversity. The establishment

INTEGRATED
COASTAL AREA
MANAGEMENT
and
AGRICULTURE
FORESTRY AND
FISHERIES

2. Interactions

TABLE C.2
Forestry-related interactions

	Types of interaction	Example
Positive interactions		
Overall economic development	Stimulation of coastal area development, employment, export of forest products, tourism	High employment percentage in Bangladesh Sundarbans
Fisheries	Provision of leaf litter and detritus for the aquatic food web, spawning grounds for fish, supply of wood (for cooking, fish smoking, boat- and house building) to fishing communities, ideal location for fish culture	In peninsular Malaysia, 30 percent of fishery production is associated with mangrove ecosystems
Agriculture	Protection of agricultural land from wind, sand and waves, improvement of carrying capacity of flood plains, provision of fodder for livestock, pollination by forest-based insects and birds, provision of game, edible and medicinal products, provision of fencing materials	In Guyana, where 90 percent of the population live in a narrow coastal area, the deterioration of the mangrove has necessitated the building of expensive sea wall defences
Tourism and recreation	Provision of shade on beaches, unique natural features to visit, excursions, bird watching, fishing, river canoeing	Proboscis monkeys in Borneo, royal Bengal tiger in Bay of Bengal, the milky stork
Human settlements	Protection against storms and coastal erosion, recreational activities, building materials	
Infrastructure	Maintenance of roads and ports, protection of ports through reduced risk of siltation	
Environment	Protection against erosion in mountainous coastal areas, conservation of biological diversity, restoration of degraded areas through reforestation, favourable microclimate and habitat to numerous plant and animal species	In Viet Nam, mangroves are planted as a protection measure against wind and waves. In Denmark, coastal forests have been planted since 1830 to stabilize the sand dunes that had moved inland and covered several villages
Complementary interactions		
Fisheries	Shared transport infrastructure	
Agriculture	Agroforestry, shared transport infrastructure	
Tourism and recreation	Protection of forests to promote tourism, research	
Competitive interactions		
Fisheries	Conversion of mangroves for aquaculture	
Agriculture	Clearing of swamps for agricultural production, irrigation that deprives coastal forests of fresh water, livestock grazing may damage forest resources, use of agricultural land for fast-growing forest plantations	Most periodic swamp forests in alluvial plains of Asia have been cleared for wetland rice cultivation
Mining	Peat, sand and other mineral extraction which can destroy forests	
Tourism and recreation	Single-purpose forest exploitation that reduces attractive flora and fauna species diversity, disturbance of wildlife, soil compaction, destruction of rare plant species by intensive tourism	
Other sectors	Land requirements for other economic development	Johore state, Malaysia: likely release of land classified as mangrove forest reserve for this purpose
Antagonistic interactions		
Direct adverse effects	Forest conversion to other land uses or to forest monoculture	Even conversion of small forest areas can have considerable adverse effects on biological diversity, soil fertility and ecosystem stability
Indirect adverse effects	Air and water pollution caused by disposal/leaching of household aquaculture, agriculture and industry waste, oil spills and mining	Eutrophication, clogging of mangroves, acid rain
Effects of poor management	Changes in water flow caused by dams, irrigation schemes, dredging, landfilling, coastal protection structures, clearing of forests	Destruction of wetlands and tidal flats, erosion leading to siltation, destruction of coral reefs and spawning grounds

PART C

INTEGRATION OF FORESTRY INTO COASTAL AREA MANAGEMENT

INTEGRATED
COASTAL AREA
MANAGEMENT
and
AGRICULTURE
FORESTRY AND
FISHERIES

2. Interactions

of forest industries may contribute to increasing demand for timber and other forest products. But it may have adverse effects on the forest ecosystem.

Forests can also be managed with a view to sustainability, such as conservation of soil and water, and biological diversity, and the enhancement of service provided for other sectors.

As far as competitive interactions within the sector go, felling of natural forests, or draining swamps for plantation crops (e.g. oil-palms, coconut) are typical examples. Even antagonistic interactions exist within the forest sector: conversion of natural forest to forest monoculture reduces biological diversity, degrades and destabilizes ecosystems, and reduces soil fertility;

opening up of roads into coastal forests will facilitate the encroachment of farmers on to forest land with many potentially harmful effects; and dragging of logs removes topsoil and damages natural vegetation and seed-bearers.

Choices will have to be made between conflicting objectives such as maximizing wood production and increasing the stock of wildlife (see Box C.5). Conflicts will also arise between industrial users of the forest and forest dwellers or those who depend on the forest for their livelihoods. Box C.6 gives an example of benefits derived from properly managed coastal forests. Table C.2 summarizes the main forestry-related interactions.

PART C

INTEGRATION OF FORESTRY INTO COASTAL AREA MANAGEMENT

INTEGRATED
COASTAL AREA
MANAGEMENT
and
AGRICULTURE
FORESTRY AND
FISHERIES

3. Information requirements

Information on the forestry sector should cover the distribution and extent of forested areas, forest composition, actual and potential production of forest resources, and ecological factors that govern forest dynamics, as well as social and economic information related to the use of coastal forest ecosystems. The complex nature of natural coastal forest ecosystems and the links between these and other ecosystems call for expertise in disciplines such as forestry, ecology, wildlife management, geomorphology, hydrology, fisheries, agriculture, tourism, economics and social science.

Alternative uses of forested lands and their resources should be evaluated using biological, physical and socio-economic data, in particular with regard to the coastal forest resource base, environmental impacts caused by actions undertaken within and outside the coastal forest ecosystems, and the organizational and institutional structure within which management of coastal forests must be undertaken.

3.1 INFORMATION ON THE RESOURCE BASE

3.1.1 Information requirements

Information on land use.[11] With respect to land-use systems, the biophysical information generally required on coastal forest ecosystems includes the geographic distribution of forests and their extent, and forest resources and their potential supporting sites.

Information on the present status of coastal forest resources. Assessment of wood and non-wood forest resources (including wildlife) includes: availability, productivity, management costs, and determination of carrying capacities and sustainable use levels. The carrying capacity of natural ecosystems is dynamic and can be reduced through human misuse or through natural catastrophes, or increased through improved management. For example, the wildlife carrying

capacity in coastal national parks can be enhanced through strict control measures such as the reduction of the impact of visitors by limiting free access areas of the park. In addition to the carrying capacity for wildlife and for recreation and tourism, sustainable levels of harvesting of forest products must also be determined and compared with existing and estimated future demand levels.

Information on the level of utilization of coastal forest resources. This includes determination of existing and estimated future demand levels for coastal forest and wildlife products and services; more specifically: local, regional and/or national demand for forest products and services (including untraded products) and the export potential of traded products; current and estimated future supply and demand trends; price trends; and factors affecting demand for and supply of such products/ services.

Information on the social situation and economic needs of the people living in the planning area includes: alternative economic activities and investments; practices/techniques used in the harvesting/collection of forest products; and social values placed on products and services provided by the coastal forest (see Table C.3).

An economic valuation of the direct and indirect benefits provided by coastal forest ecosystems is needed, especially: an economic quantification of both marketed and non-marketed products as well as intangible benefits (e.g. provision of detritus for the marine food web), improved environment, health, shelter, coastal protection, soil conservation, water, biological diversity, education, recreation and tourism, etc. (see Table C.4).

3.1.2 Tools for information collection, analysis and presentation

Collection, analysis and presentation of land cover and land-use information. Before a detailed classification of land cover within a forested area can start, the boundaries of the forest itself must be identified. A clear definition of vegetation categories must therefore be

133

---

[11] The principles and basic concepts of land evaluation are extensively discussed in FAO, 1976 and FAO, 1984. FAO, 1993 provides useful guidance on the land-use planning process.

INTEGRATED
COASTAL AREA
MANAGEMENT
and
AGRICULTURE
FORESTRY AND
FISHERIES

PART C

INTEGRATION OF FORESTRY INTO COASTAL AREA MANAGEMENT

3. Information requirements

TABLE C.3

Types of information required for coastal forest management

Demography
Size of community (number of families/people)
Composition of community (ethnic, age-class, occupation)
Map of community
Changes in population

Tenure and usufruct
Who owns the forest land?
Who owns the forest resources?
Who uses the forest and for what purpose?
Are permits needed for specific uses?
Are any uses prohibited?
Changes in rights and regulations over time

Demand
Which products and services can be obtained from the forest?
Priority ranking by different groups
For each plant and animal product:
    Which resource(s)/species is/are preferred?
    How much is currently harvested for subsistence and/or for sale?
    Is the supply sufficient to meet demand?
    Changes in use over time and season
Which forest products are currently bought?
At what price?

Resource availability
Where are the resources needed for products or services located? (scattered over the forest/in particular parts of the forest)
For each product:
    How many individuals of the preferred resource per hectare?
    What is their status now compared with earlier?
    Seasonal availability
    Is availability a constraint?
    If so, how can this be alleviated?
Which resource is most abundant?
Which resource is most scarce?

Ecological suitability
Are any uses of the forest incompatible?
Are any of the resources presently used dependent upon other resources? (for food, shelter, pollination, seed dispersal)
For each animal product or by-product:
    What are the food and habitat requirements of the animal?
    At what age does the animal reach maturity and how many offspring does it produce per year?

Ecological suitability (continued)
For each plant-derived product:
    What are the growth and regeneration requirements for the plants whose product(s) is/are harvested?
    How many years does it take before the plant produces fruits or reaches the desired size?
    Which resources are the most versatile (have the most different uses)?
Ranking of products according to ecological suitability

Technical suitability
For each forest product:
    Previous management experience (silviculture, enhancement of yield, restriction on access, size, volume or time of harvesting, religious taboos)
    Harvesting techniques employed
Ranking of products according to ease of management and impact of harvesting technique

Economic suitability
For each product and direct-use service:
    How many people are full-time/part-time employed?
    Who? (any particular group? women, children, income group, ethnic group)
    What are the costs involved in management (including harvesting and marketing of forest products)?
For each product:
    What quantity can be harvested per person/day/year?
    What is the price obtained if sold?
    Price changes over time and season
For each service:
    How many users per year/peak season?
    What is the income to the community?
    Are any problems encountered?
Which products and services are the most profitable?

Markets and trade links
For each commercial product:
    Where is the product sold? (local/regional/national/international market)
Which trade links exist?

Final appraisal
Analysis of constraints and opportunities
Ranking of management objectives

given in order to assure a consistent classification and, subsequently, to obtain reliable area figures.

Collection, analysis and presentation of information on the status and utilization of coastal forest resources. When the selection of management objectives for a given coastal forest is completed, a more intensive resource inventory is needed to determine the status and productive potential of the forest and the carrying capacities and sustainable level of resource use.

Participatory appraisal. The term is used here to include rapid rural appraisal (RRA), participatory rural appraisal (PRA) and related techniques aimed at gathering

pertinent information by drawing on the experience and knowledge of local communities.[12]

Table C.3 shows the type of information that can be elicited using participatory appraisal techniques aimed at determining the suitability of different forest resources for exploitation.

Local demand for forest products for subsistence purposes is best ascertained through the use of participatory appraisal methods, rather than by employing lengthy questionnaires and surveys.

---

[12] The different techniques or tools that may be used in participatory appraisal are described in Davis-Case, 1989 and Davis-Case, 1990. See also Part A, Box A.20.

PART C

INTEGRATION OF FORESTRY INTO COASTAL AREA MANAGEMENT

INTEGRATED
COASTAL AREA
MANAGEMENT
and
AGRICULTURE
FORESTRY AND
FISHERIES

3. Information requirements

TABLE C.4

Valuation approaches in relation to type of forest product (good or service)

Techniques	Examples
Direct market price technique	This is used to value all market-priced goods and services from the forest, unless it is believed not to reflect adequately the willingness to pay (e.g. when there are effective minimum prices or price ceilings on goods and/or services). In such cases, the techniques below are used.
Indirect market price techniques (value inferred from other market prices)	
Residual value	Stumpage value for timber is derived by looking at market prices for finished lumber and subtracting costs from stump through processing to lumber sale.
Increased production values	Increased market value of crop production over what it would have been without the windbreak provides a proxy minimum gross value for the windbreak. Associated costs are subtracted from that to arrive at net value.
Surrogate price	The value of fuelwood in a new market is estimated on the basis of the value of an alternative fuel (e.g. kerosene) in that market, after adjusting for calorific value of the two fuels.
Opportunity cost	The minimum value of a wilderness park is estimated on the basis of the market-priced value of the goods and/or services foregone.
Replacement cost (or avoided cost)	The maximum value of a watershed management programme focused only on containing sediment in a downstream reservoir is made equal to the alternative market cost of dredging the reservoir of the additional sediment that would occur without the watershed management programme.
Hedonic pricing	The market value differences for similar forest properties are used to reflect the value of some environmental service or cost that varies across the properties.
Travel cost	Differences in market-priced costs of trips by different users to a reserve are used to value nature-based tourism based on differences in use rates in relation to differences in trip costs.
Non-market price techniques (value inferred from surveys of willingness to pay)	
Contingent valuation	Value of a certain wildlife population is inferred from a survey of willingness to pay to save the population.

Source: Gregersen *et al.,* 1995.

135

Examples of different valuation techniques and their application to forests are shown in Table C.4.[13]

Analysis of resource assessments and forest inventories is described in standard textbooks and will not be covered here. Analysis of the status of forest resources, socio-economic issues, potential benefits and constraints forms part of the participatory appraisal and will reveal the values of individual user groups. Finally, cost-benefit analysis is often used to appraise alternative resource uses.[14]

3.2 INFORMATION RELATED TO ENVIRONMENTAL IMPACTS AND INTERACTIONS
3.2.1 Information requirements
Of fundamental importance is a solid knowledge of the impact of human activities on coastal ecosystems. Multidisciplinary studies to determine the biological, physical and socio-economic effects of the major users of coastal forests and adjacent areas are required. The objectives are to determine the following, where relevant:

---

[13] For a more detailed description of the theory behind, and the mechanism of applying, individual techniques, refer to textbooks such as Winpenny (1991) and Hufschmidt *et al.* (1983). Benson and Willis, (1992) may also be useful because recreation and tourism are particularly important uses of many coastal forests. FAO, 1994a provides valuable information on which approaches may be usable and contains annotated references on valuation. See also Part A, and Box A.24.

---

[14] See Part A, Boxes A.22 and A.23.

INTEGRATED
COASTAL AREA
MANAGEMENT
and
AGRICULTURE
FORESTRY AND
FISHERIES

PART C

INTEGRATION OF FORESTRY INTO COASTAL AREA MANAGEMENT

3. Information requirements

- the interrelationship between the aquatic food web and the supply of leaf litter and detritus by certain coastal forests and the effect of silvicultural practices on this;
- the effects of forest management and silvicultural practices on capture fisheries' biological diversity, coastal protection, recreation and tourism, flood control and water quality;
- the impact of wildlife management practices on tourism, biological diversity, timber production and the agricultural sector;
- the impact of recreation and tourism on biological diversity and forest management practices;
- the environmental impacts of conversion of natural coastal forests to other uses (including cumulative impacts);
- the impacts of infrastructure development, industrial and household waste disposal, oil exploitation, mining, dredging and filling activities, on the pollution of water and air and the resulting indirect effects on coastal forest ecosystems;
- the impacts of dams and irrigation schemes, flood control measures, coastal protection structures, dredging and filling, on changes in water flow and the resulting indirect effects on coastal forest ecosystems.

3.2.2 Tools for information collection, analysis and presentation

Environmental impact assessment. Environmental impact assessment (EIA)[15] is increasingly required by law for the development of new projects (e.g. sawmills, paper mills and other forest industries) and for the extension of existing ones in the coastal area.

Monitoring and evaluation. The general concern over the progressive deterioration of tropical forests and the need for reliable information necessary for management decisions and conservation measures have led several countries to initiate national monitoring and evaluation programmes. Such programmes aim primarily at the assessment of forest cover changes over time and are thus particularly useful for the assessment of the

cumulative impacts of forest degradation and conversion.

Many countries and organizations are presently developing criteria for sustainable forest management along with indicators to be monitored on a regular basis in order to ascertain that sustainable management is achieved.

3.3 ORGANIZATIONAL AND INSTITUTIONAL INFORMATION

Organizational and institutional information is here taken to encompass political and legal frameworks, institutional and administrative structures, cultural attitudes and social traditions.

3.3.1 Information requirements

Information on policy and laws. Coastal forested ecosystems are frequently overlooked in national forest policy. Specific provisions must be reviewed and included in the national forest policy in order to address adequately the complex issues of regulating the use of coastal forests.

Inappropriate fiscal and concession policies, together with lack of attention to the impact of other sectors' policies on the use of coastal forest resources, have recently been highlighted as negatively affecting the sustainability of coastal forests. Policy orientations, laws and regulations should provide effective incentives for sustainable forest management. For this reason, legal distortions and disincentives that discourage the wise utilization of forests, especially those related to landownership and tenure, should be correctly identified in the information collection exercise.[16]

Incentives and charges that are inappropriate and counterproductive in terms of achieving sustainable development of coastal resources should be identified. Recent examples of inappropriate fiscal policies affecting the forestry sector include: incentives for cattle ranches; clearance of forest lands in order to claim ownership of land (both in Amazonia); alienation of mangrove areas for fish pond construction purposes; and implementation of logging bans, which diminish the value of forested lands compared with other land uses (Southeast Asia). Subsidies leading to inefficient and wasteful forest industries or to the replacement of

---

[15] Refer to Wathern, 1988, Gregersen and Contreras- Hermosilla, 1992 and Gregersen *et al.*, 1993 on the specific impacts of forestry activities. See also Part A, Box A.6.

[16] See Part A, Section 1.6 and Box A.2.

PART C

INTEGRATION OF FORESTRY INTO COASTAL AREA MANAGEMENT

INTEGRATED
COASTAL AREA
MANAGEMENT
and
AGRICULTURE
FORESTRY AND
FISHERIES

3. Information requirements

natural forests or other valuable ecosystems with monocultural plantations should also be identified.

The information requirements thus focus on existing legal obligations, rights and privileges, and policy guidelines and the need to revise these.

The objective is to obtain the information required to:
- review and formulate policies, laws and regulations on the utilization, management and conservation of coastal forests and wildlife;
- review other sectoral policies, laws and regulations that may have an impact on coastal forest utilization, management and conservation;
- determine the extent of implementation of such policies and programmes;
- analyse the effectiveness of different policy instruments and the impact of policies and programmes on the forests and on forest-dependent populations.

Institutional information. A good knowledge of the existing administrative structures and the capabilities of the institutions responsible for the conservation and management of forest and wildlife resources in the region is essential. Information on cultural attitudes and social traditions related to the use of coastal forests must also be obtained.[17]

3.3.2 Tools for information collection, analysis and presentation

Tools regarding the legal and institutional framework (policies, legal obligations, rights and privileges and the administrative framework) will include existing sources of information such as published records, laws, regulations and policies.[18]

Strategic environmental assessment (SEA) will make it possible to evaluate the effectiveness of various policy instruments and the impact of laws and policies on coastal forests and their inhabitants. SEA is basically an extension of environmental impact assessment to the more strategic tiers of decision-making, covering policies, plans and programmes.[19]

Participatory appraisal techniques will yield valuable information on local attitudes and traditions, and the impact of laws and policies.

137

---

[17] See Part A, Section 2.4.3.
[18] See Part A, Boxes A.4 and A.21 for evaluating the legal and institutional issues, respectively.
[19] Refer to Therivel *et al.* (1994) for a discussion of SEA.

4. Policy and planning for integrated coastal area management

4.1 POLICY DIRECTIONS

There are a number of international conventions and regional directives that offer protection to coastal areas. As yet there is no international convention on forests, although a set of non-legally binding Principles on the Management, Conservation and Sustainable Development of Forests Worldwide (commonly referred to as the Forest Principles) was widely adopted at the Rio Conference in 1994.

The policy directions set out below, are drawn from regional and selected country experience.

4.1.1 Sustainable development

Sustainability needs to be addressed in the widest sense possible. Many of the issues that need to be addressed in order to achieve sustainable development originate outside the forestry sector (e.g. more general problems stemming from population pressure, poverty, inequitable access to resources, unemployment and health, and specific problems caused by adverse environmental externalities[21] generated by other sectors in the coastal area). Unless a concerted effort is made to tackle these problems, sustainable forest management cannot be achieved.

Efforts are also needed at the international level to: "assist technology transfer and the sharing of skills and information; to ensure that trade in forest products is sustainable and equitably rewarded; to coordinate forest monitoring and accounting and to compensate countries that protect forest assets for global benefits, on the basis of services supplied" (Sargent and Bass, 1992). The latter is still a controversial issue, but the principle is incorporated to some extent in the Conventions on Biological Diversity and Climate Change.

4.1.2 Land-use policy

A national land-use policy should be defined and/or reformulated and implemented. Such a policy should use sound and clear criteria for land-use classification

and for the reallocation of uses to ensure the conservation and sustainable use of coastal forest and wildlife resources and provide for the establishment of a permanent resource base.

Permanent forest and wildlife reserves. To ensure protection and conservation, coastal forests that have been classified for protection or production purposes should be constituted as legal reserves, regardless of ownership.

Reallocation of land to other uses and the need for environmental impact assessment. Activities with potentially adverse impacts on coastal forest ecosystems, in particular proposals for converting existing coastal forests to non-forest uses, should be subject to environmental impact assessment (including an assessment of cumulative impacts).[22] Such activities include: the construction of dams; coastal protection and flood control measures; housing and industrial estates; large-scale tourism facilities, marinas, ports and other infrastructure; mining activities; dredging and filling; oil exploitation; and waste disposal.

To minimize the adverse impacts generated by the forestry sector, environmental impact assessments of forestry activities suspected of generating adverse environmental effects should also be required by law (examples include the construction or extension of forest industries and the establishment of large-scale plantations requiring the conversion of existing natural ecosystems or large amounts of water for irrigation).

Increasing the resource base. Community-based coastal plantations and private wood lots should be promoted to expand the forest resource base. Concomitant measures to clarify the usufructuary rights and land tenure arrangements for rural communities should be made. A strategy for the restoration of degraded forest areas should be formulated.

139

---

[21] See Part A, Sections 1.5 and 1.6, and the Glossary.

[22] See Part A, Box A.6.

INTEGRATED
COASTAL AREA
MANAGEMENT
and
AGRICULTURE
FORESTRY AND
FISHERIES

PART C

INTEGRATION OF FORESTRY INTO COASTAL AREA MANAGEMENT

4. Policy and planning for ICAM

4.1.3 Sustainable management of coastal forest ecosystems

Multiple-use concept. Single-use management of coastal forests should be avoided as this forecloses the many direct and indirect benefits and services that the natural coastal ecosystem can offer on a continuing basis. A policy statement on the need for multiple-use management of coastal forest resources, particularly for forestry, wildlife, fishery and agriculture development and conservation should therefore be formulated and politically supported at the highest level of government.

Management plans. The continued provision of forest products and services is greatly dependent upon the effectiveness of forest and wildlife management measures. Management plans for coastal forests should therefore be prepared and implemented, integrating the production of selected wood and non-wood products and providing for forest services corresponding to the available resources and the current and projected demand. Such plans should identify the carrying capacity and maximum sustainable use levels for various activities, including allowable annual harvesting levels for wood and non-wood forest products, and ensure that these are never exceeded.

Multiple-use management should be promoted within each forest management unit involving as many different species, varieties and clones as feasible to conserve biological diversity and reduce risks. Where uses are incompatible, a classification of individual forest ecosystems or parts thereof for specific priority purposes may be needed. Such classifications should be based on resource surveys, demand for particular products and services and the ecological, technical and economic suitability of resource uses.[23]

Whereas there is already a tradition for ten-year management plans in forestry, the plans have often had a very narrow scope, concentrating on harvesting and silvicultural practices for a few commercial timber species. The scope of forestry plans should be broadened to take account of other direct and indirect uses of the forest and the interactions occurring within the sector as well as between the forestry sector and other sectors in the coastal area.

---

[23] See Box C.7.

140

> ### BOX C.7
> ### Achieving sustainability in forest management
>
> For all types of forestry, whether plantations or natural forests managed for timber or other products, sustainability can be achieved through:
>
> - **maintaining the harvest of all products at sustainable levels by:** careful control of harvesting levels, timing and frequency; minimizing damage through harvesting residual stock; and monitoring and feedback into silvicultural management;
> - **maintaining essential ecosystem processes by:** retaining continuous vegetation cover; returning nutrients to the soil (e.g. through in-forest debarking and conversion); minimizing soil compaction by the careful use of light machinery and animals; maintaining watercourse patterns; and careful control of chemical use;
> - **maintaining biological diversity at ecosystem, species and gene levels by:** adopting multispecies/variety/clone systems wherever feasible; incorporating secondary succession as far as possible, rather than treating it as a weed problem; and integrated pest management;
> - **satisfying the needs of people living in and around the forest by:** involving local people at all stages in forest boundary definition, planning, management, harvesting and monitoring of the forest, and forest product processing; employing local people; compensating for foregone rights and privileges; providing access and usufruct rights; providing recreation facilities; ensuring landscape and cultural compatibility;
> - **ensuring economic sustainability:** on the part of the *forest user*, through investing in processes that minimize external inputs of materials and energy, recycle and reduce waste and, especially, turn "waste" into products; and through investment in forestry research, species/provenance selection and breeding; and on the part of *governments*, through creating conditions that will ensure that forest users stay in business but do not reap an excessive portion of forest rent.
>
> **Source:** extracted from Poore and Sayer, 1987.

Criteria and indicators for sustainable forest management. The establishment of criteria for sustainable forest management should be promoted and indicators identified that can be monitored on a regular basis. Box C.7 provides examples of such criteria and practices recommended to achieve sustainable forest management.

4.1.4 Institutional matters

Jurisdiction. The jurisdiction of government agencies and the rights and privileges of government institutions and organizations, NGOs, communities and individuals affecting the conservation and use of coastal forests

PART C

INTEGRATION OF FORESTRY INTO COASTAL AREA MANAGEMENT

INTEGRATED
COASTAL AREA
MANAGEMENT
and
AGRICULTURE
FORESTRY AND
FISHERIES

4. Policy and planning for ICAM

should be clarified. Where existing institutions and organizations are found to be inadequate to meet the needs of effective renewable resource management, legislative and administrative action should be taken to build effective administrative structures and to provide funding for appropriately skilled staff.[24]

Devolution of power and appropriately qualified institutions. To ensure sustainability, each forest area or management unit should be managed in accordance with the local ecological and socio-economic conditions. For this to be achieved, responsibility for forest management can be, where possible, devolved to local institutions and the capability of these to manage forests for multiple purposes must be strengthened. Where traditional forest management systems exist, these should be reinforced.

Forest and wildlife service. In view of the special needs of some types of coastal forests, establishing a management unit within the forest and wildlife service (or other department holding such responsibility) that is responsible for management planning, harvesting, reforestation and protection of coastal forests may be appropriate in countries endowed with abundant coastal forest resources.

Research, information, communication and training. Important prerequisites for sustainable forest management include applied research documenting positive ideas and developments in the field of multipurpose management of forest ecosystems, diffusion of information in appropriate formats to generate support for suitable solutions, consultation and dialogue with the various partners in forest management (including forest dwellers and other forest-dependent rural groups), and human resources development to ensure that enough people are adequately trained in new approaches and practices (Salleh and Ng, 1994; Montalembert and Schmithüsen, 1994).

Additional prerequisites essential for the formulation of an ICAM strategy aimed at enhancing positive and complementary cross-sectoral interactions and

minimizing competing and antagonistic interactions include a sound knowledge of the ecological links between coastal forest ecosystems and other terrestrial and marine ecosystems, and of the impacts of human actions on such links.

Applied research, information dissemination, establishment of communication channels and consultation mechanisms, public awareness campaigns and training of government staff, local communities and other interested parties in issues related to the conservation and sustainable use of coastal forest ecosystems within the framework of an approved ICAM strategy should therefore be actively promoted.

4.1.5 Social issues
Sufficient coastal forest areas should be designated for the supply of goods and services needed by local rural communities. Equitable distribution of forest management incentives, costs and benefits between the forest authority, forest owners, rural communities and private entrepreneurs is another vital requirement for the optimum contribution of coastal forests to economic welfare.

4.1.6 Fiscal policies
Forest revenue systems that fail to capture the potential economic rent of timber production and to cover economic replacement costs (reforestation and maintenance) and that levy charges on the volume of wood removed regardless of species, grade and site conditions (leading to high-grading and destructive harvesting techniques) should be amended.

Incentives to rehabilitate degraded areas and subsidies to private owners providing public services are examples of incentives with a positive effect on the coastal forestry sector and these should be promoted further.[25]

4.2 POLICY INSTRUMENTS
4.2.1 Direct government investment
Physical infrastructure. The provision of physical infrastructure such as roads linking forests to markets may decrease the transportation costs for forest

141

---

[24] See also Part A, Section 2.3.5.

[25] See also Part A, Table A.5.

INTEGRATED
COASTAL AREA
MANAGEMENT
and
AGRICULTURE
FORESTRY AND
FISHERIES

PART C

INTEGRATION OF FORESTRY INTO COASTAL AREA MANAGEMENT

4. Policy and planning for ICAM

products, stimulate production and demand, and generate additional income for local people. However, the construction of roads can also lead to overexploitation of coastal forests and to human encroachment.

Purchase of land. Where coastal forests are privately owned and deemed to be of national importance (e.g. for biological diversity conservation) the government can purchase them to secure their protection.

Education and training. Most coastal forests and forest resources are owned by the state. Consequently, government plays a major role in the preparation and implementation of forest and wildlife management plans. Plans can also be implemented, under agreement with government, by agencies, enterprises, local communities and even individual forest users.

Education and awareness include:

- raising public awareness of the many direct and indirect benefits provided by coastal forests;
- emphasizing the ecological links between coastal forest ecosystems and other terrestrial and aquatic ecosystems;
- understanding the impacts of human actions on the forests and their resources and the need for sustainable management of these ecosystems as an important step in achieving sustainable development of coastal forests;
- developing educational material for schools and public campaigns;
- providing grants to local NGOs engaged in environmental education;
- creating educational centres in forests and wildlife reserves;
- training government staff.

4.2.2 Institutional and organizational arrangements

The creation of effective administrative structures and the provision of funding for appropriately skilled staff and for research are important prerequisites for sustainable development.

As mentioned in Section 4.1.4, specific institutional actions include: revision and clarification of jurisdiction, obligations, rights and privileges; devolution of power to local institutions and strengthening of these where

needed; and the creation of a special unit within the forestry and wildlife service responsible for coastal forest ecosystems, where appropriate. The revision of tenurial arrangements and the establishment of mechanisms for public participation are also necessary.

More imporantly, the creation of a coordinating committee for ICAM is needed for formulation and implementation of integrated forestry management.

4.2.3 Command and control measures

Command and control measures in the form of laws and regulations are very common but do require that the government has the workforce and resources necessary to enforce them.

Land-use zoning. The decision in many countries to require by law the retention or establishment of a buffer zone of trees along coastlines and waterways to provide protection against the actions of wind and waves, habitats for wildlife and detritus for the aquatic food web is an example of a specific land-use zoning measure adopted to enhance some of the existing, positive interactions between the forestry sector and other coastal sectors. Minimum distance limits between developments and natural forests such as mangroves and the creation of protected areas such as national parks and wildlife reserves with restricted access in the core zone are other examples of land-use zoning.

Environmental impact assessment. The enactment of legislation to require the carrying out of EIA prior to the approval of certain development activities is an important measure to prevent adverse environmental impacts and one that has been introduced in most developed and many developing countries.

The critical point is to ensure that the EIA be conducted early in the planning process and that the result be taken into due consideration in the decision-making process.

Pollution control. The most common form of pollution regulation is through the setting of environmental standards including the total prohibition of the use of certain chemicals. However, other methods of pollution control have recently gained a lot of interest – in particular, economic instruments.

PART C

INTEGRATION OF FORESTRY INTO COASTAL AREA MANAGEMENT

INTEGRATED
COASTAL AREA
MANAGEMENT
and
AGRICULTURE
FORESTRY AND
FISHERIES

4. Policy and planning for ICAM

Restrictions on resource use. Restrictions on resource use aim at minimizing unsustainable use of coastal forests and their resources and reducing the adverse environmental effects of forestry activities. Typical measures include placing limits on the size of area that can be cleared at one time and the imposition of appropriate timber harvesting methods in erosion-prone areas, prohibiting the felling of trees in buffer zones along coastlines and waterways, limiting the number and types of animals that can be hunted or making restrictions in the hunting season, and limiting the number and size of charcoal kilns or sawmills allowed to operate in an area.

On an international scale, restrictions on forest resource use are also found in the form of trade restrictions, such as those employed in the Convention on International Trade in Endangered Species (CITES). Requirements can also be unilaterally imposed by individual countries in the form of export or import restrictions (e.g. import restrictions on tropical timber from countries that cannot prove that the timber originates from sustainably managed forests) although unilaterally imposed import restrictions may conflict with the rules of the World Trade Organization.

4.2.4 Economic instruments
Economic instruments can also include various forms of taxation (e.g. penalties, tax incentives, subsidies, tradable permits).[26]

Charges. Charges in the form of royalty and stumpage fees for timber or a license fee to allow the harvesting of non-timber forest products are imposed in most state-owned forests and the level of this charge can be raised to reduce demand and increase government revenues. However, it is often the poorest section of the population who is affected by such measures and they should therefore be designed with care. A user charge, such as an entrance fee, can also limit the use of a recreational area or the number of visitors to a wildlife sanctuary. Import taxes are another form of charge that is frequently employed.

Subsidies and tax incentives. The removal of inappropriate subsidies (favouring inefficient and wasteful use of resources) is often required to prevent or minimize adverse externalities. Incentives can be in the form of grants to landowners as compensation for wildlife damage, subsidies for rehabilitation of egraded areas and tax incentives for plantation establishment.

Tradable permits. Although these are not often used in the forestry sector, they are becoming a more common form of pollution control measure and may be applied to forest industries, the effluence of which is adversely affecting the quality of nearby water courses.

4.3 PLAN DEVELOPMENT
The management of forests constitutes the core of any strategy or programme in the field of forestry. In its

---

BOX C.8

Different types of forest management plan

The regional management plan covers a region or province that is territorially divided into a number of forests or forest districts that are sustainable units, including coastal forests. Whereas provinces and districts are civil administrative units, which may be demarcated socio-politically, forest districts are delineated according to natural terrain features, which may or may not coincide with the administrative units above. As the area covered is extensive, the planning horizon is necessarily long-term, because large investments are needed for plan implementation. Regional forest plans often have a time frame of ten to 20 years.

At the forest management/working plan level, the management area is most likely to be a forest district, often constituted as a forest reserve. The forest management plan covers all of the forest and, although predicted removals and a felling plan are prepared for the whole rotation (e.g. 25 to 30 years), the plan period may be ten years or less as a result of the difficulties of forecasting the economic and demand situations over long periods.

The working plan, on the other hand, only covers areas in which forest operations are to be undertaken within the working plan period, which is often shorter than the forest management plan for the district in order to take account of new factors or changes (normally five to ten years). The working plan may be further divided into separate plans covering silviculture, harvesting operation, etc.

An operational plan entails a further division of the area in that it deals with detailed specifications for on-site operations to be carried out in the near future (one to three years at most) and may be prepared for each range within the forest.

Source: FAO, 1994a.

143

---

[26] See Part A, Table A.5.

BOX C.9
Steps in forestry planning

Setting the terms of reference

Define the management area, the planning horizon, the financial and human resources and the time-frame allotted to undertake the tasks. This will not be a problem in a plan revision exercise, where the area is known and past survey cost data are available. For an unmanaged area, however, attention should focus on what is practicable and affordable.

Assemble baseline information

Relevant socio-economic, ecological and resource data are collected, compiled, analysed and documented in a structured format. Existing maps, available data and past inventory records are consulted and updated.

Identify constraints

Constraints are generally inflexible but may be circumvented in some cases. For example, if the tract of forest to be managed is too small, a switch to higher value-added products or service management may justify the operating cost involved. Alternatively, where land is available, the forest estate could be enlarged through land acquisition or reservation. Constraints are categorized as follows:

- *technical/biological:* technical or biological factors may constrain the extraction methods to be applied or the products to be produced. For example, site limitations will restrict the species that can be established;
- *financial:* the rate of return on capital may be insufficient to meet the rigid standards set by lending institutions;
- *socio-economic:* a plan cannot operate in isolation. The resources allotted to its use will become unavailable for other uses. The overall benefit to the community involves employment generation, environmental impact and "invisible" benefits derived from savings in other sectors, such as improved fisheries, ecotourism and coastal protection. Local customs, culture and religious beliefs may constrain the use and promotion of certain products or services, such as alcohol from fermented *nypa* sap or wild boar meat;
- *institutional:* these are limitations imposed by the organizational and managerial ability of the body executing the plan, and include such issues as the legal framework, social patterns and attitudes, low literacy rates, etc.

Formulate objectives

Production goals should be designed to meet as many of the societal needs for each resource use as possible within the limits of sustainability. Other goals regarding the environment, soils and water protection and rural development are also considered within the framework of the global ICAM strategy.

Develop management alternatives

Where economic and financial data are available, management alternatives may be compared in terms of their cost-effectiveness, taking into account other equally valid considerations, versus social, cultural and environmental factors. The choice and ranking of priorities will depend on the alternatives that can best achieve the preferred set of objectives.

Prepare management plan

The term "management plan" is here used in the generic sense to include plans applicable to each planning level. This plan should be part of an ICAM programme to ensure sustainable multiple use of the coastal forest and wildlife resources.

Implementing the plan

An activity schedule to implement plan targets is drawn up. Further data may need to be collected, such as regeneration sampling prior to logging.

Monitoring

Periodic review of plan outputs is required to see how well objectives are being met and to make adjustments as required. To facilitate the evaluation process, indicators for measuring the success or efficiency of the adopted plan are drawn up.

Plan evaluation and revision

Ideally the forest management plan should be evaluated at least once during the planning period and revisions incorporated where necessary. However, because of the amount of work involved in such an exercise, plan evaluation is often only undertaken in connection with the preparation of the next management plan. Such an evaluation should, *inter alia,* encompass an assessment of the following:

- standing stock and growth rate compared with the estimated production and the actual yield;
- the environmental impacts of the current harvesting system and an examination of mitigation measures that could be undertaken;
- plan objectives;
- the need for changes in current silvicultural operations;
- further research needed in order to refine the present management prescriptions.

Source: adapted from FAO, 1994a.

PART C

INTEGRATION OF FORESTRY INTO COASTAL AREA MANAGEMENT

INTEGRATED
COASTAL AREA
MANAGEMENT
and
AGRICULTURE
FORESTRY AND
FISHERIES

4. Policy and planning for ICAM

broadest sense, forest management deals with the administrative, economic, legal, technical and scientific aspects of the conservation and use of forests and associated wildlife, within the framework of a technically sound and politically accepted overall land-use plan. It implies various degrees of human intervention, ranging from action aimed at safeguarding and maintaining the forest ecosystem and its functions, to favouring given socially or economically valuable species or groups of species for the improved production of goods and environmental services.

In technical terms plan development includes the formulation and implementation of forest management plans, which help control and regulate harvesting of specified goods, combined with silvicultural and protective measures applied to varying degrees of intensity to sustain or increase the social, ecological and economic values of the forest (Vantomme, 1995).

Most coastal forests and forest resources are owned by the state. Consequently, government plays a major role in the preparation and implementation of forest and wildlife management plans. Plans can also be implemented, under agreement with government, by agencies, enterprises, local communities and even individual forest users.

The levels of forest management plans are usually tied to geographical units as illustrated in Box C.8.

The basic planning steps applicable to each planning level, with minor modifications, are described in Box C.9.

PART C

INTEGRATION OF FORESTRY INTO COASTAL AREA MANAGEMENT

INTEGRATED
COASTAL AREA
MANAGEMENT
and
AGRICULTURE
FORESTRY AND
FISHERIES

5. Conclusions

Coastal forests are coming under increasing pressure as a result of population growth in certain regions and increased economic activity. Increasing and conflicting demands on natural resources require governments to establish criteria, priorities and actions to regulate the uses of coastal areas, based on available information and its analysis. Such analysis has to focus on the number of people affected and the benefits to be derived from alternative land-use options, the degree of social disruption and the economic, financial and environmental costs. The setting of priorities raises, in turn, a number of institutional issues and capability requirements.

Coastal forests are different from inland forests insofar as they consist largely of mangroves and other species whose importance for the coastal environment and ecosystems are very poorly understood by local populations and especially by newly established actors. This places such areas under great threat of destruction, with potentially disastrous consequences. In addition, forests are often seen as an obstacle to development rather than a resource to support, and the direct and indirect contributions of forests to food security and the provision of other services by coastal forests are underestimated. ICAM can serve as a framework to correct some of these misconceptions among politicians, public opinion and the media.

For successful conservation and development of coastal forest resources under an ICAM plan, people and governments alike must be convinced that the land planned to remain under forest cover is at least equally or more valuable when kept as forest than if converted into another form of land use. Social and economic benefits emanating from such forests, and their sustainable use, must be quantified, maintained and enhanced at the local as well as the national level. An essential need is therefore to develop an understanding of their direct and indirect values, in particular their positive interactions with other sectors, as a means of affording them greater protection, to the benefit of all users of coastal areas. People living in or adjacent to these forests must be closely involved in all stages of formulation and implementation of the ICAM plan.

Forest management under ICAM will therefore be concerned mainly with protecting forests and with ensuring that the full benefits are drawn from their positive effects on other sectors.

147

INTEGRATED
COASTAL AREA
MANAGEMENT
and
AGRICULTURE
FORESTRY AND
FISHERIES

PART

D

INTEGRATION OF FISHERIES INTO COASTAL AREA MANAGEMENT

INTEGRATED
COASTAL AREA
MANAGEMENT
and
AGRICULTURE
FORESTRY AND
FISHERIES

PART D

INTEGRATION OF FISHERIES INTO COASTAL AREA MANAGEMENT

INTEGRATED
COASTAL AREA
MANAGEMENT
and
AGRICULTURE
FORESTRY AND
FISHERIES

Executive summary

The fisheries sector depends on the coastal area in a variety of ways, both directly (e.g. resources and space) and indirectly (e.g. factors affecting biological productivity). This makes the sector particularly susceptible to land- and sea-based activities that have an impact on the coastal environment. To a lesser degree, the sector also generates negative effects on other activities that are concentrated on the coastal area. While many of the interactions within the fisheries sector and between the sector and other activities (e.g. agriculture, forestry and tourism) are of a competitive or antagonistic nature, a number of complementary interactions may also exist. If the fisheries sector is to make an optimal contribution to economic and social welfare, these interactions must be taken into account and the development and management of fisheries integrated within the wider context of coastal area management.

A first challenge facing fisheries authorities is to establish clearly the social value of the fisheries sector. This requires an approach to management that gives economic and social factors at least as much importance as biophysical ones. However, in the context of ICAM, objectives and strategies for the development of fisheries must be conceived as part of wider local, regional and national economic development and resource use strategies. The "best use" of coastal fisheries resources will depend on these wider strategies, which condition the value attached to the impacts generated both by the sector and by other sectors on the coastal environment (e.g. the type and degree of human-induced changes in the ecosystem that are acceptable).

These objectives, and the related management strategy, will in turn condition the selection of indicators to assess the impact of policy measures from a social and economic, as well as a biophysical, perspective. The entire process is closely linked to the institutional and organizational context in which the fisheries sector operates; a major challenge is to modify the existing context in order to achieve preferred patterns of coastal resource use.

The central problem is one of resource allocation between alternative uses and users. The difficulty of this lies in the special characteristics of renewable coastal resources, i.e. their mobility, the related issue of free and open access and the dynamic nature of their use. Within the capture fisheries subsector, the problem of limiting access and finding ways to extract resource rents is well known; in the absence of such measures, fisheries are bound to be overexploited, preventing the increase in economic welfare that they could generate. Where a fishery is already overexploited, the exploitation level will have to be reduced in order to achieve optimal use. Fisheries dynamics are subject to considerable variability and uncertainty, as is well documented. Approaches to management (e.g. the precautionary approach) must take risk and uncertainty explicitly into account.

Resource allocation problems arising from interactions that are mediated by changes in the biophysical qualities of the coastal environment appear to present similar difficulties; examples include free and open access to water, space, primary productivity, and critical habitats, and the variability and uncertainty of their evolution in response to human use. In addition to the issue of access to fish resources, management needs to consider the environment within which the fisheries sector operates. If ignored, these interactions and those more directly associated with fish resources are bound to generate conflicts between users, both within the fisheries sector and with other activities.

A central role of the fisheries authorities should be to define the trade-offs at stake clearly and in consultation with other sectors involved in coastal resources. This should be based on an assessment of the value placed on various management options, taking into account all the elements of value attached to each option, rather than only those for which a market already exists. Integrated coastal area management (ICAM) requires the potential benefits of the management process to be made explicit to the actors concerned, for them to agree on common goals and follow compatible strategies.

While research may be required for the assessment of the value and risks associated with each option, it is essential to involve stakeholders and seek public involvement in order to benefit from the knowledge of the resource dynamics already available to users, foster a common knowledge of the management process, and reach consensus and agreement on resource management.

151

INTEGRATED
COASTAL AREA
MANAGEMENT
and
AGRICULTURE
FORESTRY AND
FISHERIES

PART D

INTEGRATION OF FISHERIES INTO COASTAL AREA MANAGEMENT

Executive summary

In terms of policy measures, two broad solutions suggest themselves. One is a regulatory approach based on direct control by a management agency, where essentially very detailed plans are established designating who may do what in different areas and under what conditions. In rare cases, this may be the only option. However, a second approach is to seek to modify incentives faced by individuals through the use of various economic instruments (e.g. charges or subsidies). Of particular interest is the extension into the coastal environment of the standard resource allocation model based on use rights and prices. In fisheries some progress has been made in the development of exclusive use rights systems. The challenge is how to implement such mechanisms for other, unpriced, coastal resources. The best solution, often based on a mix of policy instruments, will depend on local circumstances and may change over time.

The variability and uncertainty linked to the dynamic nature of coastal resource use requires that management strategies remain flexible and be considered as an ongoing learning process, rather than a single, isolated exercise. Uncertainty also requires the adoption of strategies, based on the definition of thresholds beyond which the risk of unacceptable changes in the coastal environment are considered excessive. An important aspect of management strategies is to deal explicitly with the risks associated with various management options.

The monitoring system developed as part of the policy measures should be linked to this aspect. In addition to measuring the impact of policy measures, it should allow early detection of thresholds. Both the monitoring of biophysical and economic and social parameters, and the prioritization of research needs should be closely linked to the management objectives.

PART D

INTEGRATION OF FISHERIES INTO COASTAL AREA MANAGEMENT

INTEGRATED
COASTAL AREA
MANAGEMENT
and
AGRICULTURE
FORESTRY AND
FISHERIES

1. The fisheries sector in coastal areas

The fisheries sector (which is defined in these guidelines to include both capture fisheries and aquaculture, unless specifically stated to the contrary) depends on natural resources that are found in a great variety of environments, ranging from the high seas through natural inland water bodies to human-created ponds. However, for a number of reasons the sector is particularly dependent on the coastal area; most capture fisheries are based on coastal stocks, others exploit offshore stocks that spend part of their lives in inshore waters (e.g. in a nursery or feeding area). Coastal aquaculture is also heavily dependent on the coastal area for space and resources.

1.1 MAIN SOCIO-ECONOMIC AND ECOLOGICAL FEATURES

1.1.1 Food security and employment

Fish has always been a primary source of food for coastal populations and remains so today despite the difficulties the sector is facing. The transport of fresh fish over increasing distances, together with more sophisticated processing techniques such as freezing, has led to increasing demand and allowed consumption to spread ever further from the coast.

Aquaculture has been practised for centuries, if not millennia, especially in Asia. Most aquaculture activities continue to be based on traditional, small- to medium-scale operations employing mainly extensive and semi-intensive production methods. In some countries, some types of aquaculture are increasingly being transformed into semi-industrial occupations. Aquaculture is contributing to a growing share of global fish supply of both marine (primarily molluscs and seaweeds) and freshwater (primarily carps) species.

In developing countries, it is estimated that 27 million fishers (including those engaged in production, harvesting and landing site-based activities) are dependent for all or part of their livelihoods on coastal fisheries; together with their dependants, this amounts to some 135 to 150 million people (FAO, 1996c). Artisanal fisheries produce about 25 percent of the total world marine fish catch and contribute about 40 percent of the fish destined for direct human consumption. The contribution of coastal fisheries to the labour force and to local food security is important, particularly in terms of animal protein supply in isolated communities. The social relevance of coastal fisheries is important because fishing communities are often poor, geographically isolated and have very little access to the benefits of public infrastructures and services or coverage by social policies.

Artisanal fishing communities are characterized by: special patterns for remuneration of labour and capital inputs (e.g. prevalence of sharing systems rather than fixed wage); professional training within kin groups; integration of workplace habitation/profession-specific settlements; labour-intensive methods of production; usually among the poorer population groups; and high fertility. Families with an abundant labour force are at an advantage in the exploitation of open access fishery resources and a large family facilitates diversifying the sources of income (which is especially significant in view of the uncertainties surrounding fisheries' nature and decreasing productivity).

Fishing, which is almost everywhere an open access or "free" resource, may also serve as an occupation of last resort for landless and impoverished rural populations.

Where fishing is concentrated and intensive, it plays an economic catalyst role, through activities that build up around the fishing community but that are not directly related to fisheries. The employment aspect, for instance, is not limited to the act of fishing in itself but also extends to boat-building and repairs, mechanical workshops for engines and gear, net-making and repair, handling, processing, packing and transport.

In remote areas, and in countries where fish is a major resource, or where the land has low agricultural potential, the importance of the fisheries sector for employment and food security is proportionately even greater (for example in Mauritania, and in islands of the Pacific and Indian oceans).

Despite the huge catches taken by industrial fishing fleets off the richest coasts, small-scale capture fisheries

INTEGRATED
COASTAL AREA
MANAGEMENT
and
AGRICULTURE
FORESTRY AND
FISHERIES

PART D

INTEGRATION OF FISHERIES INTO COASTAL AREA MANAGEMENT

1. The fisheries sector in coastal areas

profitably elsewhere in the economy. The problems will be worse in more valuable fisheries (where the potential resource rents are higher); ironically, the more profitable the fishery and the greater its potential contribution to economic welfare, the faster it can be expected to decline. It is common to find various kinds of subsidies being granted to the fishing industry (e.g. fuel oil, investment grants, tax write-offs), leaving the impression of an industry that is a burden on society in general and is consequently of little inherent value. Where conflicts arise between fishing and alternative resource uses, the chances are that fishing will be seen as an activity of marginal economic importance. Yet the resource on which fishing is based is in fact very valuable. Fisheries represent a renewable gold mine, provided they are managed correctly.

Biological overexploitation implies that increases in effort decrease the size of the fish stock to the point where its long-term productivity declines. Increasing levels of exploitation tend to be associated with a number of undesirable features:

- the number of fish year-classes tends to decline, leading to year-to-year variability of stock size;
- the average size of fish tends to fall, resulting in less consumer satisfaction and lower returns since larger fish command higher prices;
- the environmental "niche" of the overexploited species may become occupied by less attractive species (e.g. the apparent extension of balistes in West African waters and of various small species of "trash fish" in the Gulf of Thailand);
- competitive innovation is likely to occur among fishers, but it will give low overall returns under conditions of open access;
- the fishing season often becomes shorter, decreasing consumer satisfaction where fresh fish is sought, and increasing processing costs since the high capacity required during the peak season will lie practically idle for the rest of the year.

1.3 SPECIAL CHARACTERISTICS OF COASTAL AQUACULTURE

Aquaculture can provide food, income and employment; it also contributes to diversification of primary production and compensates for the low growth rate of capture fisheries. Aquaculture can contribute to rehabilitation of coastal rural areas through the reuse of degraded land. Stocking and release of hatchery-reared organisms into coastal waters support culture-based fisheries. Culture of molluscs and seaweeds may, in certain cases, counteract processes of nutrient and organic enrichment in eutrophic waters. Conversely, productivity of oligotrophic waters may be enhanced as a result of the nutrient and organic wastes released from aquaculture farms.

Aquaculture can be extensive, semi-intensive and intensive (according to the density of cultured organisms, water supply and exchange rates, degree of supplementary feed provided and other factors), and sea- or land-based. The environmental compatibility (and performance) of coastal aquaculture may be determined by a wide range of factors: biophysical characteristics of the site (i.e. biological, hydrological, locational, meteorological and soil and water quality factors); specific characteristics of the cultured organism; the culture method (i.e. design and construction of the aquaculture site, operation and production levels); skills; access to credit and information; appropriateness of technology, etc.

In many cases, several authorities have direct or indirect jurisdiction over the use of land and water for aquaculture, which usually causes confusion. In some cases, aquaculture is still not considered as a legitimate use of land and water resources because similarities between aquaculture and agricultural practices are often not recognized. The type of tenurial arrangements, such as short- or long-term leases of land or water surface, can influence the development and life span of aquafarms. Uncertainties in the allocation of land and water resources under public domain can result in social conflicts with other users.[4] Environmental legislation, if it exists, often does not cover specific requirements and characteristics of the various coastal aquaculture practices.

Coordination of coastal aquaculture development, supported by adequate information bases and planning

_____

4 See Part A, Section 2.2.2 and Box A.2.

PART D

INTEGRATION OF FISHERIES INTO COASTAL AREA MANAGEMENT

INTEGRATED
COASTAL AREA
MANAGEMENT
and
AGRICULTURE
FORESTRY AND
FISHERIES

1. The fisheries sector in coastal areas

capacities, is still insufficient in many countries. Even though aquaculture development may be prioritized in national development plans, technical assistance to the sector and enforcement of supportive regulations is frequently not carried out as a result of lack of staff and/or financial resources. Inadequate institutional cooperation between the government authorities in charge of planned development of the various activities in the coastal area (agriculture, fisheries, urban and industrial development, sanitation, etc.) may hamper both overall development and environment protection efforts (Barg, 1992; FAO, 1997a).

1.4 DIFFICULTIES IN IMPROVING MANAGEMENT

There is overwhelming empirical evidence that, in the absence of effective management, the world's fisheries are set on a course for long-term decline. Good management of fish resources, which is still extremely rare worldwide, requires three apparently simple conditions:

- in-depth knowledge of existing fisheries and the stocks they exploit;
- agreement on well-defined policies;
- enforcement of fishing regulations.

However, a variety of risks and uncertainties pervade both fisheries exploitation and fisheries management. These include the variability inherent in numerous aspects of the fisheries system such as recruitment, biomass, spatial distribution and likelihood of catching fish, fish prices and input prices.

In seeking to explain variability, it may be difficult to separate the impact of fishing from the impact of environmental changes. This also makes it difficult to know precisely which management measures to adopt. For example, in the face of declining fish stocks, it makes sense to reduce fishing pressure. But there is no guarantee that such action will lead to recovery of the stock. On the other hand, failure to take action seems likely to worsen the situation.

In the case of mangroves, and possibly coral reefs, it may prove possible to design user-right systems, and research in this area would be worthwhile. The basic premise is that the beneficiary should pay the owner of the use right. In the absence of rights, it may seem easy to say that the remaining mangroves should be protected because of the benefits to fish production, but why should people who depend on cutting or clearing the mangroves be expected to give up their (open access) rights so that fishers can benefit? Where two or more interacting natural resources are exploited by two or more groups, some difficult resource allocation questions will eventually have to be addressed (e.g. the extent to which past involvement constitute a future right to use a resource).

In other words, the results of any fishery management process can never be foreseen with certainty. Interest groups opposed to management objectives may use this lack of certainty as an excuse for removing or not implementing a management strategy. However, in the long term, as already stressed, a managed fishery is likely to perform better, on any criterion, than an unmanaged fishery.

The challenge facing fisheries management is to design a system that will be both effective in the short term, and capable of gradual improvement with experience, drawing on the lessons of past mistakes. It is frequently claimed that, as a practical matter, management cannot be introduced until there is an economic crisis in the fishery. If the introduction of management must wait this long, then the management process will seem doomed to failure. As a general rule, the earlier the fishery development process is effectively managed, using a precautionary or preventive approach,[5] the easier it will be to achieve good results. What is required is a move towards economic management methods based on user rights.

A first requirement is to document the natural variability of the fish stock, and it will be necessary to adopt flexible management systems that can respond quickly to changes in the fish stock and in the fishery. Management decisions will also have to take account of the need of small-scale fishers to obtain their daily income (and food) from fishing, the difficulty of converting the labour force to other activities, sources of livelihood and locations and, in the case of industrial fisheries, the difficulty of reconversion of capital (vessels, equipment) to other uses.

157

---

[5] See Part A, Section 2.2.4 and Box A.5.

INTEGRATED
COASTAL AREA
MANAGEMENT
and
AGRICULTURE
FORESTRY AND
FISHERIES

PART D

INTEGRATION OF FISHERIES INTO COASTAL AREA MANAGEMENT

1. The fisheries sector in coastal areas

The development and management of the fisheries sector has tended to be pursued on the generally implicit assumption that the sector can be dealt with in isolation from other sectors of the economy. While this constitutes a working assumption in some circumstances, it has become increasingly apparent – especially in coastal areas – that pressures from, and interactions with, other sectors must be taken into consideration if rational resource use is to be achieved.

Rational resource use within the sector needs to encompass interactions: the fisheries sector may affect, positively or negatively, and other sectors (including itself) through its impact on the coastal area environment; other sectors may affect the fisheries sector through environmental impacts or spatial competition. ICAM should consider all of these aspects.

In an integrated management process, trade-offs between different uses are inevitable. A critical comparison of the benefits and costs embodied in the trade-offs is essential as a basis for developmental, environmental and natural resource policy. Where possible, this approach should be based on the valuation of alternative resource use (Japan, Government of, and FAO, 1995).

PART D

INTEGRATION OF FISHERIES INTO COASTAL AREA MANAGEMENT

INTEGRATED
COASTAL AREA
MANAGEMENT
and
AGRICULTURE
FORESTRY AND
FISHERIES

2. Interactions

Both capture fisheries and aquaculture may generate positive and/or negative impacts on the coastal area and these need to be taken into account in the definition of policy measures for the sector. Synergistic and complementary impacts tend to be similar within the fisheries sector and between fisheries and the other sectors (they are hence dealt with together). Negative externalities generated by the fisheries sector tend to be different in capture fisheries compared to aquaculture (the two are therefore considered separately).

2.1 POSITIVE IMPACTS OF THE FISHERIES SECTOR

Positive impacts of the fisheries sector can be considered according to the three broad categories of effects the sector may have on: economic development; coastal area management; and ecosystem monitoring and rehabilitation.

2.1.1 Regional and national economic development

The fisheries sector, as with other economic activities, may provide a focus for overall economic development (e.g. in island states, such as Iceland, and in coastal countries with extensive coastlines and rich fisheries resources, such as Mauritania or Peru). Most frequently the sector will have a strong regional impact.

The resource rents that the sector generates, especially the capture fisheries subsector, can be used to finance investments within or outside the sector, provided a mechanism exists for such rents to be collected by a resource owner (usually the state).

One specific contribution of the sector is the employment opportunities it generates, especially in remote and marginal areas (see Section 1.1.1).

The fisheries sector contributes to domestic food security and self-sufficiency, although this objective may conflict with the desire to earn foreign exchange. In the Philippines, the shift in the utilization of coastal ponds from the production of milkfish largely for domestic consumption to the production of the more lucrative shrimp for export has had negative consequences on domestic supplies of milkfish. Valuable rice land may also have been lost as a result of conversion into, or salinization by, shrimp ponds (Primavera, 1994).

2.1.2 Coastal area management

The fishing industry can make a positive contribution to the wider objectives of coastal area management. Fishing activities (e.g. ports, fishing boats, landing sites and fish markets) contribute to shaping the landscape, giving it attributes that are attractive to many people, both those living permanently in the area and tourists. In addition, the relative dispersion of the activity, in particular artisanal fishing, may contribute to maintaining viable rural communities and balancing the trend towards growing coastal urbanization.

2.1.3 Ecosystem monitoring and rehabilitation

The fisheries sector is also an observer of the coastal environment capable of alerting the relevant authorities in case of some major hazard such as pollution. In addition, major changes in ecosystems are often first witnessed by fishers and fish farmers.

Aquaculture can provide relief to overexploited species. Overexploitation, both biological and economical, is generally a result of the higher prices obtainable for such species, which in turn is what provides investors with good profitability from related aquaculture operations. By contributing to satisfying the demand for such species, aquaculture can have a positive impact on the state of wild species; higher supplies will tend to bring down prices, making capture fishing efforts less attractive. This effect has been noted in the case of salmon, for example.

For some species, aquaculture may also contribute effectively to conservation. Tisdell (1989) gives the example of giant clams, a species that has been overexploited to the point of being listed in the Convention on International Trade in Endangered Species. However, not all countries are signatories to the Convention and even when they are, loopholes can be found. All species of giant clam have now been successfully bred in captivity and mariculture may therefore be used as an effective means of conservation.

2.2 COMPLEMENTARY INTERACTIONS PERTAINING TO FISHERIES

There are a number of complementary interactions pertaining to the fisheries sector. These include market

159

INTEGRATED
COASTAL AREA
MANAGEMENT
and
AGRICULTURE
FORESTRY AND
FISHERIES

PART D

INTEGRATION OF FISHERIES INTO COASTAL AREA MANAGEMENT

2. Interactions

and non-market linkages and the use of collective goods and services.

2.2.1 Market linkages

Market linkages include intrasectoral interactions (e.g. between capture fisheries and ancillary activities such as net-making, or between capture fisheries and aquaculture through the supply of fishmeal), and cross-sectoral interactions (e.g. between forestry and fisheries through the supply of timber for boat-building, or between agriculture and aquaculture through the supply of feed).

2.2.2 Non-market linkages

The activity of fishing or fish farming is often included as an element of a household's wider production function. Inputs used (e.g. upstream production such as boats or gear) and outputs provided (e.g. fish caught) are exchanged within such households, outside the market. Such complementarities may in some cases determine part of the fisheries sector dynamics; for example, the supply of capital and labour of the fishing activity may evolve in close relation to agricultural activities undertaken by the household.

2.2.3 Use of collective goods and services

This includes for example, harbour facilities or road networks. Various sectors such as aquaculture, agriculture and tourism may also derive benefits from the existence of a natural (e.g. mangrove) or artificial (e.g. dyke) protection from erosion and storm surge.

2.3 NEGATIVE EXTERNALITIES GENERATED BY FISHERIES

Most of the negative externalities generated by the fisheries sector are intrasectoral, i.e. they affect mainly the sector itself.

2.3.1 Negative externalities generated by capture fisheries

Negative externalities generated by capture fisheries include an excessive decrease in biomass, modification of the coastal environment, space congestion problems, subsectoral conflicts and impacts on other sectors.

Excessive decrease in biomass. In the absence of fishing, a fish stock will tend to some average size that reflects the carrying capacity of the environment and interactions with other species (predators, etc.). Changes in environmental conditions (e.g. exceptional conditions for larval survival or the increase in a predator stock) will alter the biomass of the stock. Fishing adds another predator to the system.

The reduction in biomass is not a problem in itself, provided management measures lead to the regeneration of the resource. However, it is an issue if the reduction is so great that the fish stock faces biological (and thus commercial) extinction. It is also an economic issue if, as a result of reduced biomass, high effort levels are required to produce a given catch where lower effort levels would be needed for the same catch if the fish stock were allowed to recover.

Modification of the coastal environment. Although all fishing methods involve some perturbation of the marine environment, some have an environmental impact that extends far beyond the target species, for example the use of poisons and explosives, trawling and the use of other moving gears that tend to plough the sea bed, thereby significantly perturbing the benthos. In addition, habitat might be affected when infrastructures such as harbours are built, involving the conversion of wetlands or the disappearance of some microhabitats or critical nursery space.[6]

Efforts aimed at a target species may affect other fish and non-fish species. This kind of problem affects particularly trawling and net-based fishing generally. The optimal mesh size required for one species may be smaller than for a second species found in the same area with the result that significant by-catches are taken of the second species. Where a trawl fishery exploits many species simultaneously, as in tropical waters, this problem may prove intractable. Stocks of larger species may be consistently biologically overexploited to the point of extinction. Introducing devices aimed at avoiding such wastage can entail prohibitive costs and the alternative to the by-catch may be not to fish at all.

160

---

[6] See also Section 2.4.2.

PART D

INTEGRATION OF FISHERIES INTO COASTAL AREA MANAGEMENT

INTEGRATED
COASTAL AREA
MANAGEMENT
and
AGRICULTURE
FORESTRY AND
FISHERIES

2. Interactions

Space congestion problems. The development of capture fisheries also generates space congestion problems that may prove to be particularly stringent in the coastal area, especially near densely populated areas. This concerns the activity of fishing itself, but also fish landings, and shelter and maintenance of the fleet and gear, including associated infrastructure.

Subsectoral conflicts (industrial, artisanal, recreational). There are various sources of conflict within the fisheries sector. These include conflict for a particular fishing area or for the fish stock, or between artisanal and industrial fishers. For example, large-scale fishing vessels often operate closer to shore than the law allows. Conflicts also occur between commercial and recreational fisheries (see Box D.2).

Impacts on other sectors. Impacts on other sectors in the coastal area relate essentially to the status of marine populations, pollution and the availability of space.

Decreased biomass or modification of species assemblages brought about by fishing may have cross-sectoral consequences where other users such as local diving operators or environmental conservation associations place a value on the affected species or species assemblages. The resulting conflicts may be particularly strong if the impacts concern non-fish species, such as marine mammals, sea birds or sea turtles. Insofar as conservationist activities are in the longer-term interests of fishers themselves, dialogue is required to overcome the dispute.[7]

In addition, the fishing industry affects other sectors through pollution, e.g. water pollution from fishing vessels, air pollution from fish smoking, fishing vessels and processing plants, or noise pollution from traffic generated by fishing activity, especially relating to the movement of fish from the market to the consumer. Waste generated by fish landing sites and tar balls on beaches creates substantial pollution and discourages tourism and bathing uses of the coast.

2.3.2 Negative externalities generated by aquaculture

The long-term trend in aquaculture appears to be towards intensification and increased control over the site and species characteristics (World Bank, 1992). The

---

BOX D.2
Fisheries and ecotourism

The coastal fisheries resources available to many countries constitute not only a source of food and income but also an important tourist attraction. The concept of ecotourism centres around the use of the resources of the coastal area for water sports such as swimming and diving, and the touristic interest of fish, coral reefs and other underwater resources. Sport fishing and diving are also gaining increasing importance for tourism. Touristic uses can be beneficial, for instance, game fishing generates substantial revenues and is selective, while for many reef-dependent species, localized fishing sanctuaries can help to reduce conflict between user groups.

However, with few exceptions, exploitation of sea and fisheries resources for tourism will usually lead to conflicts with more traditional fishing activities since fishers rarely reap the benefit from this alternative use of the resource they draw their livelihoods from. Simultaneously increasing tourism and fishing will thus always lead to allocation problems. Coordination of traditional fisheries, marine reserves and various forms of tourism is the best way to avoid conflicts among different users of coastal areas. Short- and long-term resource allocation strategies will have to be established in accordance with countries' economic and social needs.

161

characteristics of coastal resources used by aquaculture, especially the fluid nature of water resources (and hence water quality) and lack of clearly defined resource-use rights[8] explain most of the negative externalities generated by the sector.

Overexploitation. Aquaculture may contribute to various kinds of overexploitation. For example by affecting populations of wild seed (when aquaculture depends on wild stocks) and fishmeal species in cases of cultured species (such as salmon or shrimp which require high-protein feeds).

In large-scale oyster culture (for example in France), where sharing the resource base implies sharing the overall trophic capacity of the coastal embayment (i.e. available primary production and other sources of nutrients), many growers assumed that by increasing individual stocks a greater share of the resource could be reaped. In fact, such competitive overstocking by

---

[7] See Part A, Section 2.3.4, Figure A.8 and Box A.20.

[8] See Part A, Section 2.2.2.

INTEGRATED
COASTAL AREA
MANAGEMENT
and
AGRICULTURE
FORESTRY AND
FISHERIES

PART D

INTEGRATION OF FISHERIES INTO COASTAL AREA MANAGEMENT

2. Interactions

growers can result in stagnation of total output (caused by excessive total biomass), decreased productivity, longer growing cycles, higher natural mortality and a greater risk of disease epidemics (Heral, Bacher and Deslous-Paoli, 1989). The main reason for this is that, while access is limited on the basis of area, productivity depends on the overall trophic capacity of the entire bay which is shared by all the sites in the area.

This example demonstrates that limiting access is not always sufficient unless the correct variable is identified. A better approach in this case would be to limit overall production according to estimated carrying capacity, and share it among growers, taking measures to ensure that quotas are not exceeded.

Pollution and habitat degradation. Aquaculture itself can generate pollution through release of organic waste, chemicals and inorganic nutrients. For example:

- the deposition of organic fish farm and bivalve waste has been shown to cause enrichment of the benthic ecosystem in the vicinity of fish farms, resulting in the formation of anoxic sediments, increased oxygen consumption by the sediment, the flow of dissolved nutrients and changes in the benthos;
- some of the chemicals used in aquaculture (antibiotics, pesticides) may have toxic effects, possibly leading to increased pest and disease resistance, and potentially posing as a threat to human health;
- inorganic nutrients (nitrogen and phosphorus) released by intensive aquaculture cages or ponds can lead to nutrient enrichment and, depending on site-specific conditions, to occasional phenomena of eutrophication of local ecosystems, especially in semi-enclosed coastal embayments (e.g. fjords, inlets). However, aquaculture is most often a victim of eutrophication caused by other sources, leading to fish deaths and a decline in fish quality.

Other negative impacts of aquaculture can arise from the clearing of mangroves, which are seen as an unproductive resource, their total goods and services being unrecognized,[9] to build fish ponds (destruction of wetland habitats). It has been estimated that in the

Philippines, severe mangrove loss occurred over the period 1967 to 1977 (WRI, 1986; Primavera, 1994). Moreover, in Thailand and Taiwan, Province of China, for example, intensive shrimp culture in coastal ponds has been observed to cause saltwater intrusion, leading to degradation of agricultural land, as well as to land subsidence (Insull, Barg and Martosubroto, 1995).

Impacts on ecosystem structure. Farmed fish may escape and pose a risk to wild species inhabiting open waters in the same area through competition for habitat and food. They may also spread disease. Also associated with the problem of escape is the effect that aquaculture might have on genetic diversity.

Subsectoral conflicts. Another source of negative impacts is linked to the economic and social effects that aquaculture development may have; large-scale aquaculture may result in the displacement of fishers, or other small-scale resource users, especially where common property resources are not regulated. Conflicts can be particularly severe between traditional aquaculturists producing for local needs, and commercial fish farming enterprises producing for export markets.

Impacts on other sectors. As with capture fisheries, the negative externalities generated by aquaculture activities are mainly intrasectoral although cross-sectoral impacts also exist. Aquaculture may limit public use of water space (e.g. physical obstructions to fisheries and navigation) or be seen as affecting landscape aesthetics in areas of natural scenic beauty, and this could lead to a decline in tourism. In this respect, it should be noted that the site requirements of aquaculture (sheltered, unpolluted waters) are often those valued by other users, primarily tourists.

2.4 NEGATIVE EXTERNALITIES GENERATED BY OTHER ACTIVITIES THAT AFFECT FISHERIES

Coastal waters are the ultimate recipient for pollutants coming from land, rivers, air and the sea. Coastal lagoons, estuaries, semi-enclosed seas and shallow littoral waters of the open coast seem to be the areas where most damage is concentrated. This will need to be considered in the definition of management strategies for the coastal area.

162

---

[9] See Part A, Section 1.6.1 and Part C, Box C.1 and Figures C.1 and C.2.

PART D

INTEGRATION OF FISHERIES INTO COASTAL AREA MANAGEMENT

INTEGRATED
COASTAL AREA
MANAGEMENT
and
AGRICULTURE
FORESTRY AND
FISHERIES

2. Interactions

BOX D.3

Fisheries institutions and the other sectors

Few coastal area management schemes neglect fisheries. However, the emphasis is often on the management of fishery habitats rather than the regulation of fishing effort or the establishment of quota schemes. The reasons for this are quite clear; fisheries are often an important economic sector in the coastal area and fishing communities reside therein. More importantly, fishing communities are often the segment of the coastal population most seriously affected by detrimental environmental effects and spatial competition with other sectors. However, there is the paradox that, as other economic sectors expand in the coastal area, the relative economic importance of fisheries declines, weakening the influence that fisheries sector institutions can exert on policy decisions.

In Trinidad, for example, the role of fisheries in terms of their contribution to national income and employment is minimal compared to that of other sectors, so it was not possible for a coastal management process to be headed by the Fisheries Department even though the latter had initiated such a process. In Sri Lanka, on the other hand, where fisheries play a relatively more important role in the coastal area, the management programme was initially located within the ministry responsible for fisheries even through the main concern was coastal erosion which threatened wider interests than fisheries. In the Maldives, integrated reef resource management has also been initiated by the ministry responsible for fisheries, but tourism interests clearly also weigh heavily.

In the United States, which promulgated coastal zone management legislation in the 1970s, fisheries management measures such as effort regulations and quotas are normally not dealt with in the coastal zone management programmes of the various states, but are handled through regional fisheries management councils. However, fisheries benefit from measures to maintain sensitive coastal ecosystems and measures to limit and reduce water pollution.

In the Philippines, fisheries sector institutions and fishing communities play a major role in coastal zone management

programmes while coordination is done largely through intersectoral agencies such as the National Economic and Development Authority and the Department of Environment. Broad government responsibilities have been decentralized and delegated to local municipalities and, where fishing communities make up a large percentage of the local population, they can exert significant influence. However, the interests of small- and large-scale fishers are often in conflict, and local-level interests can be overruled through forces from the centre. Nevertheless, the degree of decentralization and delegation of management authority need to be important considerations of any demand that fisheries sector participants (such as fishers' organizations) may make on the institutional structure of coastal management programmes.

An important lesson from the above examples is that it is in the interests of the fisheries sector institutions to take the initiative of a process of coastal area management; this will usually allow them to exert more influence on future developments. In this regard, an important principle stated in the coastal zone management legislation (or policy) of some countries is to give priority to coast-dependent development. The application of this principle provides a first rationale for allocating scarce coastal resources by giving added weight to uses (or sectors) that by their very nature are dependent on inherent attributes of the coastal area. Fisheries and fishing communities clearly fall within this category whereas many activities of other sectors may not.

When complex intersectoral management problems arise in the coastal area, and the role of fisheries declines, the influence of fisheries sector institutions may depend on the kind of alliances they can create with other sectors or segments of the population on issues of common interest.

Fisheries agencies also need to change their orientation, developing more interest in what other sectors are planning to undertake in the coastal area. Furthermore, they need to develop or acquire expertise to be able to evaluate the consequences of these undertakings on the fisheries and fishing communities.

Source: Willmann, 1996.

2.4.1 Pollution

Most aquatic pollution in coastal areas originates from land-based sources, the rest coming from shipping, waste dumping, oil production and offshore mining.[10] Land-based pollution can be transported in a variety of ways (e.g. rivers, freshwater runoff, the atmosphere).

Pollution may significantly decrease marine environmental quality. Population growth in coastal areas, which leads to urban development and changes in land and other resource uses, also induces various forms of pollution. A major factor is increased waste water discharge into the sea leading to nutrient and organic enrichment and ecosystem disruption, including adverse consequences of eutrophication and reduction of freshwater inflow caused by irrigation and urban uses.

---

[10] See also Part A, Section 1.3 for more on inland sources of pollution.

INTEGRATED
COASTAL AREA
MANAGEMENT
and
AGRICULTURE
FORESTRY AND
FISHERIES

PART D

INTEGRATION OF FISHERIES INTO COASTAL AREA MANAGEMENT

2. Interactions

Another common source of pollution is agricultural waste such as toxic compounds from pesticides. Many such compounds have long half-lives and consequently tend to have long-term effects. Industrial waste also comprises many toxic substances including heavy metals, radioactive elements, acids and industrial chemicals. Oil spills are another common source of acute pollution.

Aquatic pollution, even at low levels, may influence fish production in numerous ways: reduction of stocks by mass mortality (particularly of larval and juvenile fish); gradual decline or changes in species composition of fish populations or entire ecosystems; increased occurrence of diseases; slower growth rates; and deterioration of the food quality of fish. Long-term effects of aquatic pollution on fish should not be underestimated. Species may be disadvantaged through chronic effects such as tissue damage, impaired reproduction or abnormal larval development.

Pollution can have especially severe effects on shellfish. In Canada, for example, over 200 000 ha of near-shore waters are closed for shellfish harvesting because of pollution; in the United States, one-third of shellfish beds have been closed. On a larger scale, the crash of the entire fisheries economy of the Black Sea area as a result of pollution, overfishing and the introduction of exotic species that feed on fish larvae is estimated to cost some US$1 billion per year (Barg and Wijkstrom, 1994).

Both capture fisheries and aquaculture are affected by land-based pollution. The problem is at once "worldwide yet highly specific to different geographic, ecological, social and economic situations" (Dahl, 1993). As a result, there can be no unique solution although some general principles may perhaps be enunciated.

Many of these problems may be aggravated, if not actually caused by, coastal tourism. Tourism leads to increased sewage, much of which is left untreated, resource depletion and conflict (e.g. between recreational and commercial fishers). Such problems are likely to be especially severe in the case of islands (Bass, 1993). Because the principal gains from tourism are clearly priced and easily observable, whereas the environmental costs generally affect unpriced resources, there is a tendency to overestimate the net social benefits of tourism and, consequently, to favour this sector over competing ones such as fisheries. Rational resource use requires that all benefits and costs associated with an activity be identified.[11]

2.4.2 Perturbation of critical habitats

Civil engineering works (e.g. road construction, dams, ports) may place further stress on coastal ecosystems as a result of soil runoff and degradation of critical habitats. Similarly, agriculture and forestry activities, through their impact on soil stability, may affect coastal sedimentation.[12] Because of their importance for the productivity of marine communities and because of their particular location in the coastal area, a number of critical habitats must be considered specifically, as growing pressures on them may have significant consequences for the fisheries sector. These include mangroves, sea grass, lagoons and estuaries (see Box D.1).

The common feature of these habitats is that they provide valuable services that are difficult to observe and are unpriced. Because they are difficult to observe, there is a tendency to ignore them, for example fishers themselves may trawl through sea grass meadows despite the impact that this may have on their own future welfare. In many cases the value of such resources is grossly underestimated, pointing to an urgent need for studies and research to demonstrate their value. Given the widespread impact on the fisheries sector, the fisheries authorities should take the lead in organizing such work. More importantly, since the resources are unpriced, there is no mechanism for their value to be reflected. As a result, overexploitation of such habitat resources follows in the same way that it does in open-access fisheries.

---

[11] See Part A, Section 1.6.3.

[12] See Part A, Sections 1.1, 1.3 and 1.7.

INTEGRATED
COASTAL AREA
MANAGEMENT
and
AGRICULTURE
FORESTRY AND
FISHERIES

PART D
INTEGRATION OF FISHERIES INTO COASTAL AREA MANAGEMENT

3. Information requirements

3.1 DESCRIPTION OF THE RESOURCE BASE

The economic health of the sector is closely linked to the condition of the fish resource base. Its assessment should be a multidisciplinary exercise closely linked to policy-oriented information needs. The 1993-94 situation of the Canadian northern cod fishery and the consequences for the fishers, for the whole Newfoundland community and for the Canadian Government are testimony to the importance of knowing and understanding the resource base (see Box D.4).

3.1.1 Information requirements

The first information requirement is a sound description of the fishery resources themselves. The fisheries authorities, economists and scientists should be able to identify the most important species for the country and concentrate their efforts, at least initially, on those species. Determining these species and main issues concerning them will depend on the extent to which particular instances contribute to meeting the objectives of fisheries policy. Typical goals might include employment, contribution to balance of payments, earning foreign exchange and/or supplying domestic markets. However, research priorities often seem to have depended on the interests of particular scientists with the consequence that the best information may concern a species of relatively minor societal importance, notwithstanding its scientific interest. Such a situation represents a failure of fisheries policy. The fisheries authorities must establish research priorities, and possibly make funding for research depend on its relevance to management needs. Curiosity-driven research programmes are doubtless of interest, but they may turn out to be inadequately focused from a management perspective.

Priority issues. Priority issues will usually concern estimations of current yields, potential yields and their variability, and expected impacts of policy measures on future yields. The focus of fisheries science has traditionally been on estimating sustainable yields associated with different effort levels, and in particular on estimating maximum sustainable yields (MSY).

BOX D.4

Newfoundland cod fishery

Depletion of the North Atlantic cod stock compared to historical levels was evident as early as the mid-1970s, yet adjustments to quota levels lagged behind stock declines. A special meeting of the Northwest Atlantic Fisheries Organization (NAFO) in June 1992 recommended that catches should not exceed 50 000 tonnes, the low range of $F_{0.1}$ values. The meeting could not specify the cause of decline but, in addition to overfishing, it identified other negative influences such as the impact on cod recruitment of cold water currents in the northwest Atlantic and increased predation on young cod by harp seal populations which had expanded since culling was banned. Recent declines in capelin, the principal food organism of cod, might also be involved.

Disagreements on the management objective for this straddling stock may have been a prime cause of stock depletion, but the differences in the scientific advice based on commercial catch per unit effort versus research survey indices, also contributed to the uncertainty of advice. Possible biases in abundance trends can probably not be excluded, since the calendar of research surveys on the seasonally migrating stock was fixed, while seasonal patterns were in a period of change. Serious differences in the advice formulated, using several population dynamic models, was the main reason why it was not possible to make an agreed stock projection in June 1992.

The fact of the stock decline, about which no one disagrees, also raises a number of controversial political issues. These include the need to reinforce the roles of fisheries commissions and coastal states in regulating fisheries on those portions of straddling stocks lying beyond EEZs. Although the areas falling outside the Canadian 200-mile zone are relatively small, a more significant part of the stock, through migration, may occur in these areas at certain periods of the year. Here, there has been disagreement between the coastal states, who recommend $F_{0.1}$ management criteria, and distant-water-fishing countries wishing to fish at higher levels of exploitation. Added to this were the problems of deciding on a uniform approach by all participants to fishery surveillance. This case also illustrates the difficulties faced by commissions not having independent means to control biases in statistical reporting and surveillance, particularly when such reporting has direct implications on quotas in the following year. The inertia of the quota allocation mechanism is evident, particularly in a period when some assessments did not unambiguously reflect declining stocks. The closure of domestic fisheries by the Canadian Government in 1992, followed by a compensation package to support fishers in a province with high unemployment and few job alternatives, has had severe consequences for coastal communities.

Source: FAO, 1994b.

INTEGRATED
COASTAL AREA
MANAGEMENT
and
AGRICULTURE
FORESTRY AND
FISHERIES

PART D

INTEGRATION OF FISHERIES INTO COASTAL AREA MANAGEMENT

3. Information requirements

There has been some tendency for fisheries administrators to consider MSY as a fixed potential of the stock, and as a management target. More recently however, management-oriented research has tended to move away from the assessment of target values and single-figure estimates.

Policy objectives will determine the choice of reference points for management, which in turn condition the performance indicators used and the related data needs. In a number of cases, for example, policies may rely on the objective of avoiding severe ecological, economic and social disturbances (Willmann, 1983). Avoidance of risks of overfishing, defined in various ways, have been granted growing importance in the definition of fisheries policies. The various possible reference points for fisheries management are reviewed by Caddy and Mahon (1995) and Garcia (1996). The latter includes threshold reference points based on biological or economic considerations (see Box D.5). From a management perspective, adopting such reference points implies the definition of a monitoring system that allows early detection of risks of "overshooting" agreed thresholds.

In addition, advice offered to managers is tending towards range estimates sometimes associated with probabilities. There is a need to reinforce this approach in order to force managers to consider explicitly the risks and uncertainties inherent in the exploitation and management of multispecies fisheries and ecosystems. This is particularly true where complex coastal interactions are taken into account.

In this context, research is needed to evaluate the degree of stability of different fisheries. Long-term data sets need to be developed to deal with this kind of question. Along the same lines, consideration must be given to the resilience of the fish stock in the face of its exploitation. The search for answers to these questions may require a different approach to management whereby measures are implemented deliberately with a view to generating information about the exploited system's response to various events. This kind of experimental approach to management has long been advocated by some fisheries analysts (e.g. Walters, 1986).

Resource characteristics. An appropriate characterization of the resource base will rest on complementary biological and socio-economic information.

For the major targeted species, estimating potential yields will require assessment of key parameters, such as growth, reproduction and biomass. Given the biological/fisheries science background of many fishery research institutes around the world, such features are often among the most investigated aspects of fisheries and fish stocks. For aquaculture, in addition to information relating to the fish species, biophysical information on the resource base will also include space characteristics on land and at sea (e.g. topographic and hydrographic characteristics), related availability of water of the quality required, and availability of nutrients, food organisms, etc.

On the other hand, economic and social information is often weak for both fisheries and aquaculture, certainly in comparison with biological and technical information. Economic information has usually been collected in an ad hoc manner, meaning that few time series of data of the same quality and consistency as that developed for biological assessments are available.

Economic and social impact. Economic impact analysis estimates the activity generated in the economy from the various activities related to the fisheries sector. The anticipated impact of policy measures on the economy, both within and outside the sector, can thus be assessed. Developing the fisheries sector may have an important economic impact in terms of labour and capital employed on the sector itself and, via multiplier linkages, on other sectors related to the fisheries sector. Typical indicators of the economic impact of the fisheries sector would include gross value of production, value added, capital and labour operating in the fishery and income and employment multipliers.

Another requirement is to establish the social significance of the sector. Various indicators might be taken, depending to some extent on the objectives assigned to the sector by the management authorities. Typical variables would include earnings, employment and contribution to food security.

However, such impacts per se do not reflect the social value of the activity because the labour and capital employed have an opportunity cost (i.e. if they were not involved in fishing, they would be employed elsewhere). Because of political factors and because a

INTEGRATED
COASTAL AREA
MANAGEMENT
and
AGRICULTURE
FORESTRY AND
FISHERIES

PART D

INTEGRATION OF FISHERIES INTO COASTAL AREA MANAGEMENT

3. Information requirements

BOX D.5

Precaution and management reference points

Reference points (RPs) have always been used in management, explicitly or implicitly, and are not a particular characteristic of the precautionary approach to fisheries. Precaution will relate to the choice of reference points (and their resource-related properties) and to the way in which they are used. A management reference point is therefore "an estimated value derived from an agreed scientific procedure and an agreed model to which corresponds a state of the resource and of the fishery and which can be used as a guide for fisheries management". They are meaningful only with reference to the underlying theory, model, method and data used to estimate them, as well as species to which they apply. Thus, reference points should be reassessed periodically as new data are collected and new understandings or methods become available.

Maximum sustainable yield (MSY) reference point. For decades, MSY has been used as a reference point by research, development and management and considered as a last-resort threshold for stock "sustainability". Research has amply argued that, even at MSY, stock instability and risk of recruitment failure are sometimes already high. This, added to the fact that MSY and the fishing rate corresponding to it are usually difficult to determine accurately, should mean that MSY is not considered as being a precautionary target, particularly for stocks with low resilience or high natural variability.

Target reference point (TRP). A TRP corresponds to the state of a fishery and/or resource that is considered desirable and at which fisheries management aims. In most cases, a TRP will be expressed as a level of desirable output from a fishery (e.g. related to catch) and will correspond to an explicit objective of the fishery. When a TRP is reached during a development process, management action should aim to maintain the fishery system at its level, e.g. through establishment of total allowable catches and quotas or through effort controls (see " Precautionary use of RPs and threshold reference points", below).

Limit reference points (LRPs). A LRP indicates the state of a fishery and/or resource that is considered undesirable. Fishery development should be stopped before reaching the LRP, thus reducing the risk of inadvertently "crossing" the limit. Limits are usually expressed in biological terms (e.g. minimum spawning biomass required) but could be expressed in economic terms (e.g. minimum profitability), even though this does not seem to have been done yet. A common way to specify LRPs is to express them as a percentage of the virgin biomass below which the stock should not be driven. When a LRP is approached, management action should severely curtail or stop fishery development, as appropriate, and corrective action should be taken.

Precautionary use of RPs and threshold reference points (ThRPs). The two major sources of bad performance in a reference points system are the accuracy and precision with which the RPs

are determined and their adequacy to the fishery system dynamics. Because of the uncertainty inherent in their determination, RPs should preferably relate to probabilities (e.g. specifying both their central value and confidence limits). This uncertainty, combined with uncertainty in the current value of the fishing mortality or stock biomass, implies a certain probability that RPs be "missed" (e.g. overfishing or underfishing, reliability of statistics). Furthermore, the fishery system has its own dynamics, and fishing fleets have a high level of inertia (resistance to change), as a result of various financial, technical, cultural and administrative factors. As a consequence, stopping fleets from evolving or expanding, and reversing or only modifying historical trends, are not trivial tasks and may require time in addition to political will and incentives.

Two solutions are generally offered to deal with both of these problems: choosing more precautionary references; and using the references in a more precautionary way. It is possible to select different reference points based on the level of precaution desired, or on acceptable risk, and this is usually achieved at the expense of some potential economic benefits. It is also possible to keep the same RPs, using them differently. The probability of inadvertently "crossing" a TRP when aiming strictly at it, is 50 percent. These results could only be obtained through fishing at a level somewhat lower than otherwise possible, on average, and this second solution is therefore equivalent to replacing the reference point by a more precautionary one. Precaution will be ensured by combining TRPs and LRPs which will most often refer to different control or status variables of the fishery system.

ThRPs indicate that the state of a fishery and/or a resource is approaching a TRP or a LRP and that a certain type of action (preferably agreed beforehand) is to be taken to avoid (or reduce the probability) of the TRP or LRP being accidentally exceeded. It provides an early warning when critical reference points are being approached, reducing the risk of these points (and the management objectives they give rise to) of being violated.

Ecosystem reference points. Ecosystem management is "the maintenance of ecological relationships between harvested, dependent and related species" as well as the "prevention of change or minimization of the risk of change in the marine ecosystem which are not potentially reversible". This requirement is precautionary in nature in the sense that it requires the integrity and essential functions of the ecosystem to be preserved as a prerequisite to fisheries sustainability. In practice, however, the way of managing entire ecosystems is not yet known. Management therefore has to be flexible, adaptive and experimental at scales compatible with the scales of critical ecosystem functions. It has been proposed, for instance, that in multispecies management, a reasonable strategy would be to exploit all species in proportion to their abundance in order to maintain the overall ecosystem structure.

Source: extracted from Garcia, 1996.

167

INTEGRATED
COASTAL AREA
MANAGEMENT
and
AGRICULTURE
FORESTRY AND
FISHERIES

PART D

INTEGRATION OF FISHERIES INTO COASTAL AREA MANAGEMENT

3. Information requirements

sectoral approach is adopted, undue weight is often given to economic impacts.

Economic value. If access to the fish stock is not restricted, the economic returns on the stock will be perceived as profit to exploiters and will encourage more labour and capital to be employed.[13] If the stock were to be placed in the hands of an owner, then the owner could be expected to charge for use of the resource. Such payments would be similar to payments made to landowners for the use of land.

In the case of fish stocks, it is often argued that the government should assert ownership of the resource on behalf of society in general (trusteeship). Whatever the ownership structure, the economic value of the resource will become apparent only where there is someone who takes it into consideration.

Important elements are therefore an estimate of the resource rent potential of a fishery and consideration of the impact of different policies on such rent. Such studies might be done on the basis of simulations. Estimates should at least be made of their level in the different parts of the fisheries system, including factors of production (e.g. labour), upstream sectors (e.g. boat-building) and downstream sectors (e.g. marketing and processing). As noted by Willmann (1983), the former two will influence input costs of fishing, while the latter will influence the output value of fishing; imperfect market conditions may lead to a part of the resource rent being appropriated by factors of production, upstream activities or downstream activities through underpriced outputs or overpriced inputs. At least a qualitative assessment of these effects should be made available.

The difference between economic impact and value can be particularly important, for example, in the analysis of conflicts between different components of the fishing sector on fishing grounds, e.g. conflicts between industrial fleets and artisanal fleets. In this case, comparisons based on economic impact and those based on economic value may yield different conclusions as to the relative contribution of each component to the welfare of a country (Palfreman and Insull, 1994). From an economic welfare perspective it seems far more

---

[13] See Section 1.2.1 and Part A, Box A.2.

BOX D.6
Integrated coastal fisheries management in Trinidad and Tobago

The FAO/UNDP project, Integrated Coastal Fisheries Management (ICFM), has undertaken a pilot project in Trinidad and Tobago (Gulf of Paria) with the objective of developing improved methodologies and coordinating mechanisms for ICFM. The project's principal strategy was to strengthen the capability of the Fisheries Division of the Ministry of Agriculture, Land and Marine Resources to integrate the subsector's concerns in the wider framework of coastal area management and development planning. This entailed the following broad elements:

- consolidation of the information base on fisheries and on other sectors' impacts on them;

- creation of awareness of the socio-economic contribution of the fisheries sector and of its role as a natural monitoring unit of the environment;

- strengthening of organization and representation among fishers, fishing communities and other related occupations;

- promotion of the supportive role of the Fisheries Division in coastal area management matters.

Source: extracted from Trinidad and Tobago, Government of the Republic of, FAO/UN

---

important to estimate economic value than impact, although studies of both may be required.

3.1.2 Identification of research requirements

In addition to the impact and value studies referred to above, investigations may be required into: costs and earnings of vessels; the distribution of earnings between participants in the fishery; economic and social linkages; fish distribution margins; margins of input suppliers; and alternative employment opportunities.

Market structures should also be investigated to ascertain the degree of competition and, in particular, to identify market imperfections. In themselves, high margins are not particularly revealing since they may arise from many sources (e.g. skill shortages in particular areas such as fish trading), and profits serve a socially useful resource allocation function by signalling areas of the economy to which more resources should be devoted.

PART D

INTEGRATION OF FISHERIES INTO COASTAL AREA MANAGEMENT

INTEGRATED
COASTAL AREA
MANAGEMENT
and
AGRICULTURE
FORESTRY AND
FISHERIES

3. Information requirements

3.1.3 Tools for collecting information

The responsible authorities should be able to provide a description of the sector which would include, for example, the capture fishery and marine aquaculture subsector, its history, location, size, structure, markets and fleet dynamics.

This is not a trivial task since, in many situations, information on the sector is collected by numerous different agencies. It is common to find, for example, that different agencies use different codes for the same species. In some cases, different agencies may have different definitions of the same species and, therefore, different aggregations of species may be used. It is the role of the authorities to ensure the compatibility of collection and archival systems.

One agency should be responsible for the country's fisheries statistical system and coordinate the activities of the various agencies involved. Such agencies might include one or more research institutes (collecting biological and economic information), the customs service (collecting export and import data), the enforcement agency (often the navy), fish markets, the licensing authority, the regulatory agency (responsible for drafting regulations), etc.

Information collection and analysis will only lead to a learning process if a reliable record is kept of past data and analysis concerning the dynamics of the resource. An important task of the fisheries authorities is to establish baseline studies with which future assessments are to be compared in order to improve understanding of the biological and socio-economic impacts of policies.

The constitution of the required information will rest on the acquisition of both primary and secondary data. The former involve direct observation of the biophysical and socio-economic factors of interest (e.g. censuses, surveys, remote sensing), and can also involve some form of measuring and recording equipment. The latter involve using information that is already available, organized in various formats (e.g. data sets, maps, photographs, published or unpublished texts), from sources including government agencies, research institutes, libraries and international organizations. Tools for the collection of primary and secondary data in fisheries are described in Meaden and DoChi (1996).

For both biophysical and socio-economic information, the choice of primary data collection methods (e.g. periodic sample surveys in capture fisheries or target study sites in aquaculture, continuous monitoring schemes for key parameters) will depend on data needs and the means available. In both components of the fisheries sector, regular observation and reporting by resource users may also play an important role in the rapid detection of significant variations.

Explicit inclusion of risk and uncertainty in the information provided as an output of monitoring and analysis of fisheries data can require a large amount of information and technicality. The subjective views of participants, based on their experience, can also be useful in the policy process (Caddy and Mahon, 1995).

Biological information. Assessment of the current and potential yields from exploited stocks requires both biological data on the resources and technical data on the fisheries. Where parameters such as growth are not known, and in particular when fisheries are not developed, it may be possible to derive an idea of likely values from studies of similar species in other areas. However, local studies are to be preferred and, if not available, should be initiated.

For capture fisheries, data collection methods include research vessel campaigns and/or the monitoring of commercial fisheries. However, where a fishery is already developed, it will usually provide most of the information required.

Information on patterns and trends in magnitude and distribution of catches and landings are usually considered as the minimum requirement of an information system for capture fisheries. Most often, a catch assessment survey will be based on a sampling framework designed to monitor catches in time and space. Catch data can, however, also be collected either systematically or using sampling methods (Neiland *et al.*, 1994), as the production passes through transport and marketing.

Both in research vessel surveys and in monitoring of commercial fisheries, catch sampling frameworks will usually be designed to collect complementary data, including effort, length and age frequencies, length to weight ratios and data concerning fishing gear and operations. While some of these data will be easy to

INTEGRATED
COASTAL AREA
MANAGEMENT
and
AGRICULTURE
FORESTRY AND
FISHERIES

PART D

INTEGRATION OF FISHERIES INTO COASTAL AREA MANAGEMENT

3. Information requirements

BOX D.7

Bio-Economic Analytical Model: BEAM 4

Bio-economic models can address three basic questions.

First, they can help explain why a fishery has developed in a certain pattern, for example, why many investments were made in one type of fishery while no significant developments have taken place in other fisheries.

Second, they can help in the identification and selection of the most effective policy measures to achieve one or a set of economic and social objectives. For example, a fairly widespread policy measure is the provision of subsidies during periods of economic distress. Without a thorough analysis of the bio-economic effects of subsidies, the government may aggravate the economic crisis rather than contribute to a lasting economic recovery of the sector.

Third, they can help in determining the appropriate prescription for the selected policy measure(s). Here there are a wide variety of examples, ranging from the right minimum mesh, to the right timing of the closed season and to the right numbers and types of vessels to be allowed to exploit a particular fisheries resource. Taking the latter example, determining the optimum fleet size is, of course, also of direct relevance in the planning of investments into fishing harbours and allied onshore facilities.

The Bio-Ecomomic Analytical Model (BEAM 4) is a FAO-designed programme for deterministic bio-economic simulation models, handling several target and by-catch species and several fleets operating sequentially or simultaneously across several areas and landing in several processing plants. It takes account of migration and seasonal recruitment. The objective of BEAM 4 is to predict yield, value and a series of measures of economic performance as a function of fishery management measures such as control of fishing effort, closed season, closed areas and minimum mesh size regulations. BEAM 4 is a versatile tool for the rational management of exploited living aquatic resources.

The model behind BEAM 4 is an age-structured cohort-based fish stock assessment model combined with an economic model of both harvesting and processing sectors. The basic purpose of bio-economic modelling may best be derived from the objectives of fisheries policies at large. These objectives may include higher incomes for fishing families, better supply of fish to consumers, increased earning of foreign exchange or the creation of employment. The measures of economic performance calculated by the economic submodel include private profit, profitability, gross value added, net value added, national net value added, resource rent, employment, costs in foreign exchange and foreign exchange earnings.

BEAM 4 is primarily designed for the analysis of tropical mixed fisheries with penaeid shrimps as the target and fin-fish as the by-catch. However, in principle it may be used to analyse any fishery. It is suitable for the analysis of resources shared between artisanal and industrial fisheries.

Source: extracted from Sparre and Willmann, 1992.

---

record (e.g. length or weight), others may prove more difficult to measure accurately (e.g. age of fish).[14]

Economic and social information. Much of the economic and social information required may be available through secondary data. However, as a result of potential gaps in the data and the need for consistency in the information available, primary data should also be collected, with cost-effectiveness being the main determinant of methods chosen.

For example, where information on the main units of the fisheries system (farms, fish farmers, ports, boats, fishers, markets, transportation network) is required, tools could include land- or water-based censuses, periodic sample surveys and/or the use of remote sensing techniques.[15]

Data on income and profitability can be collected as part of a catch assessment survey or in a separate costs and earnings survey. Once the results of such studies are known, they can be used to assess the fishery and its management, for example via bio-economic simulation models, such as FAO's BEAM 4 (see Box D.7).

For the aquaculture sector, various performance criteria might be developed similar to those used for

---

[14] Basic sampling theory and sampling desig and examples of statistical procedures for the collection and analysis of capture fisheries data are presented, for example, in Caddy and Baziogos (1985); Sparre, Ursin and Venema (1992); and Hillborn and Walters (1992). Methods for the collection of biophysical information concerning the resource base for coastal aquaculture (including site requirements in terms of space and water) are reviewed by Barg (1992).

[15] Application of remote sensing tools to fisheries are presented in Butler *et al.,* (1998); see also Part A, Box A.18.

PART D

INTEGRATION OF FISHERIES INTO COASTAL AREA MANAGEMENT

INTEGRATED
COASTAL AREA
MANAGEMENT
and
AGRICULTURE
FORESTRY AND
FISHERIES

3. Information requirements

agricultural activities, in terms of profitability, rates of return on capital invested, employment, physical production, labour productivity, etc. Information on these indicators will need to be collected, as for capture fisheries, e.g. through surveys.

In the case of small-scale artisanal fisheries, in particular in developing countries, special care should be taken in defining and measuring income and profitability indicators. First, the fishing unit may not be the relevant decision unit to consider where it is only an element of a larger household production function. A growing number of studies have shown the importance of such production structures in many developing countries. Second, and partly as a consequence, the unpriced nature of a number of inputs (e.g. gear, boat, labour) and outputs (e.g. production consumed by the household or traded outside the market) must also be acknowledged. These "non-market" dimensions of the activity should be taken into account in data collection and analysis. Participatory assessment surveys are useful tools for this purpose.[16]

3.2 ENVIRONMENTAL INFORMATION

In addition to an adequate description of the resource base, the integration of fisheries management into coastal area management requires information on the environmental parameters affecting its dynamics.

3.2.1 Information requirements

The importance of coastal ecosystems for the productivity of both wild and cultivated fish stocks is now well established. Assessing the nature and the extent of human-induced changes in the biophysical environment, their origin and their consequences is essential. This will mostly be based on the evaluation of local interactions, although in some cases it may also be necessary to consider wider biophysical changes (e.g. climate change, ocean circulation patterns)[17] to explain locally observed dynamics.

---

[16] Indications on participatory appraisal methods are found in Part A, Box A.20.

[17] The potential effects of global warming would presumably affect many coastal areas through sea-level rise, water temperature increase, deviations from present patterns of precipitation, wind and water circulation. Estuaries would experience loss of habitat, intrusion of marine waters and associated organisms, changes in circulation patterns that affect retention of some indigenous species, and increased hypoxia and storm surges (Barg and Wijkström, 1994).

Biophysical information may be required concerning changes in critical habitats, in water and sediment quality and in ecosystem structure. Where possible, the value of such changes should be assessed, for example, in the case of changes in economic value of the fisheries sector associated to these biophysical changes.

Habitat characteristics. The nature of the links between the various commercial fish stocks and their productivity must be understood, and critical habitats identified. A key role for the fisheries authorities is to provide information on these areas. To begin with, it will be useful simply to identify them and the kind of benefits they provide (e.g. in the case of mangroves, coral reefs, sea grass beds, estuaries). Information should then be provided on their present status, for instance the degree (percent) to which they have been affected and the implications for the fisheries sector. The authorities should try to identify the causes of these transformations.

Changes in the water column and sediment. A major cross-sectoral interaction in which the fisheries sector is involved (and usually suffers from) is induced by the quality of water and sediment. Information is needed on the impact of changes in water quality and on the dynamics of wild and cultivated fish stocks (e.g. recruitment, growth, mortality). A distinction is usually made between "contamination" and "pollution" of the marine environment (Barg, 1992). Only the latter implies adverse effects significant enough to become unacceptable. Measuring pollution will thus rest on a preliminary definition of acceptable levels of human-induced environmental change. To a large extent, this will be related to the priorities and objectives assigned to the fisheries sector.

Social and economic environment. The environment in which the fisheries sector operate influences interactions between the components of the sector and between the sector and other sectors (e.g. economic linkages). It should therefore be possible to have information on selected regional and national indicators, such as prices of substitute products for fish, price of fuel, tax regime on inputs and outputs, employment, transport infrastructure and availability of alternative sources of income.

171

INTEGRATED
COASTAL AREA
MANAGEMENT
and
AGRICULTURE
FORESTRY AND
FISHERIES

PART D

INTEGRATION OF FISHERIES INTO COASTAL AREA MANAGEMENT

3. Information requirements

3.2.2 Research requirements

A number of issues will probably require further research, including effects of pollution on marine organisms or risk for human health posed by consumption of polluted marine organisms. More generally, research is required into the whole area of the valuation and pricing of environmental goods and services under various schemes of resource allocation,[18] as well as into monitoring and analysis of the impact of management measures where implemented.

Better measurement of the multispecies dimension of coastal fisheries and improved understanding of coastal fishing's and aquaculture's impacts on the structure of coastal species assemblages are also required. Methodologies for assessing the extent and impacts of by-catch and discards in capture fisheries are being developed (e.g. Alverson *et al.*, 1994). For impacts specific to aquaculture, environmental assessment and monitoring efforts should be related to the scale of the perceived impact of a given aquaculture operation (Barg 1992; GESAMP, 1996b).

3.2.3 Tools for collecting information

Primary data on the biophysical changes observed in the coastal environment and their causes (e.g. land use, effluents) can be collected through monitoring of key parameters, surveillance of target sites and/or species, and regular observation by resource users. Remote sensing is also very useful.[19]

Much useful secondary data concerning the economic and social environment in which the fisheries sector operates can be collected by improving links between the fisheries agencies and the other sectoral and/or governmental agencies and resource users.

The assessment of the economic value of human-induced biophysical changes in the coastal environment can rest on a variety of methods, depending on the nature

of changes considered. Cost-benefit analysis is one such method.[20]

3.3 INSTITUTIONAL AND ORGANIZATIONAL INFORMATION

3.3.1 Information requirements

Institutions determine the rules with which individual users are confronted within and outside the fisheries sector. They include national and regional legislative

---

BOX D.8

Co-management can work! Canada's Maritime Fishers' Union

The Canadian Atlantic fishery has been going through difficult times. However, not all inshore fishers depend on cod and many make a good living from lobster. Many fishers are members of the Maritime Fishers' Union (MFU) which has been successfully collaborating with government regulators and enforcers to ensure adherence to restrictions on size, egg-bearing females and limited entry to lobster resources.

Relations between unions such as MFU and the government have not always been peaceful. In the early days, one of the rallying cries of the movement was that collective bargaining rights for inshore fishers should be recognized. The demand was to include such rights in the same or similar bargaining legislation as Canada's trade union movement had won for industrial workers. However, over the past two decades, inshore fishers and their union have been caught up in the general upheavals of the Canadian fishing industry. In the case of both the cod and the herring fisheries, the Canadian Government did not prove effective in protecting either the livelihood of the inshore fishers or the resource itself against the expansion of catching capacity by the larger fleets.

Organizations such as MFU in the past were never really able to make themselves heard until the damage had already been done. However, the fisheries crisis itself has helped reinforce the demands of such organizations for more responsible fisheries policies in the future. There is little doubt that their efforts have helped to create a general consensus on fisheries management in Canada, with an emphasis on limited-entry licensing and a range of controls on fishing activities and quotas. And they have been able to prove that co-management between the government and fishworkers' organizations – for example, in the lobster industry – is both cost-efficient and effective.

Source: Belliveau, 1995.

---

[18] See Part A, Section 2.4.3.

[19] FAO has produced a manual of methods on aquatic environment research covering the methodological aspects of detection, measurement and monitoring of the impacts of pollution on marine ecosystems. In particular, Gray, McIntyre and Stirn (1991) consider the specific aspects of impacts on marine life and describe techniques used for information collection and analysis. Aquaculture-specific pollution assessment and monitoring methods are described in Barg (1992), Kapetsky and Travaglia (1995) and GESAMP (1996b).

[20] See Part A, Box A.22.

PART D

INTEGRATION OF FISHERIES INTO COASTAL AREA MANAGEMENT

INTEGRATED
COASTAL AREA
MANAGEMENT
and
AGRICULTURE
FORESTRY AND
FISHERIES

3. Information requirements

frameworks, but also the customary regimes under which individuals operate, in particular with respect to access to, and use of, coastal resources.[21]

Organizations influence the nature of the decision-making process, its structure (e.g. more or less decentralized) and its degree of integration (e.g. more or less fragmented). Interactions between fisheries organizations and other government agencies responsible for land-use planning and coastal development policy should be documented, as should the decision-making processes in all sectors that have an impact on the coastal area.

Existing institutions should be assessed with respect to their responsibilities for coordination and resource allocation in coastal areas. Most importantly, gaps in the institutional context concerning coastal resources must be identified. Also, the responsibilities of different institutions may overlap. This is particularly likely to concern the area of customary use rights, often neglected or obliterated by modern institutional set-ups, particularly in developing countries. Similar problems may arise in the case of legislation. For instance, it is not uncommon for different ministries to adopt laws and statutory instruments that are in conflict with one another.

The technical capabilities of the various agencies (e.g. the planning and economics division of the fisheries authorities) need to be assessed in order to evaluate training needs. In relation to this, a study should be undertaken of research and training organizations relevant to the sector, in order to identify possible repetition, inadequacies to the sector's needs and potential economies of scale. Areas for improving links between official government research agencies and the higher education sector should be identified.

The role of the industry itself needs to be considered. The role of non-governmental organizations (e.g. industry organizations, employers' and fishers' federations, marine conservation organizations) should be assessed. A usual approach to the preparation of

policy measures is to establish consultative committees where government officials, scientists and fishers' representatives can meet to discuss management problems and seek solutions. Such decision-making bodies should be identified and, where they do not exist,[22] they should be set up.

It can be noted that the whole area of appropriate institutional and organizational arrangements merits much thought. Aspects that particularly need to be considered are, for example: the role and structure of the fisheries administration; consultation processes and the devolution of management authority; community-based organizations and management; decentralized versus centralized regulation; and the use of economic incentives, enforcement, etc.

3.3.2 Tools for collecting information
An important part of the institutional and organizational information will usually be available in the form of secondary data obtained from legal and administrative sources and various existing documents concerning the coastal area. Participatory methods and tools[23] can give rise to primary information of particular interest in the field of institutional and organizational problems and opportunities.

It is highly desirable to store the information gathered on the fisheries sector in a way that facilitates combined use. This is particularly the case given the potentially wide variety of data sources, formats and dimensions to be considered when integrating information concerning the resource base, the environment and the institutional and organizational context of the fisheries sector. Given that important aspects of this information have a geographical dimension (e.g. location of catches or fish farms, patterns of environmental interactions and spatial coverage of institutional systems), geographical information systems (GIS) appear very useful for this purpose.[24] GIS is a particularly useful tool in integrating fisheries information into the wider coastal area management information needs.

173

---

[21] See Part A, Sections 1.6.1 and 2.2.2.

[22] See Section 4.1.1 and also Part A, Sections 2.3.4.

[23] See Part A, Box A.18 and Figure A.12.

[24] See Part A, Box A.17. Applications of GIS to the fisheries sector are presented in Meaden and DoChi (1996).

PART D

INTEGRATION OF FISHERIES INTO COASTAL AREA MANAGEMENT

INTEGRATED
COASTAL AREA
MANAGEMENT
and
AGRICULTURE
FORESTRY AND
FISHERIES

4. Policy and planning for integrated coastal area management[25]

Management of coastal fisheries, as with that of all agricultural sectors, must have the basic objective of ecological sustainability. Management will have to decide which policy measures will allow this general objective to be achieved in each local circumstance, taking account of economic and social factors as well as the condition of the fisheries resources. At the same time, management measures must take account of the dynamic nature of coastal fisheries whereby physical, ecological, social and economic processes interact constantly.

As a result of the nature of fisheries, the concept of sustainability cannot be compared with other subsectors or, indeed, with other economic activities. Fisheries resources are finite and increasingly scarce, and the biological limit of their productivity has been reached or surpassed virtually everywhere. Investing more resources in exploiting fisheries resources, with the exception of aquaculture, will no longer result in increased productivity and profitability. On the contrary, today, increased productivity for one user (thanks to improved gear or vessels, for example), will necessarily lead to decreased productivity for other users. Management actions will therefore revolve around resource allocation, trade-offs, careful monitoring and enforcement.

Management must take account of the constraints that will determine the policy options. These relate to matters such as:

- the limited biological productivity of fisheries resources;
- the importance of defining conditions of access to those resources;
- the risk factors, in particular ecological and market variability;
- the difficulty of establishing an adequate information base;
- the difficulties surrounding the establishment of a suitable and effective institutional framework.

The key issue is to achieve the stated objectives sustainably and this will depend on the condition of the resource base (stocks, habitat, environment) and the capacity of management measures to improve it, the economic performance of the fishing activity, and the effectiveness of the development and management framework.

Management strategies must be flexible, adapting to the changing nature and condition of the resource through time and concerned to improve socio-economic performance within the sector, while decreasing negative impacts deriving from other sectors and from the sector itself.

4.1 INSTITUTIONAL ARRANGEMENTS

In the coastal area, there are many interests, often conflicting, not only within the fisheries sector but also outside it, competing for limited space and resources. An appropriate framework must be found to integrate these interests into a coherent and equitable framework and overcome the current and future conflicts between them.

Each coastal area has its own characteristics, making many aspects of management area-specific. Therefore, management decisions are likely to be more efficient if they are taken locally rather than being decided at national level and simply handed down for execution. With this in mind, it is advisable to envisage devolving responsibility for management of coastal areas, as far as possible, down to the local level, assuming the necessary competence to do this exists. A system of reporting and controls can be put in place as necessary.

4.1.1 Integration

Ministries and government agencies are the group most concerned with coordination and collaboration. Conflicts can arise in cases where jurisdictions overlap or are not clearly defined. These include the ministry (or department) of fisheries, but also those of agriculture,

175

---

[25] This section takes account of the Code of Conduct for Responsible Fisheries adopted at the Twenty-Eighth Session of the FAO Conference in October 1995 (Resolution 4/95).

INTEGRATED
COASTAL AREA
MANAGEMENT
and
AGRICULTURE
FORESTRY AND
FISHERIES

PART D

INTEGRATION OF FISHERIES INTO COASTAL AREA MANAGEMENT

4. Policy and planning for integrated coastal area management

---

BOX D.9
Article 10 of the Code of Conduct on Responsible Fisheries

10.1. Institutional framework

10.1.1. States should ensure that appropriate policy, legal and institutional framework is adopted to achieve the sustainable and integrated use of the resources, taking into account the fragility of coastal ecosystems and the finite nature of their natural resources and the needs of coastal communities.

10.1.2. In view of the multiple uses of the coastal area, States should ensure that representatives of the fisheries sector and fishing communities are consulted in the decision-making processes and involved in other activities related to coastal area management planning and development.

10.1.3. States should develop, as appropriate, institutional and legal frameworks in order to determine the possible uses of coastal resources and to govern access to them taking into account the rights of coastal fishing communities and their customary practices to the extent compatible with sustainable development.

10.1.4. States should facilitate the adoption of fisheries practices that avoid conflict among fisheries resources users and between them and other users of the coastal area.

10.1.5. States should promote the establishment of procedures and mechanisms at the appropriate administrative level to settle conflicts which arise within the fisheries sector and between fisheries resources users and other users of the coastal area.

10.2. Policy measures

10.2.1. States should promote the creation of public awareness of the need for the protection and management of coastal resources and the participation in the management process by those affected.

10.2.2. In order to assist decision-making on the allocation and use of coastal resources, States should promote the assessment of their respective value taking into account economic, social and cultural factors.

10.2.3. In setting policies for the management of coastal areas, States should take due account of the risks and uncertainties involved.

10.2.4. States, in accordance with their capacities, should establish or promote the establishment of systems to monitor the coastal environment as part of the coastal management process using physical, chemical, biological, economic and social parameters.

10.2.5. States should promote multidisciplinary research in support of coastal area management, in particular on its environmental, biological, economic, social, legal and institutional aspects.

10.3. Regional cooperation

10.3.1. States with neighbouring coastal areas should cooperate with one another to facilitate the sustainable use of coastal resources and the conservation of the environment.

10.3.2. In the case of activities that may have an adverse transboundary environmental effect on coastal areas, States should:

  a) provide timely information and, if possible, prior notification to potentially affected states;

  b) consult with those States as early as possible.

10.3.3. States should cooperate at the subregional and regional level in order to improve coastal area management.

10.4. Implementation

10.4.1. States should establish mechanisms for cooperation and coordination among national authorities involved in planning, development, conservation and management of coastal areas.

10.4.2. States should ensure that the authority or authorities representing the fisheries sector in the coastal management process have the appropriate technical capacities and financial resources.

Source: FAO, 1995a.

---

forestry, tourism, merchant marine and many others. To handle the issues that will almost inevitably arise, interministerial (and indeed intraministerial) groups should be set up at the national level, to define and share responsibilities. Decisions must be relayed to corresponding local bodies, or upwards if devolution is in place, through structured and functional linkages at the various administrative levels. Authority at the highest level should sanction such joint decision-making to ensure its results are effectively applied.

Stakeholders within the sector are the second group that must be integrated into the management and planning process. Local resource users are key actors in fisheries policies, often being at the base of the local economy. They generally know the area and its

PART D

INTEGRATION OF FISHERIES INTO COASTAL AREA MANAGEMENT

INTEGRATED
COASTAL AREA
MANAGEMENT
and
AGRICULTURE
FORESTRY AND
FISHERIES

4. Policy and planning for integrated coastal area management

environment particularly well and can therefore be important allies in the monitoring of environmental impacts. In addition, traditional fishing and resource sharing techniques may show the way to more sustainable management. Social cohesion among local fishing communities provides a basis for successful implementation of management decisions, provided that traditional users have been associated with defining them. Although fishers are only one group of stakeholders, involving them is basic to success since they are the main users of fisheries resources. Since the nature of their work gives fishers little time to participate in meetings and consultations, it may be necessary to stimulate the establishment of fishers' organizations and committees, where these do not already exist; however, to be effective, the latter must truly reflect and represent a broad cross-section of views in the fishing community. They should take account of artisanal and larger-scale fishers, aquaculture interests, etc. Where rights of access have not yet been implemented, the search for consensus on resource use between those directly involved in the fishing operation will play an important role, for example when designing voluntary guidelines.

Stakeholders in other sectors. Stakeholders operating within the sector encompass all those interested in the marine and land-based coastal resources, from farmers and hoteliers to port authorities and municipalities. Relations with extra-sectoral stakeholders will also be handled at national, regional and local levels. Nationally, the fisheries authorities will be expected to defend the sector's interests *vis-à-vis* others making a claim to the resource. To do this, they should be involved in activities such as the review process for environmental impact assessment of coastal projects, in drafting laws and regulations related to coastal areas, in the spatial planning process, in awarding building permits for large projects where fisheries interests will be affected (for instance when building a hotel complex or marina) and many others. The stronger the institutional structure representing the fisheries sector, the more effectively fisheries interests will be represented.

Locally, consultative committees can be set up, with proposed solutions being submitted to higher authorities after due discussion and agreement. Such proposals must conform with national policy objectives (for instance, the government may give priority to promoting

fish production for export rather than for domestic markets, or to tourism in a particular zone rather than fisheries), otherwise they will be overridden. When proposals are accepted, they will have a greater chance of being implemented if they derive from a consensus of a large majority of stakeholders.

Analysis of roles. The first step in setting up a suitable management framework will be to analyse the roles and responsibilities of each actor and to identify overlaps and sources of real or potential conflict, as well as ensuring that no essential issue is left out. The institutional mechanism for ICAM will therefore ensure that:

• the responsibilities of each agency are clearly defined;
• suitable coordinating and integrating arrangements are established, and information on coastal policies and relevant developments flows regularly between agencies at all levels to ensure coherence in policy implementation.

4.1.2 Allocation of rights

The constraints imposed by the limited natural productivity of the stock and the open-access nature of fisheries will only be overcome by measures to limit access. Since scarcity will normally lead to price increases, allocations should be made on the basis of value, rather than quantity.

Fisheries scientists have identified the limit of physical productivity as the maximum sustainable yield (MSY). However, this maximum tends to be seen by managers as the target for fisheries development and, in the absence of access rights, this is very unlikely to result in sustainability (see Section 3.1.1).

Ideally, the implications of various levels of exploitation on major species should be researched jointly by fisheries biologists and economists. Even without sophisticated methods, it will be possible to make a reasonable working estimate of an adequate level of fishing from both the economic and biological standpoints. Similarly, the consequences of (continued) overexploitation will be estimated (risk of collapse of the stock and of the industry, for example). Explanations of such risks on the basis of research will form the basis for consultations with fishers aimed at reaching a consensus on the need for reducing the catch.

Major problems – economic, social and even political

177

INTEGRATED
COASTAL AREA
MANAGEMENT
and
AGRICULTURE
FORESTRY AND
FISHERIES

PART D

INTEGRATION OF FISHERIES INTO COASTAL AREA MANAGEMENT

4. Policy and planning for integrated coastal area management

BOX D.10
Towards integrated coastal fisheries management (ICFM) in Malaysia

The situation analysis of Malaysian fisheries, conducted by the Department of Fisheries Malaysia (DOFM) and the Bay of Bengal Programme (BOBP) in 1994, identified several broad-based issues within the project area of the Pulau Payar Marine Park. These include: general degradation of resources, particularly mangrove areas, corals and sea grass beds; overfishing; conflicts between artisanal and commercial fishers; organic and inorganic pollution from industrial development; multiuse conflicts; and loss of fishing grounds. The analysis recommended a sustainable resource management approach to emphasize the importance of marine parks as productive ecosystems contributing to fisheries and biological diversity. The project design evolved during the planning stage of the project in 1995. Outputs included the design and initiation of a Special Area Management Plan (SAMP) approach for the Pulau Payar Marine Park and surrounding areas (Kuala Kedah and Langkawi) to allow for focused management that integrates local community participation, multiple government agencies, and ecological and sociological components. Pulau Payar was the first marine park in Malaysia, established in 1995. The SAMP approach is incremental.

The first phase has been to form a working group to complete the groundwork needed to take the process to a wider audience of local decision-makers in the SAMP area. The Fisheries Resource Working Group (FRWG) was formed by DOFM in 1995 for this purpose. Policy implications of SAMP would require the FRWG to report or go through the already existing high-level Management Committee of DOFM at the HQ level. Therefore, it was useful to have this working group composed of a multidisciplinary team. Four key disciplines within DOFM are represented in FRWG: the Marine Parks Branch; the Fisheries Resource Management Branch; the Fisheries Research Institute; and the Fisheries Planning Division.

The second phase was to characterize the geographic area under the SAMP to help identify and gain a broader understanding of: 1) the list of issues and problems to be addressed under the SAMP; 2) the probable causes of the problems and issues; and 3) the possible solutions. This phase is on-going and has been guided by the FRWG and DOF Management Committee since 1995. Activities under the characterization phase include the implementation of scientific characterization studies, a socio-economic baseline study, institutional review, public outreach materials, training of fishers in alternative livelihoods from ecotourism, training of DOFM staff in integrated coastal management, and a first draft SAMP. During the second phase, the results of the early characterization provided a greater understanding of the issues for management within the SAMP area, and the issues became more focused. They include: decline in fisheries resources; impacts from tourism development; impacts from the changes in land- and sea-based development; and protection of the area's high marine biological diversity and ecosystem health.

The third phase was designed to overlap with the second phase and begin to develop solutions to the problems and issues with a wider audience of local decision-makers in the SAMP area. For this purpose, a State-level Coordinating Committee (SCC) is being established which will comprise all the government agencies at the state level that have programmes affecting the issues in the area. As the initial activity of the third phase, an integrated coastal management workshop was held in October 1997 to build consensus among the various agencies, academia and invited NGOs, who will become members of the SCC, as well as to identify and commit to roles and responsibilities for SAMP implementation. The workshop consolidated opinions and achieved consensus on the objectives of the SAMP and potential solutions for action among the participants. It laid the foundation for increased multisectoral participation. It provided the early results of the scientific studies to the seven agencies represented and gained their active participation in contributing ideas towards potential solutions to improve management of the area's environment.

A second workshop was organized for early 1998 to build on this foundation and ensure greater participation from additional agencies and the wider public on the SAMP objectives and potential actions, and identify and commit to roles and responsibilities for SAMP implementation. The wider public includes such groups of stakeholders as fishers, tour operators and investors in marine tourism activities whose activities are seen to have a different level of impact than government agencies but whose perception of management issues is oriented more towards their impact on livelihoods and direct damage to the ecosystem. The opinions and feedback from the direct users of the SAMP area resources is a vital contribution for the final development, implementation and adoption of the SAMP by the wider public and its approval by the state and federal governments. It is expected that the public-stakeholder workshop would also help to identify candidates from these stakeholder groups for representation on the SCC. The workshop will also establish the SCC as a multidisciplinary and interagency committee with local-level management responsibility for the SAMP.

It is envisioned that SAMP development and implementation will be facilitated by the SCC and supported by the national-level FRWG. The two levels of support will benefit SAMP development and implementation. The SCC will ensure local-level change, while the FRWG will support SCC with funding, legislative backing and harmonization of policy initiatives. The SAMP for the Pulau Payar Marine Park and surrounding areas will promote the conservation and sustained production and use of the area's reef fisheries resources and habitats. The SAMP will be used as a model both for other marine park islands in peninsular Malaysia and to glean lessons learned to develop a national integrated coastal management programme.

Source: Nickerson, 1997.

PART D

INTEGRATION OF FISHERIES INTO COASTAL AREA MANAGEMENT

INTEGRATED
COASTAL AREA
MANAGEMENT
and
AGRICULTURE
FORESTRY AND
FISHERIES

4. Policy and planning for integrated coastal area management

– arise when, as is often the case today, the resource is already overexploited and measures must be taken to bring exploitation down to a more sustainable level. Where still possible, it is preferable to avoid overexploitation in the first place, which is a manner of applying the preventive approach.[26]

Given the need to limit access to fisheries resources, the question is how to achieve it. For both capture fisheries and aquaculture, policy measures can be classified in two broad types; those based on regulatory instruments and those based on economic instruments. The former imply direct control of the uses by a regulating agency, while the latter are based on approaches seeking to modify the economic incentives with which users are faced. Institutional instruments are used where the former cannot be successfully put into place.[27] Choice of the instruments (which can also be used in combination) for the implementation of policy directions will depend on local circumstances, and can rest on a comparison of their relative economic efficiency (comparing total benefits to total costs including transaction costs), cost-effectiveness (comparing total costs of different instruments providing similar expected benefits) and distributional consequences (Grigalunas and Congar, 1995). In addition to these instruments, policy measures will need to be defined concerning cross-sectoral impacts and conflict resolution, and the monitoring of management effects on the fisheries sector.

Capture fisheries. Conventional management of capture fisheries has centred on measures of direct control of fishing capacity. Such measures, while they may prevent resource collapse, do nothing to prevent the depletion of resource rents, and have in some cases accentuated the overcapitalization problem. If the full economic benefits are to be achieved from a fishery, it seems clear that access to it has to be limited in some way.

Direct control of fishing activity implies that, once a target level of exploitation is fixed, the level of fishing effort required to achieve it must be determined. Various types of conservation and management direct control measures can usually be considered by fisheries authorities depending on local conditions. Typically, these will include:

- the fishing gear (e.g. mesh size limits);
- fishing areas (e.g. nursery area protection);
- fishing times (e.g. closed seasons);
- the fish stock (e.g. catch quotas, minimum landing size limits);
- the vessel or the fishers (e.g. licences or individual quotas).

The impact of such regulations has been reviewed in many places (e.g. Cunningham, Dunn and Whitemarsh 1985). If the fishery is managed only by control of the exploitation level, for instance by setting a total allowable catch and closing the fishery once this has been taken, the problem of overexploitation of the resource will be translated into a problem of overcapacity of the fishing industry. Such problems have long been documented in the fisheries economics literature (e.g. Crutchfield and Pontecorvo, 1969). The history of the United States Pacific halibut fishery over the period since the Second World War provides an example of how far this process may be pushed.

A number of palliatives might be implemented to try to improve the situation. For example, the exploitation level might be limited weekly rather than annually so as to try to make the season last longer. However, the fundamental problem will remain that, unless access is limited, effort and capacity will be excessive.

An alternative would be to try to limit fishing effort directly. This approach is difficult to implement because of the practical difficulty of defining and measuring fishing effort and fishing capacity and the relationship between them. Control often works by limiting the number of vessels that are licensed to participate in the fishery, but this approach faces at least two difficulties. First, effort may be increased by existing vessels operating more intensively as well as by the addition of new vessels, so that the impact of a reduction in vessel numbers often proves far less than hoped. Second, over time vessels will need to be replaced, but new vessels are usually more technically efficient than older vessels and allowance must be made for this if the effort is to be controlled. In theory, therefore, working via effort seems technically more difficult than operating on catch. However, there is some evidence that fishers find it more difficult to alter the configuration of their fishing vessels than has often been assumed by

179

---

[26] See Part A, Section 2.2.4.
[27] See Part A, Box A.26.

INTEGRATED
COASTAL AREA
MANAGEMENT
and
AGRICULTURE
FORESTRY AND
FISHERIES

PART D

INTEGRATION OF FISHERIES INTO COASTAL AREA MANAGEMENT

4. Policy and planning for integrated coastal area management

economic theory so that some improvement in economic performance can occur under such schemes. Whether such improvements will be permanent remains to be seen.

The best approach to the establishment of exclusive use access rights will depend on the nature of the fishery and on the legal system of the country. The fundamental question to be answered prior to the establishment of any system of use rights is who owns the resource. Frequently the response is that the government manages the resource on behalf of society in general. In this model, fishers are exploiters of the resource and access rights that they may acquire will be exploitation or use rights, not ownership rights. Regardless of how this is decided, a use-right system should improve the economic performance of the fishery; but the issue is critical for determining who receives the benefits of improved performance, in particular who receives the resource rent.

Resource rent may be captured by the management agency, either through taxation (on catch or effort) or by use of resource charges associated with use rights. Alternatively, a decision might be made to leave rents with the industry, in which case their value may be capitalized into property rights. In any event, it is unlikely that the management agency could capture all rents, so use rights will take on some value whatever the system. However, this value will be much greater under the property right scheme.

A number of approaches suggest themselves. One possibility is to grant rights in the form of percentage shares of the total allowable catch (TAC). Where rights are tradable – i.e. individual transferable quotas (ITQs) – it should be possible to allocate them efficiently between users, those who put a low value on rights being expected to sell them to those who value them more highly. For example, in many fisheries, fish prices increase with fish size. In such cases, fishers who concentrate on smaller fish would be expected to sell to those fishing larger ones. In this way, the value derived from the given exploitation level would be maximized. Clearly a key issue in the case of ITQs concerns the ability to enforce them and prevent cheating. Studies would be required of the feasibility of introducing ITQs in particular cases and of the conditions necessary for effective enforcement.

In some cases, it may prove impossible to control either catch or effort, e.g. because the fishery is small-scale with many landing points, as is the case with many artisanal fisheries. One approach in such cases is to strengthen any traditional management systems that may exist and use social cohesion and self-control. However, fairness in the distribution of access and income are more important to communities than efficiency. This implies giving (or returning) rights to traditional groups and devolving some management authority to them. Alternatively, the fishery might be divided into areas with control of each area given to a particular group of fishers, especially where social cohesion is strong. Although the mobile nature of most fish stocks probably rules out this approach as a general solution, it is useful in coastal regions and has frequently been advocated in the case of artisanal fisheries in the form of territorial use rights (TURFs) (Christy Jr, 1982).[28]

One issue to be considered is the duration of rights. If rights are granted in perpetuity, cost reductions associated with technical progress will be captured by rights holders via increases in the price of rights. Some of this might subsequently pass to the resource owner (i.e. the state) if a tax is imposed on the price of rights when these are sold. If rights are simply leased for a limited period then the resource owner will capture the benefits of technical progress through increased prices for the next allocation of rights (those with better technology will be able to afford to bid more for rights.)

One advantage of use rights is that they allow for changing resource usage over time. If catches are allocated administratively then it may prove very difficult to change allocations over time in response to

[28] Such methods are widely used in Japanese and Korean inshore fisheries for example. They have also been used in some shellfish fisheries, e.g. the Solent oyster fishery (Guillotreau and Cunningham, 1994), where the sedentary nature of the stocks simplifies the management problem. In the United Kingdom, the allocation of quotas to producers' organizations to manage is another step in this direction. In many situations, an important factor preventing fishers themselves from implementing management measures is their large number. If the numbers of fishers can be reduced, then area licensing is a possible means of achieving improved management (Wilen, 1988).

INTEGRATED
COASTAL AREA
MANAGEMENT
and
AGRICULTURE
FORESTRY AND
FISHERIES

PART D

INTEGRATION OF FISHERIES INTO COASTAL AREA MANAGEMENT

4. Policy and planning for integrated coastal area management

dynamic economic effects.[29] An additional advantage is that the beneficiary is more likely to take notice of negative impacts and report these with a view to their being tackled than when access is open to all, in which case no-one will have any sense of responsibility.

The issue of reallocation does not only affect fishers or groups of fishers. It also affects allocations between sectors of the economy. In fact, probably the strongest argument in favour of use rights is that they allow for transfers of fish between sectors and for one sector to compensate the other in a very simple manner.

Under some conditions, it may be possible to use fish prices to control fishing activity. For example, the government might establish a marketing agency to deal with all shellfish in an area. Anyone fishing shellfish would be required to sell to this organization. If the organization buys at a low price and resells at a higher one, the government can extract resource rents. Alternatively, a tax might be imposed on domestic consumers. In this way the exploitation level might be reduced and the government would collect the resource rent via the taxes. From the point of view of rent collection, a domestic tax would be more appropriate in situations where the domestic market dominates, while a marketing organization would be more appropriate in cases where much of the catch is exported. In fact, a marketing organization may provide countervailing power to foreign buyers, enabling the country to achieve better export performance. In some cases it may be possible to work via traders, although their activities are often difficult to control. If this kind of management approach is to be used, it is important that the nature of marketing arrangements is properly understood so that the best point at which the tax collector should intervene can be identified.

Where a fishery interacts with other fisheries or other coastal activities, which is almost inevitable, a taxation system will be inadequate to deal with allocation problems. In this case, allocation will have to be organized through an administrative (planning) approach or an economic approach based on use rights, or some combination of the two.

Aquaculture. In the case of aquaculture, a combination of direct intervention of the management agency through regulation and of the use of economic instruments seeking to modify individual incentives of fish farmers can usually be considered.

Legislation will be required relating to a number of aspects of the operation of an aquaculture facility, mostly public health-related issues (e.g. water quality, harvest and processing of the product). There may also be specific requirements imposed by countries to whom the output is to be exported (e.g. those within the European Union). These regulations will affect the kind of activity that can be placed near an aquaculture area and will require regulatory measures (unless some kind of market in environmental rights can be developed). The impacts of aquaculture on the coastal environment will also need to be considered.

A number of regulatory instruments can be considered, depending on the characteristics of the activity and the site. These include: land-use planning and zoning (e.g. distance limits between sites, restricted areas); control over installation and operation of the facilities (e.g. limits on production, water depth regulations, moratorium on new farms, regulations on ownership); and pollution control (e.g. waste discharge limits) (Barg, 1992). Some large-scale aquaculture projects may be placed under regulations requiring authorization by the management agency, in which case environmental impact assessments[30] may be required from large-scale operators before the authorization of an installation is granted.

In a regulatory context, economic analysis may be limited to a cost-benefit analysis (CBA).[31] One problem here is that, to date, relatively few environmental impact

181

---

[29] An example of the kind of problem is provided by the catch key of the European Common Fisheries Policy. This catch key was agreed administratively in 1983 together with a principle of relative stability. Over time, the preferences of different national fishers for different species have changed but allocations are still based on the original catch key. Various convoluted arrangements then have to be implemented to rearrange allocations among countries according to current preferences. A system of users' rights would allow such changes to occur as and when necessary with no need for any administrative intervention.

---

[30] See Part A. Box A.6.
[31] See Part A, Section 2.4.4 and Box A.22.

INTEGRATED
COASTAL AREA
MANAGEMENT
and
AGRICULTURE
FORESTRY AND
FISHERIES

PART D

INTEGRATION OF FISHERIES INTO COASTAL AREA MANAGEMENT

4. Policy and planning for integrated coastal area management

assessments or CBAs have been carried out, so that in many cases the wider economic impacts of aquaculture development are simply not known.

As for capture fisheries, economic instruments will either seek to establish tradable rights systems or rely on charging systems to adjust supply and demand for environmental goods and services. In attempting to deal with the specific problem of pollution caused by aquaculture, Soley, Neiland and Nowell (1992) suggest that economic approaches based on the polluter pays principle[32] should be implemented. They suggest three possibilities that might be considered. First, a tax (or tariff) might be applied to stocking density to encourage environment-friendly stocking decisions (this is however difficult to enforce). Second, a tariff might be applied to continuous production. The idea would be to encourage fallow periods, where these are feasible, to prevent the cumulative build-up of environmental impacts. The exact nature of such a tax would depend on the hydrological characteristics of the site, and its impact on the profitability of the enterprise would have to be considered. The third suggestion is that a system of tradable permits might be introduced. Similar schemes have been suggested for pollution control generally and the approach is simple in principle. The acceptable level of pollution (e.g. nutrient discharge) is determined and broken into many small units. Only holders of units may legally discharge into the environment and they are free to trade in these entitlements. Another instrument which could be used is fiscal incentives (e.g. tax deductions and exemptions) to promote the installation of water treatment equipment, for example.

Research will be required to determine the enforceability of various schemes. The methods do, however, indicate the way in which economic incentives might be used to regulate demands on the environment.

Aquaculture may be subject to various other externalities that limit its rate of development. One of the most significant of these is the problem of defining property rights in certain situations. Although in aquaculture the open access issue is more easily dealt with than in fisheries, there are situations where it is a problem. One example concerns ocean ranching; ocean ranching involves the release into the wild of captive bred young fish, almost invariably anadromous species such as salmon which at maturity return to their birthplace to spawn. Under international law and most national legal systems, fish in the wild have no legal owner (i.e. they are regarded as *res nillius*) and ownership is acquired by the person who captures them. This means that unless the "rancher" who releases young fish into the wild is given some form of property rights in those fish and/or exclusive or preferential rights to harvest them on maturity, a third party may freely reap the fruits of the rancher's investment simply by catching the fish. This substantially diminishes the economic incentives to invest in ocean ranching. Policy instruments need to be developed to deal with this problem, but it is not easy to see what kind of system might be used, especially for very wide-ranging species.

A second problem may concern private research into farming methods for new species. It is generally difficult to keep the results of such research secret, especially when they are of broad public interest. If matters are simply left to the market it is likely that too little research and development will be undertaken by private companies since they cannot be sure that they will benefit from the results of their efforts. In this situation national governments may want to assist research either through national research institutions or by funding research at company level.

A similar problem concerns the availability of skilled labour, especially in the early days of the sector since workers trained by one company may move on to another. In this case, training by one firm benefits all firms (actual and potential) in the sector. To resolve this problem, the government can either provide training directly via aquaculture degrees and vocational qualifications or subsidize company training programmes.

4.1.3 Conflict resolution

Conflicts are to be expected in the operation of coastal fisheries, both within the sector between sectoral actors and cross-sectorally. Given the finite and limited nature of coastal resources, it is not always easy to avoid conflicts, but they can often be handled effectively and to general satisfaction.

Conflicts will arise within the sector, for example between artisanal and commercial fishers, between

---

[32] See Part A, Box A.5.

PART D

INTEGRATION OF FISHERIES INTO COASTAL AREA MANAGEMENT

INTEGRATED
COASTAL AREA
MANAGEMENT
and
AGRICULTURE
FORESTRY AND
FISHERIES

4. Policy and planning for integrated coastal area management

---

BOX D.11

Participatory coastal area management in Soufrière, Saint Lucia

In the late 1980s, the situation in the Soufrière Bay, on the southwest coast of the island of Saint Lucia, resembled that of many other Caribbean coastal areas. With the expansion of tourism, the impact of land-based activities on coastal environments and changes in fishing technology, new and serious conflicts emerged between the different groups of users of the area's coastal resources. These conflicts had become grave and acrimonious, as pot fishers began to compete with dive operators for access to reef areas, seine fishers began to lose traditional fishing territories to permanent yacht moorings and jetties, and all sectors began to suffer from the effects of general resource degradation and overexploitation.

The initial response of government agencies and other institutions was to establish fishing priority areas, in order to secure fishing access to the most critical fishing grounds, and marine reserves for recreational diving and stock replenishment. These measures, however, failed to reduce the conflicts and, on the contrary, served to exacerbate them further; the resource users had not been consulted in the zoning and establishment of the areas, boundaries had not been clearly demarcated, and rapid changes in the local economy had created new demands and pressures on the resource.

Against this background, a process was started in July 1992. The process sought to resolve the conflicts and to identify management mechanisms that would allow desired economic and social activities to take place in the area. The Department of Fisheries, the government agency responsible for marine resource management in the country, recognized the need for such a consultative process, and collaborated with a NGO, the Soufrière Regional Development Foundation, in conducting it. A regional NGO, the Caribbean Natural Resources Institute (CANARI) assisted with design and facilitation.

The main features of the process, which lasted for a period of 18 months, included: careful identification of all stakeholders; use of both popular and scientific knowledge to assess the resources and the problems affecting them; conduct of formal and informal meetings; use of the mass media and other information channels to generate public interest and "control" over the process; and

negotiation of all decisions among all concerned parties. As a result, the Soufrière Marine Management Area (SMMA) was created as a collaborative management arrangement between government and local stakeholders, which provided for a new zoning of uses in the Soufrière coastal area, and identified a number of measures to facilitate multiple uses (fishing, recreational diving, marine transportation) whenever possible. The SMMA was formally inaugurated in July 1995.

Within Saint Lucia, the SMMA has been a unique learning experience for all parties involved, and it has also offered important lessons to coastal and marine management agencies in other parts of the Caribbean. It has shown the value of participatory decision-making processes which seek to involve all stakeholders, and it has demonstrated that it is indeed possible to restore the harmony between conflicting uses and activities. But the implementation of the SMMA has also revealed many shortcomings. It has shown that a participatory planning process does not automatically lead to a decentralized and participatory institutional arrangement, and that safeguards are always needed to prevent the return to the status quo of centralized management. It has highlighted the need for local institutional development work that can equip resource users and facilitate their full involvement in management. It has shown that resource-user communities are very diverse, and that indirect representation often leads to the marginalization of the most powerless among them. Above all, it has demonstrated that conflict over resource utilization cannot really be "resolved", but only "managed".

What is needed, therefore, in the insular Caribbean as well as in other areas where coastal fisheries are threatened by changing patterns in resource use, are conflict management institutions that allow all stakeholders to adapt to changing conditions, to prevent disputes and to gain greater control over the resources on which their livelihoods depend. This is, possibly, the most important lesson from this innovative experiment in participatory coastal area management in Soufrière, Saint Lucia.

Source: CANARI, 1997.

183

commercial fishers when different groups use incompatible gear, or when commercial and recreational fishers' interests diverge. Capture fishers and fish farmers may also come into conflict over site location or for other reasons.

Fishers will come into conflict with other resource users, including those from the agriculture and forestry sectors,[33] but also with mining interests (e.g. coral, sand, gravel), tourism and local authorities, when roads or ports are envisaged. Some conflicts will involve locally identifiable actors, others may involve parties that are difficult to pin down (e.g. oil spills, siltation resulting from erosion provoked by distant deforestation).

---

[33] See Part A, Section 1.5.

INTEGRATED
COASTAL AREA
MANAGEMENT
and
AGRICULTURE
FORESTRY AND
FISHERIES

PART D

INTEGRATION OF FISHERIES INTO COASTAL AREA MANAGEMENT

4. Policy and planning for integrated coastal area management

It is most important to establish strong and effective mechanisms for conflict resolution and this should be a concern of coastal area managers. Various approaches are possible, among which are direct or assisted negotiation and other appropriate means[34] which avoid the heavy procedures of the legal system. Administrative approaches may involve the appropriate authority making spatial and/or temporal regulations that favour one group over another or simply ban resource use at least for a period; zoning[35] is one form of administrative approach. Economic measures, especially transferable access rights, can, in some cases, enlist the market to solve conflicts; those who place the highest value on resources are able to purchase access to them from others.

The clearer the policy and regulatory frameworks, the more precise the valuation of disputed coastal resources, and the more efficient the management regime, the easier it will be to solve, or even to avoid, conflicts early on.

4.2 POLICY MEASURES

Policy measures should take account of the value of the resources to be managed, the need to reduce risks and the time-frame over which they may be used. Public awareness and participation in decision-making will greatly increase the chances of successful implementation. Finally, indicators must be designed to assist in the monitoring process.

4.2.1 Public awareness and participation

The public – including the general public but especially local populations and resource users – must be aware of the importance of protecting and managing coastal resources and be able to participate in the management process. Adequate participation in this process, provided for within the legal and institutional frameworks, will contribute to the long-term success of policy measures. A significant public input by stakeholders is especially important at local level; this will increase the likelihood of compliance as mentioned above, reduce the risk of serious errors being made, and reduce alienation of those most likely to be affected. Typical means to achieve

local participation include, among many others, consultative committees, public information meetings, discussion papers and debates.[36]

4.2.2 Valuation of resources

Decision-making on the allocation of coastal resources will be greatly assisted by a proper assessment of their value, taking account of economic, social, cultural and environmental factors. Indeed without such assessments, rational decisions will be virtually impossible. As explained in Part A,[37] however, while many coastal resources can be clearly valued, the values are not the same for every user, and some resources have values that cannot be determined in monetary terms. In other words, assessing values is not easy, and various methods proposed generally fail to give satisfactory results.

The aim will be to promote optimum use of resources taking account of the interests of users, non-users and future generations. Valuations can be derived from the clear identification of the goods and services being assessed and, when markets do not exist for them, making valuations that may be purely intuitive.

4.2.3 Reduction of risk

Reducing risk, in the context of ICAM, means identifying impacts on fisheries from both within and outside the sector, and taking measures – or negotiating, through appropriate bodies, with other sectors that have a negative impact or are affected – to reduce such impacts, preferably through preventive action. While it will be impossible to trace all possible linkages, those groups most likely to be substantially affected should be identified.

As for risk assessment, even though this may not be very precise, at least some range of most likely outcomes of particular actions is known. Where an activity is likely to have a negative impact, the user could be required to purchase a bond that would not be refunded if the impact occurs; such a system encourages prevention rather than clean-up. If no effective measures are introduced, negative impacts will continue and society will in effect be subsidizing those who benefit in the short-term from

---

[34] See Part A, Section 2.3.4 and Box A.11 and Part E, Section 4.
[35] See Part A, Section 2.2.5 and Box A.6.
[36] See Part A, Box A.20.
[37] See Part A, Section 1.6.1 and Box A.24.

PART D

INTEGRATION OF FISHERIES INTO COASTAL AREA MANAGEMENT

INTEGRATED
COASTAL AREA
MANAGEMENT
and
AGRICULTURE
FORESTRY AND
FISHERIES

4. Policy and planning for integrated coastal area management

an activity that results in degradation of fisheries resources. Where a conscious decision is be taken by the state to allocate benefits to another sector to the detriment of fisheries, adequate compensation must be provided for.

Given the above factors underlying, and providing the basis for, the state's response to risk and uncertainty there must be an appropriately flexible legal approach.

4.2.4 Indicators and monitoring

Monitoring the application of policy measures and of their effects on the fisheries sector is an essential aspect of the management strategy. A baseline study must be made, and measurable criteria established against which the success or failure of the policy can be assessed and corrective measures implemented. Such criteria will concern the impact of policy measures on the resource base, the environment, the institutional context, the reduction or elimination of conflict, and the control of pollution and other negative impacts. Most important will be the effect of policy on the economic health of the fisheries sector and on the state of the resource.

There is a need to identify those indicators that must be monitored.[38] The range will depend on particular circumstances (the nature of the problem, the budget available) but might include (FAO, 1996b):

* physical parameters, such as: mapping of land use, area of reclamation and drainage, changes in beaches, and virgin land to developed land ratios;
* biological and chemical parameters, such as: water transparency and sea bed integrity, extent of seaweed and sea grass beds, biological diversity indices, persistent organic pollutants (POPS) of aquatic production, red tide occurrences, and degree of habitat protection;
* economic and social parameters, such as: population density, employment and unemployment, income levels, regional GDP, barriers to entry and exit of main occupations, resource allocation systems, occurrence of social conflict and levels of subsidy in different sectors.

Perhaps the key issue in the success or failure of any management programme is the monitoring and enforcement of regulations. If regulations have been

designed in collaboration with the fisheries industry, including artisanal fishers, the chances of voluntary compliance will be enhanced. Equity and justice are important elements in voluntary compliance, as well as ensuring that measures are economically bearable while having the desired impact.

Monitoring the condition of the resources is also essential. This is usually the aspect that is done best because fisheries biology is the chief area of competence of fisheries research institutes. However, it is the management process that should determine which resources to monitor, not the researchers alone. The functioning of the user-rights system, and the rents extracted, will be relatively easy to monitor; monitoring the impact of policy measures on stock structure may often be more difficult.

Aquaculture will be subject to regulations and criteria relating to choice of site, quality of the water, hygiene, stocking density, waste discharge, etc., aimed partly at avoiding negative impacts on other sectors (in particular, pollution from chemicals, feeds and fertilizers) mainly on capture fisheries and on neighbouring aquaculture sites. Ideally, monitoring of the environmental and socio-economic performances of aquaculture, and of the impact policy has on it, as well as monitoring of the reduction of negative impacts received from elsewhere, should be combined and coordinated in order to facilitate integrated subsectoral information that can be compared with other sectors active in coastal areas.

4.3 PLAN FORMULATION

The coastal fisheries management plan should cover the level of resource exploitation to be allowed, the determination of access to the resources and the means of ensuring compliance with plan provisions. These objectives should be pursued while avoiding irreversible changes in the resource base. However, account must be taken of changing economic, social, technical and environmental circumstances, and evolving societal perceptions.[39] In other words, management must be willing to adapt plans over time and revise them in the light of changing conditions.

---

[38] See Box D.12 and also part A, Section 2.3.6

[39] As societies grow more affluent, they tend to attribute greater value to the environment; developed country standards cannot be expected of poorer ones.

INTEGRATED
COASTAL AREA
MANAGEMENT
and
AGRICULTURE
FORESTRY AND
FISHERIES

PART D

INTEGRATION OF FISHERIES INTO COASTAL AREA MANAGEMENT

4. Policy and planning for integrated coastal area management

BOX D.12
Indicators of sustainable fisheries development

In a fisheries context, adopting sustainable development principles requires broadening the traditional fisheries management concerns with sustainable fishing of target species (with associated concepts such as maximum sustainable yield) to consideration of the health of the total ecosystem and the social and economic well-being of all stakeholders in the fishery. The development of a framework for evaluating progress towards achieving this sustainable development of fisheries then requires: specifying what is to be achieved in terms of the fisheries resource, the environment, and the economic and social benefits; defining what is meant by success in meeting these objectives; developing performance indicators against these objectives and a basis for comparison; and implementing the system to include a decision-making framework in which management actions result from a predefined change in indicators.

Performance evaluation. Conceptually, the evaluation process consists of, first, setting clear objectives (focusing on outcomes), defining what a successful outcome would be, developing performance indicators and developing a basis for comparing the indicators (see Figure D.1).

Multiple and hierarchical objectives. In order to achieve sustainable development in fisheries, objectives are needed for all components, not just the harvesting of the resource. The objectives need to provide a framework for decision-making that will sustain both short- and longer-term development. Objectives and strategies are linked in a hierarchy, in that the strategy of one level becomes the objective of the next. One classification of objectives is to start at the top level by considering the human needs and strategies to meet these needs (see Figure D.2). Policy and legislation are then developed to implement these strategies which, in turn, form the basis for overarching fisheries management objectives for a given fisheries jurisdiction. More specific objectives are then developed for individual fisheries; these state what management is attempting to achieve for that fishery. Objectives are often developed for individual stocks based on their biological status and methods of harvesting to make them easier to manage and their performance easier to measure.

Defining success. The next stage is to take each objective/ outcome and define success. The main reason for this is that the objectives are written in very general terms and, unless success is defined, the outcomes can be interpreted differently by different people, depending on their perspective. Each outcome is taken separately and a perfect outcome described, considering issues such as cost, timeliness, relevance, accuracy, quality and quantity. Success is then defined in terms of the level of performance that can be realistically achieved.

Developing performance indicators. A performance indicator is a piece of information that focuses on important and useful information, expressed as an index, rate or other ratio in comparison with one or more criteria and monitored at regular intervals. In

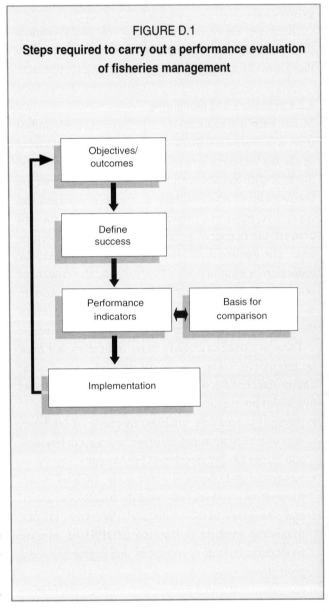

FIGURE D.1
Steps required to carry out a performance evaluation of fisheries management

PART D

INTEGRATION OF FISHERIES INTO COASTAL AREA MANAGEMENT

INTEGRATED
COASTAL AREA
MANAGEMENT
and
AGRICULTURE
FORESTRY AND
FISHERIES

4. Policy and planning for integrated coastal area management

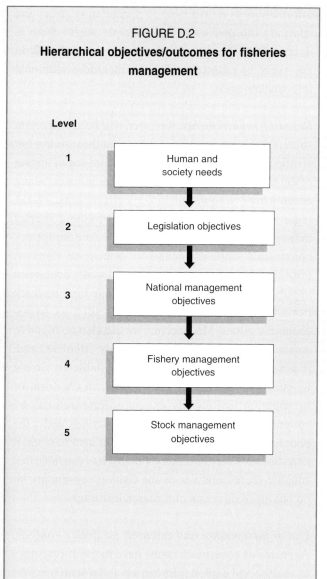

FIGURE D.2

Hierarchical objectives/outcomes for fisheries management

Level

1 — Human and society needs

2 — Legislation objectives

3 — National management objectives

4 — Fishery management objectives

5 — Stock management objectives

developing indicators, consideration should be given to who the main users of the indicators will be; the main users will probably be decision-makers in the public and private sectors as well as the general public. Indicators should therefore be highly aggregated so that they provide concise information devoid of detail. Each indicator requires a basis for comparison. Comparisons can be made: with a standard; with a target; with a threshold or limit value; before and after a change; and with a similar management objective made by another agency (a benchmark). Performance indicators should provide information on appropriateness, effectiveness and efficiency. Appropriateness is a check on how well objectives match government priorities and community needs; effectiveness measures the extent to which management achieves stated objectives; and efficiency is the extent to which the inputs to management are maximized to provide outputs and outcomes.

Implementing performance indicators. The main problems encountered during the implementation of performance indicators include achieving a simple system that is practical and useful and making rational decisions about the level of investment required to obtain the information needed for a particular indicator. A cost-benefit analysis is needed to determine the level of research and effort that should go into indicators that are expensive to monitor and assess. Another difficulty is to determine who should be introducing the performance indicators. Ultimately, it is a management responsibility but, in cases where industry is heavily involved in management decision-making, the use of a "public watchdog" may be warranted.

Use of indicators in decision-making. One of the main uses of indicators should be to guide decisions. As well as the obvious benefit of providing performance criteria against which governments can assess their rate of progress towards meeting objectives, sustainability indicators can also be used operationally to link future management to agreed actions. These decision rules can provide commitment to remedial action when objectives are not met, providing long-term benefits to both the fishing industry and the public. The process becomes proactive rather than reactive and is transparent to all stakeholders.

"Management strategy evaluation" uses several different performance indicators to evaluate alternative harvest strategies. The problem is posed within a decision-making framework, and involves the following steps: clearly defining a set of management objectives; specifying a set of quantitative performance indices related to each objective; identifying various alternative harvest strategy scenarios; and evaluating the performance indices for each harvest strategy.

In many cases, the evaluation in the last step involves simulating the future development of the fishery over a specified period under each harvest strategy. Examples of performance indices include total catch (or profit) over the period, variability in catch and the frequency with which threshold stock sizes are transgressed. The results are presented as a decision box to allow trade-offs to be made across conflicting objectives.

187

Source: extracted from Staples, 1997.

INTEGRATED
COASTAL AREA
MANAGEMENT
and
AGRICULTURE
FORESTRY AND
FISHERIES

PART D

INTEGRATION OF FISHERIES INTO COASTAL AREA MANAGEMENT

4. Policy and planning for integrated coastal area management

---

BOX D.13

Possible research topics for fisheries authorities relevant to the integration of fisheries into coastal area management

Ecological functions. These need to be understood to assess the impact of proposed projects on different users of the coastal area, including fishers, and will include studies of overall carrying capacity, impact reversibility, etc.

Resource dynamics. These include research to distinguish between the natural variability of resources and human impact, and to predict long-term trends resulting from management action and/or climate change.

Applied research. This includes research aimed at, for example, studying sectoral dynamics and developing cheap and simple ecological monitoring schemes based on appropriate environmental hazard assessment and prediction methods.

Socio-economics studies. These are carried out to identify the factors underlying the economic activities in the coastal area and impinging upon it, the application of valuation techniques, and the design and impact of economic incentive systems.

Institutional issues. These include the legal and property rights framework needed to allow market pricing, organizational arrangements for local-level management by communities and the development of co-management over larger areas.

Source: FAO 1996b.

4.3.1 Negotiation of trade-offs

Trade-offs will be needed within the plan formulation process since some objectives will always be incompatible and a choice will have to be made. Similarly, where there is conflict over finite resources, compromise between potential users will be necessary. Such trade-offs must be negotiated through appropriate channels. Handling trade-offs satisfactorily is a central aspect of the policy process. In seeking to implement trade-offs, the difficulty lies in applying fairly simple solutions to complex situations (for example, how to "zone" the coastal area seawards).

4.3.2 Capacity building

Application of the plan, monitoring and ensuring compliance with related regulations, depends crucially on capacity building.

Collection and analysis of information. Collecting reliable information on coastal areas, fisheries in particular, is notoriously difficult. As mentioned in Part A,[40] it will often be necessary to make do with such information as is available in formulating plans and applying the precautionary principle where there is doubt. Given the need for flexibility, the plan will, in any event, be adapted as changes, including additional information, arise.

Research requirements. Research will be an important source of information, especially about the resource but also, potentially, about the economic and social impact of the plan. Research should be interdisciplinary, taking account of environmental, biological, economic, social, legal and institutional aspects of coastal fisheries management. Since many countries face budgetary constraints, care is needed to determine research priorities. Fisheries authorities, traditionally concerned mainly with the fish stock, must enlarge their research horizons to cross-sectoral aspects such as socio-economic issues. Mechanisms should also be found to ensure that research results are widely circulated and, if possible, that summaries are available in simple language for use by non-specialists, in the form of information leaflets, for example. Research can be commissioned on the impact of regulations under the plan to demonstrate their benefits, but also to suggest adjustments where necessary. Finally, it is desirable that suitable representatives of the fishing community sit on boards of directors of research institutes.

Use of information and research for policy analysis. Agencies of government must have the staff resources to analyse and exploit information and research results and apply them to fisheries management policy and plans. Where necessary, training should be provided to this end since, otherwise, resources spent on research and the generation of information will be wasted. Similarly, fisheries authorities must ensure that they dispose of the capacity to use tools such as environmental impact assessment, cross-sectoral policy analysis, geographical information systems and various economic valuation techniques.

---

[40] See Part A, Section 1.6.3

PART D

INTEGRATION OF FISHERIES INTO COASTAL AREA MANAGEMENT

INTEGRATED
COASTAL AREA
MANAGEMENT
and
AGRICULTURE
FORESTRY AND
FISHERIES

4. Policy and planning for integrated coastal area management

Institutional arrangements. Institutional arrangements for integrated coastal fisheries management must begin by defining the appropriate management unit, which should be broad enough to include all the elements that play a significant role in the fisheries system. The agency with major responsibility for coordination should have a mandate to initiate cross-sectoral planning. Setting up consultative committees, stimulating the establishment of fishers' organizations where they do not exist already, ensuring that legislation avoids overlapping (a strong risk in the area of aquaculture) and allows for participation will also contribute to the physical institutional structure. Ensuring that information circulates as widely as possible, as mentioned above, is also part of the institutional arrangements.

Enforcement capacity. A strong enforcement capacity will be required if plan objectives are to be achieved, especially with respect to the environment and sustainable resources management. Legislation should be drafted in collaboration with the enforcement authorities to increase the chances of conviction in the courts when necessary. Ideally, the management authorities should control the enforcement authorities, which is difficult in cases where the navy ensures enforcement, but this is less likely to apply to coastal resources. Observers are often placed on vessels, especially foreign ones; the observer is paid for by the fishing company as part of its licence, and this could open the risk of abuse. Observers also provide very useful information about the fishing operation, including biological data which are difficult to obtain by other means.

As already mentioned, when regulations have been drawn up in consultation with users and agreed on a consensual basis, enforcement should be easier since compliance should be by common consent.

4.3.3 Integrating fisheries plans into national plans
In the context of ICAM, fisheries plans will be integrated into overall plans for integrated management of the coastal area, at both national and local levels. The process for achieving this is described in Part A.[41]

189

---

[41] See Part A, Section 2.3 and 2.4 and Figure A.7.

PART D

INTEGRATION OF FISHERIES INTO COASTAL AREA MANAGEMENT

INTEGRATED
COASTAL AREA
MANAGEMENT
and
AGRICULTURE
FORESTRY AND
FISHERIES

5. Conclusions

Integrating fisheries management into coastal area management is not an easy task and the process is time-consuming. However, without such integration, it is likely that optimum use of society's fisheries resources will not be achieved and, indeed, the future of fisheries in coastal areas is likely to be seriously threatened.

The first challenge to the fisheries management authorities is to establish clearly the value of the fisheries sector to the economy. In the case of capture fisheries, this requires an approach to management that gives equal weighting to biological and economic factors. A major issue is to find a way to avoid resource rent driving the fishery to overexploitation and making the rent available to society for use elsewhere to improve social welfare. Exploitation levels of the fishery will have to be reduced if these results are to be achieved. There are a variety of ways of achieving reductions in exploitation, in particular allocation of rights to fish. Such rights have the advantage of allowing at least some intersectoral conflicts to be resolved, in addition to their role in improving performance of the fishery itself.

In addition to the access issue, management must give consideration to the environment within which fisheries operate. Many resources in the coastal area (e.g. mangroves, coral reefs) produce valuable outputs for society but, because they are unpriced, such values are difficult to reflect. It may also be difficult to identify precisely the nature of the benefits and who the beneficiaries are. In such cases, research can attempt to identify the positive physical effects of various coastal resources.

Integrated management requires these wider issues to be duly taken into account. The problem is how the management process can achieve this. Two broad solutions suggest themselves: an administrative approach whereby very detailed plans are established determining who may do what in specific areas and under what conditions; or an approach in which the standard resource allocation model based on user rights and prices is applied to coastal areas. Under the latter conditions, overfished fisheries are unlikely to be competitive.

Conditions in the coastal environment differ in several respects from those on land, although some problems are similar (e.g. acid rain, water pollution, location of airports). The challenge is to try to design systems that will enable market mechanisms to work effectively in the coastal environment. In fisheries, some progress has been made in the development of licensing and individual catch quota systems. Now is the time to consider how such mechanisms might be implemented for other, unpriced, coastal resources.

Two things seem clear from experience around the world. One is that the management authority cannot possibly plan for all contingencies. The other is that there appears to be no better means of resource allocation than the price mechanism, given the need for safeguards and corrections. The rule therefore seems to be to rely on price mechanisms as far as possible and reserve the administrative planning process for cases where the price mechanism cannot be made to work.

INTEGRATED
COASTAL AREA
MANAGEMENT
and
AGRICULTURE
FORESTRY AND
FISHERIES

PART

E

CONFLICT RESOLUTION IN INTEGRATED COASTAL AREA MANAGEMENT

INTEGRATED
COASTAL AREA
MANAGEMENT
and
AGRICULTURE
FORESTRY AND
FISHERIES

PART E
CONFLICT RESOLUTION IN INTEGRATED COASTAL AREA MANAGEMENT

INTEGRATED
COASTAL AREA
MANAGEMENT
and
AGRICULTURE
FORESTRY AND
FISHERIES

Executive summary

Owing to the limited physical availability of resources in coastal areas (namely land, fresh water and coastal waters), and the increasing competition for them, there is a greater risk of conflict between competing users of coastal area resources than there is in other areas.

Disputes can erupt between government departments, private individuals, companies or any combination of these. In coastal areas, they can involve neighbouring states. The relative power of the disputants (e.g. large timber company versus impoverished smallholder whose remaining land is at risk) may influence the outcome. Conflict will often arise between different sectors (agricultural polluters and shrimp farmers, hotel owners and inshore fishers). It can also involve residents (or potential residents) of the area and non-residents (for example, ecologists who are aiming to protect a threatened breeding ground).

Disputes can be resolved through the courts, with the existing law being applied on the strength of the case presented by the litigants. But this will usually leave one party unsatisfied and will not relieve the tensions. Increasingly, moves are being made towards establishing other forms of dispute settlement, known as alternative dispute resolution (ADR) techniques.

ADR consists of direct negotiations between the parties, with or without some form of intermediary (conciliator, mediator or arbitrator), each having defined roles to play. When large disputes over public policy are concerned, negotiated rule-making is often introduced, whereby all the parties seek to agree on the objective and the means of attaining it.

The choice of such alternative techniques will depend on local circumstances and, while no guarantee of a satisfactory conclusion can be given beforehand, experience shows that, with goodwill and flexibility on all sides, it is often possible to reach solutions to disputes that are acceptable to all parties concerned. An essential element is that all concerned parties are involved on an equal footing. Special efforts will usually have to be deployed to bring in the weakest parties and provide them with all the instruments needed (e.g. information on the suit, the consequences of various solutions, alternative solutions) to argue their respective cases.

The conditions necessary for a successful outcome include voluntariness, opportunities for mutual gain, participation, clear identification of interests, development of options and the capability of the parties to enter into agreements and ensure that they are carried out.

Alternative dispute resolution techniques are especially appropriate in coastal areas where issues are complex, all concerns often legitimate and the scope for compromise fairly broad.

PART E

CONFLICT RESOLUTION IN INTEGRATED COASTAL AREA MANAGEMENT

INTEGRATED
COASTAL AREA
MANAGEMENT
and
AGRICULTURE
FORESTRY AND
FISHERIES

1. Introduction

As a result of the valuable resources and high level of human activity that characterize coastal areas, there are inevitably competing and conflicting claims over the allocation and use of such resources. The different priorities of different institutions in a sectoral or poorly integrated coastal area management system also tend to produce institutional conflicts. One of the fundamental goals of integrated coastal area management (ICAM) is "anticipating, avoiding or resolving conflicts that dissipate the value of coastal resources and environments", and "typically [ICAM] is concerned with resolving conflicts among many coastal uses and determining the most appropriate use of coastal resources", (Sorensen and McCreary, 1990).

The resolution of conflict is one of the central concerns of any legal system and courts may have an important part to play in resolving disputes in coastal areas. Appropriate legislation will be indispensable to the creation of institutional arrangements and the establishment of procedures that reduce the potential for conflict and facilitate the resolution of conflicts when they do arise.

However, traditional "top-down" legislative processes and litigation through the courts have often proved to be ineffective methods of regulating competing interests and addressing conflicts concerning natural resources and the environment. Dissatisfaction with conventional litigation and rule-making processes has led to a growing trend in favour of alternative dispute resolution (ADR) techniques in the context of natural resource and environmental management. These techniques include arbitration, mediation and direct negotiation, and alternative means of regulating to avoid or manage conflict, such as negotiated rule-making. Since these techniques aim to engage the disputants actively in seeking a result acceptable to all the parties involved, they are likely to be more effective in the ICAM context.

This part of the guidelines is intended to give those involved in coastal management an overview of various alternative dispute resolution mechanisms and to identify the circumstances in which such approaches can be usefully adopted. Section 2 sets out a conceptual framework for discussing conflict resolution. This is followed by a discussion on an international trend towards collaborative (as opposed to adversarial) methods of resolving conflicts in Section 3. Section 4 describes and compares various ADR techniques, and Section 5 deals with the processes involved and the issues that are typically encountered. Finally, Section 6 deals with legal and institutional mechanisms for promoting conflict resolution in the context of ICAM.

PART E

CONFLICT RESOLUTION IN INTEGRATED COASTAL AREA MANAGEMENT

INTEGRATED
COASTAL AREA
MANAGEMENT
and
AGRICULTURE
FORESTRY AND
FISHERIES

2. A conceptual framework for conflict resolution

Before examining the various techniques and their appropriateness in resolving the conflicts that arise in coastal areas, it is necessary to examine the nature of conflict and the circumstances in which it arises, as well as the meaning of, and justification for, conflict resolution.

2.1 THE NATURE OF CONFLICT

Conflict arises when the interests of two or more parties clash and at least one of the parties seeks to assert its interests at the expense of another party's interests. Conflict has also been described as "a social phenomenon that can result from instantaneous or gradual changes that create diverging interests and needs" (Chandraskhan, 1997). Conflicts can involve two parties or several parties ("multiparty conflicts") and can arise in numerous contexts, on numerous levels and over numerous issues.

Conflicts are multidimensional and frequently involve complex interactions between many parties. However, for analytical purposes it is useful to identify the following four dimensions of a conflict: the actors; the resource in dispute; the stake that each actor has in the resource; and the stage that the conflict has reached (i.e. the time dimension). The environmental dimension will be added to each of these.

2.1.1 Actors

The actors are generally the disputants (e.g. government departments, private companies and local communities) but may also include other parties, such as the state, which may have an interest in the peaceful resolution of social conflicts. The interaction between the actors is frequently crucial in determining the terms on which the conflict will be resolved, if it is resolved. This interaction will be influenced by:

- the level at which the conflict occurs (e.g. at an international level between states, at a national level between government departments or at local level);
- the relative level or status of the disputants (e.g. a conflict may occur "horizontally" between parties on the same level, or "vertically" between parties on

different levels, such as a government department and a local community);
- the relative power of the disputants (e.g. even though all government ministries may be on the same level, a ministry that is responsible for a sector that makes a major contribution to the national economy often wields more power than a less economically important ministry).

Addressing large discrepancies in the relative power of disputants may present formidable obstacles in an ADR process (see Section 3.2).

2.1.2 Resources at stake

As discussed in Part A, activities in the coastal area may be characterized as synergistic, complementary, competitive or antagonistic.[1] Of these, the competitive and antagonistic interactions are most likely to give rise to conflict (physical, biological, social or economic). Such conflicts arise primarily from competing and conflicting claims over the allocation of, or access to, natural resources, both within and between the agriculture, forestry and fisheries sectors, and between these and other sectors in the coastal area, such as industry or tourism.

The resource in respect of which the conflict arises may have certain objective characteristics that will have an important bearing on the resolution of the conflict. For example, if the conflict concerns the amount of pollution that may be discharged into a bay, the natural assimilative capacity of the bay will define the limits within which the parties will have to negotiate a settlement. A settlement that involves exceeding this limitation will fail in the long term. However, there is frequently a high degree of scientific uncertainty in relation to such issues[2] and this complicates negotiation processes.

It is also important to be aware of the interactions between the resource concerned and other components of the ecosystem, since changes to one part of a system

---

[1] See Part A, Box A.1.
[2] See Part A, Boxes A.5 and A.13.

199

INTEGRATED
COASTAL AREA
MANAGEMENT
and
AGRICULTURE
FORESTRY AND
FISHERIES

PART E

CONFLICT RESOLUTION IN INTEGRATED COASTAL AREA MANAGEMENT

2. A conceptual framework for conflict resolution

are likely to affect other resources and thereby involve other actors in the ecosystem.

2.1.3 The stake

The stake is the value, use or interest that an actor has in the resource base. It can be economic, political, environmental, religious or socio-economic, and will vary depending on the resource and the actor (e.g. a member of a forest-dependent community and a private company often associate different stakes with the same resource).

It is important to appreciate that a stake can be conceived of as having both subjective and objective elements. It can be seen as representing the actor's subjective evaluation of their relationship with the resource. The more highly the actor values this relationship, the more intensely they will assert their interests in the resource.

An actor's stake may also be assessed on the basis of objective criteria such as the percentage of income derived from the resource. Furthermore, the stake may be affected by external factors such as legal recognition of an actor's interest in a resource. Formal legal recognition can have a dramatic effect on an actor's bargaining power in relation to other actors. For example, the ability of indigenous or local communities to assert customary rights to use a resource will be severely compromised if their traditional interests in the resource are not recognized as legally enforceable rights under national law.

2.1.4 The time dimension

It is important to establish what stage the conflict has reached. A certain period of time may need to elapse before the issues surrounding a conflict crystallize to the point where they can be constructively addressed. However, as a conflict continues, it is likely that it will increase in intensity and the relationship between the parties will become more confrontational. The state of the resource(s) at issue may also deteriorate over time, thus reducing the total potential benefits available to be shared between the parties through resolution of the conflict (see Section 2.1.2). Pressure to resolve a conflict is also likely to increase over time, which may lead to a less than satisfactory conclusion being reached in haste. If damage has occurred, issues such as the payment of compensation may complicate matters further.

Early intervention in most conflicts is therefore advisable to facilitate their satisfactory resolution and to minimize undesirable consequences. This approach is also in line with the principle of preventive action, now widely endorsed by the international community, which advocates early action to prevent environmental harm on the basis that it is cheaper, safer and more desirable to prevent such harm occurring than to rectify it later.[3]

As the population continues to grow and environmental, social, political and economic conditions evolve, competition for coastal resources is increasing, resulting in situations of conflict that set different parties against each other. With growing numbers of conservationists, private companies, government and non-government projects and communities, all demanding rights to the resources for different purposes, the potential for different types of conflict is also growing.

2.1.5 Environmental issues

Many ICAM conflicts involve environmental issues, and these have certain characteristics that can make them more difficult to resolve than other types of conflict, such as:

- uncertainty as to the harm caused (e.g. the effects on human health of an incinerator or the effects of pollution on the marine environment, may not be known for many years after the event);
- uncertainty as to the parties and interests affected (e.g. the effects of activities that harm the environment are often not only felt locally or immediately but may have negative impacts further afield and on future generations);
- differences of opinion as to what risk is acceptable, to what extent the environment should be protected from change, etc., often involving value judgements;
- economic implications and uncertainties (e.g. environmental protection measures can have economic effects, and *vice versa*, yet it is often impossible to put a monetary value on the environment)[4] and the fact that simple cost-benefit analysis is inadequate in certain situations (e.g. the

---

[3] See Part A, Section 2.2.4 and Boxes A.3, A.5 and A.6.
[4] See Part A, Box A.24.

PART E

CONFLICT RESOLUTION IN INTEGRATED COASTAL AREA MANAGEMENT

INTEGRATED
COASTAL AREA
MANAGEMENT
and
AGRICULTURE
FORESTRY AND
FISHERIES

2. A conceptual framework for conflict resolution

loss of a species or a forest as a result of logging), given the global as well as local benefits provided by the resources.

Many conflicts over natural resources arise because resources have been exploited without taking into account their true value. The true value of the natural environment and the costs of damaging it, the so-called "externalities", have not been "internalized"[5] in calculations affecting the use of the environment. For example, the decision to clear an area of forest to sell timber should take into account not only the value of the timber in the market but the loss of the benefits offered by the forest (e.g. soil stability, climate regulation, biological diversity). When decisions are made that do not take into account the real value of environmental resources, they may lead to unsustainable practices and conflicts, and ultimately to the exhaustion of the resource (Chandraskhan, 1997).

2.2 THE MEANING OF CONFLICT RESOLUTION

Before considering the meaning of conflict resolution, it is useful to consider the broader term "conflict management" which has been described as a kind of proactive-reactive[6] continuum: "The proactive end of the spectrum involves fostering productive communication and collaboration among diverse interests, addressing the underlying causes of conflicts in order to prevent conflicts from recurring, developing trust and understanding and using participatory and collaborative planning in order to prevent conflicts which result from policies. The reactive end of the spectrum includes approaches to managing conflicts that involve negotiation, mediation, conciliation and consensus building. The reactive approach is used after the conflict has erupted." (Chandraskhan, 1997).

There are a number of ways of dealing with a conflict, ranging from violence at one extreme to ignoring the conflict at the other, with a variety of approaches in between. Towards the more hostile end of the spectrum is litigation, in which parties take their grievances to a court or tribunal which applies predetermined legal rules to the conflict and issues a decision that is binding upon the parties, producing a winner and a loser. However, parties are turning increasingly to ADR techniques to

settle their disputes. These include negotiation, mediation and conciliation, which are more flexible and produce results that are more acceptable to the parties as well as more sustainable in the longer term. ADR is being used increasingly in conflicts over the environment and natural resources and has considerable advantages over traditional contentious methods. ADR techniques and their suitability to ICAM are examined in some detail in Section 4.

Some analysts have used the concept of a mountain to symbolize the range of options faced in managing conflicts and explained it as follows:

"At the summit of the mountain is cooperative teamwork, with the goal of achieving a synergy of solutions of mutual advantage to all interests. At the base of the mountain, from where any climb has to begin, are isolation, the decision not to engage in the debate at all, and confrontation, in which positions have been adopted in fixed opposition to one another." (Brown *et al.,* 1995).

From isolation and confrontation at the base of the pyramid the options progress through the stages of litigation, arbitration, mediation, facilitation, conciliation, negotiation, and on to cooperation at the top (see Figure E.1).

The term "conflict resolution" has been described as "a process by which two or more conflicting parties improve their situation by cooperative action... [allowing] the parties to expand the pie, or to prevent it from shrinking, giving each party a larger slice" (Melling, 1994). This definition highlights the fact that conflict resolution aims to bring about benefits for the parties. It does not simply mean the cessation of conflict; if it did, it could include war and litigation, but war and litigation usually leave one, if not both parties, worse off. A common way of conceptualizing the process is to ask whether the conflict is a "zero-sum game", in which gain for one party causes loss for another, or a "plus-sum game", which creates the possibility of "win-win" solutions in which both parties gain overall through collaborative effort.

Conflict resolution through cooperative action aims to find win-win solutions and leave both parties better off with the outcome. However, it may not always be the best option for all the parties. In some situations a party may actually capture the largest share of the benefits through unilateral action. Some dispute

201

---

[5] See Part A, Section 1.6.3, Box A.24 and Glossary.
[6] See Glossary.

INTEGRATED
COASTAL AREA
MANAGEMENT
and
AGRICULTURE
FORESTRY AND
FISHERIES

PART E

CONFLICT RESOLUTION IN INTEGRATED COASTAL AREA MANAGEMENT

2. A conceptual framework for conflict resolution

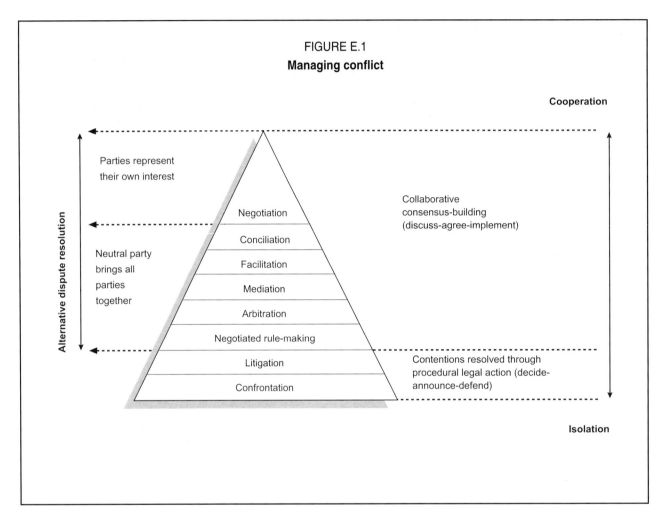

FIGURE E.1
Managing conflict

Cooperation

Parties represent
their own interest

Alternative dispute resolution

Negotiation

Collaborative
consensus-building
(discuss-agree-implement)

Conciliation

Neutral party
brings all
parties
together

Facilitation

Mediation

Arbitration

Negotiated rule-making

Contentions resolved through
procedural legal action (decide-
announce-defend)

Litigation

Confrontation

Isolation

resolution theorists refer to this as a party's "best alternative to a negotiated settlement", or BATNA. If a party's BATNA is better than any collaborative outcome, it will have no incentive to explore options and possible solutions collaboratively, but will instead simply pursue unilateral action.

2.3 THE RATIONALE BEHIND CONFLICT RESOLUTION
In determining whether conflict resolution is appropriate, an important consideration is whether it results in a better situation than if the conflict is allowed to take its natural course. Conflict is not always negative; it may be a necessary stage in progress towards a better state of affairs. It may galvanize community organizations, put important issues on the public agenda and ultimately help to bring about essential societal and institutional changes that may result in a more equitable and sustainable use of resources. It is arguable that, if conflict is nipped in the bud, these important benefits

may be lost. Early intervention in a dispute, for example, could be used as a mask behind which powerful interests work to advance their own interests. As noted by Brown *et al.* (1995) "...conflict is the inevitable accompaniment of change. The challenge is therefore not to prevent conflict arising, but to identify the outcome of the conflict and the best ways to manage it."

It is also important to distinguish between the underlying causes of conflict and the symptoms of the conflict. Sometimes a conflict may appear to have been resolved, when in fact only the manifestation of the conflict has been removed. If the police break up a violent demonstration, for example, they are removing the manifestation of a conflict between the demonstrators and the object of their demonstration, but the root causes of the conflict remain, possibly to re-emerge at a later stage. To resolve a conflict properly, it is necessary to address the concerns of the conflicting parties and seek solutions that will

PART E
CONFLICT RESOLUTION IN INTEGRATED COASTAL AREA MANAGEMENT

INTEGRATED
COASTAL AREA
MANAGEMENT
and
AGRICULTURE
FORESTRY AND
FISHERIES

2. A conceptual framework for conflict resolution

maximize the benefits to them in the long as well as the short term.

Those responsible for making and implementing coastal management policies and programmes may have a variety of reasons for intervening to resolve conflicts. These include:

• ***Promoting better and more sustainable utilization of natural resources.*** If a conflict arises from the competitive or antagonistic use of a resource by more than one party, the process of conflict resolution may lead to the discovery of solutions that can lead to the resource involved being utilized more sustainably and optimally. Sustainable development is not a simple, or even universally accepted, concept, and the issues are often complex, but the main principle behind it is that the present generation is responsible for managing the resource base in such a way as to ensure its availability to future generations to satisfy their needs while, at the same time, ensuring its own needs are met. The process of resolving conflicts presents the opportunity to address the problems at their root and to plan for the sustainable use of resources into the future.[7]

• ***Promoting equity.*** Equity or "fairness" is a relative concept and hard to define in general terms, but it can be an important reason for resolving conflicts and is also considered to constitute an important element of sustainable development. It implies fairness to present and future generations in the way the earth's environmental resources are managed and passed on. Where conflict arises out of unfair distribution of resources, conflict resolution has the potential to correct the "wrong" and result in a fairer state of affairs. However, a number of factors may complicate the implementation of equity in practice, and many considerations need to be taken into account (such as indigenous rights and previous usage).

• ***Avoiding unwanted consequences.*** Unwanted consequences may include violence and loss of life, damage to physical property or financial loss. For example, when local fishers blockaded the Valdez Narrows in 1993 in protest at the Exxon Valdez oil spill, the consequences could have included substantial financial loss and property damage, because oil tankers would have been unable to reach the oil storage tanks which would have filled, forcing the oil company to shut down the pipeline, an action that had never been attempted. Fortunately, mediation was used to persuade the fishers to lift the blockade.

• ***Promoting social stability.*** The promotion of social stability can result from the resolution of a conflict, through the avoidance of undesirable consequences (such as those referred to above) and by promoting a sense of fairness among the parties to the conflict. Where conflicts are resolved using collaborative techniques, involving the interested parties in the search for solutions, the outcome is usually more satisfactory to the parties and therefore more easily enforced and workable in practice. If conflicts are left to end in violence or litigation, however, feelings of resentment and revenge may remain and give rise to a recurrence of conflict in the future.

203

---

[7] See Part A, Sections 2.1 and Box A.11.

PART E

CONFLICT RESOLUTION IN INTEGRATED COASTAL AREA MANAGEMENT

INTEGRATED
COASTAL AREA
MANAGEMENT
and
AGRICULTURE
FORESTRY AND
FISHERIES

3. The trend towards collaborative methods of conflict resolution

3.1 THE LIMITATIONS OF LITIGATION

In most legal systems, once a conflict has arisen the courts resolve it by applying relatively inflexible legal rules in order to determine which party's case is superior in law, thereby producing a winner and a loser. In some instances courts are the most appropriate forum for resolving conflicts, for example where the conflict is governed by clear legal rights and/or obligations that define a "guilty" and an "innocent" party or where there is a need for punishment, deterrence or redress. This is particularly relevant where there is an imbalance of power (e.g. economic or political) and the less powerful party could be forced into an unfair settlement.

However, in the case of many of the conflicts that arise in an ICAM context, such as competition for the use of a particular part of the coast, it is not possible, or even desirable, to stipulate rigid rules to determine who is "right". Resolving conflicts of this nature requires a balancing of interests in the context of a wide range of flexible criteria, which themselves may not be wholly consistent.

The litigation process has been described as "decide, announce, defend" (Environment Council, 1995a). The parties to the dispute confront each other in a court, a judge or arbitrator considers the evidence and, based on predetermined legal rules, imposes a binding decision on them as to which party's case is superior in law, thus producing a so-called "win-lose" outcome. The parties relinquish control over the process by which the dispute is heard as well as the decision that is reached.

The role of the presiding judge(s) or arbitrator(s) varies in different legal systems. For example, in common law countries the judge acts more as a referee in a contest between the parties while in civil law systems judges have a more active role in determining the facts. However, the process generally involves adjudicating on the relative merits of the facts and arguments presented by the adversaries. The main disadvantage of this adversarial approach, particularly for the sort of disputes that arise in the context of ICAM, is that it produces piecemeal, incremental decision-making by a judge, based on narrow points of law, without taking wider related issues into account.

As litigation is ostensibly directed at narrow procedural and legal issues instead of the underlying policy questions, it often fails to resolve the real differences between the contending parties. For example, a challenge to a nuclear power plant may be based on the granting of a licence without holding a public hearing, but the policy questions at the heart of the controversy (e.g. should the nuclear power plant be built at all? What are the alternatives for supplying energy needs?) are rarely addressed by the courts. Furthermore, in many countries, when a court is required to review the decision of a government agency, it will typically only overrule it if the agency has failed to follow proper procedures, incorrectly interpreted the law, abused its discretion or acted arbitrarily or capriciously. Questions of policy may not even be considered.

There are a number of other significant disadvantages to applying adversarial techniques to the resolution of conflicts. For example, adversarial techniques frequently:

- encourage conflict between groups and generate anger;
- force people into entrenched positions;
- make one group suspicious of the motives of another;
- lead to long delays in decision-making;
- impose a "solution", rather than producing an efficient and equitable settlement;
- create winners, losers and divisions within communities;
- are expensive, in terms of both human energy and economic resource costs;
- take control of the outcome away from the parties, increasing the likelihood of subsequent claims of bias and of non-compliance with the rule;
- make no provision for policy review or monitoring of the decision on behaviour in the future.

Many of these shortcomings stem from the focus on rights and duties rather than alternatives. As one expert

INTEGRATED
COASTAL AREA
MANAGEMENT
and
AGRICULTURE
FORESTRY AND
FISHERIES

PART E

CONFLICT RESOLUTION IN INTEGRATED COASTAL AREA MANAGEMENT

3. The trend towards collaborative methods of conflict resolution

puts it: "Litigation is geared to rectifying the injustices of the past and present, rather than to planning for some change to occur in the future. The very notion of planning is alien to adjudication..." (Horowitz, 1977). This illustrates the unsuitability of litigation for resolving many of the conflicts that arise in the context of ICAM and require the implementation of long-term sustainable solutions.

In addition, legal rules, not to mention social status and cost considerations, may prevent a party with a grievance from having access to the courts even to have its case heard. In many jurisdictions, legal rules on *locus standi* (standing) prevent parties from bringing an action to court if they do not have some right that has been directly infringed. This is particularly problematic in cases where individuals or organizations attempt to represent the interests of the damaged environment which, itself, has no legal rights. Coupled with this dilemma of access, is the fact that the law may not provide an adequate legal remedy in any event.

Many of the disputes that arise in the context of ICAM involve parties with multiple needs or ongoing relationships over the use of a common resource over which no party has a clearly superior legal claim. In these circumstances, adversarial confrontation is inappropriate and even counter-productive. Such conflicts are resolved most appropriately through a process that can take account of these needs or relationships and involves a process of interactive cooperation or consensus, in which the participants work together in the active pursuit of "win-win" solutions.

3.2 THE ADVANTAGES OF ALTERNATIVE DISPUTE RESOLUTION (ADR) TECHNIQUES

One of the main objectives of ADR is to create consensus by satisfying the interests of the people most concerned with the outcome. In contrast to the "decide, announce, defend" nature of litigation, alternative dispute resolution and consensus-building techniques (such as negotiation and mediation) are based on a philosophy of "discuss, agree, implement" (Environment Council, 1995b). They aim to help people with opposing views to work together to seek solutions that they can all support, allowing time for trust to build up between the participants so that they all feel part of a team seeking solutions together.

The main characteristics of ADR techniques are:

- they are less formal and generally more private than court litigation;
- they permit the disputing parties to have more active participation in, and more control over, the processes for solving their own problems;
- they have been largely developed in the private sector, but are now being increasingly borrowed and adapted by courts and administrative agencies.

A number of significant advantages result from these characteristics:

- results can be gained more quickly and cheaply;
- in a non-adversarial atmosphere, communication between alienated parties can be restored, leading to increased mutual understanding;
- since the interested parties retain control, substantive issues of importance to them can be discussed and the roots of the problem tackled;
- interested parties that are involved in the issues at stake bring to the bargaining table a much deeper understanding of the technical and institutional dimensions of the problem than an external judge would, and are in a better position to explore different solutions and analyse their consequences;
- decisions can be tailored to the needs of the parties, who are free to fashion any deal that accommodates their interests, without regard to past disputes;
- the prospects for successful implementation of the decisions/solutions produced by the interested parties themselves are enhanced and, as they have a better understanding of and a greater investment in the settlement, any subsequent problems that do arise can often be expeditiously resolved, rather than becoming the subject of further litigation (lawsuits breed more lawsuits).

ADR has been viewed negatively by some critics as a submissive reaction to conflict consisting only of compromise. However, it should be noted that generating "synergy" is an important part of ADR processes, and the use of synergy in pursuit of win-win solutions is not the same as compromise, which implies negative results for one if not both parties. To synergize means to apply the technique of creative cooperation. Synergy is achieved when two sides to a dispute work together, using their creative capacities to find new options and alternatives, to come up with a solution that is better than either side first proposed. "Compromise means that one plus one equals one and

PART E

CONFLICT RESOLUTION IN INTEGRATED COASTAL AREA MANAGEMENT

INTEGRATED
COASTAL AREA
MANAGEMENT
and
AGRICULTURE
FORESTRY AND
FISHERIES

3. The trend towards collaborative methods of conflict resolution

a half. Synergy means one plus one equals three, four or five... the real essence of synergy is that the whole is greater than the sum of its parts." (Covey, 1992).

The following quote also highlights the advantages of ADR: "Behind opposed positions lie shared and compatible interests, as well as conflicting ones. We tend to assume that, because the other side's positions are opposed to ours, their interests must also be opposed. If we have an interest in defending ourselves, then they must want to attack us. If we have an interest in minimizing the rent, then their interest must be to maximize it. In many negotiations, however, a close examination of the underlying interests will reveal the existence of many more interests that are shared or compatible than the ones that are opposed." (Fisher, Ury and Patten, 1991).

3.3 INTERNATIONAL DIMENSIONS

Although most conflicts of concern to ICAM will be between parties in the same country, environmental and natural resource disputes also occur at the international level and specific methods of settlement are being developed. While some coastal disputes have a potential international dimension (e.g. by virtue of their impact on shared marine resources), many of the principles applicable to international conflict resolution can be usefully applied at other levels.

The settlement of disputes arising at the international level, between states, has traditionally been approached on the basis of state responsibility, using the variety of forms of dispute settlement machinery set out in Article 33 (1) of the Charter of the United Nations, which states that "The parties to any dispute, the continuance of which is likely to endanger the maintenance of international peace and security, shall, first of all, seek a solution by negotiation, enquiry, mediation, conciliation, arbitration, judicial settlement, resort to regional agencies or arrangements, or other peaceful means of their own choice."

Just as in disputes within states, there has, however, been a move away from the settlement of international environmental disputes through judicial institutions (such as the International Court of Justice) towards a more comprehensive regime aimed at the control and prevention of environmental harm and the conservation and sustainable development of the natural resources and ecosystems of the whole biosphere. This is in part

the result of a growing recognition of the global character of many environmental problems and the inappropriateness of according "rights" to an injured state after the event when much wider issues are at stake, such as the protection of common interests, common property or future generations.[8] In addition, many environmental problems involve harm that is subtle, cumulative and manifests itself only after a long period of time.

Experience indicates that solutions to such problems are often found most effectively not by judicial tribunals but through negotiations, allowing room for flexible or equitable solutions not necessarily dictated by international law, but accommodating as far as possible the interests of all parties. To meet these needs, there has been a move towards reliance on institutional machinery to resolve conflicts, in the form of intergovernmental commissions and meetings of treaty parties,[9] rather than the traditional bilateral forms of dispute settlement.

As Birnie and Boyle (1992) point out: "No other model offers adequate solutions to the problem of controlling phenomena of global character, such as global warming or ozone depletion, where no single state's acts are responsible and where the interests of all are at stake. In other situations too, such as the conservation of fish stocks, the allocation of water resources or transboundary air pollution, bilateral dispute settlement may be inappropriate to the polycentric character of problems involving a range of actors and a multiplicity of complex interrelated issues. Some form of international management and cooperation will usually offer a more efficient and more equitable means of allocation and conservation of such resources."

For these and other reasons (e.g. the lack of standing of states to bring international claims relating to the protection of "global commons" such as the high seas), international institutions have increasingly become a forum for dispute settlement through discussion and negotiation. Most of the more recent environmental

207

---

[8] See also Part A, Section 1.6.1.

[9] For example: The London Dumping Convention 1972; the Vienna Convention on the Protection of the Ozone Layer 1985; and the International Convention for the Regulation of Whaling 1946.

INTEGRATED
COASTAL AREA
MANAGEMENT
and
AGRICULTURE
FORESTRY AND
FISHERIES

PART E
CONFLICT RESOLUTION IN INTEGRATED COASTAL AREA MANAGEMENT

3. The trend towards collaborative methods of conflict resolution

treaties make specific provision for institutional supervision and regulation, with the aim of securing the parties' compliance with the treaty rather than adjudicating on breaches of it, and also refer to the need to ensure that parties use negotiation and other diplomatic channels to resolve their disputes before resorting to other more formal approaches.

Some of the more recent treaties (such as the 1992 Climate Change Convention) have established detailed mechanisms to settle disputes and encourage implementation non-contentiously. The 1982 UN Convention on the Law of the Sea (UNCLOS) went further than any previous environmental treaty by setting out, in Part XV, very comprehensive provisions on compulsory dispute settlement and requiring states to choose, on signing the Convention, which methods they will use in the event of a dispute arising over the application of the Convention.[10]

Chapter 39 of Agenda 21, entitled "International Legal Instruments and Mechanisms", recognizes as part of the review and development of international environmental law, the need to "...identify and prevent actual or potential conflicts, particularly between environmental and social/economic agreements or instruments, with a view to ensuring that such agreements or instruments are consistent...[and to] study and consider the broadening and strengthening of the capacity of mechanisms, *inter alia,* in the United Nations system, to facilitate, where appropriate and agreed to by the parties concerned, the identification, avoidance and settlement of international disputes in the field of sustainable development."[11]

Furthermore, Article 10 of the Code of Conduct for Responsible Fisheries (Integration of Fisheries into Coastal Area Management)[12] specifies that as part of the institutional framework for integration, states should "...facilitate the adoption of fisheries practices that avoid conflict among fisheries resources users and between them and other users of the coastal area...[and] promote the establishment of procedures and mechanisms at the appropriate administrative level to settle conflicts which arise within the fisheries sector and between fisheries resource users and other users of the coastal area."[13]

208

---

[10] As noted by Birnie and Boyle (1992), this was considered essential for UNCLOS, a convention that establishes a complex balance of rights and duties over a wide range of issues. In other purely environmental treaties, which are concerned more with facilitating cooperative solutions to common problems than with the allocation and control of power, institutional supervision is still, generally, the more appropriate means of control and development.

---

[11] Paragraph 39.3.
[12] See Part D, Box D.9.
[13] Paragraphs 10.1.4. and 10.1.5.

PART E

CONFLICT RESOLUTION IN INTEGRATED COASTAL AREA MANAGEMENT

INTEGRATED
COASTAL AREA
MANAGEMENT
and
AGRICULTURE
FORESTRY AND
FISHERIES

4. Alternative dispute resolution techniques

4.1 THE MAIN TECHNIQUES

The main "alternative" or "collaborative" techniques for resolving disputes are direct negotiation, conciliation, facilitation, mediation, arbitration and various combinations of techniques such as negotiated rule-making.[14] These techniques are discussed in this section; the main features of each are compared in Table E.1.

4.1.1 Direct negotiation

Negotiation is a process in which the parties to the dispute meet to reach a mutually acceptable resolution. Each party represents its own interests.

4.1.2 Conciliation

Conciliation is a process in which an outside party brings the parties in dispute together for discussion among themselves. Unlike mediation, conciliation usually connotes only preliminary involvement by the outside party. Conciliators do not usually take an active role in resolving the dispute but may help with setting of the agenda, record-keeping and administration, and may act as a go-between when parties do not meet directly, or as a moderator during joint meetings.

4.1.3 Facilitation

Facilitation is similar to conciliation, being a less active form of mediation. Facilitators may act as moderators in large meetings, ensuring that everyone is able to speak and be heard. They are not expected to volunteer their own ideas or participate actively in moving the parties towards agreement. Facilitation can also be applied at a one-to-one level, to guide an individual through strategic processes such as problem solving, prioritizing and planning.

4.1.4 Mediation

Mediation is a process during which the parties to a

dispute meet together and separately in confidence with a neutral and independent outside party (the mediator) to explore and decide how the conflict between them is to be resolved. The mediator assists the parties in reaching an agreement but has no power to impose a result upon them.

Mediation is commonly defined as a process of settling conflict in which an outside party oversees the negotiation between two disputing parties. The mediator is a neutral party who, although having no ability to give a judgement, acts in some way as a facilitator in the process of trying to reach agreement. The central quality of mediation has been described as "its capacity to reorient the parties towards each other, not by imposing rules on them, but by helping them to achieve a new and shared perception of their relationship, a perception that will redirect their attitudes and dispositions towards one another" (Fuller, 1971).

The main advantages of bringing in a neutral outside party to mediate in a dispute (in addition to the general advantages of ADR outlined above) are as follows:

- the mediator can facilitate communication between the parties and restore communication between alienated parties, breaking any deadlock that may otherwise block the resolution of the conflict;
- the mediator can help the parties to discover common interests, which they may otherwise be unaware of, and thus reach solutions that take these common interests into account;
- the mediator can expedite the negotiations, stimulate the parties to suggest creative settlements, help them to assess settlement alternatives realistically and generally assist them in reaching a better agreement;
- where there is a mass of conflicting scientific information and statistics which must be unravelled in order for a decision to be made, mediation techniques can be used to facilitate a more cooperative approach, because a mediator can identify the uncertainties and suggest ways of reducing them (for example, by agreeing to a research project whose terms of reference and methodology are set in advance

209

---

[14] These terms are used slightly differently by different countries or writers, etc. For example, the terms "facilitation" and "conciliation" are often used to mean mediation.

INTEGRATED
COASTAL AREA
MANAGEMENT
and
AGRICULTURE
FORESTRY AND
FISHERIES

PART E

CONFLICT RESOLUTION IN INTEGRATED COASTAL AREA MANAGEMENT

4. Alternative dispute resolution techniques

TABLE E.1

Comparative table of conflict resolution techniques

	Litigation	Arbitration	Mediation	Negotiation
Result sought	Court judgment	Arbitration award	Mutually acceptable agreement	Mutually acceptable agreement
Voluntary/involuntary	Involuntary	Voluntary	Voluntary	Voluntary
Binding/non-binding	Binding (subject to appeal)	Binding (subject to review on limited grounds)	Agreement enforceable as contract	Agreement enforceable as contract
Private/public	Public	Private (unless judicial review sought)	Private	Private
Participants	Judge and parties	Arbitrator and parties	Mediator and parties	Parties only
Third-party involvement	Judge, not selected by parties and usually with no specialized subject expertise, makes decision based on law	Arbitrator, selected by parties and often with specialized subject expertise, makes decision	Mediator, selected by parties, facilitates negotiation process	Parties communicate directly
First steps	One party initiates court proceedings	Parties agree on arbitration and appoint arbitrator	Parties agree on mediation and appoint mediator	Parties agree to negotiate
Approach/ methodology	Formal	Less formal	Flexible	Flexible
	Structured by predetermined rules	Procedural rules and substantive law may be set by parties	Usually informal and unstructured	Usually informal and unstructured
	Adversarial	Less adversarial	Non-adversarial	Non-adversarial
Advantages	Application of legal rules may help to address power imbalances	Quicker and cheaper than litigation Parties can tailor procedure to suit their needs Parties can choose subject matter experts as arbitrators	Quicker and cheaper Enables creative solutions to be found Can resolve conflicts over policy issues and/or where clear legal rights/obligations are lacking Parties retain control over process and outcome Parties work together to find win-win solutions Substantive issues of importance to parties can be addressed Decisions can be tailored to needs of parties Parties can directly contribute expert understanding and expertise Agreement more likely to be implemented and future problems solved in non-adversarial way Mediation, in particular, can restore communication between alienated parties and break deadlock	
Disadvantages	Slow and expensive Reinforces conflict between parties; may result in further litigation Decision restricted within narrow legal parameters Parties relinquish control over process and decision Inappropriate for disputes involving wider policy issues	Parties relinquish control over final decision Success depends on competence of arbitrators No appeal against decision (usually)	Power imbalances may be enhanced Agreement may not be reached Failure to implement agreement may necessitate enforcement through courts	

PART E

CONFLICT RESOLUTION IN INTEGRATED COASTAL AREA MANAGEMENT

INTEGRATED
COASTAL AREA
MANAGEMENT
and
AGRICULTURE
FORESTRY AND
FISHERIES

4. Alternative dispute resolution techniques

by all concerned – its results would be less partisan and therefore more likely to be accepted, improving the chances of the issues being discussed and resolved on their merits);[15]

- the mediator can provide new information and bring in a neutral perspective to problems of drafting.

4.1.5 Arbitration

Arbitration is usually used as a less formal alternative to going to court.[16] It is a process in which a neutral outside party or panel of neutrals meets with the parties to a dispute, hears presentations from each side and makes an award or a decision. Such a decision may be binding on the parties if they have previously agreed that it should be. Unlike in court, the parties to the dispute can participate in choosing the arbitrator (who is often an expert in the subject matter of their dispute) and in drafting the rules that govern the process. Arbitration hearings are usually held in private.

Sometimes parties to a dispute use a combined process known as "med-arb", in order to retain the advantages of both mediation and arbitration – if the mediator is unsuccessful in resolving the dispute through the agreement of the parties, then the mediator becomes an arbitrator with power to issue a binding decision.

4.1.6 Negotiated rule-making

Large disputes over public policy are increasingly being resolved using processes based on mediation and negotiation, commonly referred to as negotiated rule-making or regulatory negotiation. Representatives of interested parties are invited to participate in negotiations to agree on new rules governing issues such as industrial safety standards and environmental pollution from waste sites. Examples of how such processes have been used in practice are set out in Boxes E.1 and E.2.

In many jurisdictions, framework laws are enacted in broad terms but the formulation of regulations to govern their practical application is delegated to an administrative agency. The traditional rule-making process involves a few individuals drafting rules which are then circulated for comment and published. This process, which ignores the collective thinking of the parties directly affected by the rule, often leads to criticism, conflict and ultimately litigation, which can cost time, money and resources, and the rules are also likely to be less workable in practice.

If the consequences of a new rule are addressed before it is promulgated, by changing the rule-making procedures, conflicts can be avoided or resolved. To this end, negotiated rule-making techniques are increasingly being employed. Under these techniques, representatives of parties directly affected by the new rules are invited to participate in negotiations to agree on their content before they are made. The main advantages of negotiated rule-making are that it can reduce costs, delays and court challenges and promote policies that are more easily implemented because they are more acceptable to the parties involved. The main barrier to its implementation is the reluctance of rule-makers to relinquish control over rule-making.

The principle behind negotiated rule-making is supported in Agenda 21. For example, Chapter 28 "Local Authorities' Initiatives in Support of Agenda 21" calls on local authorities to enter into a dialogue with their citizens, local organizations and private enterprises in adopting "a local Agenda 21": "Through consultation and consensus-building, local authorities would learn from citizens and from local, civic, community, business and industrial organizations and acquire the information needed for formulating the best strategies."[17]

Chapter 23, entitled "Strengthening the Role of Major Groups", recognizes that: "One of the fundamental prerequisites for the achievement of sustainable development is broad public participation in decision-making. Furthermore, in the more specific context of environment and development, the need for new forms of participation has emerged. This includes the need of individuals, groups and organizations to participate in environmental impact assessment procedures and to know about and participate in decisions, particularly those that

211

---

[15] In any case, the independent opinion/advice of an expert may be of value in a dispute, particularly in one that raises environmental issues. In addition, some conflicts arise from ignorance, and educating the parties as to the effects of their activities may help to diffuse the conflict and find realistic solutions.

[16] However, the term "arbitration" serves a broad spectrum of dispute resolution processes; it can, for example, be used to describe a mandatory, non-consensual form of dispute resolution imposed on the parties, as well as the voluntary form described here.

[17] Paragraph 28.3.

INTEGRATED
COASTAL AREA
MANAGEMENT
and
AGRICULTURE
FORESTRY AND
FISHERIES

PART E

CONFLICT RESOLUTION IN INTEGRATED COASTAL AREA MANAGEMENT

4. Alternative dispute resolution techniques

BOX E.1
The British Wind Energy Association Guidelines

Wind energy developers are increasingly looking to the coast and out to sea for new locations for the siting of wind energy turbines. In such locations, exposed to high winds, turbines can provide maximum returns in terms of cost-effectiveness. But they can also interfere with a number of other users of the area, including wildlife, and thus give rise to conflicts.

The British Wind Energy Association (BWEA) found that their plans to build wind generators met a lot of opposition, including from environmental groups, many of which support the development of renewable energy resources. In 1994, in an attempt to improve its image by demonstrating its commitment to responsible and sensitive development, BWEA produced new development guidelines with the involvement of a broader range of interested parties, including groups opposed to wind energy. Although the process was viewed initially with suspicion from both sides, it was ultimately successful.

The process
- *Selection of a mediator.* The consensus-building began with the selection of a mediator. Financial assistance from the government helped to fund the process.

- *Interviews with stakeholders.* About fifty telephone interviews were carried out with main stakeholders such as planners, the Countryside Council for Wales and the Landowners' Association, which helped to identify the main issues.

- *First workshop.* After the interviews, a workshop was held to develop the criteria for what should be included in the guidelines. Twenty-five people attended the workshop, including all those who had been invited, among which were the strongest opposition groups. The ground rules were agreed and it was made clear that participation did not necessarily lead to endorsement of the guidelines. However, the participants agreed to express their support for the process and the end product.

- *Second workshop.* The first draft of the guidelines was prepared by BWEA and was then examined, paragraph by paragraph, at a second workshop. The final text was then agreed.

- *Monitoring.* Once the process of agreement was complete, the parties began to plan the next stage, which was to monitor the use and effectiveness of the guidelines.

Reaction of the parties
Although many participants were initially suspicious of the exercise, they found that their opinions were valued and respected, even if not always agreed with. One established opponent of all wind energy developments was even noted as stating how valuable and enjoyable the process had been. BWEA had expected to have to defend many of its positions and challenge the other participants on several issues, but this rarely happened and the participants were able to raise the issues themselves. Having agreed to create a safe and confidential environment in which they could find the best solutions, the participants were able to develop their thoughts and concerns with ease.

The end of the exercise
The guidelines produced by BWEA were produced in November 1994. Another benefit of consensus-building then became apparent. The guidelines were not attacked by opposition groups, as such guidelines often are, because the key stakeholders had been involved in the process of developing them and broadly agreed with their content.

Source: Environment Council, 1995c.

---

potentially affect the communities in which they live and work."[18]

4.2 CHOOSING THE MOST APPROPRIATE STRATEGY

It is not possible (or desirable) to lay down rigid rules as to when each method of conflict resolution should or should not be employed. The best process for a particular dispute will depend on the parties concerned, the interests at stake and the resources involved.

Although time and money are significant considerations, the quickest and cheapest method may not always be the best. The following considerations should also be taken into account in choosing a process:

- the nature of the conflict and the number of parties involved;
- the stage the conflict has reached;
- the type of relief sought;
- the extent to which a creative result is sought;
- the extent to which the parties prefer to be guided by their own notions of fairness as opposed to some objective standard;
- the present relationship of the parties and the value they place on their future relationship;
- the extent to which the parties need to cooperate in implementing or complying with a solution;
- whether the parties require to be listened to, to

---

[18] Paragraph 23.2.

PART E

CONFLICT RESOLUTION IN INTEGRATED COASTAL AREA MANAGEMENT

INTEGRATED
COASTAL AREA
MANAGEMENT
and
AGRICULTURE
FORESTRY AND
FISHERIES

4. Alternative dispute resolution techniques

BOX E.2

The 1980 Arizona Groundwater Management Act

This Act illustrates how the negotiated rule-making procedure was used to overcome some typical procedural obstacles to the resolution of conflict in the enactment of an important piece of legislation affecting the interests of a number of parties.

The history behind the Act was one of years of conflict between farming, mining and urban interests resulting from the depletion of Arizona's groundwater supplies from overextraction. After months of negotiations facilitated by the then Governor of Arizona, the affected interested parties reached an agreement and drafted the Act which was passed six days later. It was the first time that a state legislature had successfully resolved a groundwater management controversy. The procedural obstacles that had prevented agreement being reached were:

- **Strategic voting.** Sometimes legislators vote contrary to their true preferences, based on predictions of how other legislators will vote on competing alternatives, in order to achieve their second-best outcome. This creates uncertainty and can be a barrier to cooperative dispute resolution which requires open, honest communication about preferences and a willingness to accommodate the interests of other parties.

- **Bargaining through the mass media.** Politicians often appeal to the media to push their legislative agenda. The media become a filter for information but, being motivated by the desire to create a story, they tend to exaggerate differences and polarize parties' positions, consequently hindering open honest communication between the parties and limiting the opportunities for cooperation.

- **Bargaining through elected representatives.** Where interested parties do not participate directly in legislative debate over policy but through an elected representative, the latter may have

Source: Melling, 1994.

different incentives, and even conflicting interests, to the groups in conflict. Consequently, legislative decision-making is not determined by the interests of conflicting groups but by other political considerations.

These barriers were overcome, through negotiations, using the following strategies:

- **Unanimous decision.** Decisions were only taken by consensus, encouraging reluctant parties to negotiate and seek solutions that everyone could support rather than engaging in strategic behaviour and forming splintered coalitions. Because the parties had more control over the process, they also felt more satisfied with and committed to the group's decision, making its successful implementation in practice more likely. However, in order for this rule to work, the prospect of no agreement must be worse for all parties than a negotiated settlement. Parties may be tempted to use veto power to block a resolution. In addition, as the number of negotiating parties increases, the unanimous decision rule may become impractical.

- **Negotiation in private.** The negotiations were conducted in private, away from the press, whose potentially destructive influence was thus avoided. The parties could address the press together after decisions had been made. When parties are free to discuss their positions informally, out of the public eye, there is usually greater opportunity for agreement, as they can explore alternatives and find mutual interests without adopting rigid positions.

- **Mediation by a politician.** By acting as a mediator rather than an agent, a politician (the State Governor) with the requisite skills and the necessary respect and trust of the parties, was able to facilitate the negotiations, guiding the parties towards agreement, while using their political position to influence the parties.

---

participate actively in the process and retain control over the outcome;
- the need for a final result (and the avoidance of appeals or other challenges to that result);
- whether it is desirable to establish a principle to govern the resolution of future disputes, and how suitable the particular dispute is for establishing such a principle.

In addition, when dealing with disputes over natural resources, cultural values and principles must not be overlooked. Understanding and managing conflicts are culturally sensitive issues and depend on the context in which the conflicts occur. Similarly, the various approaches and tools of conflict management may not

be directly transferable from one culture or region to another; traditional practices and principles have a vital role to play in the management of conflict and must always be considered. Furthermore, as stated in the 1992 Rio Declaration on Environment and Development: "Indigenous people and their communities, and other local communities, have a vital role in environmental management and development because of their knowledge and traditional practices. States should recognize and duly support their identity, culture and interests and enable their effective participation in the achievement of sustainable development."[19]

---

[19] Principle 22.

PART E

CONFLICT RESOLUTION IN INTEGRATED COASTAL AREA MANAGEMENT

INTEGRATED
COASTAL AREA
MANAGEMENT
and
AGRICULTURE
FORESTRY AND
FISHERIES

5. The process of alternative dispute resolution

5.1 REQUIREMENTS FOR A SUCCESSFUL CONFLICT RESOLUTION PROCESS

It is possible to identify certain requirements that must be satisfied if a dispute is to be resolved successfully based on consensus or cooperation. Although they may vary slightly in the particular circumstances of each case, these requirements can be summarized as follows:

• voluntariness;
• opportunity for mutual gain;
• participation of interested parties;
• identification of interests;
• development of options;
• capability of parties to enter into and carry out agreement.

5.1.1 Voluntariness

The parties should be free to participate in or withdraw from a process. They, rather than an outsider, should come to a decision about which path to pursue to resolve the dispute. In addition, the interested parties themselves, not outsiders, should set the agenda. They are then more likely to engage in the process openly rather than defensively, thus increasing the chances of resolving the conflict permanently. Following on from this is the requirement that both or all parties want to reach a settlement. Fundamental divisions based on clashing values, where parties are divided over a matter of principle (e.g. whether a coastal tourist complex should be built at all, rather than simply where it should be built) and remain entrenched in their positions, may be impossible to resolve through ADR.

5.1.2 Opportunity for mutual gain

Linked to the voluntariness requirement is the requirement of opportunity for mutual gain. As stated above, conflict resolution is a process by which two or more conflicting parties make themselves better off through cooperative action. If one or both believe that they can achieve a better outcome through unilateral action, they will not be willing participants in a process of cooperative conflict resolution. Fuller (1971) described this, in the context of mediation, as the need

for "some strong internal pull towards cohesion" and "an intermeshing of interests sufficient to make parties willing to collaborate in the mediational effort".

5.1.3 Participation by all interested parties

In order to develop consensus, all interested parties should have an opportunity to participate in the process that creates the consensus. If an interested party is excluded from the process, it may feel it has no stake in the final result and consequently will not only refuse to support it but may even resort to the courts to fight it. It is therefore usually in everyone's interests to include anyone in the process who could later challenge the settlement and thus prevent its implementation. Furthermore, when all affected parties are at the table, there is a better chance that all the relevant issues will be raised.

5.1.4 Identification of interests

It is important, in working towards consensus, to identify interests rather than positions. Conflicting parties often engage in positional bargaining, sticking rigidly to their own positions without hearing or understanding the interests of the other parties. This creates confrontation and a barrier to consensus. It is therefore crucial to get down to the conflict's real issues and find areas of common interest between the parties which can open the way for agreement.

5.1.5 Development of possible solutions and options

A common barrier to successful conflict resolution is a psychological phenomenon known as "reactive devaluation". This is when a concession or proposal made by a perceived adversary is received less favourably because of its source, just as a compromise that is suggested by the other side is valued less highly because it comes from the other side. An important part of a conflict resolution process is therefore the neutral development of possible solutions and options in an atmosphere without evaluation and judgement. A neutral third party can be a great asset to the process, as it can put forward ideas and suggestions from a neutral stance.

215

INTEGRATED
COASTAL AREA
MANAGEMENT
and
AGRICULTURE
FORESTRY AND
FISHERIES

PART E

CONFLICT RESOLUTION IN INTEGRATED COASTAL AREA MANAGEMENT

5. The process of alternative dispute resolution

5.1.6 Capability of parties to enter into and carry out an agreement

Not only must the issue be capable of resolution through modification of perceptions, attitudes and/or behaviour, but the parties themselves must also be capable of entering into and carrying out an agreement. The enforceability of negotiated agreements is covered in Section 5.2.2.

5.2 TYPICAL ISSUES

5.2.1 Representation of interests

It can be very difficult, particularly in environmental/ natural resource disputes, to decide who should be represented in the negotiations, especially when a decision is likely to have an effect on people far removed from the locality in space and/or time (for example, future generations). Where a large number of interests are involved, coordination of a collaborative dispute resolution process becomes more complicated, unwieldy and difficult to manage. It may also be difficult to build up trust between the parties where there are too many participants. Even if the key parties reach an agreement that they are pleased with but that fails to take into account the impacts on those interests that were not directly represented in the negotiation, further conflict is likely to result in the future.

To overcome these problems it may be necessary to have a system for recognizing groups as legitimate parties for inclusion in an ADR process, and for determining who shall represent them. However, caution is needed in order to strike the right balance between, on the one hand, facilitating the negotiations by barring participants and, on the other hand, ensuring adequate participation of interested parties.

Representatives of interest groups may need to be selected to participate in the process on behalf of the groups. However, when selecting appropriate representatives for large decentralized groups, there may be difficulties, since members may have different viewpoints that cannot be expressed by a single voice or representative. If the group does not have a binding process to select a representative, some factions may object to the final outcome. Among the questions that need to be answered are whether the representative of a small community group should have a voice that counts as much as a delegate from a group with thousands of members. This will usually depend on the nature of the conflict and the circumstances of the particular case.

5.2.2 Enforcement of the agreement

Any agreement reached through cooperative conflict resolution needs to be applicable and enforceable in practice, indeed it may be critical to reaching agreement that the parties know it will be enforced. Assuming the agreement satisfies the requirements of the relevant contract law, it will be a legally enforceable contract. Ideally, the relationship of the parties will be such that failure to comply will result in a return to renegotiation rather than court action. However, in the absence of such a solution, the only recourse may be to seek enforcement of the agreement through a court, and provision may need to be made for this in the agreement itself.

5.2.3 Power imbalances

Views differ as to whether ADR techniques are appropriate when parties are grossly unequal in sophistication or resources. Differences in power may arise from differences in strength of, for example, economic resources, information, advice or personality. In environmental cases, a relative balance of power between the parties occurs only in about 10 percent of conflicts, and almost invariably the representatives of environmental interests are at an economic disadvantage *vis-à-vis,* for example, powerful industrial interests.

If the power imbalance remains, then the less powerful party risks being overwhelmed by the more powerful one, since any settlement will be based on bargaining and will accept inequalities of wealth as an integral and legitimate component of the process. It has been argued that neutralizing the power imbalance by an independent third party, risks compromising the impartiality of the third party. On the other hand, there are situations in which the balance of power must be evened out before an effective agreement can be reached (e.g. where a state proposes granting a concession to a private company in an area traditionally occupied by indigenous people without recognizing the land rights of the indigenous people). This is for reasons of equity but also to ensure effective implementation of the agreement and avoid unwanted consequences such as

PART E
CONFLICT RESOLUTION IN INTEGRATED COASTAL AREA MANAGEMENT

INTEGRATED
COASTAL AREA
MANAGEMENT
and
AGRICULTURE
FORESTRY AND
FISHERIES

5. The process of alternative dispute resolution

violence.[20] Power disparities can be minimized through awareness raising, capacity building, information dissemination, etc. to provide access to expertise (for example, legal or technical advice) to those to whom it is otherwise not available.

Sometimes, court action may better serve the interests of the disadvantaged party, as it can take inequalities into account, but this will only be the case where there is a question of protecting legal rights. Where legislation is an alternative, for example to decide on the siting of a locally objectionable project, it may not be any better for the weaker party, as legislatures often respond to the political power of lobbyists and interest groups. Negotiated rule-making may help to overcome this problem but may still require the provision of support (e.g. funding) to less powerful parties to enable their participation.

It is sometimes maintained that, where power is very unbalanced, the building of alliances to help strengthen the hand of the weaker group or working to strengthen equity through the legal structure may provide more lasting results than fostering a negotiation process that may yield "coerced harmony" in which the weaker party ultimately loses.

5.2.4 Funding

In many conflicts involving environmental and natural resource issues, the parties will often not have adequate financial resources to fund conflict resolution efforts, such as the cost of appointing a mediator or experts, or simply for running the negotiation. Consideration should therefore be given to establishing funding mechanisms for conflict resolution as part of any ICAM initiative.[21]

5.2.5 Involvement of third parties

In any conflict resolution process, consideration should be given to the requirement for the services of a neutral party to facilitate or mediate in the dispute. The following are some of the main factors that will need to be taken into account.

Number of parties. Mediation in general is best suited to disputes involving only two parties. Where there are many different interests competing for a scarce resource, for example, it is much more difficult to conduct straightforward mediation to decide on how to allocate the resource. However, such multiparty disputes over natural resources as arise in the context of ICAM can be resolved, and indeed already are resolved, through "mediative" procedures, i.e. through consultation with parties whose interests and concerns are then taken into account by the decision-maker. Mediation can also be used as a first stage in multiparty disputes, to encourage parties to come together and help them to identify common interests.

Impartiality. The mediator's impartiality is a fundamental aspect of their role in a negotiation. Any perceived favouritism may lead to the withdrawal of the party that feels prejudiced from the process, as well as undermining the integrity of any agreement subsequently reached. It is generally agreed that a mediator should ensure fairness in the way the process is conducted, but there is much debate as to whether the mediator is also responsible for ensuring that the final agreement is fair. This leads on to the question of accountability.[22]

Accountability. Opinions vary as to whether a mediator should take responsibility for the fairness of a settlement. Because the decision reached in a mediation is the voluntary product of the parties rather than the mediator, it is generally believed that the mediator's responsibility should be limited to ensuring a fair process and that they are not accountable for the final decision. However, in the United States some states have enacted legislation on liability, requiring mediators to abide by rules established by federal associations. Failure to comply can lead to the cancellation of a mediator's licence, certificate or registration, and violation of statutes or judicial decisions regarding proper mediation procedure can even lead to court action. When mediation is applied to environmental

217

---

[20] See also Section 2.3.
[21] See also Section 6.1.

[22] See Susskind, 1981; and McCrory, 1981.

INTEGRATED
COASTAL AREA
MANAGEMENT
and
AGRICULTURE
FORESTRY AND
FISHERIES

PART E

CONFLICT RESOLUTION IN INTEGRATED COASTAL AREA MANAGEMENT

5. *The process of alternative dispute resolution*

disputes, the question of accountability is more difficult. Decisions may have negative impacts on environmental quality and natural resources, as well as various interests (present and future) that were not represented in the negotiations. Some impacts may not even be known at the time the decision is made.

The guidelines for mediators in environmental disputes, which are laid down to make such mediators accountable, may involve, for example, licensing, certification or registration. The nature of the issues discussed above makes it important that such mediators possess substantive knowledge about the environmental/natural resource and regulatory issues at stake. Licensing agencies could be used to ensure a readily available source of experts and to sponsor publications and programmes to improve the quality of mediation services. Government linkages and support will usually be required to provide systems that deliver mediation and help to fund them.

Confidentiality. Conflicting parties are often more likely to enter a mediation process and participate effectively if they are ensured confidentiality. Issues to be decided in this respect may include: what should be confidential; who should be able to enforce confidentiality; and against whom confidentiality can be enforced.

PART E

CONFLICT RESOLUTION IN INTEGRATED COASTAL AREA MANAGEMENT

INTEGRATED
COASTAL AREA
MANAGEMENT
and
AGRICULTURE
FORESTRY AND
FISHERIES

6. Legal and institutional mechanisms for conflict resolution in ICAM

6.1 MATTERS TO BE CONSIDERED

Cooperative conflict resolution cannot be forced upon unwilling parties, but is a voluntary process requiring the presence of particular factors and circumstances, as already discussed. However, the use of certain legal and institutional mechanisms may facilitate its implementation. In designing these mechanisms, particular consideration should be given to the need to:

- require or encourage courts or administrative agencies to consider cases for ADR systematically. Legislation could require referral to ADR in specific categories of cases or authorize courts to refer cases to an appropriate form of ADR;
- establish dispute resolution offices or commissions to stimulate and coordinate ADR activities in the coastal area;
- establish mechanisms to provide for participation by interested parties in coastal area management and legislative decisions affecting them as well as in the resolution of existing conflicts;[23]
- make the necessary procedural and/or legislative changes to overcome obstacles to conflict resolution in the process of rule-making;
- establish administrative procedures to anticipate and resolve conflicts arising within and between government departments;
- provide for funding mechanisms (e.g. government- and/or privately funded schemes) to make alternative conflict resolution processes available to interest groups that lack the financial means to participate;[24]
- provide training and education for outside parties to mediate/facilitate/arbitrate in disputes, with schemes and guidelines for the recognition of qualified mediators/facilitators/arbitrators;
- design rules to govern alternative dispute resolution procedures, the status of decisions, etc.;

---

[23] For example, the "coastal forum" proposed by the World Wide Fund for Nature (WWF) and the United Kingdom Marine Conservation Society in their paper setting out proposals for a United Kingdom Coastal Zone Management Plan (Gubbay, 1990).

[24] See also Section 5.2.4.

BOX E.3
Protecting the Danube wetlands

In a section of the Danube wetlands near Hainburg, Austria, located between Vienna and the border with the Czech Republic, controversy erupted following publicity of a proposal to build a hydropower dam. Annual floods of the Danube have given rise to a maze of islands, gravel and sandbanks, rivulets and streams, still waters and flooded forests, steep erosion banks and swampy flats.

This diversity of biotypes has endowed the Danube wetlands with an abundance of life, pioneer habitats and a successions of forest communities unrivalled anywhere in Central Europe. The Danube wetlands are home to an estimated 5 000 animal species. Moreover, recent scientific research has furnished evidence that bank-filtered water from the groundwater reserves of river forests has become the most important source of clean, unpolluted water in the low-lying areas.

Conservation NGOs in Austria have staunchly opposed the construction of the dam because of their concerns over environmental damage. The conflict escalated when the electricity company started to clear several square kilometres of the unique Hainburg wetland. Thousands of conservationists occupied the site.

Nobel Prize laureate, Konrad Lorenz, then led a difficult negotiation with the government which resulted in the conservationists being granted an opportunity to investigate alternatives, even though powerful trade unionists and industrial leaders still wanted to see the dam built in the wetland forest. The peace pact also led to the founding of the National Park Institute, an NGO dedicated to furthering the creation of a national park on the Danube wetlands site. Following a suit by WWF, in 1985 the Supreme Court declared the dam project to be against the law on the grounds that its impact on drinking-water resources had not been sufficiently clarified.

In 1989, the National Park Institute initiated the purchase of a strategic area of wetland forest to prevent the land from being bought by the electricity company. A nationwide campaign gathered nearly US$11 million for this purpose. However, despite the success of this campaign, politicians are still undecided as to whether to save the ecosystem as a park or to build hydroelectric power dams. In this case, the struggle is not over.

Source: after Lölsch, 1996.

INTEGRATED
COASTAL AREA
MANAGEMENT
and
AGRICULTURE
FORESTRY AND
FISHERIES

6. Legal and institutional mechanisms for conflict resolution in ICAM

BOX E.4
The Negotiated Rule-making Act 1990 (United States)

Negotiated rule-making is defined in the United States Negotiated Rule-making Act 1990 as "the development of agency rules and regulations by the consensus of interested parties". The Act provides for federal agencies to convene negotiated rule-making committees if the agency head determines that negotiated rule-making is in the public interest. In doing so the head must consider whether:

- there is a need for the rule;
- a limited number of identifiable interests will be significantly affected by the rule;
- a balanced representation of those interests can be convened and has a reasonable likelihood of reaching consensus in a fixed period of time;

- the negotiated rule-making will not unreasonably delay notice of a proposed rule and issuance of a final one;
- the agency has adequate resources and is willing to commit them to the process;
- the extent to which the agency will base its proposed rule on the version reached by the negotiated rule-making committee.

An agency that decides to use negotiated rule-making must publish a notice in the Federal Register announcing its decision, describing the issues and rules to be developed, and explaining how interested participants can become members of the committee. The committee, once convened, approves the selection of facilitators by consensus.

BOX E.5
The Massachusetts Hazardous Waste Facility Siting Act

This Act was introduced in an attempt to tackle the problem of siting proposals for new hazardous waste facilities being defeated by local community opposition (commonly known as the "not in my backyard", or NIMBY, syndrome). It lays down a procedure that provides for direct negotiation between the developer of the facility and the host community and incorporates incentives as a strategy to encourage cooperation and overcome opposition. The most important elements of the Act are as follows:

- the developer has a right to construct a hazardous waste facility on land zoned for industrial use if the developer obtains the necessary permits and reaches a siting agreement with the host community;
- the siting agreement must be negotiated between the developer and the host community, the latter being represented by a Local Assessment Committee. The agreement sets out the measures to be taken by the developer to mitigate adverse impacts associated with the facility and may provide for the payment of compensation to the community;

- the siting agreement is reviewed and approved by the State Council, which may then declare it to be binding on the developer and the host community and enforceable against the parties in any court of competent jurisdiction;
- an independent body, the Hazardous Waste Facility Site Safety Council, composed of representatives of all parties involved in and affected by the siting of hazardous waste facilities, oversees the negotiation process;
- failing agreement by negotiation, the State Council may require the parties to submit the unresolved issues to "final and binding arbitration" to resolve them. The parties (or, in the absence of agreement, the Council) choose the arbitrator;
- the host community receives technical assistance from the state to participate in the negotiation process;
- abutting communities that are likely to be affected by new facilities in adjacent jurisdictions can apply to the Council for assistance grants to participate in the process, as well as compensation from the developer.

Source: Bacow and Wheeler, 1994.

- provide incentives to encourage parties to negotiate.[25]

The United States Environmental Protection Agency (EPA) has institutionalized its use of ADR in

environmental enforcement actions, adopting an ADR Implementation Plan in 1990 to establish standard operating procedures and to obtain the services of outside mediators, arbitrators and other ADR practitioners in disputes to which EPA is a party. It also

---

[25] See also Section 6.3.

PART E

CONFLICT RESOLUTION IN INTEGRATED COASTAL AREA MANAGEMENT

INTEGRATED
COASTAL AREA
MANAGEMENT
and
AGRICULTURE
FORESTRY AND
FISHERIES

6. Legal and institutional mechanisms for conflict resolution in ICAM

BOX E.6

Forest allocation and conservation in Tasmania

This case illustrates use of a consensus-building process that involved the establishment of a number of bodies to provide: the databases that had been agreed upon; independent panels of experts to provide advice; and regional advisory groups to ensure local community involvement throughout the process. The purpose of the process was to develop policies for forest land use for uncut forests outside forest reserves.

In the island state of Tasmania in southern Australia, forest land-use conflicts have arisen regarding uncut forests that are outside forest reserves. Fourteen percent of Tasmanians are dependent on forestry for their livelihoods and there is high demand for wood and wood-based products. The island's high endemism in both flora and fauna has also attracted the concern of conservationists. Efforts to resolve the conservation/utilization issues were initially carried out through a government-formed Commission of Inquiry in 1987 which was charged with investigating the land area in debate and with making recommendations on its possible designation as World Heritage status. However, this process, conducted in an adversarial, legal arena, failed to produce a satisfactory solution. The Commission's findings were rejected by the Commonwealth Government which came up with a compromise solution aimed at balancing the diverse interests. However, this decision failed to resolve the conflict. Nevertheless, some valuable lessons were gained in the process, including the importance of having expert opinion, the need for an agreed set of facts and data, and the problems related to resolving the conflict in a legal, adversarial setting.

In 1989, a parliamentary accord was signed, which subsequently led to an agreement between the major forest land-use disputants (i.e. the timber industry, private forest landholders, unions, environmental groups and government agencies) to develop jointly a Forests and Forest Industry Strategy. This agreement marked a breakthrough as it reflected each of the groups' willingness, for the first time, to recognize each other formally.

As a result of these negotiations, a new contract was drawn up in which community interests were integrated into the formulation of a protected park. For example, where grazing stock was to have been excluded from one area and phased out of two other areas, provisions were made for stock units to be reduced on a voluntary basis when alternative land was made available to pastoralists. In addition, in the initial government plan, the responsibility of the park management would have rested solely with the National Parks Board. In the subsequent arrangement, a Management Plan Committee would be formed consisting of four Parks Board members and four elected community representatives. The latter park plan also made provisions to set up a Richtersveld Community Trust to which the Parks Board would pay set fees per hectare per year and, in addition, it would channel its net profits to the community from its proposed nursery. Furthermore, residents of northern Richtersveld would get preference as employees of the park. As a result of the negotiations, all parties signed the Richtersveld National Parks contract which created the park and established the conditions under which it should be managed.

Source: Rolley and Brown, 1996.

221

maintains a list of neutral individuals who have experience in environmental enforcement, to supplement the list of dispute resolution specialists which is held on a nationwide computer.

6.2 INSTITUTIONALIZING NEGOTIATED RULE-MAKING

Negotiated rule-making procedures are already used informally in some countries to develop new laws. In the United States, EPA has used such procedures to formulate policies, rules and environmental standards in many areas. Using the so-called "reg-neg" (i.e. regulation-negotiation, or negotiated rule-making) process, they have developed rules, for example, for: granting emergency exemptions from pesticide controls; developing emission control standards for wood stoves; and regulating the underground injection of hazardous wastes. Negotiated rule-making procedures may also

be formalized through legislation, and in 1990, in response to EPA's success, Congress passed the Negotiated Rule-Making Act, establishing a framework for negotiated rule-making in the future (see Box E.4).

6.3 INCENTIVES AND COMPENSATION

One way of encouraging consensual agreement is to use incentives to persuade conflicting parties to negotiate, on the basis that "carrots" may be more effective than "sticks". A good example of this is the 1980 Massachusetts Hazardous Waste Facility Siting Act (see Box E.5), which uses incentives and compensation to encourage negotiation between the developers of hazardous waste facilities and opposing host communities.

This kind of dispute over the location of an unwanted facility typically ends in deadlock, as the only options

INTEGRATED
COASTAL AREA
MANAGEMENT
and
AGRICULTURE
FORESTRY AND
FISHERIES

PART E

CONFLICT RESOLUTION IN INTEGRATED COASTAL AREA MANAGEMENT

6. Legal and institutional mechanisms for conflict resolution in ICAM

BOX E.7
Integrating villages in a National Park Scheme, Pakistan

This case illustrates the depth of opposition/conflict that can arise when a new park is proposed that would exclude traditional grazing use of the land, and how negotiations resulted in a decision to allow some such use.

In the Pamir mountains of northern Pakistan, clashes between local people (including the Shimshali and Gojali) and government officials occurred following the establishment of the Kunjerab National Park in 1975. The national government had been pushing for this park, the management of which would exclude uses except wildlife protection. However, tremendous local opposition to the park arose as it became apparent that a part of the traditional grazing land had been included within the core of the park and that access to this land would be denied to villagers. Compensation for the loss of grazing rights had been promised by the government to the local villages but was never delivered. Consequently, illegal grazing and poaching in the park increased (with members of local security forces also implicated) resulting in the decline of wildlife.

In June 1989, a workshop was held in Gilgit in collaboration with the International Union for the Conservation of Nature and Natural Resources (IUCN), the United States Park Service and local and federal government agencies. The workshop discussed the existing park situation, developed certain management guidelines and stressed the need for preparing a detailed management plan for the park. The Government of Pakistan then commissioned the preparation of a management plan. The local communities of the park who had already lost a portion of their grazing lands and had no trust in the government agencies, developed further suspicions that, because of the workshop, they might lose the rest of their grazing lands as well.

From this situation, a series of confrontational events ensued, including a court trial over the villagers' rights to park resources, and illegal police removal, strikes and blockades carried out by local people against the park administration.. Subsequently, the Forests and Forest Industry Council was convened to engage in a multiparty, consensus-building dialogue (without the assistance of a professional, independent mediator) to develop a Forests and Forest Industry Strategy. This process involved: the establishment of a number of bodies to provide agreed databases and assessment overviews in cooperation with interested stakeholders; the establishment of independent panels of experts to provide advice on matters related to the development of the strategy; and the establishment of regional advisory groups to ensure local community involvement throughout the strategy development process.

The process broke new ground in relations between land-use adversaries to produce a win-win approach for resolving land-use conflicts. However, the final document did not gain unanimous support from all of the groups involved, notably, the environmental groups withdrew their support. Nevertheless, the state government proceeded to implement the major reforms negotiated by parties, many of which were also legislatively adopted in the Public Land Act of 1991. The key components of the strategy included protection of forested land areas of high conservation value, legislated security for wood production areas, processes to address changes to land tenure over time, greater public input to forest planning and acknowledgement by the main interest groups of the need to address community costs associated with the win-lose outcomes from past land-use conflicts.

Source: Ahmed, 1996.

---

appear to be either build or do not build, a so-called "zero-sum" dispute which produces a winner and a loser. Compensation introduces a third option; build but compensate, redistributing some of the benefits that would otherwise be distributed regionally while the social costs are borne locally. Compensation thus provides an incentive to negotiate on the basis that the recipients of the compensation will be better off than if they had simply rejected the facility outright.

Compensation, however, has its own limits. First, financial compensation may be inadequate to meet the concerns of the opponents; for example, where the objection to a development is over the loss of an endangered species, a more acceptable offer than money for the parties would be measures to avoid that loss in the first place. Second, the offer of compensation for irreversible loss of environmental quality or harm to health may be unacceptable or even morally repugnant. Third, where a number of interested parties are involved in the negotiations, all with different views of what constitutes fair compensation, it may be very difficult to agree on a solution that satisfies them all. Sometimes it may be appropriate to set up a trust fund to finance measures to mitigate the losses caused.

PART E
CONFLICT RESOLUTION IN INTEGRATED COASTAL AREA MANAGEMENT

INTEGRATED
COASTAL AREA
MANAGEMENT
and
AGRICULTURE
FORESTRY AND
FISHERIES

7. Conclusions

Conflict resolution is an integral part of ICAM; its fundamental objective being to resolve those conflicts among the various users of the coastal area that can lead to the deterioration of its valuable resources and environment.

As can be seen from the above overview of the various dispute resolution mechanisms available to deal with conflicts, ADR techniques (see Table E.1), such as negotiation and mediation, can offer particular advantages over the more traditional contentious methods, such as litigation. Furthermore, it is evident that these alternative techniques are particularly suitable for resolving the sort of conflicts that typically arise in ICAM.

The positive experience of a number of developed countries in applying alternative dispute resolution techniques in this context suggest that ICAM planners should seriously consider explicitly incorporating ADR mechanisms into their ICAM programmes. Although there are, as yet, fewer examples of the use of ADR in developing countries, the potential for its use here is great, not least because of the significant savings in time and money that it can bring about.

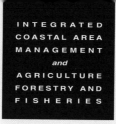

INTEGRATED
COASTAL AREA
MANAGEMENT
and
AGRICULTURE
FORESTRY AND
FISHERIES

GLOSSARY

REFERENCES

INDEX

INTEGRATED
COASTAL AREA
MANAGEMENT
and
AGRICULTURE
FORESTRY AND
FISHERIES

INTEGRATED
COASTAL AREA
MANAGEMENT
and
AGRICULTURE
FORESTRY AND
FISHERIES

Glossary

Terms are defined in the sense that they are used in these guidelines. Unless otherwise specified, the definitions were made by the editor, by modifying and adapting several definitions available in the literature to the needs of the guidelines. In the following definitions, words that appear in *bold italics* are defined elsewhere in the glossary.

Abiotic
Non-living (Lawrence, 1995).

Accretion
Build-up of the coastal land area as a result of accumulation of sediment from the sea. Horizontal accretion occurs when sediments accumulate against coastal land and extend it outward. Vertical accretion occurs when sediments accumulate on coastal land and raise its level (and, thus, counteract *subsidence*).

Anadromous species
Fish that spend their adult life in the sea but swim upriver to freshwater spawning grounds in order to reproduce (e.g. salmon).

Aquaculture
The farming of aquatic organisms, including fish, molluscs, crustaceans and aquatic plants. Farming implies some sort of intervention in the rearing process to enhance production, such as regular stocking, feeding, protection from predators. Farming also implies individual or corporate ownership of the stock being cultivated. For statistical purposes, aquatic organisms that are harvested by the individual or corporate body that has owned them throughout their rearing period contribute to aquaculture, while aquatic organisms that are exploitable by the public as a common property resource, with or without appropriate licences, are the harvest of fisheries (the definition currently used by FAO for statistical purposes).

Avoidance costs
The actual or imputed costs of preventing environmental deterioration by alternative production and consumption processes, or by reduction of or abstention from economic activities (UN, 1997).

Biomass
The total weight of all the biological material or the combined mass of all the animals and plants inhabiting a defined area; usually expressed as dry weight per area (grams per square metre, kilograms per hectare). Biomass should not be confused with productivity, the actual rate at which organic matter is created. For example, a redwood forest has a high biomass and low productivity, while phytoplankton have a low biomass (because they are continually consumed by predators) but high productivity.

Brackish water

Water containing salts at a concentration significantly lower than that of sea water. The concentration of total dissolved salts is usually in the range of 1 000 to 10 000 milligrams per litre (UN, 1997).

Carrying capacity

The point of balance between reproduction potential and environmental resistance, which is the maximum population of a species that a specific *ecosystem* can support indefinitely without deterioration of the character and quality of the resource(s). Carrying capacity is the level of use, at a given level of management, at which a natural or human-induced resource can sustain itself over a long period of time. For example, the maximum level of recreational use, in terms of numbers of people and types of activity, that can be accommodated before the ecological value of the area declines.

Catadromous species

Fish that spend their adult life upriver but descend to the lower river or the sea to spawn.

Climate

Condition of the atmosphere at a particular location (microclimate) or in a particular region over a long period of time. Climate is the long-term summation of atmospheric elements (e.g. solar radiation, temperature, humidity, frequency and amount of precipitation, atmospheric pressure, speed and direction of wind) and their variations (UN, 1997).

Coast

The geographical area of contact between the terrestrial and marine environments, a boundary area of indefinite width, appreciably wider than the shore.

Coastal area

A geographic entity of land and water affected by the biological and physical processes of both the terrestrial and the marine environments, and defined broadly for the purpose of *natural resources* management. Coastal area boundaries usually change over time without regard to enabling legislation.

Coastal zone

A geographical entity including both terrestrial and submerged areas of the *coast*, defined legally or administratively for coastal zone management.

Command and control policy instruments

Mechanisms (often laws) for implementing policies that rely on prescribing modes or standards of behaviour and using sanctions to enforce compliance with them.

Conservation

Includes protection, maintenance, rehabilitation, restoration and enhancement of populations and *ecosystems*.

INTEGRATED
COASTAL AREA
MANAGEMENT
and
AGRICULTURE
FORESTRY AND
FISHERIES

Glossary

Coordination

The process of bringing different parts or entities into functioning relationships with each other. In these guidelines, the term is used to describe the process of bringing together concerned government agencies, research institutions, municipalities, *NGOs* and resource users to agree on *objectives*, formulate *strategies* and subsequently implement them.

Deposit refund system

A policy instrument in which a surcharge is levied on the price of products that cause resource depletion or pollution; the surcharge is refunded if the product (or its residuals) are recycled.

Diversity

The number of different species, their relative abundance and the number of *habitats* existing in a particular area. Diversity is a measure of the complexity of an *ecosystem* and often an indication of its relative age, measured in terms of the number of different plant and animal species (often called species richness) it contains, their distribution and the degree of genetic variability within each species. Biological diversity is the term used to designate the variety of life in all its forms, levels and combinations and includes ecosystem, species and genetic diversity.

Earth Summit

The United Nations Conference on Environment and Development (UNCED), Rio de Janeiro, Brazil, 3 to 14 June 1992. Texts of agreements negotiated by more than 178 governments at the Conference were Agenda 21 (the Programme of Action for Sustainable Development), the Rio Declaration on Environment and Development, and the Statement of Forest Principles. The Conference also presented the Convention on Climate Change and the Convention on Biological Diversity.

229

Economic policy instruments

Policy instruments that create the economic incentives for individuals to choose freely to modify or reduce their activities, thus indirectly producing an environmental improvement (Barbier, 1992).

Ecosystem

A natural entity (or a system) with distinct structures and relationships that interlink biotic communities (of plants and animals) to each other and link them to their abiotic environment. The study of an ecosystem provides a methodological basis for complex synthesis between organisms and their environment. A complex of ecosystems is constituted of many ecosystems and is characterized by a common origin or common dynamic processes (for example, the complex of ecosystems of a watershed).

Edaphic

Of or pertaining to the soil; resulting from or influenced by factors in the soil or other substrate rather than by climatic factors (Canadian Society of Soil Science, 1972). An edaphic requirement is a requirement of the crop for a particular condition or range of conditions in the soil environment (FAO, 1996a).

INTEGRATED
COASTAL AREA
MANAGEMENT
and
AGRICULTURE
FORESTRY AND
FISHERIES

Glossary

Efficiency

In general, the ratio of a system's output (or production) to the inputs that it requires, as in the useful energy produced by a system compared with the energy put into that system. In ecology, efficiency is the percentage of useful energy transferred from one *trophic level* to the next (such as the ratio of production of herbivores to that of primary producers). Used in the context of production, efficiency is the ratio of useful work performed to the total energy expended, thus it does not count any wastage that is generated. In the context of the allocation of resources, efficiency is the condition that would make at least one person better off and no one worse off. This implies that some may get richer and others not improve their status.

Environmental impact assessment (EIA)

A sequential set of activities designed to identify and predict the impacts of a proposed action on the biogeophysical environment and on human health and well being, and to interpret and communicate information about the impacts, including mitigation measures that are likely to eliminate risks. In many countries, organizations planning new projects are required by law to conduct EIA.

Equity

Term used for the administration of justice according to principles of fairness and conscience, balancing the hardships in those cases where legal remedies and monetary damages would not suffice. Intragenerational equity is the principle by which all sections of the community share equitably in the costs and benefits of achieving *sustainable development*. Intergenerational equity is the principle by which each generation utilizes and conserves the stock of *natural resources* (in terms of *diversity* and *carrying capacity*) in a manner that does not compromise their use by future generations.

Erosion

Geologically, erosion is defined as the process that slowly shapes hillsides, allowing the formation of soil cover from the weathering of rocks and from alluvial and colluvial deposits. Erosion caused by human activities, as an effect of careless exploitation of the environment, results in increasing runoffs and declined arable layers (Roose, 1996).

Estuary

Generally the broad portion of a river or stream near its outlet that is influenced by the marine water body into which it flows. The demarcation line is generally the mean tidal level (UN, 1997).

Exclusive Economic Zone (EEZ)

A concept adopted at the UN Conference on the Law of the Sea (1982), whereby a coastal state assumes jurisdiction over the exploitation of marine resources in its adjacent section of the continental shelf, which is taken to be a band extending 200 miles from the shore (UN, 1997).

Externality

An outside force, such as a social and/or environmental benefit or cost, not included in the market price of the goods and services being produced; i.e. costs not borne by those

INTEGRATED
COASTAL AREA
MANAGEMENT
and
AGRICULTURE
FORESTRY AND
FISHERIES

Glossary

who occasion them, and benefits not paid for by the recipients. Some economists suggest that externalities should be internalized, if they are known to have a significant effect on the demand or cost structure of a product, that is, corrections should be made, to allow for externalities when calculating marginal cost. Marginal cost thus becomes a social opportunity cost, or true cost.

Habitat

The place or type of site where species and communities normally live or grow, usually characterized by relatively uniform physical features or by consistent plant forms. Deserts, lakes and forests are all habitats.

Half-life

The time during which radioactivity or some other property of substances falls to half of its original value (UN, 1997).

Human settlements

An integrative concept that comprises (a) physical components of shelter and infrastructure and (b) services to which the physical elements provide support, that is, community services such as education, health, culture, welfare, recreation and nutrition (UN, 1997).

Indicators

Signals of processes – inputs, outputs, effects, results, outcomes, impacts, etc. – that enable them to be judged or measured. Both qualitative and quantitative indicators are needed for management learning, policy review, monitoring and evaluation.

231

Institutions

The rules that operate in a society or, more formally, the humanly devised constraints that shape human interactions. An institution is formed when at least two individuals or groups create arrangements that bind more than themselves. Institutions therefore structure incentives in human exchange, whether political, social or economic. Institutions can be formal (i.e. devised rules) or informal (i.e. socially transmitted conventions and codes of behaviour). Thus, they can be created or may simply evolve over time, as does the common law. Institutions determine the opportunities in a society; organizations are created to take advantage of those opportunities and, as organizations evolve, they alter institutions (after North, 1990).

Integration

The process of bringing together separate components as a functional whole that involves *coordination* of interventions. In *ICAM*, integration may take place at three levels, system, functional and *policy* systems integration refers to the physical, social and economic linkages of land and water uses and ensures that all relevant interactions and issues are considered; functional integration ensures that *programmes* and projects are consistent with ICAM goals and *objectives*; and policy integration ensures that management actions are consistent with other development and policy initiatives.

INTEGRATED
COASTAL AREA
MANAGEMENT
and
AGRICULTURE
FORESTRY AND
FISHERIES

Glossary

Integrated coastal area management (ICAM)

A dynamic process by which actions are taken for the use, development and protection of coastal resources and areas to achieve national goals established in cooperation with user groups and regional and local authorities. In this definition, integrated management refers to the management of sectoral components as parts of a functional whole with explicit recognition that it is the users of resources, not the stocks of *natural resources*, that are the focus of management. For the purpose of integrated management, the boundaries of a *coastal area* should be defined according to the problems to be resolved. The definition thus implies a pragmatic approach to the defining of coastal areas in which the area under consideration might change over time as additional problems are addressed that require resolution over a wider geographical area.

Land-use planning

The systematic assessment of land and water potential, alternative patterns of land use and other physical, social and economic conditions, for the purpose of selecting and adopting the land-use options that are most beneficial to land users without degrading the resources or the environment, together with the selection of measures most likely to encourage such land uses (Choudhury and Jansen, 1997).

Liability legislation

Law requiring polluters or resource users to pay damages to those individual or corporate bodies affected by their actions. Damaged parties collect settlements through litigation and the court system. Examples include long-term *performance bonds* posted for potential or uncertain hazards from infrastructure construction and "zero net impact" requirements for road alignments or water crossings.

Lithosphere

Upper layer of the earth, including its crust and upper mantle.

Natural resources

Any portion of the natural environment, such as air, water, soil, botanical and zoological resources and minerals. A renewable resource can potentially last indefinitely (provided stocks are not overexploited) without reducing the available supply because it is replaced through natural processes (either because it recycles rapidly, as water does, or because it is alive and can propagate itself or be propagated, as some organisms and *ecosystems* do). Non-renewable resources (such as coal and oil) may eventually be replaced by natural processes, but these processes occur over long periods of geologic time rather than within the time-frame of current generations, and their consumption necessarily involves their depletion.

Non-governmental organization (NGO)

Any organization that is not a part of federal, provincial, territorial or municipal government. The term usually refers to non-profit organizations involved in development activities.

INTEGRATED
COASTAL AREA
MANAGEMENT
and
AGRICULTURE
FORESTRY AND
FISHERIES

Glossary

Non-compliance fees

"Additional" prices to be paid to meet the social costs arising from environmental damages caused by failure to comply with environmental requirements.

Non-point source of pollution

Pollution sources that are diffused and do not have a single point of origin or are not introduced into a receiving stream from a specific outlet. The pollutants are generally carried off the land by storm-water runoff. Non-point sources of pollutants include agriculture, urban areas and mining (UN, 1997).

Objectives

The aims of an action, or what is intended to be achieved. Any objective will include explicit statements against which progress can be measured, and will identify which outcomes are truly important and the way that they interrelate; quantified objectives are referred to as targets.

Open access

A situation in which access to a *natural resource* (e.g. a fishery or grazing land) is, for practical purposes, free, unlimited and available to everyone. This situation arises either where no one is legally entitled to deny others access (e.g. to fish on the high seas) or where the owner or manager of the resource fails to control access effectively. Because these resources are freely available or at minimal cost, they are frequently overexploited and degraded.

Performance bonds

Similar to a *deposit refund system* but categorized as an *economic policy instrument*, a bond is placed that is equal to the estimated social costs of possible environmental damage as a surety for complying with environmental requirements and is forfeited if these requirements are not met.

Plan

Amplification of the *strategy* showing the precise means by which *objectives* will be reached; the policy instruments to be employed; the financial and human resources required; and the time frame for implementation. See also **Rolling plan.**

Planning

The plotting of a course of action (involving executive action or enforcement) that is proposed to carry out some proceeding, devising the relative positions and timing of a set of actions.

Policy

The course of action for an undertaking adopted by a government, a person or some other party. The instruments that exist to support policy and the tools used to achieve policy *objectives* comprise some or all of the following societal instruments; economic or market-based instruments; command and control instruments; direct government involvement; and institutional and organizational arrangements. It is to be mentioned that, although law may be used as a policy instrument, there are cases where law may impose constraints

INTEGRATED
COASTAL AREA
MANAGEMENT
and
AGRICULTURE
FORESTRY AND
FISHERIES

Glossary

on what policies can be adopted. For example, if the constitution states that the shore is the patrimony of the nation or requires the payment of compensation for the expropriation of the land, the policies that could be adopted for *ICAM* are restricted.

Policy process
The whole process of defining goals and *objectives*, and the means to achieve them, that are formulated in *strategies* and *plans*.

Programme
Descriptive notice of series of events, including an indication of the intended proceedings. In these guidelines, the term is used for an undertaking structured around a defined *objective*, usually consisting of a number of projects.

Protected area
A geographically defined area that is designed and managed to achieve specific conservation objectives.

Rolling plan
The practice of preparing a *plan* for a number of years in annually sequentially less detail, revising the plan annually and maintaining the number of years covered by the plan.

Stumpage value
The economic value of a standing tree, equivalent to the amount concessionaries earn when a log is sold to the sawmill or the exporter, less the cost of logging. It is used as the net-price valuation in environmental accounting (UN, 1997).

Subnational government
Any level of government below the national level. In large, federally organized countries (e.g. Australia, Brazil, India and the United States), the *ICAM* responsibility rests on the state governments; in unitary countries (e.g. Kenya), there may also be a devolution of responsibility.

Subsidence
Sinking of the earth's surface in response to geological or human-induced causes (e.g. mining, extraction of water or petroleum by wells). When subsidence occurs over large areas, the resulting features are termed geosynclines. Non-linear subsidence produces basins and irregular depressions. Subsidence may be counteracted by vertical *accretion* where sediment-loaded floodwater enters the area.

Stakeholders
Individuals and groups of individuals (including government and **non-governmental** *institutions*, traditional communities, universities, research institutions, development agencies, banks and donors) with an interest or claim (whether stated or implied) that has the potential of being affected by or affecting a given project and its *objectives*. Stakeholder groups that have a direct or indirect "stake" can be at the household, community, local, regional, national or international level.

INTEGRATED
COASTAL AREA
MANAGEMENT
and
AGRICULTURE
FORESTRY AND
FISHERIES

Glossary

Strategy

A coherent statement indicating how resources will be deployed and the approach that will be taken to achieve one or more *objectives* successfully (often set out in a *policy* or *plan*).

Subsidiarity

Transfer of certain tasks of general interest to the civil society with responsibilities at a hierarchical level (minimizing economic costs and maximizing social welfare). Subsidiarity entails that each member of the social group involved shall organize their own actions towards an end that must remain part of the *objectives* pursued by the entire group (Babin *et al.,* 1998).

Sustainable development

"Development that meets the needs of the present without compromising the ability of future generations to meet their own needs" (Bruntland Report, 1987) or "...the management and the *conservation* of the *natural resource* base and the orientation of the technological and institutional change in such a manner as to ensure the attainment and continued satisfaction of human need for present and future generations. Such sustainable development in the agriculture, forestry and fisheries sectors concerns land, water, plant and animal genetic resources, is environmentally non-degrading, technically appropriate, economically viable and socially acceptable." (FAO Council, 1989).

Synergism

Cooperative interaction of two or more elements, producing a greater total effect than the sum of their individual effects.

235

Threshold

Limit below which a stimulus ceases to be perceptible or signal, indicating that a critical state of a resource has been reached. In *ICAM*, thresholds are used (e.g. in fisheries) as an early warning when a resource is approaching a target reference point or a limit reference point, suggesting that a certain type of action (usually agreed beforehand) needs to be taken. Thresholds therefore add precaution to *natural resource* management, especially for resources or situations (e.g. uncertainty of available information, inherent inertia of the management system) involving high risk (Garcia, 1996).

Tidal flat

Level, muddy surface bordering an *estuary*, alternatively submerged and exposed to the air by changing tidal levels (UN, 1997).

Tradable permits

An *economic policy instrument* under which the rights to discharge pollution or exploit resources can be exchanged through either a free or a controlled "permit" market. Examples include individual transferable quotas in fisheries, tradable depletion rights to mineral concessions, tradable pollution or resource use permits, and marketable discharge permits for water-borne effluents.

INTEGRATED
COASTAL AREA
MANAGEMENT
and
AGRICULTURE
FORESTRY AND
FISHERIES

Glossary

Trade-off

The value of something that has to be given up in order to get something else that is desired (e.g. the environmental cost incurred to obtain economic development). Sustainability can be evaluated by the sum of the various social, economic and ***natural resources*** where the degrees of use, exchange and trading among resources will vary according to the values given to each. Trade-off patterns are therefore determined by the different properties of a system and their importance to different groups. The understanding of social dynamics and resource-use systems and the evaluation of related trade-offs, in terms of ***equity***, productivity, resilience and environmental stability, are useful to envision alternative development scenarios.

Trophic levels

Classification of natural communities or organisms according to their place in the food chain.

Twin-track

As used in these guidelines, the process of working at the national (or subnational) and area levels simultaneously.

Usufruct

Right of enjoying the use and advantages of another's property (e.g. land) short of destruction or waste of its substance.

INTEGRATED
COASTAL AREA
MANAGEMENT
and
AGRICULTURE
FORESTRY AND
FISHERIES

References

ABARE. 1993. *Use of economic instruments in integrated coastal zone management.* Canberra, Australian Bureau of Agricultural and Resource Economics (ABARE).

Acland, A.F. 1995. Alternative dispute resolution: simply negotiation with knobs on. *Legal Action* (8), November 1995.

Ahmed, A. 1996. Survival in a vertical desert. In *Managing conflicts in protected areas. A manual for protected area managers.* Gland, Switzerland, IUCN.

Aksornkoae, S. 1993. *Ecology and management of mangroves.* Bangkok, IUCN.

Alix, J. C. 1989. Community-based resources management: the experience of the Central Visayas Regional Project. *ICLARM Conf. Proc.,* 19: 185-90.

Allaby, A. 1998. *Macmillan dictionary of the environment.* (Third edition). London, Macmillan.

Al Rifai, M.N.E. 1993. *Problem of seawater intrusion into coastal aquifers in ten selected countries of the Near East.* Paper presented at the Expert Consultation on Seawater Intrusion, Cairo, 10-13 October 1993. Cairo, FAO Regional Office for the Near East, Keynote Paper (KP7).(mimeo) Abstract in *FAO Water Reports,* (11): 93-6. 1997.

Alverson, D.L. et al. 1994. *A global assessment of fisheries by-catch and discards.* FAO Fisheries Technical Paper No. 339. 233 pp.

Amy, D. 1989. The politics of environmental mediation. *In* Murray, J.S., Rau, A.S. & Sherman, E.F. (eds.) *Processes of dispute resolution: the role of lawyers.* New York, Foundation Press.

Anderson, L. 1980. Necessary components of economic surplus in fisheries economics. *Canadian Journal of Fisheries and Aquatic Sciences,* 37: 858-70.

Aylward, B. 1991. *The economic value of ecosystems. 3. Biological diversity.* (GK91-03). Gatekeeper Series London Environmental Economic Center. 10 pp.

Babin, D. et al. (1998). Patrimonial mediation and management subsidiarity. In *Proceedings of the FAO Workshop: Managing pluralism for sustainable forestry and rural development,* Rome, 9-12 December 1997. Rome, FAO.

Bacow, L.S. & Wheeler, M. 1984. *Environmental dispute resolution.* New York, Plenum Press. 372 pp.

Barbier, E.B. 1989. *The economic value of ecosystems. 1. Tropical wetlands.* (GK89-02). Gatekeeper Series London Environmental Economic Center. 12 pp.

Barbier, E.B. 1990. Alternative approaches to economic-environmental interactions. *Ecological Economics,* 2: 7-26.

Barbier, E.B. 1992. *The nature of economic instruments: a brief overview.* (GK92-02). Gatekeeper Series London Environmental Economic Center. 9 pp.

Barg, U.C. 1992. *Guidelines for the promotion of environmental management of coastal aquaculture development (based on a review of selected experiences and concepts).* FAO Fisheries Technical Paper No. 328. 122 pp. (issued also in French and Spanish)

Barg, U.C. & Wijkström, U.N. 1994. Environmental management options for coastal fisheries and aquaculture: role of local authorities. *Marine Policy,* 18(2): 127-37.

Barg, U.C. et al. 1997. Aquaculture and its environment: a case for collaboration. *In* Hancock, D.A. *et al.* (eds.) *Developing and sustaining world fisheries resources: the state of science and management. Second World Fisheries Congress,* p. 462-70. Collingwood, Victoria, Australia, CSIRO.

**INTEGRATED
COASTAL AREA
MANAGEMENT
and
AGRICULTURE
FORESTRY AND
FISHERIES**

References

Bass, S. 1993. Ecology and economics in small islands: constructing a framework for sustainable development. *In* Barbier, E.B. (ed.) *Economics and ecology*. London, Chapman and Hall.

Bateman, I. & Wills, K. (eds.) 1996. *Valuing environmental preference: theory and practice of the contingent evaluation method in the US, EC and developing countries*. Oxford, UK, Oxford University Press.

Belize, Government of,. 1992. *International action programme on water and sustainable agriculture development. Outline for Action in Belize*. Government of Belize, Belmopan.

Belliveau, M. 1995. Co-management can work! Canada's Maritime Fishermen's Union. In *DEEP, a periodic review of FAO and NGO programmes and publications in agricultural and rural development*, p. 33-4. Rome, FAO.

Benson, J.F. & Willis, K.G. 1992. *Valuing informal recreation on the Forestry Commission Estate*. Forestry Commission Bulletin, London No. 104. 42 pp.

Birnie, P. & Boyle, A. 1992. *International law and the environment*. Clarendon Press, Oxford, UK.

Boelaert-Suominen, S. & Cullinan, C. 1994. *Legal and institutional aspects of integrated coastal area management in national legislation*. Rome, FAO. 118 pp.

Bonnieux, F. & Rainelli, P. 1991. *Catastrophe écologique et dommages économiques*. Paris, INRA Economica.

Brinkman, R. 1995. Impact of climatic change on coastal agriculture. *In* Eisma, D. (ed.) *Climate change: impact on coastal habitation*, p. 235-45. Boca Raton, Fl, USA, Lewis Publishers.

Bromley, D.W. & Cernea, M.M. 1989. *The management of common property natural resources: some conceptual and operational fallacies*. World Bank Discussion Paper No. 57. 66 pp.

Bromley, D.W. & Cochrane, J.A. 1994. *Understanding the global commons*. Work Paper No. 13, EPAT/MUCIA (Environmental Natural Resource Policy Training Programme/Midwestern University Consortium on International Activity). 18 pp.

Brown, V. *et al.* 1995. *Risks and opportunities: managing environmental conflict and change*. London, &Earthscan Publications.

Bryant, D. *et al.* 1995. *Coastlines at risk; an index of potential development. Related threats to coastal ecosystems*. World Resources Indicator Brief, World Resources Institute, Washington, D.C. 8 pp.

Butler, M.J.A. *et al.* 1998. *The application of remote sensing technology to marine fisheries: an introductory manual*. FAO Fisheries Technical Paper No. 295. 165 pp. (issued also in French and Spanish)

Bye, V. 1990. *Legal, political and social constraints in aquaculture*. Special Publication of European Aquaculture Society, No. 12.

Caddy, J.F. 1996. An objective approach to the negotiation of allocations from shared living resources. *Marine Policy*, 20(2): 145-55.

Caddy, J.F. & Bazigos, G.P. 1985. *Practical guidelines for statistical monitoring of fisheries in manpower limited situations*. FAO Fisheries Technical Paper No. 257. 86 pp. (issued also in Arabic, French and Spanish)

Caddy, J.F. & Griffiths, R.C. 1995. *Living marine resources and their sustainable development: some environmental and institutional perspectives*. FAO Fisheries Technical Paper No. 353. 167 pp. (issued also in French and Spanish)

Caddy, J.F. & Gulland, J. 1983. Historical patterns of fish stocks. *Mar. Policy*, 7: 267-78.

Caddy, J.F. & Mahon, R. 1995. *Reference points for fisheries management*. FAO Fisheries Technical Paper No. 347. 83 pp. (issued also in French and Spanish)

238

INTEGRATED
COASTAL AREA
MANAGEMENT
and
AGRICULTURE
FORESTRY AND
FISHERIES

References

Canadian Society of Soil Science. 1972. *Glossary of terms in soil science.* Canadian Department of Agriculture Publications No. 1459.

CANARI. 1997. Study prepared by CANARI based on Renaud, Y. & Koesten, S. 1995. Resolving conflicts for integrated coastal management: the case of Soufrière, St. Lucia. *In* Geoghan, T. (ed.) *Caribbean Protect Area Bulletin,* (2); and, Brown, N. 1997. *Devolution of authority over the management of natural resources: the Soufrière Marine Management Area, St. Lucia.* Case study prepared by the CANARI Development Administration under UNDP Caribbean Capacity 21 Project. Vieux Fort, St. Lucia, Caribbean Natural Resources Institute (CANARI).

Caughley, G. & Sinclair, A.R.E. 1994. *Wildlife ecology and management.* Boston, Scientific Publications, 334 pp.

Centre for Dispute Resolution. 1996. *Information manual.* London, Centre for Dispute Resolution.

Chandraskhan, D. (ed.) 1997. *Proceedings: Electronic Conference on Addressing natural resources conflicts through community forestry. January-May 1996.* Rome, FAO, Forestry Department, Forests, Trees and People Programme, Community Forestry Unit, Conflict Management Series. 195 pp.

Choudhury, K. & Jansen, L. 1997. *Terminology for integrated resources planning and management.* Rome, FAO, Soils Resources Management and Conservation. 59 pp.

Christy, F.T., Jr. 1982. *Territorial use rights in marine fisheries: definitions and conditions.* FAO Fisheries Technical Paper No. 227. 10 pp. (issued also in French and Spanish)

Cicin-Sain, B., Knecht, R.W. & Fisk, G.W. 1995. Growth capacity for integrated coastal management since UNCED: an international perspective. *Ocean Coastal Management,* 29(1-3): 93-123.

Clark, J.R. 1992. *Integrated management of coastal zones.* FAO Fisheries Technical Paper No. 327. 167 pp. (issued also in Chinese)

Costanza, R. & Perrings, C. 1990. A flexible assurance bonding system for improved environmental management. *Ecological Economics,* 2: 57-76.

Coughanowr, C.A., Ngoile, M.N. & Lindén, O. 1995. Coastal zone management in Eastern Africa including the island states: a review of issues and initiatives. *Ambio,* 24(7-8): 448-57.

Covey, S.R. 1992. *Seven habits of highly effective people.* New York, Simon and Schuster.

Crutchfield, J. & Pontecorvo, G. 1969. *The Pacific salmon fisheries: a study in irrational conservation.* Baltimore, Md, USA, Johns Hopkins University Press.

Cunningham, S., Dunn, M. & Whitemarsh, D. 1985. *Fisheries economics: an introduction.* London, Mansell Publishing.

CV-CIRRD. 1993. *Mangrove production and management. Central Visayas Technology Guide.* Cebu City, the Philippines, Central Visayas Consortium for Integrated Regional Research and Development (CV-CIRRD).

Dahl, A. 1993. Land-based pollution and integrated coastal management. *Marine Policy,* 17(6): 561-72.

Davis, S.H. 1997. Public involvement in environmental decision-making: the experience of the World Bank. In *Proceedings of the OECD/DAC Workshop on Capacity Development in Environment.* Rome, 4-6 December 1996. Theme paper No. 5, p. 250-264. Paris CEDEX, OECD.

Davis-Case, D'A. 1989. *Community forestry: participatory assessment, monitoring and evaluation.* FAO Community Forestry Note No. 2. 150 pp.

Davis-Case, D'A. 1990. *The community's toolbox. The idea, methods and tools for participatory assessment, monitoring and evaluation in community forestry.* FAO

239

Community Forestry Field Manual Volume 2. 146 pp. (issued also in French and Spanish)

De Graaf, M. 1997. Pre-implementation tools. Tools and challenges for donors in designing and preparing initiatives towards capacity development in the environment. In *Proceedings of the OECD/DAC Workshop on Capacity Development in the Environment*. Rome, 4-6 December 1996. Supplementary paper, p. 136-52. Paris CEDEX, OECD.

Dent, D. 1985. *Acid sulphate soils: a baseline for research and development*. International Institute of Land Reclamation and Improvement (ILRI) Publications No. 39. 250 pp.

Dick Osborne and Associates. 1993. *The prospect for institutional arrangements to promote integrated coastal zone management*. Canberra, Resource Assessment Commission. 64 pp.

Dix, M., Lee, R. & Santana, A. 1995. Land use and environmental dispute resolution: the Special Master. *Florida Bar Journal*, 69: 63.

Dougherty, T.C. & Hall, A.W. 1995. *Environmental impact assessment of irrigation and drainage projects*. FAO Irrigation and Drainage Paper No. 53. 84 pp.

Dragun, A. & Jakobsson, K. 1993. Institutions and equity as issues in sustainable development. *Borneo Rev.*, 4(1): 15-36.

Environment Council. 1995a. *Environmental resolve – beyond compromise: building consensus in environmental planning and decision-making*. London, The Environment Council.

Environment Council. 1995b. *Environmental mediation and facilitation course notes*. London, The Environment Council.

Environment Council. 1995c. *Environmental resolve: a conflict resolution guide*. London, The Environment Council.

ESCAP. 1987. *Coastal environment plan for Bangladesh. Vol. 2. Final report*. Bangkok, Economic and Social Commission for Asia and the Pacific (ESCAP).

FAO. 1976. *A framework for land evaluation*. FAO Soils Bulletin No. 32. 71 pp. (issued also in Chinese, French and Spanish)

FAO. 1981. *Manual of forest inventory with special reference to mixed tropical forests*. FAO Forestry Paper No. 27. 200 pp. (issued also in French)

FAO. 1984. *Land evaluation for forestry*. FAO Forestry Paper No. 48. 123 pp. (issued also in Chinese, French, and Spanish)

FAO. 1990. *Restoration and expansion of the mangrove belt in Guyana*. A report prepared for the Hydraulics Division, Ministry of Agriculture, Government of the Cooperative Republic of Guyana by FAO, based on the work of M.Z. Hussain. Rome, FAO, Technical Cooperation Programme TCP/GUY/8953, Technical Report No. 1. 31 pp.

FAO. 1992. *Sustainable agriculture and rural development in small island countries*. Paper presented at the FAO Interregional Conference of Small Island Countries on Sustainable Development and Environment in Agriculture, Forestry and Fisheries. Christ Church, Barbados, 7-10 April 1992. Rome, FAO, (AGR:SIC4). 21 pp. (issued also in French)

FAO. 1993. *Guidelines for land use planning*. FAO Development Series No. 1. 96 p. (issued also in French)

FAO. 1994a. *Mangrove forest management guidelines*. FAO Forestry Paper No. 117. 319 pp. (issued also in Spanish)

FAO. 1994b. *Review of the state of world marine fishery resources*. FAO Fisheries Technical Paper No. 335. 136 pp. (issued also in French and Spanish)

FAO. 1995a. *Code of conduct for responsible fisheries*. Rome, FAO. 41 pp. (issued also in Arabic, Chinese, French and Spanish)

INTEGRATED
COASTAL AREA
MANAGEMENT
and
AGRICULTURE
FORESTRY AND
FISHERIES

References

FAO. 1995b. *Review of the state of world fishery resources: aquaculture.* FAO Fisheries Circular No. 886. 127 pp.

FAO. 1996a. *Agro-ecological zoning. Guidelines.* FAO Soils Bulletin No. 73. 78 pp.

FAO. 1996b. Fisherfolk safeguarding aquatic biodiversity through their fishing techniques. In *Dynamic diversity.* Rugby, UK, Intermediate Technology Development Group. 21 pp.

FAO. 1996c. *Fishers and fisheries: population dimensions of a vital sector.* Rome, FAO, Population Programme Service. 22 pp. (mimeo)

FAO. 1996d. *High resolution satellite data for coastal fisheries. Pilot study in the Philippines.* FAO Remote Sensing Decision-Making Series No. 5. 5 pp.

FAO. 1996e. *Integration of fisheries into coastal area management.* FAO Technical Guidelines for Responsible Fisheries No. 3. 17 pp.

FAO. 1996f. *Precautionary approach to capture fisheries and species introductions.* Elaborated by the Technical Consultation on the Precautionary Approach to Capture Fisheries (including species introductions), Lysekil, Sweden, 6-13 June 1995. FAO Technical Guidelines for Responsible Fisheries No. 2. 54 pp. Issued also as FAO Fisheries Technical Paper No. 350/1 (1996). 52 pp. (issued also in French and Spanish)

FAO. 1997a. *Aquaculture development.* FAO Technical Guidelines for Responsible Fisheries No. 5. 39 pp.

FAO. 1997b. *Land quality indicators and their use in sustainable agriculture and rural development.* Proceedings of the Workshop organized by the Land and Water Development Division. FAO Agriculture Department and the Research, Extension and Training Division, FAO Sustainable Development Department, Rome, 25-26 January 1996. FAO Land and Water Bulletin No. 5. 212 pp.

FAO. 1997c. *Seawater intrusion in coastal aquifers. Guidelines for study, monitoring and control.* FAO Water Report No. 11. 152 pp.

FAO. 1997d. *State of the world's forests, 1997.* Rome, FAO, Forestry Department. 200 pp.

FAO/UNEP. 1997. *Negotiating a sustainable future for the land: structural and institutional guidelines for land resources management in the twenty-first century.* Rome, FAO/United Nations Environment Programme (UNEP). 60 pp.

Fisher, R., Ury, W. & Patton, B. 1991. *Getting to yes.* New York, Penguin.

Flaaten, O. 1988. *The economics of multispecies harvesting: theory and application to the Barents Sea fisheries.* London, Springer-Verlag.

Freeman, M. 1979. *The benefits of environmental improvements: theory and practice.* Baltimore, Md, USA, John Hopkins University Press.

Fuavao, V.A. 1994. *Coastal development in small island developing states. Case study, 4.* Paper prepared for the UN Global Conference on the sustainable development of small island developing states, 15 April-6 May 1996. New York, UN, A/CONF. 167/CRP5. 24 pp. (mimeo)

Fuller, L. 1971. Mediation – its forms and functions. *Southern California Law Review,* 44: 305.

Garcia, S. 1994. The precautionary principle: its implications in capture fisheries management. *Ocean Coastal Management,* 22: 99-125.

Garcia, S. 1996. *The precautionary approach to fisheries and its implications for fishery research, technology and management: an updated review.* FAO Fisheries Technical Paper No. 350/2, p.99-125.

Garcia, S. 1997. *Indicators for sustainable development of fisheries.* FAO Land and Water Bulletin No. 5, p.131-154.

GEF/UNDP/IMO. 1996. *Enhancing the success of integrated coastal management. Good practices in the formulation, design and implementation of integrated coastal management initiatives.* Quezon City, Philippines, GEF/UNDP/IMO, Regional Programme

INTEGRATED
COASTAL AREA
MANAGEMENT
and
AGRICULTURE
FORESTRY AND
FISHERIES

References

for the Prevention and Management of Marine Pollution in the East Asian Seas and Coastal Management Center. MPP-EAS Technical Report No. 2. 32 pp.

GESAMP 1990. *The state of the marine environment.* IMO/FAO/UNESCO-IOC/WMO/WHO/IAEA/UN/ UNEP Joint Group of Experts on the Scientific Aspects of Marine Environmental Protection (GESAMP). GESAMP Reports and Studies No. 39. 111 pp. (issued also in Spanish)

GESAMP. 1991. *Reducing environmental impacts of coastal aquaculture.* GESAMP Reports and Studies No. 47. 35 pp.

GESAMP. 1996a. *The contributions of science to integrated coastal management.* GESAMP Reports and Studies No. 61. 66 pp.

GESAMP. 1996b. *Monitoring of ecological effects of coastal aquaculture wastes.* GESAMP Reports and Studies No. 57. 45 pp.

Gillett, R. 1995. *South Pacific islands. Demand and supply of fish and fish products in selected areas of the world: perspectives and implications for food security.* Paper presented at the International Conference on the Sustainable Contribution of Fisheries to Food Security, organized by the Government of Japan in collaboration with FAO. Kyoto, Japan, 4-6 December 1995, KC/FI/ 95/TECH/10, p. 165-79. (mimeo)

Goldberg, B., Sander, F. & Rogers, N. 1992. *Dispute resolution: negotiation, mediation and other processes.* Boston, Mass, USA, Little, Brown and Co.

Gomez, E.D. & McManus, L. 1996. *Case study 4. Coastal management in Bolinao town and the Lingayen Gulf, the Philippines,* p. 57-66. GESAMP Reports and Studies.

Gommes, R. *et al* 1997. *Sea level, agriculture and population: some issues.* Paper presented at the Staring Symposium on Sea Level and Science Fiction, Amsterdam, 22 October 1997, organized by the Royal Netherlands Academy of Arts and Sciences (KNGMG). 20 pp.

Gornitz, V. 1995. Monitoring sea level changes. *Climate Change,* 31: 515-44.

Grandstaff, T.B. & Messerschmidt, D.A. 1995. *A manager's guide to the use of rapid rural appraisal.* Bangkok, FAO/UNEP Farmer-centred Agricultural Resource Management Programme, FARM Field Document No.1. 127 pp.

Gray, J.S., McIntyre, A.D. & Stirn, J. 1991. *Manual of methods in aquatic environment research. Part 11. Biological assessment of marine pollution with particular reference to benthos.* FAO Fisheries Technical Paper No. 324. 49 pp. (issued also in French)

Green, G. 1983. Use of mangrove areas as sewage treatment plants. *In* Proceedings of Interdepartment Workshop, February 1983, Suva, Fiji. *Technical Report of the Ministry of Agriculture and Fisheries, Fisheries Division, Suva, Fiji,* (5): 49-55.

Gregersen, H. & Contreras-Hermosilla, A. 1992. *Economic assessment of forestry impact.* FAO Forestry Paper No. 106. 134 pp. (issued also in French)

Gregersen, H. *et al.* 1993. *Assessing forestry project impacts: issues and strategies.* FAO Forestry Paper No. 114. 72 pp. (issued also in French and Spanish)

Gregersen, H.M. *et al.* 1995. *Valuing forests: context, issues and guidelines.* FAO Forestry Paper No. 127. 53 pp.

Grigalunas, T.A. & Congar, R. (eds.) 1995. *Environmental economics for integrated coastal area management: valuation methods and policy instruments.* UNEP Regional Seas Report Studies Nairobi No. 164. 165 pp.

GTZ. 1988. *ZOPP (Zielorientierte Projektplanung) in brief.* Frankfurt, Germany, Deutsche Gesellschaft für Technische Zusammenarbeit (GTZ), GmbH, (1/88): 2-6.

Gubbay, S. 1990. *A future for the coast? Proposals for a UK coastal zone management plan. Report for the World Wide Fund for Nature from the Marine*

INTEGRATED
COASTAL AREA
MANAGEMENT
and
AGRICULTURE
FORESTRY AND
FISHERIES

References

Conservation Society. London, Marine Conservation Society.

Guillotreau, P. & Cunningham, S. 1994. *An economic appraisal of the Solent oyster fishery: historical and institutional aspects.* Centre for Economic Management of Aquatic Resources (CEMARE) Research Paper No. 65. Portsmouth, UK, University of Portsmouth.

Hanemann, W.M. 1991. Willingness to pay versus willingness to accept: how much can they differ? *American Economic Review*, 81: 635-647.

Hardin, G. 1998. The tragedy of the Commons. *Science, Washington*, 162: 1243-1248.

Heald, E.J. & Odum, W.E. 1970. The contribution of mangrove swamps to Florida fishieries. *Proceedings, Gulf Caribbean Fisheries Institute*, 22: 130-5.

Hemocque, Y. *et al.* 1997. *Guide, méthodolique d'aide à la gestion intégrée de la zone côtière.* IOC Management Guides No. 36. 47 pp.

Heral, M., Bacher, C. & Deslous-Paoli, J. 1989. La capacité biotique des bassins ostréicoles. *In* Troadec, J.P. (ed.) *L'homme et les ressources halieutiques*, p. 225-59. Brest, France. IFREMER.

Hillborn, R. & Walters, C.J. 1992. *Quantitative fisheries stock assessment: choice, dynamics and uncertainty.* London, Chapman and Hall. 570 pp.

Hoang Hoe. 1991. Some facts of agroforestry in Vietnam. *In* Mellink, W., Rao, Y.S. & MacDicken, K.G. (eds.) *AgroForestry in Asia and the Pacific*. FAO Regional Office for Asia and the Pacific Publications.

Hodgson, G. & Dixon, J.A. 1988. Logging versus fishing and tourism in Palawan. *Occasional Paper, East-West Environment and Policy Institute, Honolulu,* (7).

Horowitz, D. 1977. *The courts and social policy.* Washington, DC.

Huber, R., Ruitenbeek, J. & Seroa da Motta, R. 1997. *Market based instruments for environmental policymaking in Latin America and the Caribbean: lessons from eleven countries.* Washington, DC, World Bank. 79 pp.

Hufschmidt, M.M. *et al.* 1983. *Environment, natural systems and development: an economic valuation guide.* Baltimore, Md, USA, John Hopkins University Press.

Huizenga, C.& Nieuwenhuis, D. 1993. *RAICE: a rapid appraisal of institutional capacity for environments.* Utrecht, the Netherlands, IDEM Consult.

ICAMS Consortium. 1998. *Integrated coastal analysis monitoring system for operational application in coastal regions. Technical annex to Project Plan. Project funded by EU under DG XII Environment and Climate Programme of the Fourth Framework Programme.* Integrated Coastal Analysis Monitoring System (ICAMS), London, Earth Observation Sciences Ltd. Internal document (IC-EOS-111-PL-001).

ICSU Scientific Committee on Oceanic Research for J-GOOS. 1997. *GOOS Coastal Module Planning Workshop Report.* University of Miami, 24-28 February 1997. IOC Workshop Report No. 131.

ILO. 1998. *Economically active population estimates (1950-1980) and projections (1985-2025). Vol. 5.* Geneva, International Labour Organisation (ILO).

Insull, A.D., Barg, U.C. & Martosubroto, P. 1995. Coastal fisheries and aquaculture within integrated coastal area management in East Africa. *In* Lindén, O. (ed.) *Proceedings of the Arusha Workshop and Policy Conference on Integrated Coastal Zone Management in Eastern Africa, including the Island States.* Arusha, United Republic of Tanzania, 21-23 April 1993. Manila, SAREC Marine Program, Coastal Management Center.

IOC/ICSU/WMO. 1997. *Report to J-GOOS IV.* Paper presented at Joint Scientific and Technical Committee for the Global Ocean Observing System (J-GOOS) Coastal Module Planning Workshop, University of Miami, Fl, USA, 24-28 February 1997. Paris, UNESCO/IOC/GOOS. 53 pp.

243

INTEGRATED
COASTAL AREA
MANAGEMENT
and
AGRICULTURE
FORESTRY AND
FISHERIES

References

IPCC. 1994. *Preparing to meet the coastal challenges of the twenty-first century. Conference report. World Coast Conference 1993,* Noordwijk, The Netherlands, 1-5 November 1993. The Hague, National Institute for Coastal and Marine Management, Intergovernmental Panel on Climate Change (IPCC).

IUCN/UNEP/WWF. 1991. *Caring for the earth: a strategy for sustainable living.* Gland, Switzerland, IUCN/UNEP/WWF. 228 pp.

Japan, Government of, & FAO. 1995. *Safeguarding future fish supplies: key policy issues and measures.* Paper presented for the International Conference on the Sustainable Contribution of Fisheries to Food Security, organized by the Government of Japan in collaboration with FAO. Kyoto, Japan, 4-6 December 1995, KC/FI/95/TECH/1. 50 pp. (mimeo)

Jelgersma, S., van der Zijp, M. & Brinkman, R. 1993. Sea level rise and the coastal lowlands in the developing world. *Journal of Coastal Resources,* 9(3): 958-72.

Jones, C. 1996. *PRA tools and techniques pack.* Brighton, UK, University of Brighton, Institute of Development Studies.

Jones G. *et al.* (eds). *Dictionary of the environment.* Glasgow, Collins.

Kam, S.P., Paw, J.N. & Loo, M. 1992. The use of remote sensing and geographic information systems in coastal zone management. *ICLARM Conference Proceedings,* (37): 107-32.

Kapetsky, J.M. 1986. *Conversion of mangroves for pond aquaculture: some short-term and long-term remedies.* Paper presented at the Workshop on the Conversion of Mangrove Areas to Aquaculture, Iloilo City, the Philippines, 24-26 April 1986. (mimeo)

Kapetsky, J.M. & Travaglia, C. 1995. Geographical information systems and remote sensing: an overview of their present and potential applications in aquaculture. *In* Nambiar, K. & Singh, T. (eds.) *Aquaculture towards the twenty-first century,* p. 187-208. Kuala Lumpur, INFOFISH.

Kelleher, G. 1996. *Case study 2. The Great Barrier reef, Australia.* GESAMP Reports and Studies No. 61, p. 31-44.

Kuyateh, M., (ed.) 1995. *Report on the training of selected government officers and fishing community members on the participatory rapid appraisal method (PRA), and, Conduct of PRAs in selected fishing communities of the Gambia.* Rome, FAO, Integrated Coastal Fisheries Management in the Gambia, FI:DP/INT/91/007, Field document No. 7. 69 pp.

Lal, P.N. 1990. *Ecological economic analysis of mangrove conservation; a case study from Fiji.* UNDP/UNESCO Regional Mangrove Project RAS/86/120. Mangrove Ecosystem Occasional Paper No. 6. 64 pp.

Lantieri, D. 1998. *Use of high resolution satellite data for agricultural and marine applications in the Maldives – pilot study on Laamu Atoll.* FAO Remote Sensing Series No. 45. 47 pp.

Le Blanc, H. 1997. Tools and challenges for donors in the monitoring and evaluation of CDE initiatives. In *Proceedings of OECD/DAC Workshop on Capacity Development for the Environment,* Rome, 4-6 December 1996. Paris, CEDEX, OECD, Theme Paper No, 3, pp. 201-218.

Lölsch, B. 1996. Battle over the Danube wetlands: Austria's "mini-Amazon". In *Managing conflicts in protected areas. A manual for protected area managers.* Gland, Switzerland, IUCN.

Løyche, M. 1991. *Protection of sea dykes through planting of trees. Appraisal of the forestry component of WFP Project Vietnam 4617 Rehabilitation and upgrading of sea dykes.* Rome, World Food Programme.

Løyche-Wilkie, M. 1995. *Mangrove conservation and management in the Sudan. Consultancy report.* Rome, FAO, FO:GCP/SUD/047/NET.

Macnae, W. 1974. *Mangrove forests and fisheries.* Rome, FAO/UNDP Indian Ocean Programme, Indian Ocean Fishery Commission. IOFC/DEV/74/34. 35 pp.

INTEGRATED
COASTAL AREA
MANAGEMENT
and
AGRICULTURE
FORESTRY AND
FISHERIES

References

Martosubroto, P. & Naamin, N. 1977. Relationship between tidal forests (mangroves) and commercial shrimp production in Indonesia. *Marine Resources of Indonesia,* 18: 81-6.

Mathiews, D.R. 1995. Commons versus open access: the collapse of Canada's east coast fishery. *Ecologist,* 25: 213.

McCrory, J.P. 1981. Environmental mediation – another piece of the puzzle. *6Vt. Law Review,* 49(1981): 63-4.

Meaden, G.J. & DoChi, T. 1996. *Geographical information systems: applications to marine fisheries.* FAO Fisheries Technical Paper No. 356. 335 pp.

Melling, T. 1994. Dispute resolution within legislative institutions. *Stanford Law Review,* 46: 1677.

Melling, T. 1995. Bruce Babbitt's use of governmental dispute resolution: a mid-term report card. *Land Water Law Review,* 30(1): 57-90.

Mitchell, R. & Carson R. 1989. *Using surveys to value public goods: the contingent valuation method.* Washington, DC, Resources for the Future. 463 pp.

MNS. 1991. *Draft. Kuala Selangor nature part management plan.* Kuala Lumpur, Malaysian Nature Society (MNS).

Moffat, D. & Lindén O. 1995. Perception and reality: assessing priorities for sustainable development in the Niger River Delta. *Ambio,* 24 (7-8): 527-38.

Montalembert, M.-R. de & Schmithüsen, F.S. 1994. *Policy, legal and institutional aspects of sustainable forest management,* p. 153-72. FAO Forestry Paper No. 122.

Moragos, J.E. et al. 1983. Development planning for tropical ecosystems. *In* Carpenter, R. (ed.) *Natural systems for development: what planners need to know,* London, Macmillan.

Murray, J.S. Rau, A.S. & Sherman, E.F. (eds.) 1989. *Processes of dispute resolution: the role of lawyers.* New York, Foundation Press.

Neiland, A. & Nowell, D. 1991. *Aquaculture development and coastal zone management strategies: a comparison of leading issues from the UK, Canada and the USA.* Centre for Economic Management of Aquatic Resources (CEMARE) Research Paper No. 48. Portsmouth, UK, University of Portsmouth.

Neiland, A. et al. 1994. *Design and implementation of a statistical monitoring system for fisheries in northeast Nigeria: preliminary evaluation.* Centre for Economic Management of Aquatic Resources (CEMARE) Research Paper No. 29. Portsmouth, UK, University of Portsmouth. 47 pp.

Nicholls, R. J. 1993. *Synthesis of vulnerability analysis studies.* Keynote speech delivered at the World Coast Conference 1993, Noordwijk, the Netherlands, 1-5 November 1993.

Nicholls, R.J. & Leatherman, S.P. 1995. Global sea level rise. *In* Strzepek, K.M. & Smith, J.B. (eds.) *As climate changes: international impacts and implications,* p. 92-123. Cambridge, UK, Cambridge University Press.

Nickerson, D. 1997. *Prospectus for the Integrated Coastal Management Workshop.* Alor Star, Malaysia, 20-22 October 1997.

North, D.C. 1990. *Institutions, institutional change and economic performance.* Cambridge, UK, Cambridge University Press. 152 pp.

OECD. 1991. *Report on CZM: integrated policies and draft recommendations of the Council on Integrated Coastal Zone Management.* Paris, CEDEX, Organisation for Economic Co-operation and Development (OECD).

OECD. 1993. *Coastal zone management: selected case studies.* Paris CEDEX, OECD.

INTEGRATED
COASTAL AREA
MANAGEMENT
and
AGRICULTURE
FORESTRY AND
FISHERIES

References

OECD. 1995a. *Developing environmental capacity – a framework for donor involvement.* Paris CEDEX, OECD.

OECD. 1995b. *Donor assistance to capacity development in environment.* Paris CEDEX, OECD, Development Assistance Committee, Development Cooperation Guidelines Series. (bilingual English/French)

Oliver, J. 1996. *The suitability of mediation to the resolution of disputes with regard to the experience of family mediation.* London, University College.

Olsen, S.B. 1993. Will integrated coastal management programs be sustainable?: the constituency problem. *Ocean and Coastal Management,* 21: 201-25.

Olsen, S.B. 1996. *Case study 3. Ecuador's coastal resources management programme.* GESAMP Reports and Studies No. 61, p. 45-56.

Olsen, S.B. *et al.* 1997. *Survey of current purposes and methods for evaluating coastal management projects and programs funded by international donors.* Coastal Management Report of the Coastal Resources Centre University of Rhode Island No. 2200. 28 pp.

Ong, J.E., Gong, W.K. & Wong, C.H. 1982. Productivity and nutrient status of litter in a managed mangrove forest. *Biotrop Special Publication,* (17): 33-41.

Palfreman, A. & Insull, D. 1994. *Guide to fisheries sector studies.* FAO Fisheries Technical Paper No. 342. 101 pp.

Palmer, D. 1992. Methods for analysing development and conservation issues: the Resource Assessment Commission's experience. *Resource Assessment Commission Research Paper, Canberra,* (7).

Pearce, D.W. 1991. An economic approach to saving the tropical forests. *In* Helm, D. (ed.) *An economic policy towards the environment.* Oxford, UK, Blackwell Scientific Publications.

Pearce, D.W., Markandya, A. & Barbier, E.B. 1989. *Blueprint for a green economy.* London, Earthscan Publications. 192 pp.

Pearce, D.W. & Turner, R.K. 1990. *Economics of natural resources and the environment.* Hemel Hempstead, UK, Harvester Wheatsheaf Publishers.

Pelt, M.J.F. 1993. Ecologically sustainable development and project appraisal in developing countries. *Ecological Economics,* 7: 19-42.

Penning-Rowsell, E.C. *et al.* 1992. *The economics of coastal zone management: a manual of assessment techniques.* London, Belhaven Press. 380 pp.

Pernetta, J.C. & Elder, D.L. 1992. Climate, sea level rise and the coastal zone: management and planning for global changes. *Ocean Coastal Management,* 18: 113-60.

Pernetta, J.C. and Elder, D.L. 1993. *Cross-sectoral integrated and coastal area planning (CICAP): guidelines and principles for coastal area development. A marine conservation and development report.* Gland, Switzerland, IUCN in collaboration with World Wide Fund for Nature. 63 pp.

Peters, C.M. 1994. *Sustainable harvest of non-timber plant resources in tropical moist forests: an ecological primer. The Biodiversity Programme,* Landover, Md, USA, Corporate Press Inc. 45 pp.

Pétry, F. 1990. *Multicriteria decision-making and rural development.* Rome, FAO, Policy Assistance Division (TCA), Agricultural Policy Support Service (TCAS), Internal document No. 13. 32 pp.

Pido, M.D. & Chua, T.-E. 1992. A framework for rapid appraisal of coastal environments. *ICLARM Conference Proceedings,* (37): 133-48.

Pomeroy, R.S. (ed.) 1994. *Community management and common property of coastal fisheries in Asia and the Pacific: concepts, methods and experiences.* ICLARM Conference Proceedings No. 45. 189 pp.

INTEGRATED
COASTAL AREA
MANAGEMENT
and
AGRICULTURE
FORESTRY AND
FISHERIES

References

Poore, D. & Sayer, J. (1987). *The management of tropical moist forest lands: ecological guidelines.* Gland, Switzerland, IUCN, Tropical Forest Programme. 63 pp.

Populus, J. & Lantieri, D. 1991. *Use of high resolution satellite data for coastal fisheries: 1. Pilot study in the Philippines; 2. General review.* Study implemented by GCP/INT/458/FRA with the assistance of the Government of France. FAO Remote Sensing Centre Series No. 58. 43 pp. Issued also as FAO High Resolution Satellite Data Series No. 5. 43 pp.

Post J.C. & Lundin, C.G. (eds.) 1996. *Guidelines for integrated coastal zone management.* Environment Sustainable Development Studies Monograph Series No. 9. 16 pp.

Pretty, J.N. *et al.* 1995. *A trainer's guide for participatory learning and action.* London, University College, International Institute for Environment and Development, IIED Participatory Methodology Series. 267 pp.

Pretty J.N. 1997. Capacity development and capacity challenges: learning methodologies and mechanisms for adaptive aid management. In *Proceedings of the OECD/DAC Workshop on Capacity Development in Environment,* Rome, 4-6 December 1996, pp. 223-45. Paris CEDEX, OECD.

Price, A.R.G. & Humphreys S.L. (eds.) 1993. *Applicaton of the biosphere reserve concept to coastal marine areas.* Papers presented at the UNESCO/IUCN San Francisco Workshop of 14-20 August 1989. A marine conservation and development report. Gland, Switzerland, IUCN. 1114 pp.

Primavera, J. 1994. Environmental and socio-economic effects of shrimp farming: the Philippine experience. *INFOFISH International,* (1/94): 44-9.

Resources Assessment Commission. 1992. Multicriteria analysis as a resource assessment tool. *Resource Assessment Commission Research Paper, Canberra* (6).

Richardson, J. & Nurick, R. 1994. *Environmental valuation: theory, techniques and applications.* Wye College External Programme Course Material. London, University of London, Wye College.

Rolley, E.R. & Brown, M.J. 1996. Forest allocation and conservation in Tasmania: can both win? In *Managing conflicts in protected areas. A manual for protected area managers.* Gland, Switzerland, IUCN.

Roose, E. 1996. *Land husbandry components and strategy.* FAO Soils Bulletin No. 70. 123 pp.

Ruitenbeek, H.J. 1992. *Mangrove assessment: an economic analysis of management options with a focus on Biutuni Bay, Irian Jaya.* Environmental Management Development Indonesia (EMDI) Environment Report Dalhousie University, Halifax, Canada, No. 8. 90 pp.

Saenger, P., Hegerl, E.J. & Davie, J.D.S. 1983. *Global status of mangrove ecosystems.* IUCN Community Ecology Paper No. 3. 88 pp.

Salleh, M.N. & Ng, F.S.P. 1994. *Research for sustainable forest management,* p. 185-192. FAO Forestry Paper No. 122.

Sarch, M.T. 1996. *Participatory research methods: a toolbook.* Portsmouth, University of Portsmouth, CEMARE. 56 pp.

Sargent, C. & Bass, S. 1992. The future shape of forests. *In* Holmberg, J. (ed.) *Policies for a small planet.* London, Earthscan Publications.

Sassone, P. & Schaffer, W. 1978. *Cost-benefit analysis: a handbook.* New York, Academic Press.

Scott, J. 1993. Urban agriculture: a response to the impact of structural adjustment measure. *In* Goodland, R. *et al.* (eds.) *Feeding urban Africa.* London, University of London, Wye College Press.

Scura, L.F. *et al.* 1992. Lessons for integrated coastal zone management: the ASEAN experience. *ICLARM Conference Proceedings,* (37): 1-70.

Shackleton, L. 1987. A comparative study of fossil fish scales from three upwelling regions. *South African Journal of Marine Science*, 5: 79-84.

Sharma, P. (ed.) 1997. *Participatory processes for integrated watershed management.* Participatory Watershed Management Training Asia, Farmer Centre for Agricultural Resource Management (PWMTA-FARM), Kathmandu, Field Document No. 7. 96 pp.

Shogren, J.F. *et al.* 1994. Resolving differences in willingness to pay and willingness to accept. *American Economic Review*, 84(1): 255-70.

Silbey, S. & Merry, S. 1986. Mediator settlement strategies. *Law Policy*, 8: 7.

Simpson, R. 1976. *Land law and registration.* Cambridge, UK, Cambridge University Press.

Singer, L. 1994. *Settling disputes: conflict resolution in business, families, and the legal system.* Oxford, UK, Westview Press.

Smith, I. 1985. Social feasibility of coastal aquaculture: packaged technology from above or participatory rural development. In *Consultation on social feasibility of coastal aquaculture,* Madras, India, 26 November-1 December 1984. Madras, FAO Bay of Bengal Programme, Development of Small-Scale Fisheries, BOBP/MIS/2, Appendix 3, p. 12-34.

Smith, V.K. 1993. Non-market valuation of environmental resources: an interpretive appraisal. *Land Econ.*69(1): 1-26.

Soley, N., Neiland, A. & Nowell, D. 1992. Aquaculture pollution: who pays, who should pay? Centre for Economic Management of Aquatic Resources (CEMARE) Research Paper No. 54. Portsmouth, UK, University of Portsmouth.

Sorensen, J. 1997. National and international efforts at integrated coastal management: definitions, achievements and lessons. *Coastal Management*, 25: 3-41.

Sorensen, J.C. & McCreary, S.T. 1990. *Institutional arrangements for managing coastal resources and environments.* Second edition (revised). Renewable Resources Information Series Coastal Management Publications No. 1. 193 pp.

Sorensen, J.C. & West, N. 1992. *A guide to impact assessment in coastal environments.* Naragansett, RI, USA, University of Rhode Island, Coastal Resources Center. 100 pp.

Sourji, A. *et al.* 1995. *Land resources appraisal report. District of Xai-Xai. Vol. 1. Main report.* Maputo, Mozambique, Instituto Nacional de Investigaçáo Agronómica, Ministério da Agricultura e Pescas (MAP)/UNDP/FAO. 93 pp.

Soutar, A. & Isaacs, J. 1969. A history of fish populations inferred from fish scales in anaerobic sediments off California. *CALCOFI (California Cooperative Oceanic Fisheries Investigations Report)*, (13): 63-70.

Sparre, P., Ursin, E. & Venema, S.C. 1992. *Introduction to tropical fish stock assessment. Part 1. Manual.* Revised edition. FAO Fisheries Technical Paper No. 306/1. 376 pp. (issued also in French, Portuguese and Spanish)

Sparre, P.J. & Willmann, R. 1992. *Software for bio-economic analysis of fisheries BEAM 4. Analytical bio-economic simulation of space-structured multispecies and multifleet fisheries. Volume 1. Description of model. Volume 2. User's manual.* FAO Computer Information Series (Fish) No. (3). Volume 1, 186 pp. Volume 2, 46 pp. (issued also in French)

Staples, D. 1997. Indicators of sustainable fisheries development. *In* Hancock, D.A. *et al.,* (eds.) *Developing and sustaining world fisheries resources: the state of science and management. Second World Fisheries Congress,* p. 719-725. Collingwood, Victoria, Australia, CSIRO.

Sugden, R. & Williams, A. 1978. *The principles of practical cost-benefit analysis.* Oxford, UK, Oxford University Press.

INTEGRATED
COASTAL AREA
MANAGEMENT
and
AGRICULTURE
FORESTRY AND
FISHERIES

References

Sukardjo, S. 1995. *Study of the mangrove ecology in the estaurine area of the Gambia.* Rome, FAO, Integrated Coastal Fisheries Management in the Gambia, FI:DP/INT/91/007, Field Document No. 6. 35 pp.

Susskind, L. 1981. Environmental mediation and the accountability problem. *6 Vt. Law Review*, 49 (1981): 14.

Tang, H.T. *et al.* 1984. Mangrove forests of Peninsular Malaysia: a review of management and research objectives and priorities. *In* Soepadmo, E. *et al.* (eds.) *Proceedings of the Asian Symposium on Mangrove Environment and Resource Management.* Kuala Lumpur, University of Malaya.

Therivel, R., *et al.* 1992. *Strategic environmental assessment.* London, Earthscan Publications.

Tietenberg, T.H. 1994. *Environmental economics and policy.* New York, Harper Collins College Publishers.

Tisdell, C. 1989. *Aquaculture as a use of the coastal zone: environmental and economic aspects. Giant clam farming as a development.* University of Queensland Department of Economics Discussion Paper No. 20. 22 pp.

Townsley, P. 1993. *Rapid appraisal methods for coastal communities: a manual.* Madras, India, Bay of Bengal Programme for Fisheries Development, BOBP/MAG/6. 105 pp.

Trinidad and Tobago, Government of the Republic of/FAO/UNDP 1994. *Inception report: project objectives, strategies and activities. Integrated coastal fisheries management.* Port of Spain, Government of the Republic of Trinidad and Tobago, FAO/UNDP, FI:DP/INT/91/007, Project Report Trinidad and Tobago No. 3. 31 pp.

Turner, R.K. & Jones, T. (eds.) 1991. *Wetlands; market and intervention failures for case studies.* London, Earthscan Publications.

Turner, R.K., *et al.* 1995. *Coastal zone resources assessment guidelines. LOICZ (Land-Ocean Interactions in the Coastal Zone) Reports and Studies,* London, (4): 101 pp.

UK Department of the Environment. 1994. *Mediation: benefits and practice. Seven habits of highly effective people. Information for those considering mediation as a way of resolving neighbour disputes.* London, HMSO, Department of the Environment.

UN. 1985. *Estimates and projections of urban, rural and city populations, 1950-2025: the 1982 assessment.* New York, United Nations.

UN. 1994. *World urbanization prospects: the 1994 revision. Annex tables.* New York, UN, Department for Economic and Social Information and Policy Analysis, Population Division. 67 pp.

UN. 1996. *Indicators of sustainable development: framework and methodologies.* New York, United Nations. 428 pp.

UN. *1997. Glossary of environment statistics.* Department for Economic and Social Information and Policy Analysis, Statistics Division. UN Study Methods (Series F) No. 67. 83 pp.

UNEP. 1990. *An approach to environmental impact assessment for projects affecting the coastal and marine environment.* UNEP Regional Seas Report and Studies, Nairobi No. 122. 35 pp.

UNEP. 1995. *Guidelines for integrated management of coastal and marine areas, with special reference to the Mediterranean basin.* UNEP Regional Seas Report and Studies, Nairobi No. 161. 67 pp.

UNEP. 1996. *Guidelines for integrated planning and management of coastal and marine areas in the wider Caribbean region.* Kingston, Jamaica. UNEP Caribbean Environment Programme in cooperation with Island Resources Foundation. 141 pp.

US Department of Commerce, National Oceanic and Atmospheric Administration. 1993. Proposed rules: national resource damage assessment. Guidelines for

INTEGRATED
COASTAL AREA
MANAGEMENT
and
AGRICULTURE
FORESTRY AND
FISHERIES

References

surveys for valuing public goods. *Federal Register,* 58(10): 4601-14.

US Environment Protection Agency. 1993. *National estuary program guidance: basic program analysis.* Washington, DC, Environment Protection Agency (EPA 842-B).

Van Herwijnem, M., Jansen, R. & Nijkamp, P. 1993. A multicriteria support model and geographic information system for sustainable development planning of the Greek islands. *Project Appraisal,* 8(1): 9-22.

Vantomme, P. 1995. Forestry within integrated coastal management (ICAM) in East Africa. *In* Lindén, O. (ed.) *Proceedings of the Arusha Workshop and Policy Conference on integrated coastal zone management in eastern Africa including the Island States.* Arusha, United Republic of Tanzania, 21-23 April 1993. Manila, SAREC Marine Program, Coastal Management Center.

Vatn, A. & Bromley, D.W. 1995. Choices without prices without apologies. *In* Bromley, D.W. ed. *Handbook of environmental economics,* p. 3-25. Oxford, UK, Blackwell.

Vestal, B. & Reiser, A. 1995. *Methodologies and mechanisms for management of cumulative coastal environmental impacts. Part 1. Synthesis with annotated bibliography.* Washington, DC, US Department of Commerce, NOAA Coastal Ocean Program. 150 pp.

Walters, C. 1986. *Adaptive management of renewable resources.* New York, Macmillan.

Warwick, R.A. *et al.* 1996. Changes in sea level. *In* Houghton, J.T. *et al.* (eds.) *IPCC 1996 Report on climate change 1995: the science of climate change. Contribution of Working Group I to the Second Assessment Report of the Intergovernmental Panel on Climate Change,* p. 362-405. Cambridge, UK, Cambridge University Press.

Wathern, P. (ed.) 1988. *Environmental impact assessment: theory and practice.* London, Academic Division of Unwin Hyman Ltd.

Weber, J. 1996. Conservation, développement et coordination: peut-on gerer biologiquement le social? In *Colloque Panafricain; Gestion communautaire des ressources naturelles rénouvelables et développement durable,* Harare, 24-27 June1996.

Weber, J. & Reveret, J.-P. 1993. La gestion des relations societés-nature: modes d'appropriation et droits de propriété. In *Une terre en renaissance.* Paris, ORSTOM and Le monde diplomatique, Collection Savoirs No. 2.

Whitmore, T.C. 1990. *An introduction to tropical rain forests.* Oxford, UK, Clarendon Press Ltd. 226 pp.

Wilen, J. 1988. Limited entry licensing: a retrospective assessment. *Marine Resource Economics,* 5: 313-24.

Willmann, R. 1983. *Economic information needs for small-scale fisheries management,* p. 23-35. FAO Fisheries Report No. 284.

Willmann, R. 1994. *Inception report. Integrated coastal fisheries management in Bolinao, Lingayen Gulf, Philippines.* Rome, FAO, FI:DP/INT/91/007, Field Document No. 4. 26 pp.

Willmann, R. 1996. *Fisheries management within the framework of integrated coastal area management.* Paper presented to the South Asian Workshop on Fisheries and Coastal Area Management: Institutional Legal and Policy Dimensions. Madras, India, 26-29 September 1996. Madras, International Collective in Support of Fishworkers (ICSF). 22 pp. (mimeo)

Willmann, R. & Insull, D. 1993. Integrated coastal fisheries management. *Ocean and Coastal Management,* 21: 285-302.

Winpenny, J.T. 1991. *Values for the environment: a guide to economic appraisal.* London, HMSO, Overseas Development Institute. 277 pp.

Winpenny, J.T. 1995. Evaluating environmental impacts: the process of unnatural selection. *In* Picciotto, R. & Rist, R.C. (eds.) *Evaluation and development. Proceedings of the 1994 World Bank Conference.* A

INTEGRATED
COASTAL AREA
MANAGEMENT
and
AGRICULTURE
FORESTRY AND
FISHERIES

References

World Bank Operations Evaluation Study. Washington, DC, World Bank.

World Bank. 1978. *Employment and development of small enterprises.* Washington, DC, World Bank, Sectoral Policy Paper.

World Bank. 1992. *A study of international fisheries research.* World Bank Policy Research Series No. 19. 103 pp.

World Bank. 1993. *The Noordwijk guidelines for integrated coastal zone management.* Paper presented at the World Coast Conference, 1-5 November 1993. Noordwijk, the Netherlands. Washington, DC, World Bank, Environmental Department. 21 pp.

World Research Institute. 1986. *World resources, 1986.* Washington, DC, World Research Institute. 353 pp.

World Resources Institute. 1996. *World resources, 1996-97.* Oxford, UK, Oxford University Press. 365 pp.

Young, M.D. 1992. *Sustainable investment and resource use: equity, environmental integrity and economic efficiency.* Paris CEDEX, UNESCO. 176 pp.

Young, T.R. 1995. Legal and institutional issues in the creation and implementation of integrated coastal zone management programs in East Africa. *In* Lindén, O. (ed.) *Proceedings of the Arusha Workshop and Policy Conference on Integrated Coastal Zone Management in Eastern Africa.* Arusha, United Republic of Tanzania, 21-23 April 1993. Manila, SAREC Marine Program, Coastal Management Center.

INTEGRATED
COASTAL AREA
MANAGEMENT
and
AGRICULTURE
FORESTRY AND
FISHERIES

Index

INTEGRATED
COASTAL AREA
MANAGEMENT
and
AGRICULTURE
FORESTRY AND
FISHERIES

Index

INTEGRATED
COASTAL AREA
MANAGEMENT
and
AGRICULTURE
FORESTRY AND
FISHERIES

INTEGRATED
COASTAL AREA
MANAGEMENT
and
AGRICULTURE
FORESTRY AND
FISHERIES

Index

WHERE TO PURCHASE FAO PUBLICATIONS LOCALLY
POINTS DE VENTE DES PUBLICATIONS DE LA FAO
PUNTOS DE VENTA DE PUBLICACIONES DE LA FAO

• ANGOLA
Empresa Nacional do Disco e de Publicações, ENDIPU-U.E.E.
Rua Cirilo da Conceição Silva, Nº 7
C.P. Nº 1314-C, Luanda

• ARGENTINA
Librería Agropecuaria
Pasteur 743, 1028 Buenos Aires
Oficina del Libro Internacional
Av. Córdoba 1877, 1120 Buenos Aires
E-mail: olilibro@satlink.com

• AUSTRALIA
Hunter Publications
P.O. Box 404, Abbotsford, Vic. 3067
Tel.: (03) 9417 5361
Fax: (03) 914 7154
E-mail: jpdavies@ozemail.com.au

• AUSTRIA
Gerold Buch & Co.
Weihburggasse 26, 1010 Vienna

• BANGLADESH
Association of Development Agencies in Bangladesh
House No. 1/3, Block F,
Lalmatia, Dhaka 1207

• BELGIQUE
M.J. De Lannoy
202, avenue du Roi, 1060 Bruxelles
CCP 000-0808993-13
E-mail: jean.de.lannoy@infoboard.be

• BOLIVIA
Los Amigos del Libro
Av. Heroínas 311, Casilla 450
Cochabamba;
Mercado 1315, La Paz

• BOTSWANA
Botsalo Books (Pty) Ltd
P.O. Box 1532, Gaborone

• BRAZIL
Fundação Getúlio Vargas
Praia do Botafogo 190, C.P. 9052
Rio de Janeiro
E-mail: valeria@sede.fgvrj.br
Núcleo Editora da Universidade Federal Fluminense
Rua Miguel de Frias 9
Icaraí-Niterói 24
220-000 Rio de Janeiro
Fundação da Universidade Federal do Paraná - FUNPAR
Rua Alfredo Bufrem 140, 30º andar
80020-240 Curitiba

• CAMEROON
CADDES
Centre Africain de Diffusion et Développement Social
B.P. 7317 Douala Bassa
Tel.: (237) 43 37 83
Fax: (237) 42 77 03

• CANADA
Renouf Publishing
5369 chemin Canotek Road, Unit 1
Ottawa, Ontario K1J 9J3
Tel.: (613) 745-2665
Fax: (613) 745 7660
Website: www.renoufbooks.com
E-mail: renouf@fox.nstn.ca

• CHILE
Librería - Oficina Regional FAO
c/o FAO Officina Regional para América Latina y el Caribe (RLC)
Avda. Dag Hammarskjold, 3241
Vitacura, Santiago
Tel.: 33 72 314
E-mail: german.rojas@field.fao.org
Universitaria Textolibros Ltda.
Avda. L. Bernardo O'Higgins 1050
Santiago

• CHINA
China National Publications Import & Export Corporation
16 Gongti East Road, Beijing 100020
Tel.: 6506 30 70
Fax: 6506 3101
E-mail: cnpiec@public.3.bta.net.cn

• COLOMBIA
Banco Ganadero
Vicepresidencia de Fomento
Carrera 9ª Nº 72-21, Piso 5
Bogotá D.E.
Tel.: 217 0100

• CONGO
Office national des librairies populaires
B.P. 577, Brazzaville

• COSTA RICA
Librería Lehmann S.A.
Av. Central, Apartado 10011
1000 San José
CINDE
Coalición Costarricense de Iniciativas de Desarrollo
Apdo 7170, 1000 San José
E-mail: rtacinde@sol.rassa.co.cr

• CÔTE D'IVOIRE
CEDA
04 B.P. 541, Abidjan 04
Tel.: 22 20 55
Fax: 21 72 62

• CUBA
Ediciones Cubanas
Empresa de Comercio Exterior de Publicaciones
Obispo 461, Apartado 605, La Habana

• CZECH REPUBLIC
Artia Pegas Press Ltd
Import of Periodicals
Palác Metro, P.O. Box 825
Národní 25, 111 21 Praha 1

• DENMARK
Munksgaard, Book and Subscription Service
P.O. Box 2148
DK 1016 Copenhagen K.
Tel.: 4533128570
Fax: 4533129387
Website: www.munksgaard.dk; e-mail: subscription.service@mail.munksgaard.dk

• DOMINICAN REPUBLIC
CUESTA - Centro del libro
Av. 27 de Febrero, esq. A. Lincoln
Centro Comercial Nacional
Apartado 1241, Santo Domingo

• ECUADOR
Libri Mundi, Librería Internacional
Juan León Mera 851
Apartado Postal 3029, Quito
E-mail: librimul@librimundi.com.ec
Universidad Agraria del Ecuador
Centro de Información Agraria
Av. 23 de Julio, Apdo 09-01-1248
Guayaquil
Librería Española
Murgeón 364 y Ulloa, Quito

• EGYPT
The Middle East Observer
41 Sherif Street, Cairo
Tel.: 393 97 2
Fax: 360 68 04
E-mail: fouda@soficom.com.eg

• ESPAÑA
Librería Agrícola
Fernando VI 2, 28004 Madrid
Libreria de la Generalitat de Catalunya
Rambla dels Estudis 118 (Palau Moja)
08002 Barcelona
Tel.: (93) 302 6462
Fax: (93) 302 1299
Mundi Prensa Libros S.A.
Castelló 37, 28001 Madrid
Tel.: 914 36 37 00
Fax: 915 75 39 98
Website: www.tsai.es/MPRENSA
E-mail: libreria@mundiprensa.es
Mundi Prensa - Barcelona
Consejo de Ciento 391,
08009 Barcelona
Tel.: 301 8615
Fax: 317 0141

• FINLAND
Akateeminen Kirjakauppa Subscription Services
P.O. Box 23, FIN-00371 Helsinki
Tel.: (358) 0121 4416
Fax: (358) 0121 4450

• FRANCE
Editions A. Pedone
13, rue Soufflot, 75005 Paris
Lavoisier Tec & Doc
14, rue de Provigny
94236 Cachan Cedex
Website: www.lavoisier.fr
E-mail: livres@lavoisier.fr
Librairie du Commerce International
10, avenue d'Iéna
75783 Paris Cedex 16
Website: www.cfce.fr
E-mail: pl@net-export.fr
WORLD DATA
10, rue Nicolas Flamand
75004 Paris
Tel.: (01) 4278 0578
Fax: (01) 4278 1472

• GERMANY
Alexander Horn Internationale Buchhandlung
Friedrichstrasse 34
D-65185 Wiesbaden
Tel.: 37 42 12
S. Toeche-Mittler GmbH Versandbuchhandlung
Hindenburgstrasse 33
D-64295 Darmstadt
Tel.: 6151 336 65
Fax: 6151 314 048
Website: www.booksell.com/triops
E-mail: triops@booksell.com
Uno Verlag
Poppelsdorfer Allee 55
D-53115 Bonn 1
Tel.: 49 (0) 228 94 90 20
Fax: 49 (0) 228 21 74 92
Website: www.uno-verlag.de
E-mail: unoverlag@aol.com

• GHANA
SEDCO Publishing Ltd
Sedco House, Tabon Street
Off Ring Road Central, North Ridge
P.O. Box 2051, Accra

• GREECE
Papasotiriou S.A.
35 Stournara Str., 10682 Athens
Tel.: (+301) 3302 980
Fax: (+301) 3648254

• GUYANA
Guyana National Trading Corporation Ltd
45-47 Water Street, P.O. Box 308
Georgetown

• HAÏTI
Librairie «A la Caravelle»
26, rue Bonne Foi
B.P. 111, Port-au-Prince

• HONDURAS
Escuela Agrícola Panamericana Librería RTAC
El Zamorano, Apartado 93, Tegucigalpa
Oficina de la Escuela Agrícola Panamericana en Tegucigalpa
Blvd. Morazán, Apts. Glapson
Apartado 93, Tegucigalpa

• HUNGARY
Librotrade Kft.
P.O. Box 126, H-1656 Budapest
Tel.: 256 1672
Fax: 256 8727

• INDIA
EWP Affiliated East-West Press PVT, Ltd
G-I/16, Ansari Road, Darya Gany
New Delhi 110 002
Tel.: 32 64 180
Fax: 32 60 538
Oxford Book and Stationery Co.
Scindia House
New Delhi 110 001
Tel.: 91 11 331 5310
Fax: 91 11 371 3275
Oxford Subscription Agency
Institute for Development Education
1 Anasuya Ave., Kilpauk
Madras 600 010
Periodical Expert Book Agency
D-42, Vivek Vihar, Delhi 110095
Bookwell
Head Office:
2/72, Nirankari Colony, New Delhi - 110009
Tel.: 725 1283
Fax: 91-11-328 13 15
Sales Office:
24/4800, Ansari Road
Darya Ganj, New Delhi - 110002
Tel.: 326 8786, 325 7264
E-mail: bkwell@nde.vsnl.net.in

• IRAN
The FAO Bureau, International and Regional Specialized Organizations Affairs
Ministry of Agriculture of the Islamic Republic of Iran
Keshavarz Bld, M.O.A., 17th floor
Teheran

• IRELAND
Office of Public Work
4-5 Harcourt Road, Dublin 2

• ISRAEL
R.O.Y. International
P.O. Box 13056, Tel Aviv 61130
E-mail: royil@netvision.net.il

• ITALY
FAO Bookshop
Viale delle Terme di Caracalla
00100 Roma
Tel.: 5705 5688
Fax: 5705 5155
E-mail: publications-sales@fao.org
Libreria Commissionaria Sansoni S.p.A. - Licosa
Via Duca di Calabria 1/1
50125 Firenze
Tel.: 64 54 15
Fax: 64 12 57
E-mail: licosa@ftbcc.it
Libreria Scientifica Dott. Lucio de Biasio "Aeiou"
Via Coronelli 6, 20146 Milano

WHERE TO PURCHASE FAO PUBLICATIONS LOCALLY
POINTS DE VENTE DES PUBLICATIONS DE LA FAO
PUNTOS DE VENTA DE PUBLICACIONES DE LA FAO

6/98

• **JAPAN**
Far Eastern Booksellers
(Kyokuto Shoten Ltd)
12 Kanda-Jimbocho 2 chome
Chiyoda-ku - P.O. Box 72
Tokyo 101-91
Tel.: 03 3265 7531
Fax: 03 3265 4656
Maruzen Company Ltd
P.O. Box 5050
Tokyo International 100-31
Tel.: 81 3 3278 1894
Fax: 81 3 3278 1895
E-mail: h_sugiyama@maruzen.co.jp

• **KENYA**
Text Book Centre Ltd
Kijabe Street
P.O. Box 47540, Nairobi
Tel.: 330 342
Fax: 22 57 79
Inter Africa Book Distribution
Kencom House, Moi Avenue
P.O. Box 73580, Nairobi
Tel.: 21 11 84
Fax: 254 2 22 35 70

• **LUXEMBOURG**
M.J. De Lannoy
202, avenue du Roi
1060 Bruxelles (Belgique)
E-mail: jean.de.lannoy@infoboard.be

• **MADAGASCAR**
Centre d'Information et de
Documentation Scientifique et
Technique
Ministère de la recherche appliquée
au développement
B.P. 6224 Tsimbazaza, Antananarivo

• **MALAYSIA**
Electronic products only:
Southbound
Sendirian Berhad Publishers
9 College Square, 01250 Penang

• **MALI**
Librairie Traore
Rue Soundiata Keita X 115
B.P. 3243, Bamako

• **MAROC**
La Librairie Internationale
70 Rue T'ssoule
B.O. Box 302 (RP), Rabat
Tél./Fax: 212 7 75 01 83

• **MEXICO**
Librería, Universidad Autónoma de
Chapingo
56230 Chapingo
Libros y Editoriales S.A.
Av. Progreso N° 202-1° Piso A
Apdo. Postal 18922
Col. Escandón, 11800 México D.F.
Mundi Prensa Mexico, S.A.
Río Pánuco, 141 Col. Cuauhtémoc
C.P. 06500, México, DF
Tel.: 533-5658 al 60
Fax: 514-6799
E-mail: 1015452361@compuserve.com

• **NETHERLANDS**
Roodveldt Import b.v.
Brouwersgracht 288
1013 HG Amsterdam
E-mail: roodboek@euronet.nl
Tel.: 622 8035
Fax: 625 5493
Swets & Zeitlinger b.v.
P.O. Box 830, 2160 Lisse
Heereweg 347 B, 2161 CA Lisse
E-mail: infono@swets.nl
Website: www.swets.nl

• **NEW ZEALAND**
Legislation Services
P.O. Box 12418
Thorndon, Wellington
E-mail: gppmjxf@gp.co.nz
Oasis Official
P.O. Box 3627, Wellington
Tel.: (+64) 4 499 1551
Fax: (+64) 4 499 1972
E-mail: oasis@clear.net.nz
Website: www.oasisbooks.co.nzl

• **NICARAGUA**
Librería HISPAMER
Costado Este Univ. Centroamericana
Apdo. Postal A-221, Managua

• **NIGERIA**
University Bookshop (Nigeria) Ltd
University of Ibadan, Ibadan

• **NORWAY**
Swets Norge AS
P.O. Box 6512, Etterstad
N-0606 Oslo
Tel.: (+47) 2297 4500
Fax: (+47) 2297 4545
E-mail: nicagen@swets.nl

• **PAKISTAN**
Mirza Book Agency
65 Shahrah-e-Quaid-e-Azam
P.O. Box 729, Lahore 3

• **PARAGUAY**
Librería Intercontinental
Editora e Impresora S.R.L.
Caballero 270 c/Mcal Estigarribia
Asunción

• **PERU**
INDEAR
Jirón Apurimac 375, Casilla 4937
Lima 1
Universidad Nacional "Pedro Ruiz
Gallo"
Facultad de Agronomía, A.P. 795
Lambayeque (Chiclayo)

• **PHILIPPINES**
International Booksource Center,
Inc.
Room 720, Cityland 10 Tower 2
H.V. de la Costa, Cor. Valero St
Makati, Metro Manila
Tel.: 817 9676
Fax: 817 1741

• **POLAND**
Ars Polona
Krakowskie Przedmiescie 7
00-950 Warsaw

• **PORTUGAL**
Livraria Portugal, Dias e Andrade
Ltda.
Rua do Carmo 70-74
Apartado 2681, 1200 Lisboa Codex

• **SINGAPORE**
Select Books Pte Ltd
03-15 Tanglin Shopping Centre
19 Tanglin Road, Singapore 1024
Tel.: 732 1515
Fax: 736 0855

• **SLOVAK REPUBLIC**
Institute of Scientific and
Technical Information for
Agriculture
Samova 9, 950 10 Nitra
Tel.: +42 87 522 185
Fax: +42 87 525 275
E-mail: uvtip@nr.sanet.sk

• **SOMALIA**
Samater
P.O. Box 936, Mogadishu

• **SOUTH AFRICA**
David Philip Publishers (Pty) Ltd
P.O. Box 23408, Claremont 7735
Tel.: Cape Town (021) 64-4136
Fax: Cape Town (021) 64-3358
E-mail: dpp@iafrica.com
Website: www.twisted.co.za

• **SRI LANKA**
M.D. Gunasena & Co. Ltd
217 Olcott Mawatha, P.O. Box 246
Colombo 11

• **SUISSE**
Buchhandlung und Antiquariat
Heinimann & Co.
Kirchgasse 17, 8001 Zurich
UN Bookshop
Palais des Nations
CH-1211 Genève 1
Website: www.un.org
Van Diermen Editions Techniques
ADECO
41 Lacuez, CH-1807 Blonzy

• **SURINAME**
Vaco n.v. in Suriname
Domineestraat 26, P.O. Box 1841
Paramaribo

• **SWEDEN**
Wennergren Williams AB
P.O. Box 1305, S-171 25 Solna
Tel.: 46 8 705 9750
Fax: 46 8 27 00 71
E-mail: mail@wwi.se
Bokdistributören
P.O. Box 301 61, S-104 25 Stockholm
Tel.: 46 8 728 2500
Fax: 46 8 31 30 44
E-mail: lis.ledin@hk.akademibokhandeln.se

• **THAILAND**
Suksapan Panit
Mansion 9, Rajdamnern Avenue
Bangkok

• **TOGO**
Librairie du Bon Pasteur
B.P. 1164, Lomé

• **TUNISIE**
Société tunisienne de diffusion
5, avenue de Carthage, Tunis

• **TURKEY**
DUNYA INFOTEL
100. Yil Mahallesi
34440 Bagcilar, Istanbul
Tel.: 0212 629 08 08
Fax: 0212 629 46 89
E-mail: dunya@dunya-gazete.com.tr
Website: http://www.dunya.com

• **UNITED KINGDOM**
The Stationery Office
51 Nine Elms Lane
London SW8 5DR
Tel.: (0171) 873 9090 (orders)
(0171) 873 0011 (inquiries)
Fax: (0171) 873 8463
and through The Stationery Office
Bookshops
E-mail: postmaster@theso.co.uk
Website: www.the-stationery-office.co.uk
Electronic products only:
Microinfo Ltd
P.O. Box 3, Omega Road
Alton, Hampshire GU34 2PG
Tel.: (01420) 86848
Fax: (01420) 89889
Website: www.microinfo.co.uk
E-mail: emedia@microinfo.co.uk

• **UNITED STATES**
Publications:
BERNAN Associates (ex UNIPUB)
4611/F Assembly Drive
Lanham, MD 20706-4391

Toll-free: 1-800-274-4447
Fax: 301-459-0056
Website: www.bernan.com
E-mail: info@bernan.com
UN Bookshop
The United Nations Bookshop
General Assembly Building Room 32
New York, N.Y. 10017
Tel.: 212 963 7680
Fax: 212 963 4910
Website: www.un.org
E-mail: bookshop@un.org
Periodicals:
Ebsco Subscription Services
P.O. Box 1943
Birmingham, AL 35201-1943
Tel.: (205) 991-6600
Telex: 78-2661
Fax: (205) 991-1449
The Faxon Company Inc.
15 Southwest Park
Westwood, MA 02090
Tel.: 6117-329-3350
Telex: 95-1980
Cable: FW Faxon Wood

• **URUGUAY**
Librería Agropecuaria S.R.L.
Buenos Aires 335, Casilla 1755
Montevideo C.P. 11000

• **VENEZUELA**
Fundación La Era Agrícola
Calle 31 Junín Qta Coromoto 5-49
Apartado 456, Mérida
Fundación para la Investigación
Agrícola
San Javier
Estado Yaracuy, A.P. 182, San Felipe
Fax: 054 44210
E-mail: damac@diero.conicit.ve
Fudeco, Librería
Avenida Libertador-Este
Ed. Fudeco, Apartado 254
Barquisimeto C.P. 3002, Ed. Lara
Tel.: (051) 538 022
Fax: (051) 544 394
Telex: (051) 513 14 FUDEC VC
Librería FAGRO
Universidad Central de Venezuela (UCV)
Maracay
Librería Universitaria, C.A.
Av. 3, entre Calles 29 y 30
N° 29-25 Edif. EVA, Mérida
Fax: 074 52 09 56
Tamanaco Libros Técnicos S.R.L.
Centro Comercial Ciudad Tamanaco
Nivel C-2, Caracas
Tel.: 261 3344/261 3335/959 0016
Tecni-Ciencia Libros S.A.
Torre Phelps-Mezzanina
Plaza Venezuela
A.P. 20.315, 1020 Caracas
Tel.: 782 8697/781 9945/781 9954
E-mail: tchlibros@ibm.net
Tecni-Ciencia Libros, S.A.
Centro Comercial
Av. Andrés Eloy, Urb. El Prebo
Valencia, Ed. Carabobo
Tel.: 222 724

• **ZIMBABWE**
Grassroots Books
The Book Café
Fife Avenue, Harare;
61a Fort Street, Bulawayo
Tel.: 79 31 82
Fax: 70 21 29

• **Other countries/Autres pays/**
Otros países
Sales and Marketing Group
Information Division, FAO
Viale delle Terme di Caracalla
00100 Rome, Italy
Tel.: (39-6) 57051
Fax: (39-6) 5705 3360
Telex: 625852/625853/610181 FAO I
E-mail: publications-sales@fao.org